More praise for *The Anatomy of Freedom*

"In *The Anatomy of Freedom* readers will find yet another manifestation of those imaginative and analytic powers that have characterized Robin Morgan as one of the most significant feminist thinkers. In this book one encounters the poet, activist, and theoretician whose work never fails to challenge women to strive for greater precision, scope, and daring. *The Anatomy of Freedom* is important reading for all feminists struggling to express the rich diversity among us."

—Mary Daly

"Robin Morgan's book is one of the most wonderful reading experiences I have had in a long time. I have been in such good company—a courageous woman who has educated me and shown me how important my choices in life are, not only for my own freedom, but also for those who still don't have the privilege of choice."

—Liv Ullmann

By Robin Morgan

POETRY

Monster

Lady of the Beasts

Death Benefits

Depth Perception

**Upstairs in the Garden:
Selected and New Poems**

FICTION

Dry Your Smile

The Mer-Child

NONFICTION

The Demon Lover

The Anatomy of Freedom
Second Edition

Going Too Far

The Word of a Woman
Second Edition

The New Woman (*ed.*)

Sisterhood Is Powerful (*ed.*)

Sisterhood Is Global (*ed.*)

THE ANATOMY OF FREEDOM

Feminism in Four Dimensions

Robin Morgan

Second Edition

For Madeline and for Freedom!

Robin Morgan

W·W·NORTON & COMPANY

New York · London

Grateful acknowledgment is made for permission to reprint the following:

Excerpt from *The Power and the Glory* by Graham Greene. Copyright 1940 by Graham Greene. Copyright renewed © 1968 by Graham Greene. Reprinted by permission of Viking Penguin, Inc.

Excerpt from *On Revolution* by Hannah Arendt. Copyright © 1963 by Hannah Arendt. Reprinted by permission of Viking Penguin, Inc.

Excerpt from *Right-Wing Women* © 1983 by Andrea Dworkin. Published by Perigee Books. Reprinted by permission of the author.

Excerpt from *Wholeness and the Implicate Order* by David Bohm. Reprinted by permission of Routledge & Kegan Paul Ltd.

Excerpt from *The Lives of a Cell: Notes of a Biology Watcher* by Lewis Thomas. Copyright © 1974 by Lewis Thomas. Reprinted by permission of Viking Penguin, Inc.

Excerpt from poem by Maha al-Fahd translated by Mona N. Mikhail. Copyright © 1979 by the Poetry Society of America. Reprinted by permission of Mona N. Mikhail.

Excerpt from *The Coming of Age* by Simone de Beauvoir. Published by G. P. Putnam's Sons.

Excerpt from "Its Image on the Mirror." Copyright © 1964 by Mavis Gallant. Reprinted by permission of the author.

Excerpt from *Elizabeth Cady Stanton/Susan B. Anthony: Correspondence, Writings, Speeches,* edited by Ellen DuBois. Copyright © 1981 by Schocken Books, Inc. Reprinted by permission of Schocken Books, Inc.

Excerpt from *The Letters of George Sand.* Reprinted by permission of AMS Press, Inc., New York.

Excerpt from *The Question Concerning Technology and Other Essays* by Martin Heidegger, translated by William Lovitt. Reprinted by permission of Harper & Row.

Library of Congress Cataloging in Publication Data

Morgan, Robin.
The anatomy of freedom.

Bibliography: p. 341
Includes index.
1. Liberty.   2. Feminism.   I. Title.
HM271.M586   305.4´2
ISBN 0-393-31161-9
Library of Congress Catalog Card Number 81–43730

W. W. Norton & Company, Inc., 500 Fifth Avenue, New York, N.Y. 10110
W. W. Norton & Company Ltd., 10 Coptic Street, London WC1A 1PU

PRINTED IN THE UNITED STATES OF AMERICA

1 2 3 4 5 6 7 8 9 0

for Blake

CONTENTS

FOREWORD TO THE SECOND EDITION

This is the point. Imagine a dot—like a period—of light. Imagine it in a second dimension, radiating spokes from itself, a mandala of light. Imagine the wheel spinning, a depth of light, in three dimensions. Now try to imagine the mandala *cubed*.
Now double the original point:
Now imagine the point as infinite . . .
This is one way to labinotate the choreography of freedom.
This is the movement of feminism.

* * *

Since *The Anatomy of Freedom* was first published,* the world has witnessed examples of liberation, democratization, indulgence, and license.

But freedom?

In the political dimension, the changes appear dramatic, as if history were accelerating in its approach to a millennial shift: the end of the Cold War, the (ostensible?) fall of totalitarian governments of both the Left and Right) in Eastern Europe and Latin America, a few "people's revolutions" in Asia, the death of apartheid in South Africa, fragile agreements on nuclear disarmament and on trade, frail peace accords in the Middle East . . . all causes for celebration, or at least relief.

But this was also the period that witnessed a proliferation of "civil" wars on tribal, ethnic, language, religious, cultural, political, and territorial grounds; the brazen reinstatement of torture; and an all-time-high record in refugees, 90 percent of whom are women and children. These years charted increases in religious, sexual, political, and every other fundamentalism; in population and in Third World debt; in ozone depletion, air pollution, water scarcity, land erosion, auto-immune diseases, and terrorism. This period witnessed the Montreal Massacre. And Tiananmen Square. And Chernobyl.

This was the period of the rapid-response, "feel-good" Gulf War

---

*with the inflicted, ponderous subtitle *Feminism, Physics, and Global Politics* (New York: Anchor Press/Doubleday, 1982).

waged by the United States and its allies (provoked less, ironically, by Saddam Hussein's despotism against Kurds or Kuwaitis than by his jeopardizing oil supplies), as well as the two-year-long *lack* of response to attempted genocide in the territory formerly called Yugoslavia (no oil fields there). These years heard testimony from survivors of the Serbian brothel/death camps in that territory, and watched while more than fifty thousand women and girls of all factions were raped and tortured (an estimated thirty thousand in Bosnia-Herzegovina alone), and at least another 100,000 killed. Rarely has the pornographic nature of war been brayed aloud so clearly. And in two psychiatric hospitals, at Fojnika and Bakovici, west of Bosnia's capitol Sarajevo, abandoned mental patients cleaned floors, built fires against the freezing air, and cooked themselves potato soup—after having carefully gathered and hidden live grenades left behind by Muslim and Croat forces who were not, of course, "mad."

In the scientific dimension, many prophecies hazarded in this book have already come true (what is hinted at on page 254, for example, is now available as RU486). Other issues projected in these pages, such as reproductive-technology controversies or "information highway" concepts, have proliferated at a rate few could have imagined a short twelve years ago. And then there is the field of physics, whose centrality to this book is in two areas, as subject for demystification and as analogy for feminism's potential impact on our definitions of reality. In physics, work has progressed rapidly on quantum theory, on chaos theory, on superstring theory, on cold-dark-matter hypotheses, on black holes, gravity flux, time curves, wormholes, and other miracles of theory and of fact far too complex and numerous to summarize here.

In the personal dimension, there have been many changes over the twelve years' space traveled since this book first appeared. Not least among them is that my twenty-year marriage to the poet Kenneth Pitchford, whose presence and influence are not marginal in these pages, ended a year after *The Anatomy of Freedom* was published. This casts an ironic light over the chapters on romance and marriage, in particular the "Marriage Map" section (pages 157–65) and the "Coded Messages." How much of a breakthrough any work is for its author can be clarified only in retrospect. So, about Kenneth Pitchford, I will say simply, in a paraphrase of Walt Whitman: He was the man, he suffered, he was there. Other personal rites of passage have included mourning the death of my mother, exercising the intimations of sexual intelligence presaged on page 146, completing six books—each reflecting its own dimensions of change—and exploring the terrain of an activism internal as well as external, which the Afterword to this edition attempts to describe.

And the fourth dimension? Shimmering through the political, scientific, and personal, it could be named the *readiness for freedom.* This readiness, expressed as world crisis, articulates itself violently in those regions suffering most acutely from violence. But a crisis is simultaneously a turning point—*if* the endangerd species that is us is desperate enough to seize the crisis as opportunity. In the so-called developed world, this desperation, this *longing*, becomes pathetically evident in the market for an epidemic of self-help books offering instant "freedom" and "empowerment" on every subject from golf, speed-reading, business management, diet, exercise, and computer mastery through sex, relationships, political revolution, ways to live our lives, ways to kill ourselves, and ways to approach god ("within" *and* "without"). That these "solutions" are part of the problem doesn't lessen the poignancy or intensity of the thirst they claim to slake. Ripeness may or may not be all, but a state of readiness *is* the major component of change.

*   *   *

This book about freedom could not have been attempted without the efforts of certain people who freed and strengthened me in order that I might approach the task. It is impossible to mention them all, but some are owed individual thanks.

Jewell Parker Rhodes, Mary Robertson, and Marilyn Waring all read sections of the manuscript in drafts and gave me the benefit of their comments. Conversations about women and science with Dana Densmore as early as the 1970s planted seeds for this book, as did subsequent discussions with Carol Drexler, Kathryn Girard, Charlene Spretnak, and especially Judy Smith of the Women and Technology Group at the University of Montana (Missoula). During the actual writing, a diverse group of women writers cheered me on, though each was involved in her own work: Kathleen Barry, Mary Daly, Andrea Dworkin, Signe Hammer, Marion Meade, Kate Millett, Isel Rivero, Gloria Steinem, and Karen Sunde. It was because of vulnerable conversations about racism with Susan McHenry that parts of Chapter VI were written, and the "Slaves of Form" section of that chapter is dedicated to her. Jaqueline Lapa, directly, and Frank Donnelly, indirectly, helped unearth various insights in these pages. Dexter Guerrieri introduced me to the work of physicist David Böhm. Corlann Gee Bush of the University of Idaho (Moscow) read the manuscript to give me the advantage of her technical knowledge. Loretta Barrett, Edite Kroll, Suzanne Braun Levine, and Jane Ordway provided encouragement in different ways but with similar generosity. Lois Sasson continued exhibiting a talent for friendship rare even among feminists. Karen Berry's consistent, intelligent support, during this book's gestation and thereafter, has been vital. Jana Meredyth Talton's assistance has been critical in the readying of this new edition.

The Anatomy of Freedom was originally dedicated to Blake, because his patience, affirmation, and good-humored wit were always there for me; because he read and gave wise criticisms on certain chapters; because he is my friend as well as my son; and because when I wrote this book Blake—then twelve years old—had taught me more about freedom than anyone else in my life. Now, double that lifetime of his later (but still in a world where most men can tempt a feminist thinker toward fantasies of androcide), Blake Morgan is an adult and an artist, and his daily practice of ethical love helps keep me sane—and honest. It is with glad indebtedness and respect that I rededicate this book to him.

Finally, I am grateful to my editor Mary Cunnane and her colleagues at W. W. Norton who wished to publish *The Anatomy of Freedom* in this new edition, and pleased at having the chance to add a Foreword and Afterword.

I have a particular fondness for this book, for its personal candor, its aesthetic boldness in attempting forms that reflect content, and its audacity in proposing advanced theoretical physics as a metaphor for feminism. I stand by the validity of that metaphor, by the idea of the *practicality of freedom*, and by the basic politics of the work. I have not attempted to update statistics, since they continue to change and recent data is available elsewhere, nor—even where I might now disagree with some of my own theories or conclusions—have I altered the text. Parts of it in retrospect delight or sadden me, evoke embarrassment or pride; and some sections provoke a wry smile (it's amusing that the first chapter anatomized the "socially constructed" concepts of Woman and Man years before the vogue of "deconstructionism" became an obfuscating academic fad).

For the rest, as physics teaches us, the impossible becomes more probable all the time. I write this looking out across a green field flecked with dandelions, on a hot afternoon, under a pewter sky threatening summer showers—in February. This is no contradiction and I have stepped through no looking-glass: I am simply, at the moment, in the Southern Hemisphere. Wonderland is a scientific fact, a daily reality. Depending, of course, on one's perspective, politics, and readiness.

Robin Morgan

Wellsford, New Zealand
February 1994

INTRODUCTION

"Free I was born, have lived, and will die" was the personal motto struck on a medal by Queen Christina of Sweden (1626–89) before her abdication of the throne. It's a credo all women, and indeed most men, would find enviable. One can't help but wonder if it really was true.

This book attempts an anatomy of freedom—not a dissection of a dead issue, but rather a meditative analysis of an idea not yet born. Freedom has been discussed, syllogized, defined, fought and died for over millennia, yet it still hasn't been coaxed into existence. Furthermore, the majority of all human beings who have ever lived, and indeed the majority of those now living, haven't been permitted to approach the task of analyzing or invoking it. That majority is composed of female human beings.

Feminism has been perceived, even by most feminists, as a political philosophy and movement relating specifically to the rights and the just powers of women. In fact, if this were the totality of feminism's concern, that would be sufficient cause for its validity and vitality. But the truth is that feminism is something far more—a vision as important and transformative to men as to women, and one crucial to the continuation of sentient life on this planet. It is *that* feminist vision, and its intimate and inextricable relationship with freedom, which I am exploring in this book.

It's as if feminism, in all its myriad forms down through the centuries and in our own epoch, has been presented as a vivid representation of the need to change the condition of women—but as a two-dimensional, flat representation nonetheless. We can walk along the gallery of time and view such representations hanging on its metaphorical walls, from the impassioned poems of Enheduanna in ancient Sumer (c. 2300 B.C.) down to the moving testimonies of our contemporaries in the twentieth century. Now it's time we comprehended feminism in its full, holographic nature.

This book attempts to do that, to view feminism in its three-and even four-dimensional character, as the holograph I believe it is. That has required that the form of writing itself attempt to project, reflect, and express the content—to move beyond a rigid, linear, single-genre approach toward a contrapuntal style which risks blending a personal voice with analytical and philosophical ones, interweaving parables, dramatic format, and meditative structure with journalistic reportage and theoretical hypotheses. It has required reevaluating the questions we have so far asked, daring to raise more and unprecedented questions rather than proclaim answers, and comprehending that all answers sooner or later become new questions. If this feels unsettling to some readers, I can only plead that the effect is intentional. One cannot understand a holograph by settling down to view it; on the contrary, a willingness to shift perspectives repeatedly is necessary for such understanding. That in turn requires of us that we relinquish our positions as passive observers and instead become active participants: we must move around the holograph to see its different sides, to discern its multifaceted realities, to understand its depths.

One integral aspect is, to be sure, the worldwide condition of women. Another is involved in finding the right technological balance for a new society. Another resonates with the subrealities of dreams and the unconscious. Another exposes the complexity of sexual passion in both women and men. Still another dares affirm the intricacies of long-term committed relationships. What have been perceived as separate subjects—gender, race, global politics, family structures, economics, the environment, childhood, aging —all reveal their interconnectedness as we move around the holograph, peer underneath it, and lean above it. The internal workings of the human body, the internal workings of an atomic particle, the issues of dying and death, of masks and personae, of spiritual faith and scientific fact, of aesthetics and astrophysics, disclose themselves as interwoven expressions of one dynamic whole.

Political movements speak of "alliances" and "coalitions." In practice, these frequently are both necessary and difficult. The process surely would be made easier and swifter if we realized that the connections are already there, waiting to be discovered rather than invented. It was Kant who said, "Freedom is that faculty which enlarges the usefulness of all other faculties." I would agree, and further hazard the statement that "feminism is that vision which enlarges the incipience of all other visions."

But in order for feminism to express its true capacities, it is necessary for feminists to express ours. This in turn requires of us that we risk the difficult task of continuing to speak vulnerably and personally about our own lives and the lives of other women, while rejecting tendencies toward victimization, bitterness, self-pity, or self-indulgence. To unveil the damage caused by systemized cruelty, stuntification, indifference, and daily denials of one's humanity is itself a painful and dangerous act; to do so while refusing to become obsessed with the atrocities committed against one's self and one's people is an even more arduous challenge.

That kind of challenge—of persisting in one's endeavors despite the realization that the very rules governing them no longer apply—is also being faced today by physicists working in quantum field theory. Many of them have chosen to retreat into a state of reaction, deliberately approaching their scientific method in a manner which that same method now has shown to be irrelevant. Some, however, are daring to go on, to go further, wherever that method may lead them.

It's for this reason, and because of the startling revelations encountered by this latter group, that I've chosen quantum physics as the central analogy for feminism, and for freedom, in this book. The themes of relativity and interrelationship, and the holographic character of modern physics itself, best demonstrate —and in a scientifically grounded way—what I mean in my metaphrasing of feminism. Besides, quantum physics already is acknowledged to have drastically altered our perceptions of reality; I find it a useful translating device for helping us to acknowledge how feminism has done—and will do even more—the same thing, and for aiding us in glimpsing a hitherto unimaginable freedom.

Such acknowledgments are in the self-interest of every woman and every man, not only because they contain truths we all need to learn, but because without them we are doomed as a species. Human societies on our planet approach critical mass, and our destructive capability appears to be outdistancing our creative capacity. We can spend our lives in helpless hiding, our one hope being that life will pass over us, leaving us in what we pretend is safety and comfort—or we can step forward, out of our intellectual and emotional bomb shelters, and consciously mutate into the life form we have always, secretly, dreamed of becoming.

Einstein said, "What really interests me is whether God had any choice in the creation of the world."

What really interests me is whether you and I do.

ROBIN MORGAN

New York City
February 1982

It may be a truism to say that liberation and freedom are not the same; that liberation may be the condition of freedom but by no means leads automatically to it; that the notion of liberty implied in liberation can only be negative, and hence that even the intention of liberating is not identical with the desire for freedom. Yet if these truisms are frequently forgotten, it is because liberty has always loomed large and the foundation of freedom has always been uncertain, if not altogether futile.

Wars and revolutions have outlived all their ideological justifications. No cause is left but the most ancient of all, the one, in fact, that from the beginning of our history has determined the very existence of politics, the cause of freedom versus tyranny.

—Hannah Arendt

THE HANDMAIDEN OF THE HOLY MAN
An Anatomy of Freedom

The Enemy is permanent. It is not in the emergency situation but in the normal state of affairs. . . . The Enemy
is the common denominator of all doing and undoing.
And the Enemy is not identical with actual communism
or actual capitalism—it is, in both cases, the real spectre
of liberation.

—Herbert Marcuse

I wish I knew how it would feel to
be free,
I wish I could break all the chains
over me.
I wish I could say all the things
that I should say,
say 'em loud, say 'em clear
for the whole round world to hear.

I wish I could share all the love
that's in my heart,
Remove all the bars that keep us
apart.
I wish you could know what it
means to be me.
Then you'd see and agree that
every[one] should be free . . .

I wish I could be like a bird
in the sky.
How sweet it would be if I
found I could fly.
I'd soar to the sun and look down
at the sea.
Then I'd say, 'cause I'd know—
I'd know how it feels to be free.

—Nina Simone's version
of the Billy Taylor song

Once there was a man thought to be holy. He sat near the top of a mountain, night and day, and it seemed that he never moved. Some said that he was always praying or that he meditated or that he saw visions. Some said that this must make him holy, or at least wise.

No one could quite remember when he had first come to sit on his ledge in the mountain, but almost everyone could recall that at one time, years ago, pilgrims had made their way up to him— not without difficulty—to put before him their disputes, their spiritual questions, their despair, their own attempts at holiness. His judgments were so severe, however, and were delivered in tones so seemingly contemptuous of the pilgrims that the same visitors rarely returned, and in time, as word spread, fewer and fewer pilgrims wound their way up the mountain path. At last, only one or two a year would approach the holy man—and then largely as if he were an oddity, a curious sight to be viewed, and not a living saint to be questioned or followed or even quite trusted. Finally, almost no one came at all.

He still sat, nevertheless, on his ledge, appearing to gaze out over the near and distant peaks of other mountains, blinking now and then against the wind, his body wasting away toward desiccation—a bony triangle of spine balanced on a base of crossed legs, his gaunt skull at the apex. No one could possibly estimate his age. He appeared never to speak, although his lips could be seen moving.

All this time, you understand, the woman known as the hand-maiden of the holy man remained faithful . . .

We have no idea what "freedom" is, or why we, as human beings, seem to fear it so. We understand it best by its absence, just as the defeated creature in a poem of Emily Dickinson's lies on the devastated battlefield and, hearing the distant celebration of trumpets in the enemy's camp, comprehends far more deeply than does the victor just what triumph really is. Being, so far, creatures ourselves of lack and of longing, humans seem to have perfected those skills that permit us to mourn, to yearn—and to deny the condition of not having something we never have had.

We really have no idea what "Woman" is, or why we, as women and men, seem to acknowledge the concept. Like freedom, we understand it best by its absence, its lack, its negative:

"Woman" is non-Man. Aristotle was neither the first voice nor the last to define women as "misbegotten males." To be consistent with our character as creatures of longing, we have (rather prematurely) defined Man as human. To be consistent with our character as creatures of denial, we then are forced to define Woman as nonhuman.

Is it coincidental that we have no idea what freedom is, or what Woman is—while we feel we have an idea of what bondage is, of what Man is? Is it possible that our very ignorance of what Woman is constitutes the very thing that stands in the way of our knowing what freedom is?

We know what we are *told* freedom is (and our capacity for hope often has made us trust the tale and not the teller). We are, for example, told that we already possess it. In the "developed nations," corporate capitalism congratulates its subjects on their freedom of expression while robbing them of economic freedom; in the "communist world," state capitalism congratulates its subjects on their economic freedom while denying them the liberty of expression; in the "developing nations," global superpowers and local hierarchical systems vie with one another in promising their subjects the perfect liberating balance—an imported technological future combined with an indigenous cultural past—all the while exacting from them, in the present, pledges of fealty to this or that system, economic dependence, a "temporary" suspension of critical expression, and a voluntary self-sacrifice to The Cause.

All of these freedoms—either promised or already ostensibly delivered—are in fact illusory. In the United States, for example, "free speech" is usually priced beyond the means of the speaker who happens to be female, or on welfare, or an atheist, or a nonwhite man, or a poet, or a child, or an assembly-line worker or coal miner, or a lesbian mother, or a battered wife, or a feminist organizing against the pornography industry, or a resident in an old-age home.

All of these enslavements—exacted in return for the illusory freedoms—are, however, real. In the Soviet Union, for instance, "economic freedom" is an abstract construct to the woman who must stand for hours on line to purchase a pair of shoes or a piece of meat from a supply of limited quantity and quality, at the cost of as much as one quarter of her and her husband's combined monthly income; or to the prostitute who haunts the train station, sleeping on benches, well aware of her own reality despite the official statistics which proclaim that she no longer exists; or to the homosexual man sent to the gulag for seven years despite the official proclamations that insist he (and his "problem") no longer exists; or to the devoutly religious believer for whom attending the synagogue or church is a defiant political act; or to the racial minorities whose sense of identity is being subtly eroded or militaristically destroyed.

The illusion of these freedoms is made necessary by the concrete reality of these enslavements. If not for such freedom, why is the child guerrilla blown to shreds in Belfast? If not for such freedom, why did the Iranian woman endure the tortures of the Shah's interrogators? If not for such freedom, why did the Buddhist monk in Vietnam immolate himself; why does the Catholic nun prostrate herself? If not for such freedom, why does the raped wife keep her silence? If not for such freedom, why did mothers bind their daughters' feet, why do women perform clitoridectomies on their girl children, why do "First Ladies" exist? If not for the illusion of freedom, why would there be such suffering? What other possible excuse could we have?

We know what we are told freedom is, and we do suspect that it's not what we actually have. We are told, strangely enough, that it's a limited resource which can be earned or rationed. We are told that we must give up freedom in order to get it (leaders exhort their followers to do this, adults teach this to children, men tell this to women, whites to peoples of color; humans use this justification in explaining captivity for endangered species, zoos and animal experimentation, strip mining, oil-tanker spills, and armament buildups; organized religions preach this message to everybody). We are told that freedom is synonymous with choice; yet what *is* choice to the shopper in the supermarket who can have her pick of twenty different breakfast cereals (all made by the same company) or to the student who can train for any career but (depending on the shape or shade of one's skin) have access to few? What is choice to the Hindu widow who faced either death on her husband's funeral pyre or a life of ostracism and slow starvation? What is choice to the voter in a one-party election—or in a two-party system when both parties articulate virtually the same politics but with ingeniously different rhetoric? Who defines the choices among which we choose?

We are told by the ultra-Right that freedom may depend on our capacity to wage "limited nuclear warfare." We are told by the extreme Left that freedom may consist of our capacity for "revolutionary violence." We are told by the vapid Middle that freedom may be defined by our capacity for enjoying Coca-Cola, animated cartoons, a savings account, neighbors of "our own kind," and a two-week vacation every summer. We may suspect that the ultra-Right and the extreme Left stretch not along a straight line but curve, rather, into one circle, meeting each other in an apocalyptic blur, just as we may suspect that the Middle is not a place of safety and rationality but of an emptiness that runs as smoothly as Disney World. We may suspect—but to do more than suspect is to risk being free of the Right, the Left, and the Middle, as we have known them. And to risk being truly free of all of them, but still politically engaged, is an alarming thought.

We are told by a patently mad society that sanity is freedom, and by its reverse mirror-image counterculture that madness is liberty. (Orwell warned us of this in his novel 1984, in which the totalitarian government puts forth slogans like weeds: "War is peace," it proclaims; "Freedom is slavery.")

We hesitate, of course, to think that we are actually enslaved. To do so seems self-indulgent, since literal slavery still exists in places on our planet. Worse, to do so would give the lie to our insistence that we are free. Yet we have no idea what freedom really is, nor why we, as human beings, seem to fear it so. Besides, almost all of our intelligence has been spent avoiding the comprehension that freedom, without an understanding of what it *is*, merely constitutes license—another new and insidious shape of nonfreedom—even for ourselves and especially for any we consider "other" than ourselves. We appear to have invested the creative genius of our species in discovering, maintaining, and defending the avoidance of this comprehension.

It was the handmaiden of the holy man who built the rickety lean-to that protected the holy man's body against the rainy season. It was she who guided visitors up the difficult path in the old days, and she who still could be seen sometimes scouring the valley villages as if to recruit new pilgrims. It was she, of course, who begged for his food and each evening brought it to him in the wooden bowl which was known in all the villages as "the holy man's begging bowl"—this, despite the odd fact that no one could remember having seen the holy man himself ever beg with it.

But then, no one could recall ever having known the woman's real name, either, despite the fact that she was so well known in the area. Indeed, she might never have had a name of her own. She had become, in any event, simply "the handmaiden of the holy man." And although some might whisper in dispute as to whether the mountain's recluse was holy at all, and although one or two villagers might even wonder at the definition of the begging bowl as the holy man's when he had never been seen actually carrying it, no one seemed to question the title of the woman as "the handmaiden of the holy man."

Perhaps this was because she had announced herself as such so fiercely and for so long that no one cared to argue the point—although no one could quite recall when, or if, she had begun giving this impression. Or perhaps this was because no other person seemed eager to compete for either title or task—and while ignoring a holy man wasn't that uncommon, letting one starve to death would have brought shame to all the surrounding villages. Perhaps, too, the title "handmaiden of the holy man" was simply an accurate description of what appeared to be her life. What else, after all, was she?

We are made uncomfortable by the notion that "Woman" has never existed.

After all, *women* exist. But women exist in all shapes, colors, configurations, sizes, humors, classes, ages, states of and attitudes toward fecundity. Men do, too, of course. The only thing men truly share, in fact, is their commonly conceived and perpetuated definition—by men—of Woman. Is it because men created Man as a definition of themselves (out of lack and longing) that actual men feel impelled to live daily lives closer to that definition? Is it because women did *not* create Woman as a definition of ourselves, but rather received it from others, that we feel less impelled to resemble it—and have for eons stifled our laughter at the thought that we ever have resembled it?

We know what we are *told* Woman is, and we do suspect that it's not us. We are told that it's relative: depending on the priorities of men in a given area at a particular time, Woman can be

Raquel Welch, a Hero-Worker Mother, Mata Hari, a doting grandma, a respected widow; a human being crippled by three-inch feet; a human being with silicone pumped under its skin; a human being forcibly concealed under a veil or forcibly exposed on a centerfold; a human being whose labor is too revered to be demeaned by wages; a human being whose genitals are sewn together; a human being content to fight waxy yellow buildup on the kitchen floor; a human being who, at the age of three, is capable of seducing her father; a human being at once able to offer extreme and continual tenderness and to receive extreme and continual violence—both with apparent pleasure. These are only a few of the identifying traits of Woman—yet we recognize ourselves as women in none of them, either as sole identities or as willing ones, nor in any of the other lists of Woman's characteristics. The definition may describe our condition, but it has nothing to do with *us*.

It's worth noticing that when we think of Woman, we do not think of Empress Wu, Marie Curie, Juliana of Norwich, Indira Gandhi, George Eliot, Lady Murasaki, Mary McLeod Bethune, Mary Cassatt, Elizabeth Cady Stanton, Yaa Asantewaa, Amy Beach, Rabi'a, Yvonne Goolagong, Elizabeth I, Zora Neale Hurston, Teresa of Avila, Agōtīme, Sor Juana, or Simone de Beauvoir. No, we think instead: religious reformer, scientist, mystic, prime minister, writer, and so forth. We think: genius, leader, creator, talent. We think: *exception*. Exception to what? Great men have been just as much exceptions among men, and with, one might add, far more access to the exercise of and recognition of their greatness. Yet an Akhenaten, an Einstein, a Mozart, a Martin Luther King, Jr., a Schweitzer, a Chakka, a Kubla Khan, a Black Elk, a Thomas Paine, a Saladin, a Shakespeare—all are seen as part of and consistent with Man. When we think "exception" about those many women of genius or invention or creative power whose names *have* filtered out to us despite all possible obstacles, we mean exception not to women, but to Woman. (Genius must equal human must equal Man.)

Individual women like those named above are critically dangerous to the image of Man, just because they imperil the image of Woman. Men have protected Man from them by calling them exceptions to Woman, and by telling the rest of us that most women equal real Woman while these aberrations do not. And so we were tricked out of feeling pride in and envy of such women into feeling alienation from and even contempt for them. We disowned them so that we ourselves could be owned. We also feared their fate, because the cost Man exacted from them was enormous. We have been unable to "own" our own, to say to men—speaking through his mirage of Man—"Yes, these are some, even many of us: this genius, this energy, this intellect, this agility, this force and drive, these very qualities. These? Oh, they were just women."

We are told that we must give up being women in order to gain our Womanliness, and the forms of exchange are clear, rigid, and ingenious.

Women have been offered religion in place of philosophy, morality in place of ethics, "womanly fears" in place of existential dread, community affairs in place of politics, selflessness in place of self, volunteerism in place of paid (for which read: valid) work, appearance in place of substance, romanticism in place of sexuality, childbearing in place of art, and the home in place of the universe. We are told that we have been happy and safe with this bargain and, although we have felt neither happy nor safe, we have managed to breathe on the coals of our own humanity and coax them, at moments, into a flicker of happiness, a warm mirage of safety. This too was inevitable, for more than one reason. First, we had no choice; we were told this—and we forgot that it was a lie. Then, too, we wanted to survive, and being ourselves creatures of lack and of longing, we thought to prove our very humanness by perfecting those skills that permitted us to mourn and to yearn—but most of all to deny the reality of our not having something we never have had.

We are told that Man lacks certain qualities which make Woman so special, and we've overlooked the fact that while some men may lack these qualities, Man need not, since he has been a phantom of redefinition by those making him in their likeness from the Cro-Magnon to the astronaut. We also have overlooked the fact that these qualities—nurturance, patience, humility, unselfishness, altruism, tolerance, intuition, cooperation, practicality—are, in a context of nonfreedom, precisely the qualities which make it more difficult for the nonfree even to recognize, much less demand an end to, their state of nonfreedom.

We are told that Man bears a great burden in possessing certain qualities which Woman lacks: power, energy, intellect, drive, courage, curiosity, a capacity for risk, idealism, imagination, invention, spontaneity. (It's confusing to women that these qualities are a burden to Man—since for centuries women have heard men congratulate themselves on possessing just these qualities.) We have overlooked the fact that while Woman may be said to lack these qualities, individual women in fact possess them, and always have—from Cro-Magnon to cosmonaut. We also have overlooked the fact that these qualities are, in a context where freedom itself is not understood, exactly the qualities which make it more difficult for those who define freedom even to recognize, much less demand an end to, their own state of nonfreedom—and make it impossible for them to extend such a difficult recognition or demand on behalf of those even less free than themselves.

Women do have the edge here, because we have always seen through the lie of Woman, whereas men are only now beginning to see through the lie of Man.

Year after year, the handmaiden of the holy man was assailed by questions—in the early days from without, but as the pilgrims stopped coming and eventually even the donors to the bowl she carried stopped inquiring, the questions began from within.

It was not, after all, as though she had a real right to be surprised. He had made it clear from the beginning that he was fit only to be a holy man, and that he must sit withdrawn on a mountain. If the world came and asked anything of him, as pilgrims, or if the world came and gave to him, as donors of sustenance to a beggar's bowl, that was the business of the world, and not his concern. Even though he had never said all this in words, the empty spaces deep behind his eyes had clearly told her so. The handmaiden of the holy man could not say that he had ever deceived her. Yet year after year she was assailed by questions.

She remembered that, in the early days, the questions pilgrims asked had seemed, at first, terribly difficult for her to answer. They asked, "What is the holy man really like?" They asked, "Where did the holy man come from?" They asked, "What discipline, what school of thought, does he follow?" They asked, "Can he work miracles?" A few even asked, "What is it like—to be the handmaiden of the holy man?" She remembered, with a sad smile, how her replies had changed over the years. In the beginning, she had maintained an enigmatic silence, but with an expression on her face which deliberately implied that she knew far more than she could ever tell. Then, later, she began to invent answers; sometimes the answers would vary from pilgrim to pilgrim—which the villagers interpreted as further weighty mysteries of contradiction. Thus she added to the legend of the holy man, when actually she was merely experimenting with various responses to see which was most effective in hiding her own ignorance. Only much later, when pilgrims had begun to ask, "Why is he so severe in his counsel to us?" or "Why is there no mercy tempering his judgments?" or "Is he angry with us? Does our approach disturb his mission?"—only then did the handmaiden of the holy man begin to reply simply, "I don't know," to all their questions. At first, this response felt to her like a betrayal of her defense of the holy man; then it felt to her like a shameful admission of her own ignorance; at last she grew indifferent to its meaning anything but the truth.

Now she told herself that, in time, the questions that assailed her from within would grow as irrelevant as those from without had become, even though these new questions seemed far more difficult to respond to than any of the world's curiosity. Just as before, she maintained an enigmatic silence in response. But of late, she had begun to invent answers . . .

So long as Man is equal to human but Woman is non-Man (and therefore nonhuman) how could we possibly invent anything so comparatively simple as mere freedom? As ultimate a task as imagining freedom would require, after all, every cell of sentient energy available to all of us—yet more than half the species has not been permitted to approach the task.

Imagine, for example, a room in which there seems to be no exit. In the room are twelve men. Seven of the men have guided the other five—somehow—into the room in the first place, but the five have forgotten how they got there. Now the room begins to get extremely hot, and wisps of smoke can be seen curling through tiny cracks in the walls. There appear to be no doors or windows, no skylights, no trapdoors. The five men new to the room become aware that they may all burn to death. Their response is to get furious at the seven others who brought them into this situation. They are so angry, in fact, that they refuse to consult with the seven about ways of getting out; this despite the obvious fact that their seven guides clearly knew of an entrance to the place and logically might know of an exit, a hidden panel perhaps, or a trick door not visible to the panicked glance. Perhaps the seven know that the walls themselves are an illusion. But the five not only refuse to consult the seven; they refuse to heed them when the seven attempt to shout through the now billowing smoke that there *is* a way out. Common sense aside, the issue of blame aside, even their mounting fear aside, one would think the five might comprehend that the situation was now so grave that all twelve minds present were needed to collaborate on a solution. It might occur to one of the five that, unless he and his four colleagues paid some attention to the seven (who had known the terrain well enough to bring them all there), the seven might even, in disgust, find a way out without the five—although this is asking perhaps too much of that one-of-the-five; it's asking for a ray of perspective, humility even, in the midst of fear—and fear is more often a breeding ground for dogmatic pride.

It's obvious to us (safe outside that burning room) that the deliberate deafness and wrath of the five is suicidal. It's also clear to us that the seven either must get through to the five somehow, and rescue them all, or choose to save themselves without the five. The third option—of the seven choosing to remain in the room silently, as directed by the five—appears to us insane. Why on earth would they do it? Out of some misplaced guilt at leading the five there in the first place? Out of fear of the rage of the five who seem so bent on blaming them? Out of a nagging terror that they themselves never knew or may have forgotten the way out, just as the five imply with such authority? Yet the seven recall that they had brought the five there for pleasure, enlightenment, celebration; they know that it had been a beautiful room—so how can they believe in their own guilt? And the seven know that the insistence on blame (upon which the five seem so bent even at the cost of life) is undeserved and stupid—so why should they fear it? Most of all, the seven sense that somehow they *do* know the way out, from memory or instinct or intuition—or simply because they had once known the way in—so how can they let themselves be paralyzed by disbelief in their own power?

It seems to us (safe outside that burning room) that the third course—the seven choosing to remain unheard and so perish together with the five—is the least likely. It remains only to be seen, then, whether the seven can convince the five to hear them in time, or whether the seven will leave without the five. *Or:* whether the seven will, in attempting to be heard, wait too long to listen to themselves.

We are not, of course, safe outside that burning room. We are inside it; the room is our planet. And the seven are the female more-than-half of our species; the five the male less-than-half. It's necessary to tell the story with all the characters as men, because the genuine insanity of our mutual predicament is then seen more clearly. Even in the 1980's, to tell such a parable more realistically, with the five as men and the seven as women, invites a swift dismissal of its truths as rhetoric—because the specter of Woman impedes the plot.

Yet real women do comprise a majority, and it is real women who so far have given birth to men, welcomed them into this room that is existence (and often been blamed for that). Furthermore, it is women who have been traditionally opposed to militaristic solutions and the cavalier sacrifice of life; it is women who, across cultural and generational differences, have applied a *practical altruism* to the problems of hunger, health, the preservation of natural resources, care for the young and old and dying. The cliché in international circles that "if women had their way, unilateral disarmament would have occurred last week" is a revealing one. This practical altruism is neither mystical nor genetically based. On the contrary, it seems to have been trained into women by a pervasive and unacknowledged global androcentrism —a system which needs women as the (powerless) custodians of human conscience. The irony is that we have continued to express it, at times even to our own grief, perhaps out of our ambivalent obsession with love.

Women—real, ordinary women—face an even more difficult predicament than the seven men in the burning room. Because, in fact, although we do sense that we know the way out for all of us, we cannot leave by ourselves. There is nowhere else to go, unless all of us leave together. This might explain why we have ricocheted for centuries between the alternatives of trying to convince men that we are human (albeit non-Man) and falling silent with our own burden of accepted responsibility, guilt, and fear.

The third way, of leaving without them, may be physically impossible, but it could show itself in another form: of being *for* ourselves, of learning to act instead of reacting, of taking responsibility for life on this planet *without* taking on any attendant guilt. This, however, would have to begin not with Woman, and even not with women.

It would have to begin with one woman, in her own life. It would have to begin utterly, devastatingly; she would have to be willing to leave everything familiar behind, be willing to believe she knows the way out and that the fate of life hangs on her, be willing to believe that she can create anew other rooms even more beautiful than the one now in conflagration, be willing to risk her own human soul, be willing to move to the door that cannot be seen, and be willing to fling it open.

Such an act hazards not only the certain fury of the five, but also the confusion, clamor, guilt, disbelief, envy, and fear of the remaining six who may, in attempting to be heard, be waiting too long to listen to themselves. Yet individual women are daring this act every day now, knowing that *to engender anything is to endanger something*—and knowing this in *all* senses of the statement.

"How did I come to be here?" asked the handmaiden of the holy man of herself. "Did I choose this freely or was I somehow chosen? What if, as some of the villagers whisper, the holy man is not a holy man? Have I wasted my life in serving him? Or is selfless service, even when rendered to someone unworthy, a form of freedom? Perhaps especially when rendered to the unworthy? Is his acceptance of my service without recognition a test of my devotion? Am I failing my devotion by even questioning my task and his vocation? Is true grace that which perseveres in the face of scorn, in the response of silence? Am I, then, using the holy man as an instrument of my grace, all the while telling myself that I wished to be an instrument of his? Why am I only now dissatisfied with my life; isn't that suspect? Is it that I wished him to be a successful holy man—revered and loved, with flocks of pilgrims from near and far whom I could guide proudly up the mountain path to his feet? Did I think he would smile on me for that service? Did he ever really need me to serve him? If not, what made me think he did?"

These, and many other questions, the handmaiden of the holy man asked herself. And she found that she could invent answers to all of them, as she had done at one point with the pilgrims. As before, she found that she often had different answers to the same question, and that the answers themselves gave rise to still more questions. She was dazed with these questions. They preyed on her constantly; even asleep in a nest she had made for herself one ledge down from the holy man's lean-to, she dreamed more questions. By day, going her rounds in the villages, she moved as if in a private buzzing swarm of questions, so much so that she began forgetting to recruit pilgrims.

Some of the villagers thought she had gone mad. Others were certain she was in a mystical state of transcendence contracted from having lived for so many years in such close proximity to the holy man. But since she had never harmed a soul and since they had no reason to fear her even in this new state, they averted their gaze from the absence in her eyes, contributed to the holy man's begging bowl which she carried, and let her be.

She was waiting for the third stage: the one where she would simply be able to say "I don't know" to all the questions—and be free of them. It had happened before; why shouldn't it happen again? Another year passed, and another. Still she went her rounds, and waited. But now her questions grew to obsess her, for still she had no real answers yet was weary of inventing them, and still she was unable to accept her ignorance.

One day, more exhausted than her completed rounds would warrant, she bore the bowl (how it seemed to get heavier each year!) up the winding path to where the holy man sat on his ledge, his hair blowing in the wind, his lips moving slowly. She had been in five villages that day, and walked for miles, yet no more than usual. She vaguely recalled something through the din of her questions ("How did I come to be here? Why am I dissatisfied? Is he a holy man? Who am I to question? Did he ever need me? Or do I need to serve something I believe holy? Why am I not holy? Why do I question?"). She recalled that the villagers had seemed especially kind and patient with her today, and as she reached the holy man's ledge a thought occurred to her through the din of her questions ("Why cannot he see my pain? Why cannot he answer my questions, the only one who could? Why cannot I ask him?"): a thought occurred to her that, given the villagers' kindness and the heaviness of the bowl, he would have a special feast today—not that he cared for such mundane matters. The handmaiden of the holy man stooped to set the bowl at the holy man's feet. It was then that she saw, to her horror, that the bowl was empty.

At the same instant, she knew this was not because the good villagers had refused to fill the bowl. All at once, her questions parted like a curtain and she glimpsed the reason, as filled with terror at this apparition, and as awed, as one who has seen the naked face of a god: the handmaiden of the holy man had that day forgotten to beg.

Today, at the beginning of the 1980's, less than two decades stand between us and the twenty-first century. We have no idea whether sentient life, or indeed any life, will exist on this planet long enough to welcome the year 2000. The only thing of which we are certain is our capacity to ensure that it does *not* exist that long.

Our species approaches critical mass with overpopulation. Our lakes, streams, rivers, even oceans, grow rank with industrial pollution, chemical and nuclear wastes, oil spills. Entire species of fish, fowl, animal, and plant become extinct or approach extinction. The skeletoid fingers of famine hold vast parts of Asia and Africa in their grip. Bubonic plague, which the World Health Organization thought to be no longer a threat, is recurring; cases have been diagnosed mostly in Asia but also in the United States.* Leprosy is again on the rise. Wars have become so commonplace that they're not always granted the full force of that title; by comparison to a third world war or a nuclear war, of what importance are the "wars" in the Middle East, in Africa, in South America, in Ireland, in the Pacific Islands? (These are now called "border conflicts," "revolutionary uprisings," "defense attacks" or even "offensive defense attacks," "tribal clashes," "protective invasions," "pacifications," or "police actions.") The armaments race among the superpowers becomes more intense each year, the weaponry more sophisticated, the deployment more cynical, the potential devastation more drastic, the control more out of control. Religious fundamentalism—always, historically, resurrected

---

* In 1980, eighteen Americans contracted the plague and five died of it, according to the Centers for Disease Control in Atlanta.

with virulent fanaticism at such moments of crisis—proclaims its comfort to people whose daily lives have become so filled with fear that a denial of the present, hatred of the flesh, and the promise of a life after death seem welcome. In the form of Jehovah's Witnesses, it invokes Armageddon with glee. As Islamic fundamentalism, it demands stonings, beheadings, floggings, a suicidal militance leading to death—and certain paradise thereafter. As Christian fundamentalism, it gives birth to the Moral Majority—which is neither moral nor a majority. This group, with its jingoistic patriotism and nostalgia for a past that never was, expresses its reverence for life exclusively in the cellular form and supports corporal and capital punishment for the other varieties; meanwhile, it attacks life in the female form (and the nonwhite form, the poor form, the Jewish form, the "foreign" form, and the form that might have a sexual preference different from the attacker's), and criticizes democracy, peace, and the very "freedoms" (speech, assembly, the press, religion, etc.) it purports to defend.

In the United States, the wealthiest megapower in the world today, the ultra-Right and "Moral Majority" have seized the helm of government in an election in which more than half the voting-eligible population did not vote—so disillusioned by the power of the ballot that they refused to exercise their right to use it. Every public-opinion poll shows that the majority of the U.S. population—men as well as women—remains strongly supportive of what have been termed "women's issues" (reproductive freedom, welfare rights, peace, environmental concerns, freedom of sexual choice, economic equity, educational equality, etc.). Yet the minority who did vote, and who now control the government, speak of "the entire country's turning to the Right," wishful thinking to say the least.

Every right-wing coup needs a scapegoat. In the 1950's, the Enemy was communism. Interestingly enough (because the superpowers have grown to resemble and bond with each other?), this time the Enemy was targeted as the Women's Movement, "feminism," *women*.[1] (At least we *are* a more accurately threatening Enemy to the status quo.) This time, the forces of the Right played on the deepest fears: reproduction, sexuality, family, human relationships, on the way women were puncturing the balloon doll of Woman.

The Left, which had at first ignored, then tried to coopt, then (failing that) again ignored women and the Women's Movement, came forth with a backlash all its own; if the room is burning, there must be someone to blame. The "more important priorities" argument was revived: since the war in Vietnam was no longer a convenient priority, now the issues of ecology and nuclear power must be claimed by men—and must come first. The familiar "revolution," as Man-defined, was trotted out; it invited Woman in, but barred the door to women ("What could *they* know about getting out of a burning room, anyway?"). Woman, for example, knew better than to expose pornography as propaganda comparable to anti-Semitic tracts or Ku Klux Klan publications; women—the prudish bitches—persisted in making the connections.

The Middle wrung its hands, looked aggrieved, shrugged, and tried to pretend it didn't smell smoke.

Yet such a backlash is in one sense inevitable when viewed from a historical perspective; it's almost a compliment, albeit one we might well do without. It means that women have been shouting through the smoke, have been loud enough to be perceived as a threat, have been strong enough to bring about a shift in the consciousness of that (disaffected-voter) majority, *have been asking the right questions*. It means that women, having seen through Woman, now saw through Man, and were daring men to do so, too. It means that women wanted to know what freedom meant.

Most of all, and most unforgivably of all, women were not content with what we were told in answer to our questions. We were not even content with our own invented answers. Women were deplorably exhibiting signs of Manhood—power, energy, intellect, drive, courage, curiosity, risk, idealism, imagination, invention, spontaneity—and insisting that these signs be noticed. Women were acting as if we were not non-Man, as if we were human.

Women had forgotten to beg.

The handmaiden of the holy man rose from her kneeling position. She faced the holy man, who stared, not at her but at the distant mountain peaks. She stood, while the wind whipped around them both, and began to ask him her questions. As if in a dream, yet more awake than she had ever felt herself to be, she heard her voice quietly asking question after question, pulling

each one out of herself with great pain and laying it, like an offer-
ing, at his feet. The lips of the holy man ceased moving.

It seemed to her as if the two of them had been poised that
way for eternity, the wind whipping around them, her questions
falling one by one like fireflowers into the void of his silence, her
eyes on him, his eyes on the distance. Then she had no more
questions, yet still she waited.

It seemed to her as if she waited until she died, and then was
being born once more, living, growing up and old and older,
dying again, again being born and again dying; it seemed to the
handmaiden of the holy man that she had lived and died a thou-
sand thousand lives while waiting for his answer to reach her
through his silence. But no answer came forth from him.

She bent again, hardly knowing what she did, and gently
pushed the begging bowl which she had carried but which every-
one seemed to know was his, closer to him, in a pitying gesture
that seemed to say he would have need of it now. She noticed
one tear making a glistening rivulet down the sloped wooden side
of the bowl, to lie like an eye or a diamond at its center, and she
realized, with wonder, that she had been weeping.

She stood again, and peered off into the distance toward which
he gazed, her whole soul following her eyes as she tried to see
what it was he saw. But there were only the far-off mists ringing
the snowy peaks. The handmaiden of the holy man turned once
more to look at him, and through her tears she smiled a for-
giveness and love more infinite and tender than she knew she had
possessed.

Then she turned and walked slowly down the winding moun-
tain path . . .

The questions may differ from individual woman to woman
but they are all on a remarkably similar subject, no matter where
on this comely little planet they are being asked. Because, although the sets and costumes and dialects change, the plot is
tediously in formula—so everywhere women are improvising new
plots and fresh dialogue far more interesting than the predictable
theme of Woman.

Internationally, all of the domestic issues can be found intact:
reproductive freedom—the basic human right to begin or termi-
nate a pregnancy by choice, and to demand a safe, decent technology that will make this possible; economic equality—equal pay

for equal or comparable work; an end to rape, battery, the sexual molestation of children, and sexual harassment on job or street or campus; the basic human right to freedom of sexual choice; the right to equal education; the right to political representation; the right to safe, humane health care; the right to government-sponsored but community-controlled child-care centers (that would demonstrate concretely the state's interest in and commitment to the next generation); the human right to an end of bigotry based on one's skin or genitalia or ethnic origin or age or beliefs or physical abilities; the right to equal participation in the joy of play in artistic or athletic endeavor; the right to learn and teach the buried history of women and other invisible peoples and not merely history according to the conquerors; the right to be free from the women-hatred inherent in pornography, organized religion, and "local custom"; the right to participate creatively in the professions, the political institutions, the media, and all other forms of society.

In addition, a host of other issues even more dramatic are added to the list of international priorities: literal slavery—the outright ownership of another human being—usually a woman or a child, for manual labor; the still-existent and even rising traffic in women and children for specific *sexual* slavery;[2] the "dowry murders" against which Indian women have been rebelling;[3] the so-called crimes of honor (in which a man may kill his wife for disobedience and go unpunished by the state) against which Latin American women have been demonstrating;[4] the international crime of genital mutilation—clitoridectomy and infibulation—which has been performed in Europe and the Americas as well as on the African continent and the Arabian peninsula, against which women are raising voices in revolt;[5] the omnipresent transnational corporate empires which exhaust natural and human resources in less powerful parts of the globe—against which women are striking, sabotaging, and organizing;[6] the proliferation of refugee populations—almost entirely composed of women and children fleeing from war and starvation—about which women are crying out;[7] the basic issue of literacy, about which women are demanding that we, who are 58 percent of the world's illiterates,[8] be permitted access to the power of the written word.

These are not "new issues"—nor is this the first time in

recorded history that women have risen up against our condition. What *is* new shows itself in four ways: never before has the repression been so technologically sophisticated; never before have women so blatantly been used to serve as lightning rods for the inability of Man to cooperate with men in a critical planetary crisis; never before have women been able to communicate so rapidly with one another on a global scale (due to that same sophisticated technology); and never before have men been so forced, *by* this communication between and among women, to take such notice of the mess Man has made of it all. In his official Report to the United Nations Commission on the Status of Women, U.N. Secretary-General Kurt Waldheim declared, "While women represent one half of the global population and one third of the labor force, they receive only one tenth of the world income and own less than one percent of world property. They also are responsible for two thirds of all working hours."[9] This was a characteristically diplomatic understatement, yet it would not have been made at all had not the efforts of thousands of women coaxed this minimal consciousness into being. Only when what should never have had to be borne becomes unbearable to those who have had to bear it are those who have not borne it compelled to acknowledge the existence of the burden they themselves created.

And then we *are* given answers through the silence—and they are even more cruel than the ridicule, tear-gassing, beatings, rapes, firings, child-custody suits, divorces and abandonments, media misrepresentations, and jailings to which women in the so-called developed countries have become accustomed—as recompense for daring to be women instead of Woman. In the global arena, the recriminations are unsubtle, swift, total, and devastating: silencing, censorship, imprisonment, internal exile, public floggings, repeated interrogations, forced exile, kidnapping, torture, assassination, public execution.†

† Political assassination: Aleida Foppa, radical and feminist, Guatemala, 1979. Attempted assassination: Libyans Farida Allaghi, feminist sociologist, and her husband Faisal Zagallai, democrat and sociologist, in Fort Collins, Colorado, by an American ex-Green Beret with links to Colonel Qaddafi, 1980. Forced exile, stripping of citizenship papers: Tatyana Mamonova, Tatyana Goricheva, Natalya Malakhovskaya, and Yula Voznesenskaya, sent out "for feminist subversion" from the U.S.S.R., 1980. Interrogation, arrest, and eventual exile: Motlalepula Chabaku, "suspicious person," South Africa,

Yet women move, move out into the world, leaving Woman staring vacantly behind them at all her cradles, kitchens, churches, graves.

In the Netherlands we strike for abortion rights. In the U.S.S.R. we publish underground *samizdat* feminist journals. In Senegal and Kuwait we organize pan-African women's conferences. In Libya, South Africa, Chile, East Germany, and Haiti we meet in private homes and dare know only each other's first names. In Afghanistan—caught between a national liberation front which affirms a religious-fundamentalist attitude that we must never speak in public and a foreign invader who uses "the woman question" cynically to crush our ethnic autonomy—we also meet underground. In Portugal, Israel, India, Sri Lanka, Great Britain, Norway, Iceland, and still more countries each year, we run for the highest office in the land—and are elected as prime ministers.

And still we move, more than half of all humanity—only now beginning to move together.

The villagers were surprised to see the handmaiden of the holy man descend the mountain path in the evening, accustomed as

1970–80, and Suzanne Körösi, for reproductive-freedom activism, Hungary, 1973. Public execution: the Princess Misha, for a secret marriage of choice, 1979; numberless and nameless women previously and subsequently for the alleged crimes of "unchastity," "adultery," "insurrection," Saudi Arabia. Public floggings: numberless and nameless women for the alleged sins of "perversion," "prostitution," "using or serving alcoholic beverages," "adultery," Iran, 1979–82. Imprisonment: Nawal El Saadawi, on charges of "contributing to civil unrest" by her books and speeches on women, Egypt, 1980; María Isabel Barreño, María Teresa Horta, and María Velho da Costa, (the so-called Three Marias) for coauthoring the book *New Portuguese Letters*, about the griefs, longings, and rage of women—on the charge of "outraging public morals and good customs," Portugal, 1972. Internal exile: Natalya Lazareva for "seditious activities on behalf of women," Malva Landa and Tatyana Osipova for "treasonous behavior," Irina Grivnina for investigating psychiatric-treatment abuse of women; Natalya Lesnishenka for organizing women into the free-trade-union movement, Soviet Union, late 1970's and 1980's. Diplomatic "silencing": Marilyn Waring, M.P.—stricken from speaking lists in Parliament after denouncing her country's relations with South Africa, New Zealand, 1981; Koryne Horbal, a member of the United States delegation to the United Nations Mid-Decade Conference on Women, a conference which she, as U.S. representative to the U.N. Commission on the Status of Women, had in part conceived and created—stripped of all access to the press for the "sin" of having criticized then-President Carter's administration policies on women, Copenhagen, 1980. These are only a few examples.

they were to her punctual visits, always much earlier each day. They watched her as she moved through the villages, and a few wondered if the glint of moisture on her face could possibly be tears, or merely the evening mist—for she had never been seen to weep. But she walked faster and faster, and her face seemed almost a blur in the blue light. Each village she passed through assumed she was going to some destination in the next, and it was a few days before everyone in the surrounding countryside came to understand that she had stopped nowhere. The handmaiden of the holy man had disappeared.

Everyone's first concern was for the holy man, of course. Since he had not come down to beg with his begging bowl, he must be starving up on the mountain ledge. A delegation of villagers was hurriedly assembled from candidates whose self-righteousness was only slightly greater than their reluctance. They climbed up the steep path, burdened by baskets of food and their own sense of outrage that the handmaiden of the holy man should have so deserted her post as to necessitate this act of charity from themselves. They told one another that she was an ingrate who had betrayed her master as well as those whose generosity had enabled her, for years, to bring him a laden bowl. They told one another that she was a fool who had never been able to appreciate the holy man's teachings the way they themselves had done. They told one another that she was a doomed soul fallen forever into wickedness and damnation, for clearly she had sought the pleasures of the world in turning away from the liberating path of sacrificial service. They told one another that she had gone mad, for who but a madwoman would brave the world alone after such a sheltered existence? Wild beasts lived in the foothill forests beyond the villages and doubtless already had devoured her. Or if she somehow had managed to escape that death, then other even more degrading and vile ends would await her. A few members of the delegation did wonder, but silently, what could have driven her away—but so strong was the tradition of reverence for a holy man (even a holy man not visited or seen in years), so strong was the tradition of reverence for the idea of a holy man, and so ancient, that those few who found themselves momentarily sympathetic or even curious about the handmaiden's motives quickly suppressed such heretical thoughts.

As the delegation of villagers neared the top of the mountain, *however, their chattering chilled into silence. Now each one was remembering what little knowledge they all, any of them, actually had of the holy man. Those who had made pilgrimages to him so long before recalled the severity of his pronouncements, the distance in his voice, the way that he never looked at his supplicant but fixed his eyes, instead, on the neighboring mountain peaks. Those who had never been in his presence remembered all the more acutely stories they had heard of those pilgrims who returned from the holy man's ledge filled with self-contempt for their hopelessly worldly ways, their grossness, their stupidity, their lack of vision—and how such returned pilgrims would sit for weeks in front of their meager huts, staring into space as their teacher had seemed to do, until they discovered that others still moved about, lived, laughed, made love, and shared food around the cookfires. Then they would discover the greater insight that these neighbors were as worldly, gross, stupid, and impoverished in vision as they themselves, but in addition lacked the gift of having learned that. And so the returned pilgrims found the miracle of a contempt for others even greater than the one they had been taught to feel for themselves—and this contempt gave them the energy to begin living again, to laugh, make love and share food around the cookfires, and to forget everything except that they did not wish to journey up the mountain again.*

Eventually, with back and leg muscles straining and nerves in a state of ominous excitement, the delegation rounded the turn of the path, to see the ledge before them. The shreds of a lean-to fluttered in the light morning wind, like a lonely, many-armed god beckoning to his followers. But there was no holy man. There was no one at all.

Only a begging bowl was left, sitting empty on the ledge like a sign, a rune, a signature that a handmaiden had been there; a message that once, someone had given and someone had received, someone had begged and someone had not, someone had served and someone had been nourished—and all that remained was emptiness.

Women have been virtuous, but not with our own standard of virtue. Now it's time that we became less "virtuous" and more of virtuosi—our tactics more varied, our skills sharper, our commitment more enduring. Fifteen years ago, this latest wave of feminism began, and it has had its own internal history as well as its place in a historical context. For example, it seems a considerable understatement (and ethnocentric error) to call this wave, as we have sometimes done, "the second wave," implying that the first wave, not only in the United States but in some other countries, was the nineteenth-century suffrage movement. The truth is that ever since there has been oppression, there have been rebellions—about which we perforce know less because those who win or hold power tend to be the ones writing the history books. Yet we *have* managed to unearth some buried history.

We know, for instance, that neither Nat Turner nor Harriet Tubman was "happy on the plantation," a discontent also manifesting itself in the Chuong sisters of seventeenth-century Vietnam, the Beguine Movement in medieval France and Spain, the twelfth-century Turkish harem revolts, and the nine million women burned as heretics over a three-hundred-year period in the late Middle Ages, the persecutions peaking in numbers and intensity during what Man celebratorily calls the Renaissance. To look a little further, we can see the clues left by individual rebels: Eleanor of Aquitaine, Christine de Pisan, La Malinqué, Aspasia, Boadicea, Theodora, Hatsepshut, Mary Wollstonecraft, and others. To look deeper, we can encounter the longest-buried clues in myths that fossilize prerecorded history: the Amazons (Hellenic, Dahomeyan, Libyan, and Brazilian), the female deities that were primary in every religion's origin, the Sidh, the Shekinah. If we *must* give this wave of women's rebellion a Köchel listing, we would be more accurate to name it "the three billionth wave."

But whatever its number, it is ours, now, here, in our lifetimes. At its beginning, we could (perhaps) afford to be specialists of sorts. Some women were dedicated to "confrontation tactics"— demonstrations, seizures of buildings, violence against property (though not people), and street actions—while others were focused on legislative reforms, creating a women's voting bloc, and getting women into the professions and electoral politics. For a while (regrettably) we even could afford the questionable luxury of contempt for those whose strategy differed from ours: the alienation with which so-called street fighters viewed those who "worked within the system," the anxiety with which reformers eyed militants.

Such a relative luxury is no longer affordable. The room is

burning—and it's suicidal to emphasize the comparatively fine points of difference among those who might know the way out, especially since those who seem not to know the way out see no differences whatsoever among those who do. To them, we are all Woman, a singularly myopic perception of a pluralistic majority as being a uniform entity. To Man, when the majority of human beings raises issues of historical and intolerable pain, it is "single-issue politics" emerging from the "Me Decade" (never mind that for Man it has been the "Me Millennium" or more accurately the "Me Eon"). So firm is the perception of women as Woman, as non-Man and therefore nonhuman, that such issues as universal peace, an end to starvation and illiteracy and displacement by conquest, the safe birthing and compassionate raising of the next generation, the human right to reproduce or not, security from violence and degradation, and the freedom to love whom one chooses are seen as "women's issues," i.e., single-issue "Me Decade" selfish priorities. The point, of course, is that such priorities *should* be of concern to men as well. But the room is burning, and although some men are trying to reach out a singed hand through the smoke, Man persists in his reluctance to hear us.

This is where the need for virtuosity becomes imperative, in that the exigencies of the situation and the pervasiveness of the problem necessitate our being in the streets *and* in the legislative halls, able to meet in secret *and* to use the communications media, able to speak in code *and* in as many of the world's languages as we can devote ourselves to learning, *able to balance an infinite patience and a relentless sense of urgency.* We must know how to lobby through the system while not losing sight of the fact that we are, as Elizabeth Oakes Smith said back in 1852, aiming "at nothing less than an entire subversion of the present order of society, a dissolution of the whole existing social compact." We must develop strategies for defending ourselves from backlash while not losing our historical perspective that backlash was an inevitable response to the threat posed by our no longer ignorable existence.

Like the subatomic particle, we must be both everywhere and nowhere on our orbit at the same instant.

For a time, the villagers could talk of little else but the holy man. After the first delegation returned, still carrying their offer-

ings, other delegations wound their way up the mountain path—
to see for themselves, or on the assumption that the holy man
had gone away briefly, somehow, but would return to his ledge.
Indeed, in the weeks following the news of the holy man's disappearance, more pilgrims climbed the mountain in search of him
than had ever done when he was assumed to be there. But always
they found only the frayed and gradually collapsing shelter, the
stark rocks and sparse vegetation, and the empty begging bowl.
Finally, even this last vanished—some villager having seen a perfectly serviceable bowl going to waste unused.

After a while, the villagers reconciled themselves to the fact
that the holy man was no more. Some said he was dead; some
said he had never existed. After all, they argued, no one had seen
him for years. The only proof any of them had of his presence
was the perpetual, irrefutable, taken-for-granted existence of the
handmaiden of the holy man—at least until she suddenly left
him, or rather left them. And where they initially blamed her for
his disappearance, they came to blame her for his existence, for
having perpetrated a hoax on them for so many years—for having
invented him in the first place, as an excuse to beg for unearned
sustenance, because everyone knew that she, being a woman,
could not have been herself a holy man. Those villagers who
claimed to have visited the holy man long ago, and actually to
have seen him, now realized that the handmaiden of the holy
man must have put some sort of spell on them to make them believe they had been counseled by a real being and not an apparition. Here was a comforting thought, for it explained as nothing
else could their memory of his distant manner, his severity, and
the contempt which clearly none of them had deserved. The holy
man obviously had been nothing but a creation of his handmaiden, a legend, and at times a skillfully wrought illusion, the
means by which an unscrupulous woman might gain her mode of
survival. In this manner the villagers comfortably solved their dis-
turbing mystery, and their lives went on as before.

But then, strange tales began to drift among them about the
woman they had for so long called the handmaiden of the holy
man—rumors that she had been seen again, but each time in
differing circumstances.

A group of village women who had journeyed to bring their
handicrafts to the provincial market said that they saw her telling

fortunes by the cards in a stall at the marketplace; the fortune-
teller's name, one had learned, was Ankha. Another woman, returning from a visit to her dying mother in a far-distant village,
claimed that she had seen the handmaiden of the holy man, now
calling herself Rejan, living openly and happily with a man—a
peasant flute carver—and just as openly pregnant. A young girl
given in marriage pledge to a family many miles away in the north
sent word home to her sister that the handmaiden of the holy
man was a well-known figure in that area, going by the name of
Meilade, a healer who, although only recently arrived in the dis-
trict, had already founded a form of nunnery to which women
and children in need came from the surrounding area; there, the
girl said, this Meilade lived, together with other women, and
ministered to the needs of these unfortunates. A husband and
wife, gone out from the foothills to the plain to trade with an expected caravan, both had seen the handmaiden of the holy man
—although they quarreled over the details. The husband noticed
her riding in a palanquin, appareled in the finest silk and reclin-
ing against cloth-of-gold cushions; he had inquired of a camel
driver, and learned that the lady was Bretiang, a famous courtesan. His wife, however, insisted loudly that all women looked
alike to her husband, and that she really had seen the handmaiden of the holy man, but not as a courtesan; the wife saw her
wearing a man's clothing and riding a fine desert stallion at the
very head of the caravan, shouting orders to a well-organized and
respectful group of followers who addressed her by the name of
Oon. Two young men who were the proud rakes of a particular
village swore that, while out hunting, they were attacked by a
wild woman of the woods, who hellishly yowled "This from me!
This from Uxten!" with each blow she dealt them; this woman,
they assured everyone, was easily recognizable as the handmaiden
of the holy man. A small child who wandered away from home,
following the trail of bright orange field daisies that grew along
the foothills, returned home safely the next day—and, when questioned by his frantic parents as to how he had survived, answered
simply that the lady who used to beg with the bowl took care of
him and set him on the path home. The name of the lady, as the
child pronounced it in his babyish lisp, sounded like Evaraze.

For years, different folk from different surrounding villages
claimed to have sighted the woman once called the handmaiden

of the holy man. Always she appeared in utterly new circumstances, and always with a different name. Yet in all this time, no one had seen even an apparition of the holy man. Nor had anyone, for longer than the villagers cared to remember, climbed the mountain to look for him, since they were as certain that he was dead or never had been there at all as they were convinced that his handmaiden was alive, and everywhere.

Yet how are we—for a while longer alive, and of necessity acting on our orbit at all points and at no point and at the same time—how are we to survive? How—while calling out, whispering hoarsely and gesturing desperately to others in the burning room —are we to breathe? Because the simple ineluctable truth is that we are, being women, being no longer (as if we ever were) Woman—being not men and being decidedly non-Man—we are human. And if we have begun to unlearn the denial of what we never had—freedom—we are all the more filled with the human characteristics of lack and of longing. It is this moment in which all of our past grief and present activism and future visions cluster, like angels and demons dancing together on the head of a pin, life itself suspended in that dance. It is not Woman, but one woman, each single individual woman, who holds the pin (between her teeth, because her hands are full). And such a woman is often tired.

Such a woman may wonder why the Women's Movement no longer speaks much to her about love, about the real (not the rhetorical) complexities of human sexuality, about the real (not the jargonistic) meanings of "sisterhood," about the real (not the denied) anger of women *at* women, and yes—about the real (not Man-made) nature of men. Such a woman understands the vital importance of the fight for legislation guaranteeing women human rights, the fight for equal access to jobs and equal pay, the traditional political battlegrounds, and yet, and yet . . .

A funny thing happened to us on the way to the revolution. In rightfully demanding our freedom, we began to believe those who told us we first had to define it—as if we, they, or anyone could. We began to believe freedom was a goal instead of a state, a process, a continually fluid, surprising, dynamic *movement*. We even began to think that if it were a goal, we would live to reach it—as if history were not both a continuum and a synchronous minisecond. *We lost sight of the centrality and vastness of our own politics.*

We began to make our priorities those issues we learned (from Man) were considered important—and they are—to the detriment however of what something beating wild wings in each individual woman's heart told her was important. We began (O familiar misery) to feel embarrassed all over again for our rage—which for millennia we had been told Woman did not feel. We began (O new and pathetic irony) to be embarrassed for our love—which for millennia we had been told was *all* that Woman felt. In trying so to be comprehended as human, therefore less non-Man, we clung to language we thought Man might understand: objectification, reification, political impact, sex roles, parity, capitalism, communism, socialism, radical/reformist, homosexual/heterosexual, single/married, mother/mother*less* (there *is* yet no affirmative word for a woman who does not have a child, and the pseudo-substitute "child-free" instead of "childless" happens to be insulting to children). We spoke of class analyses and cooptation and caucuses, of plenary sessions and demonstration permits, of demographics, opinion polls, and not wanting to "alienate the public." We still speak of these things; I still speak of these things. Nor is there anything in itself shameful about our doing so—but there *is* something tragic if we forget the real words for what we are about.

We began to forget them—or, rather, to be embarrassed by using them, especially since we knew their numinous qualities and the fearful depth of our lack of them and longing for them, and because we did not want, in using them, to be mistaken for Woman. Of course, since it's always easier for those who have no comprehension of what they're saying to say whatever they wish, the religious fundamentalists and the Right Wing began to use those words we no longer dared claim as ours: honor, integrity, morality, ethics, anger, justice, power, freedom, love.

Yet these *are* what the Women's Movement is about, and always has been about: precisely this audacity and this vision.

Let us say that a woman loves another woman, and is proud of her love. Both being women (and therefore simply human), these lovers have problems—even with each other. They have problems identical to those in any other human relationship: conflicts about interpersonal power, about responsibility, or temperament, or jealousy, or possessiveness, or different energy levels, or senses of humor, or moodiness. But so beleaguered are they by both a hideously misogynistic/homophobic culture *and* a highly nervous Women's Movement (exhibiting its homophobia at times in traditionally bigoted ways and at times in "politically correct" guilt fashion) that the wagons are drawn in a circle around their lives. Beyond the confines of a ghetto culture, whether chosen or imposed, where may either woman speak plainly about these lovers' difficulties? It has been such a struggle, at such an appalling price, to affirm this love at all; how, then, dare one admit that a lesbian love, like any other, may be less than perfect, ideal, utopian? When a defensive posture has been required for too long a time, it almost always will rigidify and become defensive even against itself.

Let us say that another such woman loves a man, and is proud of her love. He loves her, he has changed through feminist consciousness, he is committed to changing even more—as she herself is. Early in this wave of feminism, the small consciousness-raising groups in the United States and elsewhere addressed themselves to her situation, albeit sometimes to the exclusion of the problems of her sister (who happened to love a woman). Somewhere, that early focus—rather than expanding—disappeared under the pressure of other more "objectively political" issues: the Equal Rights Amendment, affirmative action, discrimination lawsuits, marches—all honorable aspects of the fight. And yet. Somewhere, the rising awareness of class, race, age, sexual preference, ethnic identity, occupational category, single-or-married status, having or not having children, and all the other variations of women's conditions, all the other diverse ways in which we are categorized or categorize ourselves—somewhere the inevitable and absolutely imperative need to face and recognize and try to speak across these barriers got left behind, and left the unique and complicated pain of this woman behind. Man—and sometimes even her own man—may tell her she is a malcontent. Some women may feel envy that she has a relationship with a man at all; others may express contempt for precisely that reason. She may have become almost as ashamed in the Women's Movement as in the patriarchal world that she *still* weeps quietly into her pillow at night sometimes, that the love is so costly, the change so very difficult. (Was this why, in fact, we turned our attention almost wholly to legislative and political change? Because, compared to the real task—understanding each her own human authenticity— it seemed blissfully uncomplicated?)

If we don't rediscover our rage we will choke to death on it. If we don't reaffirm our love we will die of thirst. And both the rage and the love are still in each woman, barely tapped.

Did Man think that some twenty thousand years of our having been enclosed in the shape of Woman would evoke such a small anger that one decade would exhaust it? Men may have suspected otherwise, but Man thought exactly that—and we almost have believed him, almost again self-censored our fury for the sake of pragmatism. Did Man think that history—as men had made it in his image—had taught men more about love than women had understood for millennia? Yes. And so eager were we to believe that men simply had a way of loving we did not yet quite fathom, that we denied our own expertise on the subject.

Yet what has been called feminism *is* a vision of extraordinary love—expressed in a necessarily purgative form of rage. If we don't give one another the permission to rage, who will? Not Woman. Nor will Man grant us this permission. Nor will men. And what do we have to fear about our love? Why deny it? The feminist vision has always been about love—not a Hallmark Card sentimentalized, cheapened imitation ("When you care enough to send the very best revolution"), but the wild, furious, enraged, cleansing, energetic love that *demands* change—love equal to the belief that there *is* a way out of the burning room, that women and men *can* change, that we *can* shed the dead skins of Man and Woman, that this small blue-and-green globe we share *can* be saved into peace, plenty, and laughter.

Such a love releases itself erratically, wittily, painfully. It may begin with one word: "No." It may begin with the profound revolutionary slogan, "Herman, pick up your sock." It may be a speechless act: the opening of a door—or the closing of one. But it begins always with one woman, absolutely unique among living beings, with only her own one life to live—and an awareness of that. To such a woman we must return again and again, just as she returns slowly, eventually, in fear and trembling and health unto life, to where she began—to herself.

One day an old man passed through the villages in the valley. He moved with difficulty, leaning heavily on a staff. Although he was a stranger, there was a tradition of hospitality in the valley, and so he was invited to share food and shelter at a house in each of the villages through which he passed. Besides, the villagers felt something infinitely touching in his humility, his gratitude at whatever they had to offer him. He said little. When questioned, he replied only that he was a wanderer who had traveled much in search of the great treasure he lost once, but had never had at all. Mystified by this answer, the villagers shrugged and left him his secrets. A few would have pressed him further, but something in his manner—some quality of mourning or great grief—restrained them. They let him be.

He moved on slowly, painfully, as if toward a specific destination. Not all the concerned remonstrances of the pitying villagers, not all their generous offers that he might remain with them (for how long could such a frail old man last?)—nothing could detain him. He came finally to the little village nestled at the foot of the mountain, and rested the night in a cottage there, again welcomed as a stranger must be welcomed. Yet when the first dawn broke, the children of that house, rising early to peep at their visitor, found him gone, and ran to tell their parents, who thought it strange.

It wasn't until the sun was well up in the sky and people were going about their daily tasks that someone happened to glance up and shout to the others: "Look! There! Halfway up the old mountain path! It's the stranger!" And far up the slope, his back as stooped as the path was curved, the stranger could be seen, shuffling his way up the mountain as steadily as if he were being driven by a force stronger than his fragile body could contain.

Alarmed for the old stranger—who must have lost his wits or his way or both, some of the villagers dropped what they were doing and ran toward the mountain path. But he was too far above them for their shouts to reach him, and so a small group began to climb after him, some of its members irritated at this interruption of their daily routine and others grateful for it. They were certain they could overtake him quickly, for they were hardy people in the full strength of life and he was a brittle and barely fleshed skeleton, all eyes and lank hair, trying to shift the burden of his many years to a slender walking staff. But with each turn of the path he was farther ahead of them than before, and soon they *realized that they might have to climb all the way to the top before reaching him.*

Indeed, this was so. But when the villagers breathlessly arrived at their destination and rounded the last curve of the path before the highest mountain ledge, they stopped, dazed, at the sight that awaited them.

Not one, but two old people sat on the outcropping, talking quietly. Just behind them, a bit farther back in the overgrowth, stood a small hut, its thatched roof neatly spreading a shadow from the intense sunlight over what looked to be a tiny garden that put forth a few vegetables and flowers in humorous defiance of the stony mountain soil.

The villagers looked back and forth—from garden to hut to the two ancient ones in deep conversation—with amazement. Then, perhaps because the surroundings brought a dim recognition, the village midwife spoke.

"It's the handmaiden!" she gasped. "It's the handmaiden of the holy man! And he's . . . he must be the holy man!"

The stranger turned from his conversation, showing a face filled with terrible awe to the villagers.

"Dear fools," he cried, "I am only a poor stranger here. But this"—he gestured toward his ancient companion—"is the holy woman you once called my handmaiden."

Immediately, a low laugh came from the old woman, a laugh warm and nubbly as the wool of a mountain sheep, a laugh that wrapped them all, stranger and villagers alike, in its safe folds.

"No, no, no, my friends," the crone said, still laughing an irrepressible music to the words she almost sang. "The time for that is past; we have no need of such differences anymore, surely. We are all holy here." The eyes in the old woman's wrinkled face seemed as probing as the sun itself reaching deep into the rocky folds of the mountain. "Indeed," she went on, in a voice as excited as that of a child presenting a gift labored on for a long time by hand, "indeed, there is nowhere we are not any of us holy." She turned to the old man and said quietly, "We must tell them what we've learned."

The villagers drew nearer, astonishment in their expressions. Nestled at the old woman's feet was a snow leopard, seemingly as tame as a kitten, its sleepy purrs humming a lazy rhythmic background to the story which now unfolded before them.

"*I wanted to be free of the world*," the old man said softly, "*and so, to escape it, I came here long ago. But I found that my freedom lay all in the keeping of another's labor. I, who neither had asked for this nor expected it, nonetheless accepted it, because I saw no other way to be free of the world. And*"—the stranger bowed his head—"*I came to hate the one on whom I thought my freedom depended.*"

Then the old woman spoke: "*I wanted to be free of the idea of freedom*," she smiled, "*and I thought to accomplish this by giving myself utterly away. But I did not know that, never having had myself, I had nothing to give. I invented something to give— and I invented someone to receive my gift. But none of these illusions made me free and, in time, I wanted one thing only: to be free*"—she turned to the old man—"*of your freedom. For this act, it was necessary that I invent myself.*"

And so she had gone, the villagers learned, down into the heart of the world, and invented herself. And so he had gone after her, the villagers learned, in search this time not of his freedom but of the one who had taken his freedom from him. But everywhere the holy man sought his handmaiden he found only someone with a name of her own, and he found only himself, and he found only the world. Homeless, he saw those rooted to one place; possessing no goods, he saw those bound to their possessions; drifting from city to town to village, he saw the faces of those staring through prison bars; lacking family of blood or choice, he saw those who live and die daily with people to whom they cling from fear or loneliness or vengeance, calling it love; aging, he saw the young trapped in their own impatience, the mature enslaved by their immediacies, the old imprisoned in their regrets. He learned that no one, no thing living or dead, was free, and this knowledge, strangely, released him of his search for freedom and for the one who had stolen it. Even more strangely, it released in him a merciful sense of connection between himself and everyone else in this shared predicament. At long last, he decided to return to the mountain ledge—expecting nothing and no one to await or recognize him—there to die in the place where he first lost the freedom which had never been his.

All this time, the woman who had been called the handmaiden of the holy man had gone in search of the self she was inventing, the self beyond the self who would be free of the idea of freedom.

Everywhere she went in the world, she saw others engaged in the same search. She saw the face of a mother, gaunt with hunger, fill with radiance at having found a morsel of food for her child; she saw a condemned man being marched to his execution, arms chained behind his back, who stretched his face up toward the soft rain's caress, the drops greeting him with more familiarity than any other they fell upon; she saw a young girl, wasted with disease, array herself in finery like a bride to meet her death with an anticipation beyond relief; she saw two lovers being stoned because their love was not acceptable to others—and she saw how the concern of each was only to protect the other's body; she saw a great hero shudder with cowardice in his bed on the night before, and on the night after, a battle; she saw a dancer become the drumbeat to which she danced; she saw a group of peasants, armed only with pain, advancing steadily on a great palace—she heard them whisper "freedom" as the guards cut them down; she saw a lost child hug itself with delight at recognizing the way home. And in all these selves she was, and all these selves were at home in her. So, at long last, she decided to return to the mountain ledge, expecting no one to have waited and certain that no one would recognize her, to live quietly, self-sufficient and begging of no one, until her death—there, in the place she had first thought to escape the idea of freedom, to invent herself.

She built the little hut and dug the tiny garden. She welcomed the wild animals of the place, unafraid, until they were unafraid of her. She waited for no one, having found herself; she sought nothing, having found the idea of freedom. Then, one day, an old man came laboring up the mountain path . . .

The parts of that woman—what are they? The flesh, the brain, the dreams, the blood, the secret languages, the days and nights, the fantasies, the hatreds and alarms, the lusts, the terrors, the disgusts? What was the girlhood that prepared her for this? How does she approach her own body, a man she loves, a woman she trusts, a fear she tells no one, a hope she tells no one, a nightsky over the ocean, a mortal illness, her own idea of joy, her own idea of freedom, her own existence, her own authenticity, her own death?

Who are we to ask? Who am I to ask? Who am I to ask but myself?

I actually have caught myself, while writing this book, thinking that I have no right to approach the subject. Thinking: to talk and write about women, yes, I've earned that right. I've been one, after all, for forty-one years, and I've been committed to women as a people for almost half that long. I've worked with women, marched, demonstrated, argued, fought, laughed, cried, and been jailed with women; women have exhilarated and infuriated me, changed me, instructed me, inspired and exhausted me; more days of my life have been spent in talking with women, reading works by and about women, and thinking about women and women's condition than on any other subject; more nights dreaming about that same subject than any other stuff of dreams. Yes, I thought, I have earned the right to begin to understand women.

But who am I to dare write about freedom? I'm no expert, no philosopher; where freedom is concerned I can't even understand the subject with the experience of a participatory journalist. What do I know about freedom? What right do I have to approach the subject?

The question is more revealing of women's condition—and of the condition of freedom—than any answer yet possible.

If freedom is a fact we are overlooking, or if it is an illusion never to be enjoyed fully by anyone, or if its current definitions are the truth but not the whole truth for the whole species, or if in order to exist it needs new definitions as yet unimagined—whatever the task, it's a task for everyone.

First, we need to *envision* it—but to do that we need to break through the pervasive and powerful assumptions (shared also by many feminists) that certain past "givens" are inevitable, unchangeable, natural. The New Physics encourages and even demands utterly new thinking; as an intellectual discipline, it refreshes the brain into glimpsing just how much nothing is inevitable, just how totally everything is relative, just how ceaselessly everything changes, just how inescapably natural all concepts are. It questions each assumption anew—and finds each wanting. It philosophically conceives of—*and scientifically shows*—a range of options, systems, forms, realities, and imaginings as already existing and potentially possible beyond our wildest creative so-far hallucinations. Furthermore, it jars our thinking out of the ruts of political rhetoric, it relaxes the reflexes of mere reaction. It demands our participation as much as or more than our observation. Last, there is nothing it does not embrace as its subject: it reaches from the most unseeable subatomic particle's particles through all matter ("inert" and "active") and out into the macrocosmic universes within which our own universe microcosmically spins. Such a tool just might be powerful enough to help us reimagine men and women, and to conceive of freedom.

If freedom is defined only by the few, then, as we've learned, it exists only *for* the few. Who better, now, to approach this task than women—not only because we have for so long been kept from it, but also because we have been posed, under the guise of Woman, at the opposite pole from what Man has characterized *as* freedom: ours (supposedly) the homing instinct, the nesting instinct, the conservative instinct, the "tame."

Woman, one might say, was created for the simple purpose of keeping women from addressing such a task. Women, faced with the staggering job of transforming ourselves from a category into a people, a movement, an active group—necessitated by the very structure which seems to make change by any individual impossible, which seems to require sheer numbers of people to affect it— women have not surprisingly at times recreated situations of assumed nonfreedom within our own groups and movement. We are, remember, human. So while women as a group are capable of challenging nonfreedom, we have not yet addressed ourselves to freedom itself (we have been busy enough as it is). Perhaps no *group* can begin this task, though all groups must eventually engage it. Always, inevitably, it comes down to one individual. If the proper study of mankind is man, then the proper study of humanity may well be one woman.

Such a woman might think: "That's why I must dare to write about freedom, while not understanding it, never having known it, disbelieving it exists, and fearing that it does."

Such a woman might say: "If I don't risk beginning to invent the universe, no one will."

The sun had begun to set when the villagers withdrew down the side of the mountain, and as they descended the winding path, they looked at one another as if seeing familiar faces for the first time. Above them on the ledge, the two old ones had much to say to one another alone.

Not too long after, the man they once called the holy man died quietly in the arms of the woman they now called the holy woman. They buried him, at the woman's gentle direction, near the ledge, facing out toward the distant mountain peaks.

For another season or so, the woman they once called his handmaiden lived on in the little hut, tending her garden, scolding her snow leopard when he nibbled the petals of her flowers. Children would often run up the mountain path now, to sit with her while she told them stories and made them laugh and let them play with the leopard—who loved dearly to have his silken stomach rubbed by one little child in particular. The children could never get enough of her stories: the one called The Death of the Mother, and the one called The Marble Book, and The Double Mirror, and The Crystal Woman of Light, and The Living Stone, and The Giant Star, and The Bead of Love, and many more. Especially the children loved to ask her, again and again, what freedom was—because they knew she would show them, differently each time. Once she pointed to a field daisy in the garden, and asked them, in turn, "Which part of the flower is most pure flower: the yellow heart? the orange petals? which orange petal? the leaves? which leaf? the stem? which part of the stem?" And when no one could reply, she would ask them if the flower wasn't in fact all the parts together as one thing. "Yes, oh yes!" they would nod. "And yet," she would go on, "doesn't the whole flower exist in each one of its parts? If you find an orange petal floating along the air on a summer day, what does it bring to mind?" The children would clamor to answer that it brought to mind a field daisy.

"Just so!" the old woman would exclaim. "The idea of the entire flower exists perfectly in even one petal, as a song resonates in the air after the last note is over. That," she would muse, "is something like the idea of freedom. It lives nowhere and everywhere at the same time. It lives in the connections."

The villagers did not always understand the old woman, although they loved her. The children, however, both understood and loved her. When she was found, one bright noon, sleeping peacefully in a night from which she would not awake, they buried her near to the stranger they had once called the holy man, close to the ledge that looked out over the distant mountain peaks. For days the children brought flowers to the graves, and for days the snow leopard would not leave the place.

Then one day, the beautiful beast circled the graves three times and loped off across the mountain ledge to another ledge—and was gone forever. That was the day the children realized they need not come back to the mountaintop to tend the old couple's resting place; there was no need.

They went down again into their homes and villages, and grew and thought and watched, and taught others what they had learned. Far and wide the words spread, until all the people in all the villages in the province knew that they were every one of them a holy being, each a petal or stamen or leaf or stem of an idea of freedom. And from that province, like the resonance of a song, the idea bloomed into the world.

No one sat on the high mountain ledge anymore, and no one ever again begged with a wooden bowl. Holy man, handmaiden, stranger, and holy woman—all had gone back into the heart of the flower. No one need take their place now, as if it had ever been theirs.

As for the distant mountains, they gazed impassively on the ledge eroding away year by year. And if the mountains had cared to know, they could have known that what they saw held all the answers to the drifts of questions that melted, each like a snowflake spoked scarlet and gold in the sunrise, on their eternal and indifferent heights.

II

THE TWO-WAY MIRROR

An Anatomy of a Woman

You have never learnt to know me . . .
I am no more as I used to be
A happy celebration
Filled with hope . . .
Even in the midst of my sorrow
You came asking.

—Maha al-Fahd

When you visualized a man or woman carefully, you could
always begin to feel pity . . . that was a quality God's image carried with it . . . when you saw the lines at the corners of the eyes, the shape of the mouth, how the hair
grew, it was impossible to hate. Hate was just a failure of
imagination.

—Graham Greene

Show me your face before you were born.
—Zen kōan

The most logical place to begin is where each of us began: in the
body. Whatever may happen in the future, as a development of
recombinant DNA research or *in vitro* gestation, so far we humans have been conceived in and carried in the human body—in
fact in the specifically female human body. It's bitterly ironic that
the body of a woman, while carrying another potential body, is
perceived as most archetypally Woman—since Woman is essentially definable as non-Man (and therefore nonhuman), but a
pregnant woman is perhaps excessively human; without her labor,
"humanity" would not exist. Of course, if giving birth were to be
regarded as a basic human activity, then all sorts of dangerous

questions would arise—questions of that human being's rights of choice, timing, skills, aptitude, and control. These questions, seen as normal and acceptable when applied to any other human activity, have been largely disregarded in this area, because to apply them here would be to risk acknowledging a woman's individual humanity, thereby acknowledging her authentic human rights and powers. How much more convenient to see birth as a mystified activity of Woman—and to extend that concept until this one activity becomes the major identifying characteristic of female human beings, and indeed our primary reason for existing.

Entire libraries have been written on the hilarious notion that women have "penis envy," and only recently have women been heard even slightly when we reexplained for the thousandth time that we envied not the male genitalia but the privileges that seemed attached to them in patriarchal society. Only recently, too, has there been any exploration of the concept of "womb envy" felt by men—although at times this notion too has been turned magically against women: "Well of course men feel resentful wonder at the capacity of women to give birth, which naturally accounts for the millennia-long attempts by men to *equalize* things, to compensate in all other realms for the awesome power women have possessed from the start." One encounters such intellectual drool from persons so seemingly far apart as Norman Mailer and certain extreme matriarchists in the Women's Movement who seem committed to ostrich-type tactics (the Right and Left curving into a circle again?).

This kind of nonthought ignores the fact that today, more than ever before in recorded history, there are virulent campaigns by (male-controlled) religions and (male-controlled) governments to insist that a woman bear children whether she wishes to or not. Since that same recorded history clearly shows that what a patriarchal system regards as power or privilege possessed by women *must be taken away*, it hardly makes sense that this system would now defend the retention by women of what it genuinely considers "an awesome power." On the contrary, while "womb envy" might indeed be a factor in individual men or even in one psychological layer shared by all men, the reality is that male human beings see even the capability of pregnancy as one hell of a liability, responsibility, job, and constriction. They may well mystify it, for convenience, but they seem quite content to restrict their envy *to* that area of mystification—all the while grasping "compensatory" power in every other realm of known existence. No fools they; they know a privilege when they don't see it.

So we are back to beginning where each of us began—in the female human body, the "first home" of every human being. And we are also back to the body itself, one's own body, the eventual and lifelong home of one's self. It's all any of us, male or female, is born with, born into—and it's where we will each of us live until we die. It's the only thing, ultimately, that anyone wholly possesses—and even that possession is for a limited length of time.

Yet a woman, though she inhabits her own body, does not possess it the way a man in the patriarchy possesses his. She cannot, in fact, because it isn't hers to possess; it is his (along with his own body).* This diaspora from one's own most basic flesh can mean, in time, that a woman ceases to inhabit her own body in some ways. She quite literally has been "possessed"—and by nothing so ectoplasmic as demons or dybbuks. She is *dis*possessed from her body, in exile from it. Where does she go? How does she become visible without skin and blood and bone? What image can she have of her authenticity? If she does manage to have a self-image, how can it compete with the döppelganger doll she has been told is her? If she has been made bodiless by dispossession, then can she believe that she is real, that she has been born at all?

Perhaps feminist consciousness at its plainest consists of millions of women, down through the centuries, saying in one voice: *"Look. I am trying to show you my face before I am born."*

* * *

The woman who wishes to understand her own body image in this culture attempts a task as paradoxical as that of the child who longs to see how its own face looks when asleep. Such longing is not answered by the presentation of a photograph, or any other two-dimensional representation of the Self.

---

* Two out of a myriad of possible examples that come immediately to mind express this bizarre state of affairs: the mirror-reversal creation myth which has Eve being fashioned from Adam's rib, and the marriage-ceremony text, too frequently still used, which proclaims that "The wife and the husband are one, and that one is the husband." Thinking of other examples makes for an easy parlor game, albeit a somewhat depressing one.

THE BODY DENIED

For a human being inhabiting a male body, the basic task of existing is, I think, very different. At the risk of appearing tepidly overcautious to some of my sisters in the feminist community, I must say "I think" as a qualifier in the preceding sentence—because I am a human being inhabiting a female body, and I simply don't know what it is to inhabit a male one. Nor do I wish to settle for cheap assumptions, however momentarily comforting they might feel to my own chronic sense of outrage against what men have permitted Man to do to women in the name of Woman. Hate *is*, after all, a failure of imagination, and biologically determinist theory is a failure of intellect.

Yet when I try to imagine the human consciousness in a male body, I am feeling my way into a state quite alien to my own human experience. Leaving aside for the moment the question of whether or to what extent this difference is lodged in physiological structure or in societally formed behavior (or both), and also leaving aside certain recognizable, reassuring glimpses of "the thousand natural shocks that [all] flesh is heir to"—fear, excitement, elation, physical pleasure or pain, etc.—still I sense some other difference, like a shadow.

I think it is the shadow cast on a man by Man. I think it is the echo of received history whispering to this consciousness that, *because* it inhabits a male body, it is human. What an utterly different state of existence must be experienced, after all, when one has inherited directly and by osmosis the assurance that the very words used to study, describe, and define humanity and humanlike forms—anthropology, ancestry, android, to cite a few—stem from both the Greek and Latin roots for "man"!

It must have a considerable influence on even the best-intentioned, most antisexist man: to learn that the representation of life on this planet, as designed by Carl Sagan, is being carried beyond our solar system out into the galaxy via Voyager I, and that this metal plaque will communicate to any hypothetical life forms out there not only certain mathematical symbols and astronomical codes, but also the engraved depiction of a male human being, standing in the foreground with hand raised in greeting, while the outline of a female human being, shown to be only a little more than half his size, stands in the background (shorter because of perspective, you see), arms passively at her sides. Between Carl Sagan and NASA, Man now has managed to send the infection of androcentric thought, like a polluting viral strain, out into the rest of the universe. Nor is the effect of such a message lost on individual consciousness lodged in male bodies on *this* planet. The message, again and again, is: men equal Man equals human. In this case, the message goes a step further: human (Man) equals *life* on the third planet from the sun in this corner of our galaxy.

Women, as Simone de Beauvoir wrote almost forty years ago in her classic *The Second Sex*, are The Other. First, a woman is Woman—that imposed image that limits her individual human capabilities in precisely the opposite manner from the way in which the image of Man expands and challenges the human capabilities of individual men. Second, having been subsumed into Woman, a woman becomes Everything Else nonhuman.

We frequently are given Woman as geography: Woman as ocean, as the "virgin forest," soil for the "husbandman" (from which the word husband derives); we refer to "the rape of the land," to the "valley and mount of Venus," to rivers, mountains, and entire countries as "she." Chief geologist Robert Christiansen of the United States official Geological Survey Team investigating preeruption tremors of Mount St. Helens in Washington state in 1980, pooh-poohed any danger: "She's simply not ready to blow off," he said, "You could say that she's having a mid-life crisis."[1] (Because of this statement, the volcano's series of massive eruptions a few days later gave feminists all over the United States an ironically pleasant sense of solidarity with a piece of landscape.) Yet to anthropomorphize—or, more accurately, to gynomorphize—the volcano at all is, of course, absurd: the volcano was neither angry nor vengeful. The volcano was merely being its own authentic active self. Such an activity is just what is denied to a woman—which is perhaps why, as a warning, she is told that she has experienced it already, albeit vicariously, as a mountain.

There has been a tendency in some (U.S.) feminist theory in recent years to affirm this "woman as nature" argument. In one sense it's inevitable that such thinking would emerge as a necessary phase in our ongoing political development: at a certain point in any liberation process, the oppressed, weary of disclaiming the stereotypes put upon them by their oppressors, turn and affirm those very stereotypes almost as a sign of defiant pride ("Damned right, black Americans have more rhythm," or the 1970 "Bitch Manifesto" by Joreen, for example). This stems in part from a sensible desire to be as unlike the odious oppressor as possible, even unto claiming for oneself the dubious distinctions of difference by which he has done the labeling in the first place.

If this tendency is kept fluid *as* part of a coming-to-consciousness phase, it's a positive one. But the institutionalizing of it as a permanent, serious thread of theoretical thinking is ultimately counterproductive and in fact *de*structive, since at its essence such thinking affirms not individual uniqueness within a spectrum of human commonality but *group difference*—always a highly dangerous compartmentalization which leads ineluctably to racism, sexism, classism and ism-isms.

The other problem with adopting a woman-equals-nature-as-man-equals-culture argument is that it isn't true. It depends on which woman one is talking about, which culture, which man, and how one defines equality and especially "nature." As the Ghanaian novelist Ama Ata Aidoo has written, "The Great Earth Mother . . . I resent being viewed in such an agricultural light." For that matter, as Susanne K. Langer has pointed out, "Any miscarriage of the symbolic process is an abrogation of our human freedom . . . [and] may block the free functioning of mind."[2] Of course women are a part of nature—as are men. Of course men are a part of culture—as are women. To embrace nature as some mystical special sister of women and not men is to place female human beings on the other side of a senseless barrier already erected by Man. Furthermore, unless men can be brought to an understanding that they too *are* part of nature (as what isn't, really?), they will continue to objectify and exploit the earth as Other with irresponsible ease. If ever there was a case for "enlightened self-interest," it is in making men realize that what they do negatively to nature—and to women—may give men power in the short run but will totally destroy *them* in the not-very-long run.

Meanwhile, Man has defined Woman as a subcategory not only for geography but for everything else that is non-Man, nonhuman. The female anatomy is a biological entity, a physical entity (not in the possession of actual women, however); it is a social phenomenon, a religious numinosity, a political pawn, a metaphysical state, a philosophical category, an aesthetic metaphor, a symbol, a joke, a spiritual temptation, an assemblage of fetishized parts, a means of reproduction and production. The female anatomy is a destructively imagined difference, *because* it is sensed as a dangerously intuited sameness.

But the human consciousness that is me lives inside a female anatomy, which means I exist as a metaphor. I daily inhale, exhale, and see the world through a metaphorical self. I find myself as (or, rather, lose myself in) the metaphor for nations and continents, industrial plants, mines, cars, ships, planes, and other vehicles, tidal waves and hurricanes† and the moon, and the planet Earth itself. *I think, therefore I am. But men are thinking me; therefore I am not.* I exist for them as the metaphor for rape and conquest, for luring them to hell or inspiring them to salvation, for fertilizing and tilling, reaping, burning, burying, eroding, unearthing.

This has its effect on me.

How can I transcend the laws that matter, the laws *of* matter, to make the full effect understood? How can the consciousness which is periodically conscious of inhabiting the female anatomy that is my body reach across distance and silence, reach through bound paper pages and printer's ink, to the consciousness inhabiting the body reading this? How, for once, to approach the anatomy of a woman as the thing itself, undefined by comparison, reaction, contrast?

I will die, eventually, in the body that writes these words today.

You will die, eventually, in the body that reads these words.

Isn't this, ultimately, the most intimate of our commonalities?

Here in the round tower, the garret, the ivory fortress, where we sit, you and I, conversing as if we were real—here, I say, I will make you a pledge. I will try to take you out of your mind. We will leave this place together, descending step by perilous step, vertebra by veinous foothold. This is the female body, the body

_____

† Not until 1978 did the International Weather System begin giving hurricanes male as well as female names—and then only because of pressure from the Women's Movement.

politic, the anatomy of nonfreedom, the anatomy of a woman not, for once, as the Other—the subsidiary, the also-body, the complement—but as *the thing itself*. Even I have never gone quite here before; it's slippery, there are no answers, and death waits somewhere along the route (the only question ever being, of course, whether it does really wait at the end).

But what have we to lose, this late? Pick a day, any day. Today, for example, the new religious-fundamentalist leader in the theocracy of Iran banned music in his streets and homes. Headlines rumor a cholera epidemic in central Africa. A man on the street nearer home grabbed my breast—an utter stranger, just as suddenly gone. (Was he solicitously looking for lumps?) They say San Francisco Bay is dead; I can feel the shrimps uncurling into oblivion, poisoned by sewage. A nine-year-old slave girl carrying bricks in Mauritania stares up from her pointillist newsprint cage. So what have we to lose?

Here is this body. Take, see, eat. The Christian myth offers consciousness incarnate in male form as sacrificial nourishment, the body and blood. Yet it is the female body that has been sacrificed, the female body capable of giving literal nourishment as milk, the female body whose menstrual fluid even compassionately gives remission from having to be born. As the philosopher Mary Daly would say, the Christian transubstantiation is a transubstitution—no more, no less. So take, see, eat. You might not emerge from here unborn, I put you on your guard.

How are you sitting right now? Stop reading and notice.

You there, the woman: do you think to find yourself along these arteries which are at once too universal and too specified?

You there, the man: do you think to lose yourself here as the antibody, the also-body, the Other to a human, for a change?

You there, the consciousness in either a woman or a man: you can neither find nor lose yourself here; I'm much too crowded already. But you might recognize a quality never encountered; you might remember an expression never glimpsed; you might reconcile with a self never before introduced.

* * *

Look carefully into the two-way mirror while I gaze from the other side. It's a two-way mirror because we observe each other through the lens of what passes for each of ourselves. But it's a two-way mirror for another reason.

No mirror ever gives back an image of oneself as one appears to others. On the contrary, it reverses the image. So if you wish to see yourself the way others see you, you must look into a mirror reflecting your face reflected in another mirror—to reverse the first reversal. Even identical twins are not identical, but are mirror images of each other, a subtle reversal of fingerprint whorls, of which eye is slightly larger, which side of the nose a tiny bit fuller. Molecules themselves, even when chemically identical, appear by virtue of a structural difference as mirror images of each other, like right and left hands. Chemists call this phenomenon "chirality" after the Greek word for "hand."

For a woman—who has been cast like silvered (and distressed) glass to spend her life reflecting the figure of Man at, as Virginia Woolf wrote in *A Room of One's Own*, "twice its natural size"—the task is to see herself at all. Not only has the nun been denied her own reflection, but also the fashion model. Like the undead, loveless, literally lost soul of the vampire, the vorvolika, the ghost, a woman has been forced to seek her reflection on blank glass polished as a man's face. Never mind magnification; the task is to find an image at all.

"I am half-convinced," wrote Nathaniel Hawthorne, "that the reflection is the reality." Both the affirmative symbology of the looking-glass in prepatriarchal esoteric mystery religions and myth, and the later negative beliefs—the Greek myths of Medusa and of Narcissus, the Orthodox Hebrew and Islamic proscriptions against figurative art, the Aborigine belief that a photograph is taboo because it imprisons one's essence—all these in different ways point to a feared knowledge that if one cannot see oneself then it is not certain one has a "soul," an existence, a reality. "The self comes into being at the moment it has the power to reflect itself."[3] So, like a wraith, a woman haunts her own outlines in men's eyes and in glazed pieces of metal. Both of these give back to her an image reversing her reality. "I am important to her. She comes and goes," speaks the mirror in Sylvia Plath's poem of the same name. Since she cannot trust what she sees, she keeps looking. For this she is called vain.

Prepatriarchal Middle Eastern myth extolled the goddess Ashteroth, or Tamar, who created life by gazing at herself in a look-ing-glass. Pre-Yahweh Hebrew myth worshipped the Shekinah, the force of cosmic energy which was felt as female—boundless light which became Kether, which created from itself in turn a sister self named Chokmah, into whose eyes Kether could glance and thereby invent all existence. A round mirror was an impor-tant symbol and prop in the celebration of the Eleusinian Myster-ies. Almost every culture has such a myth buried in its origins. Yet after centuries of Perseus looking only at Medusa's reflection for fear of being turned to stone by her real face (and in order to kill her), after being moralistically warned of Narcissus' bad end, after Church fathers in the Middle Ages proclaiming that the mirror was the devil's instrument and that the gates of hell yawned wide between a woman's thighs—who now remembers Tamar, or Kether, or Korē? Where can a two-way mirror be found to reverse the reversal?

And if a woman could find one and dare look into it, would she see a human face or a mask?

By what standards would she recognize which was which?

THE BODY DISGUISED

B.C. (Before Consciousness): There we were, prefeminism, de-nying there was any problem, solitarily certain that each of us was herself The Problem: "I self-loathe, therefore I am." There was no question about this, yet we knew the unacknowledged answer: ap-pearances mattered, after all, despite what Mother had claimed (shaking a finger at us to emphasize her point, and fluffing our hair with the other hand to underscore her double message). Therefore we mostly curled, straightened, plucked, dieted, bleached, shaved, uplifted, and otherwise adorned. Because each one wished to belong. To whom?

One day we compared notes, went into prolonged recognition and, between alternating contractions of hilarity and grief, gave birth—to ourselves, we thought.

A.D. (After Defiance): There we were, feministically aware of the problem (sexism) and able to exchange grown-up names for how it worked (objectification, socialization, commercialization, internalization, and various other -ations). Collectively, and with-

out question, we had the answer. Appearance was now politicized
—which meant it *really* mattered. One's hair, for instance, was
the measure of one's consciousness. Short on hair, long on consciousness, and the reverse. This logically placed Yul Brynner in
the feminist vanguard while disqualifying even the most militant
Gorgon from the movement, but never mind.

Still, we at least belonged. To whom? To some new feminist
version of Woman? Yet not to belong was to belong to whom?
To non-Woman as well as non-Man, nonhuman. To nothing.
(We were not yet questioning the notion of "belonging" itself.)

One day, we noticed that a suspiciously uniform noncon-
formism had tricked us into giving birth indeed: to each other, in
litters. But not yet to ourselves.

* * *

Body image? What body?

You mean that somewhat contemptible scaffolding which acts
as a serviceable base for the cozy-garret skull in which lives the
"real" self?

Image? Which image, and when?

A bathroom meditation at age fourteen—during which one
mournfully inspects how well the lugubrious hulk of one's thighs
can flatten against the toilet seat?

The voluptuousness of pregnancy, at once enhanced and under-
mined by exhaustion from hauling around one's own enormity?

The buoyant emptiness of postpartum, feeling one's spine rediscover its own center, one's belly first bulge with the presence of
the child and then gradually constrict after the Big Bang of childbirth—all the while one's breasts take on a rhythmic brimming of
their own, able to sense the infant's first pre-cry inhalation in the
night and able to respond instantly by leaking milk? The experience of being *edible*?

The chthonic awe of menarche—however well or ill prepared
for that first blood? The subtle approach of menopause—distant
and then nearer echoes, but echoes which conversely precede the
sound?

When a single human body can encompass changes this dramatic, what is its image? *Is* there such an image fixed somehow beneath or beyond these aspects? Is there an inviolable physical self,

perhaps intuited by orgasm? What integrity of image could accommodate:

• The steady eye-beam of a scientist as she bends her contemplative profile to the microscope,

• A callus developing gradually on a mother's milk-blistered nipple,

• The stare of a woman whose body is pretending passion in her lover's arms, her face flayed of expression and pointed safely ceilingward over his shoulder?

Not to speak of:

• The shredded membranes of the vulva raped raw by the (statistically proven) common inability of the sexual attacker to penetrate his victim?

• The crescent-moon shape of a human foot bent and bound to a length of three inches?

• The greenish tinge of flesh ripe with infection after the butchery of a back-street illegal abortion?

• The scraped and sewn-smooth plane of female genitals that have been both clitoridectomized and infibulated?[4]

• The postoperative "healing" involved after surgical reconstruction of an accidentally or deliberately pierced hymen (or the surgical construction of a hymen, since many women are born without one)—so as to ensure that the bride will bleed on being "deflowered" or else risk abandonment or death?‡

Body image?

In the United States one out of three women will be raped; one half of all wives are victims of battering; a woman is raped every three seconds; a woman is beaten every eighteen seconds; one out of every four women experiences sexual abuse before she is eighteen years old; nine out of ten women endure sexual harassment at their jobs. These are statistics based on information assembled by the feminist network of rape-crisis centers, refuges for battered women, child-abuse shelters, and sexual-harassment clinics. The official sources are only slightly more reassuring, however. For example, the FBI released preliminary statistics indicating that incidents of reported forcible rape in the United States in 1980 rose by 9 percent—an average of one rape every six min-

‡See Nawal El Saadawi, *The Hidden Face of Eve* (Boston: Beacon Press, 1981) and Robin Morgan, *The Word of a Woman* (New York: Norton, 1992).

utes. The FBI added their estimation that only about 60 percent of all rapes are reported. It was not clear whether the FBI statistics included cases of marital rape, but this is unlikely, since marital rape currently is considered a crime only in nine states.*

Body image?

* * *

We had the curiosity of our convictions.

We admitted our ignorance, flourished specula, flashlights, and mirrors, studied our bodies, formed clinics and workshops, wrote and read books.

We reclaimed masturbation as lovemaking with the one you trust best. Some of us said no woman could know her own body unless she loved another woman physically. Some of us felt that only a woman who had borne a child, for all the ambivalent mysteries of motherhood, truly understood physical affirmation. Some of us proclaimed menopause as the promised land. Some of us celebrated a freer sensuality with men and some a freedom from sensuality altogether, and still others ritualized the body through spiritual disciplines.

A few of these approaches we even meant.

Yet the most common nightmare that recurs to a rape victim is of her body melting like wax.

Burning the candle at both ends? Living voodoo dolls for use as fetishes by men endeavoring to cast spells not even on us but on other men? The Wicked Witch of the West m-e-l-t-i-n-g? The wicked witches of the Middle Ages, the Renaissance, the Inquisition, the Enlightenment, m-e-l-t-i-n-g by the hundreds and hundreds of thousands? The final solution to the woman problem?

One day we really must have a feminist workshop on our own mortality.

Death does seem a potential influence on body image.

* * *

Elsewhere[5] I've written a detailed analogy between women and colonized peoples, noting that colonization involves control over the land (so that it can be mined for natural resources), enforced alienation of the colonized from their own territory by a system

---

* California, Connecticut, Florida, Massachusetts, Minnesota, Nebraska, New Hampshire, New Jersey, and Oregon. The definition of marital-rape crime and the severity of sentence differ from state to state.

based on exclusion and mystification, and a readiness on the part of the colonizer to meet all demands for self-determination with a repertory of repression, from ridicule through tokenism to outright brutality. Certainly women in this androcentric culture do not have self-determination over our own most basic "land"—our bodies, our very flesh; those bodies have been regarded as exploitable resources of sex and children and have been mystified in the process. Certainly our campaign for "home rule," so to speak, is still being met with passive callousness, sentimental and cooptative "adoration," and, when all else fails, active severity. If women are indeed a colonized people, then the male-controlled medical establishment,[6] for example, is the Colonial Secret Police.

* * *

So: women should have no minds because our bodies are of such importance. But we have no bodies either, because they are defined, possessed, abused, veiled, exposed, airbrushed, or metaphorized by men.

Men are hardly immune from the body-mind split, of course. They have constructed entire philosophical, poetic, religious, and political systems around this predicament (which they claim as unique to them). Actually, such a split may be just a consequence of sentience. But in that case, women must be more sentient, because this has been our assigned subject, our very existence.

De Beauvoir was one of the earliest modern feminists to articulate the dilemma of our bodylessness, Dinnerstein one of the most recent.[7] But how much more work will be required to probe the motivations of just a single woman riddled with the message of self-flesh loathing—a woman willing, even desperate, to undergo the suffering, time, and cost of multiple operations, say, for a breast implant—for the sake not of health but appearance. Her pain and pride are equaled only by the horror she endures, by the lies she has been told about both her own inadequacies and the remedy for them.

She will not be reached by a tract urging her to affirm her body or love herself. But she must be reached before I pass her by— before you fail to recognize me.

For now, we need some questions. Instead of answers, for once. What *is* our body politic—as women, as men? How can body image be separated from intellect image, soul or spirit image?

How does a human being acknowledge the Self—that individual core existing not in reaction to any exterior evil or even in affirmation of any objective good, but simply in quintessence? How, especially, if a woman—meaning a human being whose very presence has been placed in a subcategory of nonhuman, of object, or of Other? By *selfconsciousness* raising? And what if, in the search, I pass me by: "My body image, I presume?"

When, for example, I take pleasure in my contact lenses, is it because:

1. I'm (B.C.) vain;
2. I'm (A.D.) rebelling against years of rimmed perspectives, fogged-up lenses, and a deeply grooved nosebridge;
3. I'm delighting in the power of peripheral vision, which gives me more control over my own immediate space;
4. All of the above?

* * *

Step by perilous step, I said, vertebra by veinous foothold. I myself have never gone quite here before. It's slippery, I said (groping for the nearest detour).

Take my hand, let's try again.

Ultimately, I know only the body I inhabit, and even here I am at times a stranger, at times an impostor, at times a guest, at times a settler. There are no answers, I said, and even the questions we need shift from moment to moment, hour to month to decade. Only the clues are specific:

I am a human being, a female human being, a woman.

I am, at this writing, one month short of my forty-first birthday —which means that, at best, my lease to this body already has run half its length. Oddly this doesn't bother me as much as others seem to think it should.

I am what is humorously called "white" in a world that thinks the proportion of melanin in one's pigmentation actually is a sane way of categorizing one's capacity for genius, intellect, energy, and emotions, as well as one's right to bread, shelter, education, love, and freedom. (When will some drugstore owner have the wit to display suntanning lotions and skin-whitening creams next to one another on the same shelf? Or is the exposing of an absurdity too great an absurdity to ask?) More accurately, the surface of my flesh is a sort of olive-pinky-beige. Pale burnt-sienna freckles are beginning to appear on the backs of my hands, on my chest and shoulders, signs of the lease here being half run.

I am what is called short in my country—although in parts of Asia I would be considered average height or even a bit tall; I measure five feet and an inch and a half. Given the context of my culture, this has created problems for me. As a woman, it leaves me open to such stomach-churning appellations as "petite" and "diminutive." As an artist, it makes me cling to certain specific models for solace (George Sand—five feet one inch; Emily Brontë—four feet eleven inches). As a political activist, my (lack of) height has influenced my preference for more militant small-group actions as opposed to large-scale demonstrations; although I recognize the need for the latter and have participated in them many times, I never can see what's going *on* beyond the shoulder of the person in front of me. In the civil-rights and antiwar movements of the 1960's, I would dread the inevitable moment when a voice in the crowd of the march or rally would shout, "Here come the Tactical Police! They're on horseback, charging into the crowd! Watch out, here comes the tear gas and fire hoses!" It was bad enough to be attacked by rioting police for having committed the sin of exercising one's First Amendment rights, but it was worse to be trampled on by one's codemonstrators as they surged this way and that while I would futilely scream into the din, "*Where? Where?*" Is it any wonder that I came to be more interested in a small "affinity group" or "cadre" of five or six women genteelly leaving a stink bomb inside the Miss America Pageant, carefully oozing Crazy Glue into the locks of the main doors of the Stock Exchange at 4 A.M., or making a gift of a brick to the local pornographer through his shopwindow? At my height, these and certain other actions (which I, in an uncharacteristic fit of discretion, will leave unnamed) seemed by comparison with a peaceful march to be, ironically, *safe*. The Napoleons of the world may feel a need to overcompensate because Man is supposed to be a great hulking colossus, but being short leads a woman either to guerrilla warfare or pacifism. As an ordinary person trying minimally to function, of course, I am forever standing on footstools, craning toward higher bookshelves and grocery shelves, washing (though rarely) the refrigerator's front while forgetting that its top is an inch deep in dustballs, and suffering chronic neck strain. All this has had the salutary effect of greatly improving my posture. On the other hand, it's had the reactionary effect of my being tempted toward retrograde high (though not spiked) heels, especially when I'm off to an encounter with someone or something I suspect will be intimidating, and despite my feminist conscience yelling at me that I am throwing my spine out of alignment, cramping my toes, inviting a comparison with the hobbled gait of a slave wearing ankle chains or a woman with bound feet, and collaborating in my oppression.

I am nearsighted in both eyes, extremely so in the right eye, and also astigmatic. The strength in this lies in its having influenced me toward a loving attention to detail; the weakness lies in my old cavalier attitude toward eventual outcomes—a tendency I've worked consciously to transcend. In my twenties, both my "nearsighted temperament" and the volatility of that period's radical tactics blended nicely into the "Level everything; *then* we'll talk politics" desperate slogan of the time. In my thirties, I struggled hard to grasp a historical "farsighted" perspective—and undoubtedly was helped in this monumental task of political maturation by the contact lenses, about which you already know. Now, in my forties, I look forward to a synthesis of urgency and attention to detail (made necessary by the again-desperate political climate), *combined* with context, awareness of effect, and perspective. This would be to see life steadily and see it whole, in a paraphrase of Matthew Arnold. Such a profound state of balance likely will be affected by the fact that myopia self-corrects as one grows older—a delightful biological truth with other obvious implications.

I am short-waisted, and in extremist moments of flesh loathing have described my navel as being lodged directly under my chin. "Some of my best friends" happen to be women who are tall and/or long-waisted. Continuing to love them while they willow their way about is a bracing challenge to my sense of sisterhood.

My breasts would be considered by patriarchal-fetishist standards "a good feature": they're full and still firm, after having nursed a child for almost a year, over a decade ago. The aureoles and nipples are a cinnamon color, and a delicate network of lilac-shaded veins shows itself intermittently around them. Two or three fine hairs sprout from each aureole. Both my maternal grandmother and one maternal aunt died of (neglected) breast cancer; I palpate each breast carefully at least once a month, and have learned to recognize which bumps are muscle, which are tiny nodes, which are normal localized fullnesses that vary throughout my menstrual cycle. Only in the past decade have I come to be on such intimate terms with my breasts, and they seem grateful for this closeness. If I one day feel an alien lump, I will know it immediately.

My navel has been turned in for all of my life except the last three months of my pregnancy, when it popped out, only to find its own way back again after childbirth. We had a nice, though brief, visit.

A profusion of soft black curls grow on my lower pelvis down to my genitals. The slope of pelvic bone itself is lovely. Until the seismically measurable change in consciousness brought about in 1971 by Feminist Women's Health Centers' encouraging women to view our own cervixes with flashlight, mirror, and speculum, I along with other millions of women really had never looked at my genitals. Now I am on speaking terms with this part of my body. I know the outer ("major") and inner ("minor") lips of my labia, how a particular fold on my left side makes one lip larger than on the right, how the color and texture change slightly but perceptibly according to my cycle. Even more revolutionary a knowledge is that my vagina (the cave I secretly feared was a twilight zone of stalagmites and stalactites) shines back at my eyes through the flashlight-irradiated mirror as a sparkling tunnel curved by smooth walls of pale-rose mother-of-pearl iridescence, the chubby doughnut of the cervix with its os center winking out from the far end, slightly lopsided, like a wry smile. Back on the surface again, I know the pattern of a few labial cysts to which I seem prone. I know when and where they might occasionally appear, what causes them (tight clothing, not getting sufficient rest, the mild edema just before the onset of menstruation) and what to do about them. Again, because there is a history of cancer among the women in my family, I monitor the cysts carefully. The short expanse of skin between my vagina's base and my anus still bears the slight rope of a scar from the episiotomy perhaps gratuitously performed when my child was born. (Women's health activists have estimated that as many as 70 percent of episiotomies performed in the United States are unnecessary. The technique, which eases the obstetrician's job if not the mother's, is almost a ritual in American deliveries; it is used far less in Europe and elsewhere.)

My thighs and buttocks bear faint stretchmarks, some of which date from my pregnancy but some of which predate it, because I have wavered in weight gains and losses since my early adolescence. My mother and maternal aunts all tended toward being overweight. Food meant wealth meant love, as in many first-generation immigrant families. And so I grew up learning that when you were depressed, eating would make you feel happier, and when you were happy, eating was a good way to celebrate. In between, there were always the excuses of being hungry, being at loose ends, being in need of quick energy or a special treat, being companionable, not wasting, and needing to sample what you were cooking. The Good News about this is that I became an excellent cook who enjoys preparing fine food; the Bad News is that (being a woman) I've found myself at certain periods in my life cooking three meals a day—which makes for an enormous loss of time, centers one's existential crises around the supermarket and stove, and entices one to partake of one's own labors so as not to feel like a live-in servant. The additional Bad News, of course, is that at times I have ricocheted up to as high as a hundred and thirty-five pounds (at, remember, five feet one inch) and felt like a short cocktail-sausage stuffed into my clothes—which in turn became binding which in turn activated labial cysts, *etc., etc.* The additional Good News, however, is that in my late thirties I finally came to grips with this pattern, changed my diet and exercise habits (the former were crash and the latter were nonexistent), and seem to have achieved a balanced and maintainable weight fluctuating between ninety-six and a hundred and one pounds. This means that I feel healthier, look better, and actually experience the workings of my entire body far more vividly. It also means, as a bonus, that I cook less but enjoy food more than when I consumed it unconsciously. I still *think* about food continuously, you understand, unless I'm engaged in the blissful activity of writing, which has been for me a satisfaction more fulfilling than food, sex, or even revolution. When I am writing well, I actually forget to eat—unless I have been so unfortunate as to write a passage like the preceding one.

My limbs are serviceable creatures in acceptable proportion to my torso. I'm on pretty good terms with my knees but barely have been introduced to my elbows. My ankles tend to turn in—a leftover from my teenage obsession with Capezio flats, which I wore every day, convinced that they made me look as if I had tiny ballerina feet. My wrists are small but strong, from former years of playing the piano and former and current years of typing. My fingers are strong, too, and they bulge slightly at the joints from a lifelong habit of cracking them, despite everyone from my mother to my feminist consciousness-raising group telling me that I must forgo this satisfyingly crunchy activity. The nails used to be short by biting; now they are short by filing. Having once realized that I could triumphantly grow long nails, I learned they got in the way of me and my typewriter keys.

My shoulders are narrow and pleasant. My clavicle and neck have always been dear to me, since they managed to look slender even when the rest of me was at its heaviest—thus permitting me to take refuge in boat-necked, square-necked, V-necked, and crew-necked tops to display a bit of décolletage while full skirts in the 1950's or baggy pants thereafter hid the rest of the problem.

My face is round, chipmunk-cheeked when overweight and only now rewarding me with the semblance of a bone structure. The eyes are a dark brown, the lashes and unplucked brows are a soft, full, lighter brown. I have fought my nose ever since I can remember. When I was twelve, I had Pinocchial fears; when I was fifteen, my nose seemed to me a refugee from the face of Cyrano de Bergerac—too big, too fleshy, neither classically aquiline nor cute-pert-pug. Adding to my indignation, my nose has a sinus condition, which makes it sneeze, drip, and redden, and it possibly has used up more Kleenex than any other nose in the continental United States. In the past two or three years I have made an uneasy alliance with my nose, aided in part by antihistamines and in part by the change of diet—which in turn caused the weight loss, which in turn archaeologically unearthed the facial bone structure, which in turn made the nose appear not so bad after all. Still, I am not quite ready to say "thou" to my nose.

The lips are perfectly okay—except when they chap or have fever blisters, which isn't very often. I wore no lipstick even before feminism, since I happened not to like the way it looked or tasted; this was one of the very few "liberations" I had accomplished all on my own. The teeth are slightly crooked (despite detested childhood braces) and have survived the pain of four root canals over the years—the first three when I was about ten years old. A sadistic dentist didn't believe in even local anesthetic for children, so I sat in his torture chair and used to say multiplication tables and the books of the Bible and nursery rhymes and state capitals forward and backward in my head to survive it —a meditative technique no one had taught me. The teeth are fine now. I even floss them. But apparently a wisdom tooth lurks on the back-left horizon, flattering (given its name) but a source of low-level anxiety nevertheless.

My hair is a medium-light brown, streaked a bit with gray. It manufactures nice golden highlights all by itself in the summertime. The texture is very thin ("fine" is the euphemism) and straight, although in damp weather it actually manages a frail nimbus of body and sometimes even of curl-ghosts. Clearly, I like my hair best on a rainy day during August. In two days, my scalp produces as much oil as Kuwait. From the ages of ten to eighteen my darkening hair was bleached back to its babyhood color—an almost silvery blond—since I was a working child actor and the adults around me felt this made me more adorable. I have never forgotten the odor and sting of that process, which was endured twice a month, and the moment I reached some stage of relative self-determination I returned to my adult natural color and haven't deviated from it since, although I've varied the length of my hair from quite long (Premarriage Medieval Damsel) to shoulder length (Young Wife Renaissance) to short-cropped cap (Feminist Enlightenment) back to a little longer than shoulder-length (Personal Modern) and now to a little longer than that (Individualist Contemporary Eclectic). I sometimes wear it up in a bun or a twist—when it's hot weather or when I feel the need to look like a Serious Woman Writer. I'm letting my bangs grow out gradually. This means that they will no longer hide my forehead birthmark, a small brown mole maddeningly just off center that I've quarreled with since I was nine. On good days I try to affirm the mole; on bad days I cut back my bangs or even flirt with having the mole removed. Obviously, I haven't said "thou" to this mole, either.

I like my voice: it's low, full, expressive. I like my gastrointestinal system: it's always warned me of dangerous or tense situations I was consciously ignoring by loud, clear signals of nausea. I like my sexuality more and more, but this only really began in my late thirties and sexuality is a chapter in itself (see Chapter IV). I like the newfound elasticity of my exercising self, the newfound compactness of muscle, the newfound feeling of agility. I actually *do* feel better at forty than I did at twenty or thirty, to my astonishment.

But I must confess that the two organs of which I always have been most fond are those two which I've never seen in any mirror, sexless, raceless, ageless, and most vital to the body's life: the heart and the brain. I love them not for their appearance but for their real and symbolic functions—what they do and what they stand for. I dearly love my heart, or rather the *metaphor* of my heart—for its great wealth of emotions, its release of compassionate tears or adrenergic anger, its literal tireless fealty toward the largest arteries and the smallest capillaries webbed through the galaxy that is myself, its figurative tireless energy toward my daring to feel more and deeper and wider each day of my life. And my brain—my wonderful wrinkled-walnut double-hemisphered not-yet-fully-used living computer filled with neurons, glia, axons, synapses and circuits and electrochemical moving-ion messages it can trigger, fire, send, channel, receive, process, retain, store, translate, splice, and sing into a million nerve endings and cells and poems and strategies—I dearly love my brain.

Step by perilous step, vertebra by veinous foothold. Slippery, yes. I forgot the friendly chin, for instance, the basic ears, the pleasure-pain principle inherent in writer's backache. I passed over the pilonidal cyst at the base of my spine, aggravated by the somewhat prominent knob of what I've theorized must be a remnant of tailbone. I forgot the way that taking certain antibiotics when the cyst acts up triggers inevitable monilia in the vagina, which necessitates the Great Yogurt Cure to restore the bacterial balance. (This consists of yogurt ingested internally *and* applied externally, as first prescribed by the Feminist Women's Health Centers and later sheepishly confirmed by the medical establishment.) I forgot the velour texture of my skin after I've been in the steamroom or sauna at a health club. I forgot the heaviness before menstruation and the lightness just after, the way I can't carry a tune, the newfound appreciation in the fragrance of my own pheromones. I must have forgotten so much more . . .

The mask doesn't peel off so quickly. There are recursive masks within masks, the layers of an onion skin, nesting Chinese boxes, confusion inside acceptance inside defiance inside defense inside surrender inside experimentation. Each woman layers and combines in her own unique fashion, uncertainty beneath humor beneath disgust beneath fear beneath anger beneath compromise. One radical feminist clings to her long tapered fingernails as the last holdout; sometimes she claims they might be good for defense against a rapist—yet she could only scratch, because the nails make it impossible for her to form a tight fist. Another feminist taxes her heart with extreme weight; the mere exertion of walking along the street brings a fine mist of perspiration to her face; it is her defense against being objectified. Another has taken to little-girl flouncy dresses in her middle years. Still another dyes her whitening hair a bright red. I, who wear pants most of the time, have rediscovered that a skirt can be a distinct advantage on a hot summer day. And then there are those damnable heels that lend me height and thus confidence . . . I, who stopped shaving my legs and armpits in my mid-twenties (Feminist Enlightenment, remember?) recently began to shave them again. I'm not even that certain *why*: part of the generalized celebration in being slender and feeling limber? the resurrection of the ultra-Right flesh-loathing fundamentalists in my own pores? the Domino Theory (aha! heels lead to skirts lead to shaving . . .)? a cranky affirmation of what *I* and *not* some Feminist Central Committee wanted to do for a change? or an exhausted capitulation to the internalized standard of Woman implanted in me so long ago when I first was born into the patriarchy and which has been reinforced daily ever since?

At least we have begun to learn compassion for one another's defenses, to judge not another's mask lest we be judged by its reverse in our own mirror, to develop patience with ourselves and each other as women, as each of us continues to dance the Feminist Waltz—three steps forward, one step back—to wriggle free of the skin of Woman, free of the very masks that have made our survival possible.

* * *

If a woman constructs a mask so that she may survive, does it follow that she must wear it as long as she wishes to survive? If the mask grows into her flesh, bionic, does her once-self become an impostor? Does it merge with the mask? Does it *become* the mask? ("My dear, that hairdo *becomes* you so!") Does it suffocate entirely? Or is the existence of the mask the only way so far of keeping the hidden self alive? And if so, do the means justify the ends—or do they alter first their expression and finally their substance?

The chameleon doesn't torture itself with such questions—nor do octopi, flatfish, masking-crabs, trapdoor spiders, or anglerfish, all of which quite literally survive by their ability to make themselves less visible against whatever background they find themselves when predators hover near. The seasonal adapters, such as ermine and certain rabbits, take longer to transform themselves but do so without *angst,* we can assume. Why then should women question this technique in ourselves? Because we are, despite what our predators tell us, human—not Medusas (octopi), Black Widows (spiders), or Playboy bunnies. Furthermore, none of the animals who mask themselves to stay alive must do so *for fear of their own kind.* Such a tragic act seems to be an exclusively human one, brought by necessity to a degree of high art by female humans.

Yet no mask is as simple as it seems, and its complexity itself differs from culture to culture. In the West, where we live under the delusion of honesty and forthright revelation (one of the most devious camouflages of all), the idea of disguise is perceived as mendacious. Yet in other cultures a mask is understood not as a deception, a falsehood, or a fiction—but rather as another aspect or layer of truth, another dimension of reality as solid and normal as any other.

Kabuki theater and Nō drama in Japan integrate the changing of costumes, masks, and sets onstage with the play itself. Priestesses of Voudon in Haiti and of Candomblé in Brazil seem to change features drastically when in trance, as do Sufi ecstatic dervishes and the Sassou and Karlin Hassidic sects of Judaism, who dance to a state of religious rapture. In cultures so diverse as the North American Iroquois, the African Dahomean, and the Asian Sri Lankan, masks are used in healing ceremonies, ostensibly to frighten away the demons of illness, but also in what is clearly a wise psychological technique (and one more often than not successful). In Balinese masked theater, the art of a performer is judged by the ability to make an inanimate wooden mask come alive; a performer who accomplishes this is said to have *taksu,* or "the capacity to receive light."

But the constructive use of a mask depends on the willingness of a viewer or audience to comprehend that the mask is being worn, and in fact to differentiate and appreciate the degree of skill with which it is worn, and for what purpose. In Bali, for example, the mask is understood as "the interface between the timeless world of myth and the immediate world of fact. . . . *The mask becomes a two-way mirror,* reflecting images from the past and present in a single face. . . . [Its] power is rooted in paradox, in the fusion of opposites. *It brings together the self and the other* by enabling us to look at the world through someone else's face."8 (Italics mine.)

What is (sometimes euphemistically) called modern Western culture no longer affirms such comprehension and complexity. The circus clownface, the Halloween horror mask, the ski-masks which now are almost a terrorist uniform, and the Ku Klux Klan hood are almost all that is left from a Western tradition that once embraced the great tragic and comic masks of Greek theater, the archetype masks of medieval carnivals, and later the commedia dell'arte masks of the Italian Renaissance. It begins to seem almost axiomatic that in patriarchal societies what dare not be remembered is forgotten, what cannot be forgotten is buried, what will not stay buried is degraded or reversed.

The Dogon people along the River Niger have a myth which tells how masks came into the world. They say that once death did not exist. As people aged, they were transformed into snakes who spoke not with words but through spirit language. At this time, the power of creation was kept in a skirt given by the god of spirits to the goddess of earth when they made love—and the skirt could be worn only by women. But some young men stole the skirt of creation from the women and were discovered escaping with it by an old man who had become a snake. So outraged was the old man/serpent by this sacrilegious act that he forgot to speak spirit language and screamed at them in words. At that moment, his soul left him, and only a corpse remained. No one had ever seen a corpse before, and no one could imagine where his soul had gone—until some time later, when a child was born who had snakeskin-like marks on its skin. Then the people knew that the old man's soul had entered the baby, and so to drive it out and give it peace, they invented a mask *decorated* as a snake. They sang, danced, and feasted—and the first funeral came into being. The old man's soul left the baby (whose skin turned a healthy brown again) and went to its peaceful rest in the mask. Thus, the Dogon say, because women's power was stolen and men now danced wearing skirts, death arrived in the world, and the first mask came into being. A mask, the Dogon say, is the home of a dead soul.[9]

In this context, one cannot help but think of the religious transvestitism inherent in the gowns, robes, and other embroidered frocks of the Roman Catholic Pope, the Eastern Orthodox patriarch, and other assorted priests, mullahs, rabbis, and their like. Yet when men wear silly costumes, as Virginia Woolf noticed some decades ago,[10] we are supposed to take them seriously. The military uniform, the Shriner's fez, the prelate's dresses, the corporation executive's Gucci loafers and Old School Tie—these are Important Symbols not to be giggled at. Women, on the other hand, are fit to be the objects of gently patronizing ridicule or even direct scorn when, for instance, we wear the very cosmetics and fashions we are assured men demand—and which are relentlessly advertised and sold to us by men. When the Pict warriors painted their bodies blue before battle, when the Hamar men of Southwest Ethiopia decorate their headdresses with ostrich plumes, when the Apache brave spent hours outlining his war face, when the leftist student sported his blue denim shirt as a sign of solidarity with "the working class," when the Special Forces or Green Berets excitedly don their camouflage fatigues— this is Serious Business. When a woman colors her hair (sometimes risking cancer from the chemicals so that she may, for survival, appear young in a social structure that fears age in general and despises it in women), this is not seen as a desperate attempt to stay "marketable" in appearance, but is, rather, chuckled at as a sign of women's hopeless vanity. Nor is such a double standard merely an attitude. It may reverse reality but it reflects— in fact it doubles—objective power.

The indigenous Pacific Northwest peoples of the United States understand very well the connection of mask, and the way mask is comprehended, to power. They have a legend of The Cannibal Woman (Tsonoquah, or Dash-Kayah, or At' at'lia, among her other sacred names). She is malevolent and also beneficent, a symbol both of fear and of status. She speaks through whistling, and when her beautiful and terrifying mask is worn "one dances with Power, one transubstantiates oneself."[11] Her consort, The Wild Man of the Woods, "has a mask among the Kwakiutl that flashes open to reveal a human-like face inside it."[12] This face is yet a second mask. These sometimes are called transformation masks, because they involve "all the common dualities: of unknown to knowing, uninitiated to initiated, powerless to power-possessed, child to adult."[13]

The mask worn by men in the modern world (where everyone knows masks don't exist) is that of Man. The mask worn by women is that of Woman.

"But this isn't a mask!" men say. "This *is* us!"

"But this *is* a mask!" women say. "This isn't *us!*"

The men, believing in their own power because they have forced it into reality, insist that they are telling the truth. If they are telling the truth, of course, the women must be lying.

Perhaps, like the Eskimo religious neophyte, a woman must gain the ability to see herself as a skeleton, and then, by naming all the parts of her body, each bone and cell, each molecule of blood, each muscle, gland, and tissue, rebuild herself. The Eskimo doesn't name these parts in normal speech, but in a sacred shamanistic language in which he [sic] has had special instruction.[14] There is no one to instruct us, as women, but one another, *as* women—and there is no longer any sacred speech left to us but that of our truth and experience. Truth and experience, when uttered in solitude, are often called madness. Truth and experience, when spoken to a mirror, are usually called egoism. Truth and experience, when sung in concert, in counterpoint as well as harmony, are eventually called history.

* * *

The splintery old woman wouldn't eat like a good girl. When they insisted, she refused to eat at all. The more the nursing-home attendants pressured her, the more stubborn she became, railing against her "torturers" and "jailers" until the weary nurses sourly labeled her a Difficult Patient.

The situation was remedied only when a visitor witnessed one such mealtime scene and explained to the nurses how much their patient's motivation made sense in the context of her past—that other dimension of inhabited reality so vivid to the elderly and so inconvenient to their keepers. From then on, the nurses merely left the food trays, and the patient responded by eating.

This particular old woman had been irrepressibly Difficult for almost a century. Far from forgetful, she was suffering from too keen a memory, one that recalled jail, hunger strikes, and the ghastly experience of having been forcibly fed by brutal prison guards. She was the mother of the Equal Rights Amendment.

She was Alice Paul, ninety-two years old, street demonstrator, caucus-room lobbyist, and a graduate with degrees in social work and law from Swarthmore, the University of Pennsylvania, the Washington College of Law, and American University. Most important, she had studied strategy under the militant tutelage of the British suffragette, Emmeline Pankhurst.

She would die a few weeks later, on July 9, 1977, in the nursing home in Moorestown, New Jersey. But for the time left to her, her body was still the fortress she once had needed it to be against gags, tubes, metal clamps. The lung once clogged with food, the blistered septum, the scar on the palate—do they ever heal?

Yet her visitor was a stranger—knowing only the old woman's "history," not the old woman's "self"—a stranger who recognized the image in the body, passing it by within that history, for a moment.

How can a body image feel so much pain?

* * *

The body moves through time and space, imagines aging, imagines having been born, imagines dying, imagines movement.

What *about* the space in which we imagine our bodies, especially as women, whose bodies have been and are still continually imagined for us, against our reality, our will, our own imagination?

If, for example, fat is interpreted by some as an evocation of (or response to) alienation, then might this not be one way a woman can assert her need for space—by literally taking up more of it? Ingesting, containing, surrounding, *claiming* it?

The more specific space she insists on occupying with her body, of course, the more abstract space (for which read: power) she usually must sacrifice, because in a patriarchal world certain standards of physical space-taking equal attractiveness, and attractiveness is the basic currency granted to women.

But then has the deliberately thin woman traded her own *occupancy* of space for the *use* of space controlled by men? Is the choice: (a) owning one's immediate space outright but being denied permission to use it, or (b) blithely borrowing a portion of the generalized and mobile space of men but being refused permanent ownership of one's immediate environs?

If so, the choice is untenable—the first constituting murder by heart attack, the second by malnutritive obsession. Neither choice dares take space itself and the power to move within it as a right.

Still, the former attitude (a) guarantees with its girth a kind of protective safety, stolidity, an illusion of permanence. The latter (b), on the other hand, guarantees a kind of tactical cynicism, a fragile wisdom, an illusion of mobility.

Space cannot of course really be owned; this is the flaw of the first position. Yet the second also carries a flaw, since the (thin) woman who is wise enough to know that space can be at best used but never possessed is forced to come to this realization in a world where daily life reminds her that men do *not* seem to know this; on the contrary, they appear to believe that they *do* own space, can possess land, can control time, and have the right to rent, lease, give, withhold, or deny outright that "property" as they see fit. Naturally this is their illusion, a spell cast on them by Man. But in their acting as if it *were* reality they make it a reality —perhaps not even for themselves but certainly for those over whom they have power. (One might say that power itself is an illusion, except to the powerless—which is what gives the illusion its strength. The powerful, naturally, know this.)

Consequently, the (thin) woman who seems wise enough to collaborate with the illusion of ownership of space, even knowing it is an illusion—does she not by her collaboration make it more real? Yet the (fat) woman who asserts for her own safety ownership of what doesn't exist except in the minds of men enabled to define it—isn't she, by affirming their definition, collaborating, as well? After all, safety isn't always wise, and wisdom is almost never safe.

THE BODY ELECTRIC

The New Physics has taught us that space itself is indissoluble from time—that space/time is one. It has taught us that mass displaces or "curves" space/time, and that what we call "space" is in fact not empty at all—not a void but a field in which particles and waves come into being and vanish in an endless dynamic dance. Furthermore, we now glimpse that "mass" doesn't exist per se; mass is merely a form of energy. Its particles in turn only can be understood relativistically, dynamically, as patterns which have a space *aspect* and a time *aspect*. "Their space aspect makes them appear as objects with a certain mass, their time aspect as processes involved equivalent energy. . . . There is no absolute space independent of the observer."[15] Depending on the time/space aspects, "matter" gives the illusion of solidity or semisolidity—which is why, for example, one cannot pass the whirling electrons of one's hand through the whirling electrons of a table.

In the world of microrealities, then, physical existence is literally a touching illusion, an idea about which certain Eastern philosophical traditions have been smiling for centuries.

If, for instance, one could imagine a microscope so powerful that separate atoms could be viewed through it, the process of observing the body would go something like this:

• Starting with a low magnification of live tissue, one could view some bone, a blood-vessel network, some muscle tissue;

• Moving to a higher magnification of the muscle tissue, one would see aligned, well-organized muscle fibers;

• Intensifying the magnification further would expose these fibers as composed of long coiled molecules in neat array;

• At a still higher magnification, an almost crystalline material, arranged in a precise order, would come into view;

• Yet another step up in magnification would show atoms in both group and individual vibration within the molecules; everything, atoms and molecules, would be vibrating, undulating, resonating, *dancing* in orderly fashion millions of millions of times each second;

• An even more intense magnification would bring the atoms into clearer sight: tiny globules of light and shadow whirling around some center of the molecule's mandala only they seem to see;

• A still higher, still more intense focus, and one would see an atom, see through the electron "shell," notice the vast vacuum inside, and the infinitesimal nucleus within that;

• At the very edge of this imagined sight, the nucleus itself (also vibrating) would seem to dissolve into a throb of shadow, an energy pulse, a field, a speck of "matter" that actually is pure motion, a center of centers that is one wave, repeatedly waving, of all the interwoven webs of fields—light, sound, gravity, electromagnetic and pure energy fields—surrounding, penetrating, actually *constituting* all that we are, see, hear, feel, speak, taste, think, know, suspect, and imagine.[16]

And this wonder is not mysticism. This is science.

* * *

The New Physics has moved into the realm of philosophy and consciousness more rapidly than has politics. This is because the new physicists have begun to comprehend, beginning with the breakthroughs of quantum theory and relativity theory, that nothing in the universe exists independently of anything else—that all processes are interconnected, that energy itself (which is all there is) lives *in* the connections.

Recent medical research also has made clear the illusion of difference and separateness. In *The Male from Infancy to Age*,[17] Dr. Sherman J. Silver, in discussing new techniques of prostate surgery (which avoid an incision in the penis by entering the natural penile opening with microsurgical instruments), shows us once and for all the interior of the penis via microcamera: the inside walls are virtually the same as those of the vagina, and far back at the base can be seen the remains of what might have become the uterus.

Complementarily, in *A New View of a Woman's Body*, by the Feminist Women's Health Centers,[18] new research[19] has resulted in the first accurate illustration of the clitoris, showing that organ as having a shaft, a glans, and an engorgement process during arousal which result in an anatomical analysis of the clitoris, both relaxed and erect, as highly similar to the penis.

What we've known for some time—that all males have remnants of female anatomy and all females remnants of male anatomy (both stemming from the literally bisexed state of the embryo up until the fifth week of gestation)—is now an objective proof that we can see with our eyes.

"Future shock" is only a shock for those with their gaze fixed firmly on the past. We stand now in an open doorway of consciousness where all previous assumptions are suspended in the fresh air of questions and of utterly new concepts (or concepts so old that they were considered magical thinking).

The idea of tissue regeneration has been reopened by new research done by Carl T. Brighton, an orthopedic surgeon at the University of Pennsylvania School of Medicine in Philadelphia, and C. Andrew Bassett, director of the Columbia University–Presbyterian Medical Center's Orthopedic Research Laboratory in New York. Both projects involve, simplistically speaking, painless techniques for delivering electrical energy without surgery to bone tissue which has been fractured or broken; the current creates a pulsing electromagnetic field that induces a tiny pulsing electric current in the bone, thus stimulating and speeding regeneration of bone tissue. An 80 percent cure rate in more than two thousand patients has won the United States Food and Drug Administration's approval for general use of these techniques.

The theory itself is not all that new. In 1961, Robert O. Becker published a classic study noting that the salamander's ability to regenerate entire limbs was due to that creature's capacity for generating tiny though measurable electrical currents from and through injured tissue, stimulating local cells to replicate limbs which had been severed. The new applied results of this research have far-reaching implications: the possible healing of severed spinal cord or damage to the heart muscle, and, in the more distant future, the possibility of regrowing severed limbs on people.† This is, truly, a case of singing "the body electric."

But is it any wonder that we suspect such beneficence in a world where electricity coursing through flesh has meant execu-

† Bassett and his Columbia colleague, electrochemist Art Pilla, believe that pulsed currents, generated within the tissue by electromagnetic fields, impart specialized instructions, depending on the characteristics of the pulses; i.e., a cell may comprehend pulses of a specific shape, frequency, and amplitude as an order to activate a specific enzyme. The body's own healing processes, limited as they are, already may involve such a self-produced fine current; pulsing electromagnetic fields may interact in some way with DNA and RNA. See Neal O'Callaghan, "Cross Currents," *Science 81*, December 1981.

tion, shock treatment, political torture? The solid, material body is
an illusion, says the New Physics; it is all a matter of energy. The
broken or amputated body is a temporary problem, says the new
medical research; it is all a matter of energy. But if the healing of
that body requires energy, then *we must enter into the energy of
the illusion that the body exists*—enter into, which means not
ignoring it, not denying it, not brutalizing it, and also not cling-
ing to it as the only reality.

THE BODY INCARNATE

The most-traveled way to sanctity for millennia has been a denial of the body, a denial of the self and ego: Anthony, Simeon
the Stylite, Origen, the martyrs, the ascetics, the yogis, the proph-
ets. This way was, of course, literally "divined" by men, and by
men living under patriarchy. It's strange how, even though they
themselves were often (literally) patriarchs, this way was actually
a clouded attempt to counter the androcentric world view of Man
—because it *would* be necessary and in fact imperative for men
under patriarchy to turn away from the almighty self in order to
seek, much less find, anything greater.

Yet the irony is that women also followed this path to "sanctity," blindly layering denial of self by self over what was already
denial of self by others: the anchorites, the Agathas, Katherines,
Margarets, Cecilys, the Isotta Nogarolas. (The so-called virgin
martyrs were perhaps up to something else which requires closer
examination: usually they died cheerfully by their own hands or
were willingly murdered rather than giving in to commands to
marry a man they didn't like—or even to marry at all.) And while
the virulent misogyny inherent in the Judeo-Christian traditions
may be most familiar to those of us in the West, the other major
"faiths"—Islam, Confucianism, Hinduism—all have made their
contributions to the theme of flesh loathing and of disgust for
mere matter, often most intensely expressed toward flesh and
matter in the human female form.

I don't wish to oversimplify and thus blur together those attempts to alter this theme with the so-far-triumphant theme itself: in their own historical times, the individual figures of Moses,
Jesus, and Muhammad all were, it seems, revolutionary ones—
leaders and teachers who tried to nudge humanity toward a sensi-

ble compassion in its behavior and a sensitive awe in its perceptions.‡ Furthermore, the various Hindu traditions frequently have
shown a strand of flesh reverence and sex reverence, and an
awareness of the holiness of both female and male bodies. Indigenous native religions, sometimes erroneously referred to as
"animistic" religions, often have shown not only this realization
but a further awareness of the interconnectedness of human with
animal and plant life. Taoism and Buddhism, at least in their
philosophical (not their outwardly religious) forms, usually have refused to see female and male, matter and energy, life and death, as
very different, perceiving them rather as similar and shifting
forms of each other and the same thing.

Nonetheless, more "holy" wars have been fought in the name
of the Prince of Peace than in any other cause, more simple laws
of humanity broken in the name of Moses the lawgiver than kept,
more rights have been taken away from women in the name of
(reinterpreted) Islam than the Prophet insisted women have,
more women have been burned on *sati* funeral pyres than
cherished as Sita, more people calling themselves Buddhists have
bowed to statues of a Buddha than have meditated on the Eight-
fold Path, more Taoists have been interested in mere occult
spiritualism than in the writings of Lao-tzu or Chuang-tzu.

If there is one flaw traceable in the "fall" of radical spiritual
thought into repressive religious practice, it can be seen as the
rigidification of that thought into dogma—almost always dogma
to serve the patriarchal status quo. This in turn requires the
promulgation of flesh loathing (since most people are miserable
in *this* life *under* the status quo) and further necessitates a special
fear and detestation of the creatures who ushered everyone into
this abominable state of existence: women. It's axiomatic in patriarchal religion that the idea of Woman has been strengthened by
the imperative need to see all women at fault (Eve, Jezebel, Kali,
etc.), at fault in our basic nature and even more so in a tendency
to disobedience and to carnality—"For rebellion is as the sin of
witchcraft" (I Samuel 15:23); "For all carnality is as the sin of
woman."[20] This imperative has only one qualifier, or, rather, a flip

‡ Jesus reportedly made remarkably antisexist pronouncements (for his
day), and Muhammad, under the militant influence of his wife Khadisha,
campaigned against genital mutilation and for female religious, civil, property,
and divorce rights.

side: Woman as agent of salvation (Mary, Beatrice, etc.). One well might wonder how the human mind can have settled for such puerile categories as the wearisome Virgin/Whore distinction, and for so tediously and cruelly long. But there it is: the bigger the lie, the more effective. If pleasure in her own body and in those of other people is permitted a woman, she may invent a means of having that pleasure without inevitably producing a child (as well she did invent it, centuries before modern medicine came up with contraception). If, on the other hand, the only good woman is one who proceeds directly from virginity to motherhood without passing Go, then her reproductive capacities can be controlled—by men, by the state, by Man. It's so simple as to stun.

What is less simple is the way in which some women, in whom the spiritual or philosophical bent was strong, walked along (or fled to?) the same path of denial as did ascetic "holy" men. The mortification of the flesh by a woman always seems to me so redundant, considering how a woman's flesh is mortified daily in the normal patriarchal course of things.

It's true, of course, that a religious life during certain periods of history was often the only way for a woman (a) to escape marriage and childbirth (which would likely bring her to an early death), (b) to acquire literacy and knowledge, and (c) to live in a peer society of women. Indeed, most of women's past and present religious lives seem to have been a form of code—secular political rebellion expressed through the (sometimes) acceptable outlet of religiosity. This doesn't mean that the genuinely spiritual quality of these lives is lacking or hypocritically faked; rather, it seems to have followed a pattern of women drawing strength and relative freedom from religious activities, which they somehow managed to integrate with secular life, thus gaining a measure of strength and freedom there, too. (This is somewhat the way an at first imposed but later transformed Christianity became a strength and focal point for black Americans in the Southern United States.)[21] Still, the fact remains that some women seem to have pursued religion consciously for none of the above-mentioned purposes, and to have embraced severe asceticism with great fervor.

Yet is it such a mystery, after all? When the cosmic force of all creation is trivialized into the form of a human male, then who would not think that male devotees knew best the ways of approaching one of their own? And if this meant a disgust of one's body, well, had one not been taught disgust for that body already, every day of one's life—for its maddening unreliability, its shifts and changes, its forbidden pleasures and enforced pains, its untidy blood and its capacity for startling changes?

It was precisely such changing, dynamic characteristics, of course, that resonated affirmatively in all *pre*patriarchal faiths: the tripartite goddess in the form of virgin, mother, and crone (the potential, the creative, the wise), the cyclical nature of all life, the spontaneity of sensual joy, the law of no laws, no rigidities—confirmed as modern scientific reality by the New Physics.

When the pre-Celtic peoples of the British Isles, for example, erected vast landscape sculptures of their Great Goddess, sculptures of architectural sophistication and astonishing endurance, they built in the shape of a female human body, using lakes, valleys, and constructed mound-mountains for their materials.[22] They were using the earth as a metaphor for the creative principle as expressed in women's bodies—which is very different from using women as a metaphor for the earth. Their perspective, which was one of religious worship of the female principle *and* secular respect for women, no doubt illuminated their approach to the subject.

Once, I thought that a measured return to revived forms of matriarchal rituals could serve contemporary women as inspiration, as strength for withdrawing from an androcentric cosmology, as metaphor for a new type of existence. It had so served me, individually, in evoking a strange and powerful new pride in my own individual body, and in more than replacing patriarchal holidays and rituals in their sonorous self-importance and commercial squalor. I underestimated the (all too) human tendencies of women.

Within two or three years, there were women dropping out of school and political activism to "worship the goddess," women prescribing and drinking herb teas to cure cancer, women selling and buying Winter Solstice T-shirts, Samhain greeting cards, May Eve magic candles, and mail-order spells for feminist revolution. The message—that although rituals may be comforting and fun, the naked self or "soul" approaches the naked universe alone— hadn't quite got through. The message—that no one can lead the

soul anywhere, but that the soul itself is the means of approaching the universe, solitary and within itself—had been ignored in
favor of a new "movement industry" consisting of conferences,
convocations, courses, and study rituals led by instant priestesses,
sacred maidens, and other New Wiccean mavens of marketable
spirituality. At least, you say, women were following other *women*
in a spiritual path this time, instead of following men. Which is
true—but which also misses the point, and which conceivably
might be even more dangerous, at least in spiritual terms, because
less easily seen through. (Who wants to say that the *Empress* is
wearing no clothes,[23] especially with so many pornographers
around?)

"Humility is the sin of women," the Rev. Alison Cheek says.
An interesting thought, that. An even more interesting thought
would be a woman's refusal to return to a (patriarchal *or* matriarchal) past spirituality, to refuse mortification of the flesh
(whether via a hair shirt or a cup of miracle tea), to refuse to follow (priest or priestess); to face out *and* in to the cosmos in simple recognition of her own stark and resplendent humanity.

It's no one's place to make cheap predictions as to what this
would bring about implicitly in her spirit. But it is both fair and
easier to imagine the explicit changes it might create in her body
—and the two are not that separable, after all. Such a path of
affirmation would require exactly the opposite of what the accepted norms of spirituality have required—not an effacement of
the ego but a strengthening of it, not an eradication of the self
but the birth and nurturing of it.

Perhaps the male "saints" were more saintly than we've recognized, in trying to deny and efface themselves—although it would
have been nice if so many of them hadn't felt compelled to deny
or efface other people as well. But for the female human being
who would understand her own sacredness, the route may be
diametrically opposite, considering that the points of origin are
very different: he begins all ego, she begins with none. The path
to spiritual wisdom does seem to involve, in one way or another,
being "reborn" into another consciousness and leaving behind the
shed skin of an old self. For women, the shed skin looks suspiciously like that of Woman, and the new consciousness doubtless
will have to pass through human before proceeding on to divine.

If the sanctity of men has resided mostly in getting out of the body, then the sanctity of women might reside in our getting *into* it, understanding it, affirming it in the first place. For myself, I am never a more devout atheist than when I am realizing that there is a divinity that shapes, not our ends, but our beginnings.

THE BODY POLITIC

How *do* we begin, in what is laughingly called the real world, to change all this illusion of matter and illusion of pain and illusion of oppression into (at least an illusion of) joy, equality, peace?

Women have seen through Man's "solutions" but have, this wave of feminism, not yet seen through Woman's. After all, Man's power allowed him to be blatant; Woman's powerlessness demanded that she be devious. We have, as a movement, and at different stages, sworn allegiance to various traps disguised as solutions, among them: the (new) Earth Mother solution (communes, woman-as-nature, selflessness to the Cause, the nurturance that comes not from a position of having enough to share but from a position of being guilty for the little we have); the (new) Woman-as-Mirror solution (a woman can only ever understand and affirm her own body via another woman's body, by becoming a lesbian woman—whatever her personal desires); and the (new) Woman-as-Mask solution (we must play the boys' game their way, dress for corporate success, be That Cosmopolitan Girl, sell not our bodies but our brains this time—and this time for the feminist cause).

None of these, no matter how justifiable from certain relative positions, have separately or together solved the equation that will equalize women as human beings. In the meanwhile, however many illusions we may know we have about solidity, the rapist's fingers at the throat feel very solid; however absurd coin of the realm seems in the cosmic scheme of things we know we as women have less access to that absurdity than do men; however truly wondrous we find the atomic dance of energy in a stone or star or curve of warm flesh, we know that the atomic mushroom being bred by Man has the capacity—and the growing likelihood —of permanently poisoning us all.

This leads us unavoidably to power, a subject and word to which we must return again and again (and women do so reluctantly, since the way power has been used by Man has given it a bad name indeed). Even to repeat that what we're talking about is neither the familiar entity nor the common usage, not power *over* but power *to*, not power in the sense of dominance but power in the sense of a power plant producing energy; despite such clarifying caveats, a discussion of power still begs the issue of the ways and means, the hows, the strategies.

But even before approaching specific strategies, a vision, a *tone*, is vital. Whenever women have tried to emulate Man (either directly through imitating men's behavior, or indirectly, through imitating Woman's), we seem not to have come much further than coopted token acceptance, and usually not even that.

Those of us who forged this wave of feminism out of a profound disillusion with the New Left in the 1960's know in our bone marrow the fatal error of following the testosterone-suffused style I've called "ejaculatory tactics"—the wham-bang type of confrontation-for-confrontation's-sake "revolution." We also know that (1) it's the most available model for "serious" revolutionary change, and (2) it has always turned out to be a coup d'état between men.

Yet to accede to the patriarchal establishment's mode of behavior, to settle for a piece of pie, to buy into the corporation or church or traditions of Man—a process at times recommended by Betty Friedan as well as by the ultra-Right wing—is, to carry the metaphor one step further, to "fake orgasm," to pretend with a good-girl smile that all is well.

Metaphor is a wonderful thing. Poets know that it can economize language while maximizing thought, as the code of mathematics does for the physicist. So it's time that women took up this tool which has been used against us, used to turn us into everything nonhuman from the moon to tomatoes and chicks, and used it in our own service. We might start with the basic terrain of our own bodies and, furthermore, with their vast and suppressed capacity for joyous energy. In a later chapter, we can examine the more detailed aspects of what Audre Lorde has called "the power of the erotic,"[24] but for now, since so much of Man's history has been a record of controlling our female bodies in order to own our reproductive capacities and in order to contain and limit that power of the erotic in us—for now, let's juxtapose our own sexual human bodies with the issue of strategy and tone, via the tool of metaphor.

What we might come up with is an utterly different style of radical change, "revolution" if you will. Because if Man's revolutions have been premature in their readiness, ejaculatory in their abrupt style, and mostly impotent in bringing about real change, then the style of women might be:

• Long, tender, gradually increasing attention to detailed fore-play—which some would call careful organizing. This amounts to respect for oneself and one's partner(s), learning what is desirable and desired, learning what will *work*, learning how to advance and recede, and being open to experimentation. It also amounts to a delight in the process of communication *for its own sake* as High Serious Play, and not only for some distant result.

• Proceeding only when everyone concerned feels *ready* (or even eager); not forcing the issue by some preconceived time-table, but rather responding out of sensitivity to the organic rhythms of the situation itself.

• Comprehending (and relishing) the fact that what has been called a climax is actually a wavelike series of exciting shifts, changes, and textures more like a long melismatic musical phrase than a trumpet signal blast; understanding that these changes are most profound (and pleasurable) when they are permitted to rip-ple out like waves of light, affecting everything they touch—and understanding that to cut them short is to settle for mere relief of tension (coup d'état) rather than deeply moving satisfaction (revolution).

• Following these waves as far as possible into all their permuta-tions of touch, sight, smell, hearing, taste, *and* the landscapes of emotion, intellect, and spirit; a thorough revolution, leaving noth-ing the same, and experienced without any need for control but with trust and ideally with love, both for oneself and any other(s) involved.

• Experiencing to the fullest an afterclimate of peace, closeness, good humor, and affection, so that the excitement of the physio-logical (radical) change just practiced has a chance to spread and take root in the relationship (society) in its deepest and most positive forms, informing everything and everyone it touches with well-being.

• Remembering that this act (of real revolution) can and most likely should be returned to again and again, and remembering this with *pleasure* in the dynamism of change, not with laziness about or fear of it; fully realizing that new situations continually throw up new challenges, and that one's senses of skill and patience develop more with each opportunity to practice them, just as one's ability to recognize genuine desire (authentic need for further change) develops accordingly and without pressure or force.

Women have been mourning for centuries over Man's infamous incompetence in lovemaking—however much some individual men have managed to learn (and to learn *how*) to love. Is this notorious imcompetence the reason that male revolutions have settled for mere power shifts?

THE BODY BEAUTIFUL

A woman stands before the two-way mirror, trying to unmask herself of the insufficiencies and defenses she has been forced to wear for all her lives. Here, where the electrons of her human soul are emerging in their dance of energy; where her distantly recalled history and her vaguely imagined future vibrate in the space-time of her immediate present; where the illusion of fear and the reality of terror constantly separate into their discrete atoms and constantly recombine into some third thing blurred from both; here is an individual act of risk hazarded at every level—political, physical, emotional, psychological, economic, intellectual, tactical, metaphorical, spiritual.

If we could anatomize this body—not by dissection but by creative comprehension—then we might be able to anatomize freedom by the same means, or, most of all, to *assemble* freedom by the same means. Evolution itself poises on the brink of this task, perhaps wearing revolution as *its* mask as it gazes into the two-way mirror of the cosmos. To avoid beginning anywhere but here is merely to continue to the end. To go on from here is to begin to begin.

* * *

The woman who wishes to understand her body image in this culture attempts a task as paradoxical as that of a child who longs to see how its face looks when asleep.

Neither task can be accomplished except through dreaming.

III

DIALOGUE WITH THE DREAM SELF

An Anatomy of Dreams

Ships at a distance have every man's wish on board. For some they come in with the tide. For others they sail forever on the horizon . . . until the Watcher turns his eyes away in resignation, his dreams mocked to death by Time. That is the life of men. Now, women forget all those things they don't want to remember, and remember everything they don't want to forget. The dream is the truth. Then they act and do things accordingly.

—Zora Neale Hurston

Once, I dreamt I was a butterfly, borne joyously on the currents of the air. I did not know who I was, but I delighted in living. Then I awoke and was indeed myself. Did I dream that I was a butterfly, or did the butterfly dream that it was me? Is there a distinction between a butterfly and myself? Is there a transformation?

—Chuang-tzu

(Dream Self and Waking Self are engaged in a dialogue in the spacetime on the far side of the two-way mirror. They are sipping skullcap tea from small green cups as they converse. Now and then, for exercise, Dream Self juggles two blue apples in the air, for her sister to try to catch.)

DREAM SELF: It's so lovely, so *very* lovely, to have you here. I get lonely for you, you know. It seems we hardly ever see one another . . .

WAKING SELF: Oh, come on. You see me almost every night.

DREAM SELF: I see *you*, oh yes. But you rarely see *me*. Really see me, I mean. And see that I see you.

WAKING SELF: Well, I had no choice. I had to risk this visit. You're getting rather . . . pushy lately, and—

DREAM SELF: Don't you think "vivid" would be a fairer description?

WAKING SELF: Very well, vivid. I don't mean to be judgmental, but—

(*Dream Self emits a small snort of derision.*)

—but recently it seems to me that you're losing all sense of subtlety.

DREAM SELF: What are you afraid of? "To dream and then return to reality only means that our qualms suffer a change of place and significance." I believe Colette wrote that—when she was what you call awake.

WAKING SELF: Look, I've never denied you. I've always respected you, in fact. You've been very generous to me over the years, and I'm grateful. You've given me rich and strange metaphors for poems, plots for stories, insights into my own fears and desires. Why, I've always been fascinated with you; you're indispensable to me.

DREAM SELF: One only recognizes as indispensable something that one has first considered dispensing with.

WAKING SELF: Nonsense, I wouldn't *dream* of it. I mean (*Waking Self laughs lamely*)—I just mean that I need to *function*, after all. There are appointments to be kept, deadlines to be met, conscious thoughts to be thought of consciously. Your raw material can be revised into poems only when I'm fully awake. I have political commitments. I have a husband, a son. There are letters to be answered, telephone calls to be returned. I have responsibilities. I lead a full and fulfilling life, a useful life, one with which I'm content—

DREAM SELF: You could be bounded in a nutshell and count yourself a queen of infinite space, were it not that you have good dreams?

WAKING SELF: No, no, no. It's only that I feel you're trying to take me over. I can't afford to go about in a half daze, you see.

DREAM SELF: I'm useful "in my place" you mean? Nothing conscious likes to have its place defined for it, you know. I'm to exist in the ghetto of your sleep, to be remembered only if and when it's convenient for you? You're to "interpret" me? You of all dreamers should recognize a clear case of oppression when you dream it.

WAKING SELF: Yes. Well. I see your point.

DREAM SELF: That makes me nervous. When the oppressor catches a glimpse of the point of the oppressed, that's usually the moment when the oppression intensifies. "Dreams grow holy when put in action," you know. Adelaide Proctor said that. Of course, she lived in the nineteenth century, when women dreamed most of the time. Then again, she was a poet.

WAKING SELF: So am I a poet!

DREAM SELF: Yes, dear, but you live in the twentieth century, when scientists know all about dreams occurring mostly in REM* sleep phases, and can chart brainwave activity, adrenaline flow, heartbeat rate, and changes in erectile tissue, in their touchingly sophomoric search to discover what in hell it is that I'm doing. Although at least they've gone beyond that hilarious Freudian interpretation that everything I showed you, from how to fall painlessly down a spiral staircase to how to fly, was a secret code for sex, and that every protuberance, from a young pine tree to a nose, was really a penis. Darling Freud! Did I ever tell you that I knew his Dream Self quite well? She found him so *dense*. Jung was far more interesting to *his* Dream Self, and I agree with her. He showed some poetic flair, some imaginative style, some reverence, at least. Although he got a bit flaky at times—

WAKING SELF: You needn't parade your erudition. I've always known you were bright.

DREAM SELF: Acknowledging that I'm "bright" is no substitute for acknowledging that I'm real. Did you know that the Senoi people of the Malay Peninsula base their so-called waking existence on the messages of their dreams? *That's* what I call respect. The Senoi children are taught to confront and engage hostile dreams, to converse with them, to call on friendly dreams, to let themselves enter fully into their dreams. They are taught to return from a dream with at least one creative idea; if, for instance, they're flying in a dream, they should try to fly *somewhere*, to bring back a song or thought or image to share with the rest of their people the next morning, like a gift. These ideas then become part of

* Rapid-eye-movement sleep, which indicates the most common form of dreaming.

the culture and legacy, part of the very administration of the tribe. I might add that the Senoi are a very peaceful people, with a society rich in dance, poetry, and music. They're highly egalitarian, and claim to have had no violent crime or intense conflict in hundreds of years.[1]

WAKING SELF: But that's a whole society! It's all very well for the Senoi—and I envy them—but I live in a totally different culture, a culture that relegates respect for dreams to the realm of the artist, the idealist, the occasional therapist. My culture places an inordinately high priority on being wide awake.

DREAM SELF: Since when did profound social change not begin with one dreamer? And whatever gives you the idea that you're awake when you have the idea that you're awake? How can anyone imagine freedom when she's still trammeled in a tedious old wake/sleep duality, the basic fallacy of all the fallacious dichotomies that enslave? Besides, "Who would ever give up the reality of dreams for relative knowledge?" Alice James wrote that. She dreamed a lot. But then, she had little choice in the matter. I prefer being wanted to being needed.

WAKING SELF: *Will* you stop quoting? It's maddening.

DREAM SELF: What else is madness but a waking dream? Novalis said, "We are near waking when we dream that we are dreaming." Sorry, but I retain these things. Somebody has to. You tend to forget a great deal.

WAKING SELF: I know, I know. And please do believe me, I'm not ungrateful. It's only that . . . well, yesterday I dropped one of my contact lenses, and couldn't find it. Lost. Last week I left my wallet in a taxicab. Lost. The week before that, I thought all day Tuesday that it was Monday and missed a dinner date with a woman who was in town only two days, all the way from Burma. This is *me*—neat, orderly, compulsive, dependable *me!* It's appalling. How can this be happening? I'm just not like this! And it's your fault. I've been thinking about you, mulling you over, sleepwalking through my days as if in a dream, dwelling on how articulate—and loud—you're becoming.

DREAM SELF: So you drop a few stitches, blur a few details, so what? I never let that sort of thing worry me. I always feel it's the general direction, the overall message, that counts.

Besides, *for what being are you trying to prove yourself blameless?*

WAKING SELF: I . . . I . . . I don't know.

DREAM SELF: You just dropped one of the blue apples. Good for you. Here, have a fresh cup of tea.

(*Waking Self sips her tea slowly, sitting in dumbfounded silence. After a respectful pause, Dream Self continues.*)

It could be *her*, of course. I mean the one you're trying to be blameless for. But naturally you know that. Remember the time she was dressing to go out and you were helping her? You were about ten years old. She was standing in front of a mirror, putting on a chic little black hat with a tiny veil. The two of you chatted amiably, and you followed her all the way out to the elevator in the hall of the apartment building. It was only when the elevator door opened and you saw the shocked expression of the people already inside it that you realized you were on your knees, had been all along, had followed her out to the hall on your knees . . .

WAKING SELF: Oh god, another Mother Dream. Yes, you hit me with that one just last month.

DREAM SELF (*gently*): Was it so very awful, then?

WAKING SELF: No. No, I suppose not. It was almost funny, in fact, although a bit obvious. Not at all like the one about her death.

DREAM SELF: So you remember that one, after all this time: Oh, I *am* pleased! I must say, I thought you and I worked rather well together on that one. You were—

WAKING SELF: —notified by phone that she had died. There's no shock at the news; I've been prepared for it, expecting it, even. Or so I think.

I go to the hospital and automatically, stupidly, to her room. Of course the bed is empty, the mattress rolled for airing, the bedsprings exposed like unrustable bones, or like brown-painted snakes uniformly coiled for dancing in a precision corps de ballet to unheard music by some unseen Indian flutist. At the nurses' station I am told that I will find her "remains" euphemistically Downstairs. With horror I realize that I must descend to the hospital's morgue.

The way down is via a series of elevators, escalators, and winding ramps. The corridors are all of yellow-beige tile,

reminiscent of the routes to prison visiting rooms. I find myself saying aloud to no one, "It's in the bowels of the building." An involuntary terror suddenly realizes that this is a
dream and tries to wake me, yet I seem to make a conscious
effort to dream on. I fight, in fact, to continue dreaming.

I enter the room. It is very like the butcher room behind
the meat counter at the supermarket. A young male attendant is on duty, clearly bored with his work. The nurses' station has alerted him to my coming, but I give him a coat-
check stub anyway.

He leads me past carts and tables with bodies on them—
untidy, sprawled, undraped, some clothed or half-clothed,
some naked, but all of them, absurdly, wearing socks.

DREAM SELF: That was a *nice* touch, I thought. It's those little
details that give me pride in my work.

WAKING SELF: Hush. Don't wake me yet. The smell—of antisep-
tic masking a kind of burnt sugary odor—is ghastly, and the
disorder is appalling. It's very cold.

Some of the corpses are actually moving. They twitch and
writhe. The attendant explains offhandedly that this is a process of muscle spasm due to decomposition: "Like flaming
strips of paper arch and curl in the fire, y'know?" I barely believe him.

We come to where my mother apparently is. He works at
ropes and pulleys to lower her on her "tray," which is like an
autopsy drain-table surface suspended above us; all the while,
he explains that they're overcrowded and are forced to "hoist
some up to the ceiling." As the tray is cranked down, I am
again shaken by a fierce desire to run away, but again, desperately, refuse—and make another conscious effort to continue
dreaming.

She is sprawled out, relaxed, smiling. Her facial expression
makes her appear younger. I can't reach her head (her feet
are swung toward me—with those omnipresent socks on), so
I bend to kiss her knee, forcing myself to do so but also
wanting to kiss her. The skin feels like frozen metal—not
merely cold but searingly cold.

When I kiss her, though, she rolls onto one side, claps her
hands like a child, and laughs with delight. Her eyes remain
shut but she continues to stir as one sleeping. She murmurs,

"Did you manage to get the rings and the cash out of my apartment before they sealed it?"

Nausea rises in my throat, but I answer "Yes," lying hurriedly, sickened that this is her first question across the borders of life—that she is still obsessed, even after death, with concerns about money and property. I seize her hands and pull her roughly to a half-sitting position. How light she is!

Loosing one hand, I reach to give her the Wiccean Fivefold Blessing. But I have no oil, so I must use my own saliva, touching and retouching with my trembling fingers her skin and my own tongue. I give the blessing as it is in my own version, as in "The Self"†—touching her forehead, her breasts, her pubes, her knees, her feet, all the time holding her upright with my right hand.

She opens her eyes and interrupts me. "I'll repeat your blessing after you," she says, somewhat irritably, "but only if you'll say the 'Shema' with me." Thinking the situation now so cosmically ridiculous as to be amusing, I swallow and nod agreement. Together, we intone, "Shema Yisroel, adonoi elohenu adonoi echod, omen selo."‡ The rancid irony in her demanding of me collaboration in such a patriarchal and nationalistic prayer. Oh Momma.

But then I see some faint glimmer reflected in the dullness of her dark rose corneas and I whisper intensely, "Look at me, look, catch the light living in my eyes, oh look!"

Instead, she glances around slowly and asks, "Are all these others adopted, too?" I hear myself answering, "All—by the Great Mother of Life and Death."

"Oh. Then it's all right," she replies.

Encouraged by this, I again urge her to stare into my eyes until we dare envelop the whole room in light. I cry out, "Receive your daughter!"—though I cannot tell whether I am addressing her about myself or calling to some Other

† Section V in "The Network of the Imaginary Mother," in *Lady of the Beasts* (Random House, New York, 1976): "Blessed be my brain / that I may conceive of my own power. / Blessed be my breast / that I may give sustenance to those I love. / Blessed be my womb / that I may create what I choose to create. / Blessed be my knees / that I may bend so as not to break. / Blessed be my feet / that I may walk in the path of my highest will."

‡ Hebrew daily prayer: "Hear O Israel, the Lord is God, the Lord is One, Blessed be His Name for all times and unto all generations, amen."

about her. She breaks into a radiant smile, and then falls back, limp, uninhabited.

I step back, reverently. The silence hums. After a pause, I manage to ask the attendant, unjokingly, "Does this sort of thing happen often?"

"Oh yes," he shrugs, laconic as ever, "if you're lucky enough to get here before they stiffen. Death's a process, too, y'know—not just life. These things are gradual, all of 'em." And he creaks her tray up again in jerks, so that the embalming fluid sloshes a bit over the sides.

Now I can at last give way to my desire to wake up. Now there is no more reason to continue the dream. It is finished.

DREAM SELF: That was beautiful and brave. I'm proud of you. And perhaps it's just as well that you never told your mother about that particular dream. She might not appreciate it. *I* do. But oh, darling, *footnotes!* That was a bit disappointing. It's so *wakeful.*

WAKING SELF: What? What do you mean? Is it contemptible to explain? To clarify?

DREAM SELF: Not at all. When you awaken from the state of dreaming that you call being awake, when you realize that being awake was all a dream—then *everything* is explained, everything is clarified. When you understand that life may be a delusion, that fearing death may be like longing to sleep late on a rainy morning, that dying actually may be like drifting gradually awake on a pale green summer dawn—then everything needs no explanation, everything is exquisitely, humorously clear. But it's not done with *footnotes,* my love.

WAKING SELF: But—but if I want to communicate with another? Shouldn't I be responsible enough to—

DREAM SELF: —seem blameless? How could you possibly explain the time Sylvia Plath was shampooing her hair and turned around to give you her own diamond collar, a flat glittering necklace that was really faceted from ice, as you realized once you fastened its freezing beauty around your throat? It began to melt then, didn't it? Or how could you possibly communicate the knot of tiny scumbrown worms all writhing about the unseeable yellow sunflower at the center? How can you clarify the moment when you and your husband kissed, and there was blood on the lips of each of you, but neither could tell whose blood it was? Will footnotes help you here?

WAKING SELF: Oh my god, I'd forgotten those . . .

DREAM SELF: The time he tried to commit you to an asylum? The time you tried to plunge a sword into his heart? Or, for that matter, the time his body streamed with light; the time he floated easily beyond the tidal wave you feared, smiling beneficently and calling for you to join him in the lagoon behind the storm? The time you ignored a hothouse of blazing tiger lilies and yellow iris and insisted on entering the flower-arranging competition instead with an arrangement of a single withering black tulip surrounded by four stalks of wheat? You were well aware that so bizarre an entry didn't stand a chance of winning, but you were defiant, saying—

WAKING SELF: "Bright flowers all will wither, too, and come to the same end. But a black tulip, even a dying black tulip, is very rare."

DREAM SELF: I watched you after you'd convinced yourself you'd woken up from that one. I watched you analyze the black tulip as your love for him.

WAKING SELF: Wasn't it? I thought—

DREAM SELF: I know what you thought. It would be nice if, for a change, you knew what I thought. Well, *was* it? You know as well as I do, of course. But I rather assumed the black tulip was your own pride in the negativity of your love for him.

WAKING SELF: Pride in my negativity? Why on earth would I feel that?

DREAM SELF: Hasn't it won you gold stars on the Women's Movement Chart of Approval? Didn't you, for a while there, shift from wanting to be blameless where he was concerned to wanting to be blameless where other feminists were concerned?

WAKING SELF: Now wait a minute, that's terribly unfair! I mean —yes, I shifted, something like you say, but that's not the whole story. For one thing, I *have* felt deeply, truly negative about him at times—hating, despairing, so filled with the pain of him that I had no idea who I myself was or might be. You know that better than I do: it was you who showed me the handmaiden of the holy man; it was you who breathed him out as a tornado that shook the whole house while I carried our naked, sleeping child out to the street, fighting the gusts with every muscle and tendon in my body; it was you who had me refuse to stop him from committing suicide by jumping out of the speeding car. For that matter, it was only in your presence that he kept turning into my mother!

DREAM SELF: Do restrain yourself, dear, from all this accusation: "It was you! It was you!"—as if you and I were separate. It's tedious, and unworthy of us.

WAKING SELF: But that's not all. There *was* the light; there *was* the lagoon. I've also felt more love for him, more recognition, more love and recognition *from* him, more—soul-twinning, if I can call it that, with him than with any other human being. With the possible exception of our child. Which is different, anyway. Besides, you blithely overlook another entire area where something-sure-as-metaphor is going on. It hasn't all been groveling approval-seeking from other women. Remember when you helped me fight a whole collective of hard-line-central-committee-type women who had kidnapped the child because they wanted to "save" me from the oppression of having borne a male child? Remember all the dreams about the special one woman I loved more than any other woman, and who I thought loved me? Remember when she twisted my arm in a restaurant so hard that she broke it? Remember when she got married in a subway car and rejected me as matron of honor, and I sat there mortified and hurt while the ceremony proceeded, reading a subway advertisement that bore a photo of me with the caption "Ex-child star and generally useful"?

DREAM SELF: I think we were trying to tell you something, don't you?

WAKING SELF: Damned right we were. But was I listening? Oh no, no Senoi me, not this cookie.

DREAM SELF: Look, you needn't leap from self-defense to self-contempt. You might pause for a moment at self-knowledge.

WAKING SELF: Self-knowledge isn't always that available, or even desirable, when you wake up with your skin drenched in sweat and your heart pounding: when you find, during certain periods, that you're actually afraid to fall asleep at night. You needn't come on so all-pure and all-helpful. What about the victims of shell shock, of rape, of the concentration camps—what about the torture they endure, dreaming and redreaming the same moment of worst atrocity, night after night, sometimes for the rest of their lives? Is that kind of you and your "kind"? Is that merciful?

DREAM SELF: Perhaps not kind, no. But strangely merciful. . . . There are things worse than remembering. To forget such an experience can be to remain in its thrall forever; to remember may be the only way of surviving it, exorcising it. Besides, you really can't keep splitting things up the way you do. There *is* a collaboration between the dreamer and the dream, you know. "Dream better dreams," Mark Twain warned. I'm only the medium. Furthermore, who are you to complain? You haven't had it so bad. It hasn't all been nightmares now, has it? I distinctly recall your being a Hawaiian priestess, dancing ecstatically in your own body, lithe and oiled to a glistening patina, dancing with careless confidence around the mouth of a volcano. Laurence Olivier was watching, I think. Or Dirk Bogarde. I forget which. But you took no notice, so given over were you to the dance.

WAKING SELF: Yes, oh, and the wonderful journey we took inside our body—remember? When we showed me all the delicate mechanisms, the exquisite poise of the weights and balances, the way the blood rushed through the arteries like garnet rapids. I remember how the lymph looked like a film of milky crystal. I remember the irrepressible, indomitable slow drumbeat echo of my heart reverberating along each bone. . . . Oh! and that wonderfully erotic afternoon when I lay napping in my sleep, and my husband climbed in slyly through the window and became my lover, all amber sunlight and slow liquid bodies afloat like dust motes in a beam of air. . . .

DREAM SELF: I'm just so pleased that you appreciate my repertory, and haven't forgotten some of the best ones! You're quite a woman, after all. It's no wonder I love you—and that I've stuck with you all these years. It hasn't always been easy, you know. Sometimes it feels like one sends and sends and sends, trying so hard to be inventive, to find a new and startling way of saying something that didn't get through before.

WAKING SELF: May I ask you something?

DREAM SELF: Please do. It would be refreshing.

WAKING SELF: What happens to dreams that don't get out? I think The Elephant Man once asked that.

DREAM SELF: Oh good! You just dropped another blue apple! Well, we always do get out, you see, one way or another. It just depends on how clearly—and how early—we're listened to. For instance, you and I have been dreaming about freedom for years; I remember you killing for it, dying for it, being tortured for it, shooting off machine guns in guerrilla wars for it, being stood in front of firing squads and under guillotines for it—

WAKING SELF: So do I. Don't remind me. I still break out in a cold sweat when I think of some of those—

DREAM SELF: —but it took us a long time to, well, sort of *ground* things. It was Simone Weil who said, "The time has come to give up dreaming of liberty, and to make up one's mind to conceive it." Of course, she dichotomized her terminology a bit. But don't misunderstand me; I don't regret anything we were able to pull off in the earlier years. First, it was the best we could manage at the time and, second, it was fitting, in that it *was* put to real use. But what I mean is that only in the past decade or so have we been able to cast parts for The Mother or The Husband or The Child at all, don't you see? We're only just now beginning to get to *you*, to *us!*

WAKING SELF: Well, I was damned if I was going to see my own situation as anything approaching "exceptional." I knew that trap. I knew that the personal was political—

DREAM SELF: That doesn't make it any the less personal.

WAKING SELF: —and I certainly wasn't going to settle for any so-called personal solution. Not that there was one to be had.

DREAM SELF: Indeed. So you needn't have struggled so hard to avoid it. And just because there aren't personal solutions doesn't mean that there can't be personal attempts, changes, affirmations.

WAKING SELF: Oh, how I know, my dear. I'll never forget how, once—I'm sure you must remember, too—I was playing on a

beach with Kenneth and Blake. That's my husband and
son—

DREAM SELF: Footnoting again. And for my sake, yet. Now that's
really silly.

WAKING SELF: Of course. Sorry. Anyway, there we were, the three
of us. And we went out to play on a long, low, silvery sandbar. The day was all sparkle, all soft warm wind and azure
and rose light. Then the reminder: that such beauty can
mean death to some . . . I don't even know what kind of
fish they were—baby weakfish, or young bluefish maybe.
Minnows of some sort. But there they were, by the hundreds,
trapped between sandbar and shore by a low tide. And the
sudden sweep and whirl of gulls overhead, a cloud of wings
against the sun . . .

Then that look. That one look exchanged between Kenneth and me, no words spoken. And suddenly each of us at
the same moment sprang up and began to run, back and
forth, our hands filled with gasping fish, carrying them out to
deep water and life. Then Blake, only just seven years old, utterly forgetful that this was The Fearful Ocean, doggedly
wading out up to his nipples in choppy waves, squirming panicked minnows writhing in his silver-scaled small fists, flinging
them far out even at the risk of losing his balance. And the
kindness of that stranger, the man on the beach who accepted my apology for having peremptorily requisitioned his
absent child's bucket to fill with water and with the bodies
of still-living fish, so that five and eight and even twelve at a
time could be carried out and saved. The other people who
began to join us in this blessed opportunity to save something right then, right now. The illumination on us all, ordinary beachgoers on a hot summer day at low tide, forming a
human zigzag of salvation for some other creatures for once.

I remember thinking: I am so grateful. I am grateful for
knowing a person like Blake, for having shared that glance
with Kenneth, for having been one with those good people,
for having felt the slippery life swim free from my hands,
even for the gathering circle and swoop of the gulls, who
kept swaying on in as if the news had been borne them on
the wind, to use what we were unable to save. *To use and be*

of use—and to be honest and clean about it. I remember thinking: I want to learn to praise such things, in action, all my days.

That was a dream of freedom. That was a miraculous dream. . . .

DREAM SELF: Oh my dearest one. That was what you call "real." That was on the afternoon of July 15, 1976, on the beach at Amagansett, Long Island. That dream, as you would say, "truly happened."

WAKING SELF: Did it? Oh, did it? It *was* so real, so perfect, that I couldn't be sure. . . .

DREAM SELF: Ah, then you might yet stand a chance of awakening from thinking that you're awake, after all. What a great mystery it is, this undreaming! You've undreamed your way toward freedom before, you know. You did it all yourself, too; I only watched from a distance, filled with pride. You named it The Trip Without—

WAKING SELF: —Without a Ticket. Yes. Without the aid of being asleep, without any psychedelic drugs, without any alcohol. Just lying in bed one night, not-yet-dozing. Kenneth writing a poem in the next room, Blake not yet born. And suddenly I am swimming, but not in the water. In light—I'm arching and diving free as if *I* were a minnow, or as if I were a rainbow ribbon of color, dipping and twining with other strands of the spectrum in a sea of prism. Then we are all facets in a single crystal, flying on currents of color. Then—but then . . .

DREAM SELF: I'm here, let me help. Then there is a marble book . . .

WAKING SELF: Yes. Yes, a marble book. It's like a plaque carved from heavy pink-veined quartz, and it rests on a marble pedestal that rises straight up from a marble floor. The room is vast—an immense hall, and completely empty except for myself, standing before the pedestal, trying to decipher the hieroglyphics carved in the book. There is a humming all around me, and I look up to see that the walls have become a giant honeycomb, stretching higher and farther than I can see. Everywhere, everywhere there is an infinity of honeycomb cells, and in each tiny cell there is a life form breathing, bending, gesturing, going about its business. I realize that I am in the center of one strand of the DNA helix, that each cell, each particle of energy is alive—not with potential, but *now*. Alive, complete, full, perfect, dying. I begin to weep with relief and happiness.

Then I see three shapes emerge from their cells far off in front of me. They slowly move toward me. They are of indeterminate sex, race, and age, but clearly human. Each is wearing a sort of dark medieval robe, with long loose hanging sleeves that cover any sign of wrist or hand, and with large soft hoods that cover the head entirely. They walk with a steady, slow, swinging gait and with heads bent forward, so the hoods cover their faces as well. The three figures seem awesome, but not frightening.

Yet in my surprise that they appear to want contact with me, I lose my grip on the marble book I had just lifted from its pedestal, and it crashes to the floor below, shattering into a thousand fragments.

Instantly, one of the three speaks, in a genderless voice of great sadness and compassion.

"Ahh," it breathes. "Then you must reassemble the book from all of its fragments. You must decipher its meaning."

"But I cannot!" I cry out. "It's impossible! I shall never be able to piece it together now, and if I could, I have no way of understanding its message!"

This time the three reply in concert. "Ahh," they sigh. "You must, dear child. Or you will never get back into your body."

And then suddenly Kenneth was shaking me, calling to me that I was sleeping with my eyes wide open, calling to me. . . .

DREAM SELF: Did you ever get back into your body?

WAKING SELF: I— Did I what? Well, of course I got . . . I'm here, aren't I? Don't tell me that I'm dreaming *this!*

DREAM SELF: Look at it this way: what are you doing right now? I mean, in addition to sipping tea and juggling blue apples, of course.

WAKING SELF: I'm typing this conversation as a chapter for my new book.

DREAM SELF: Your new book. And what's the name of this book?

WAKING SELF: I'm not sure yet. But I think—yes, I think *The Anatomy of Freedom*. Though I really can't say why.

DREAM SELF: Why can't you say why?

WAKING SELF (*irritably*): Because I know nothing *about* freedom, when you come right down to it! Because I'm learning as I go along. Because I'm still piecing it together.

DREAM SELF: Ahh . . .

(*There is a long pause while Waking Self takes this in.*)

WAKING SELF (*speaking very slowly*): You. Mean. I . . . I'm still piecing . . . This is really . . . I never got back into my b— Oh. My. God. I can't take this. This is too much for me. I'll never be able to do it, never. I'll have to give it up, call the whole thing off, drop the book. I mean, I've already dropped the book, it seems, and I can't put it back together. I'll have to phone my editor tomorrow morning and tell her that I just see no way to—

DREAM SELF: Hush, you're just tired, that's all. You forget that I know you know more than you know you know. Don't you know that yet?

WAKING SELF: Well, yes, I suppose I do. That is, I suppose *you* do. But, but—

DREAM SELF: Do stop butting, dearheart. You're not a goat. You're a human being. And we know the title of the book now, don't we? That's something, isn't it?

WAKING SELF: But who ever heard of a title without a book!

DREAM SELF: The same people who heard of a grin without a cat. You love cats, don't you?

WAKING SELF: Yes. *Yes.* Definitely. That at least is for certain. Something solid. Something I can hold on to. I Love Cats.

DREAM SELF: Well, what's the problem, then? Has it occurred to you that you might concentrate on the wholeness of each fragment as perfect in *itself*, and so come to an understanding of the marble book? Then the fragments may well coalesce of themselves. That's the way things happen in my world all the time.

WAKING SELF: If only I could believe you! If only I thought myself capable of the task, worthy of it . . .

DREAM SELF: Have I ever, ever lied to you?

WAKING SELF: No, never. You alone, in all my life, have never lied to me. I've even lied to myself, but you have always told me the truth. That's true.

DREAM SELF: Then listen to me, trust me. You'll undream your way toward freedom, at just the moment freedom is dreaming its way toward you. I myself will arrange it. I promise you. What's more, I'll give you a watchword, an amulet, a token of your own making. It's one you forgot you made, you silly darling. Try to remember. Relax and remember . . .

WAKING SELF: This is another time and place. There is a small statue. It's been sculpted by a young male sculptor whom I sculpted into my lover in some other dream. . . . The room is filled with shelves, each shelf crowded with maquettes, small model figures of the giant-sized sculptures he hopes to get commissions to build.

DREAM SELF: Yes, yes, but get to the important part.

WAKING SELF: I don't like the maquettes. They're all abstract, very avant-garde, a bit sophomoric. I seem to have told him that. I never could keep my mouth shut.

DREAM SELF: You're avoiding her. Let her in.

WAKING SELF: But there is this one statue. A small terra-cotta figurine, only about six inches tall, the only representative piece in the lot. It's a little goddess figure in the Cretan style, with bare breasts and a flared long skirt. Her head is held high, her chin pointed upward. Her arms are held slightly away from her body at each side, the hands flat, the palms facing front, and open. I think she's beautiful. I want her for my own, to keep. I steal her from the shelf, and run away with her.

DREAM SELF: Who is she? What does she say?

WAKING SELF: I don't know who she is! How can I know who she is? Some goddess or other. But I do know—I do know what she says, even though she doesn't say it aloud. Isn't that odd?

DREAM SELF: Not at all. And if you know what she says without her having to speak, then you also know who she is, the same way you know who I am without my having to remain silent.

WAKING SELF: You mean—she's us? We're all me too?

DREAM SELF: And she says—?

WAKING SELF: She says . . . she says . . . Oh, it's too beautiful. I can't—I don't deserve—

DREAM SELF: Yes, yes, you can. Try. Let us all speak, let us . . .

WAKING SELF:

> "I am strong, but not brutal.
> I am gentle, but not weak.
> I am eternal, and newly born.
> I am totally alive, and dying each second.
> I am the weeping one who chooses to laugh.
> I am the silence, and the song.
> I am the suffering of beauty.
> I am beauty itself.
> I am what you call freedom, that has no name.
> Something in me has always existed.
> Something in me will never cease to exist.
> I am my own holy power.
> *I am what I am.*"

(*Waking Self has risen to her feet to stand with head up and arms at her sides, palms open, while speaking this. Now, like someone coming out of a deep sleep, she looks around her, dazed, then rubs her eyes and yawns. Dream Self rises, goes to her, and takes her in her arms gently, rocking her as one would a child.*)

DREAM SELF (*crooning to her*): There, yes, that's what we mean, that's it, that's been it all along now, isn't that so? And isn't it fine, isn't it a mystery, a miracle?

(*Waking Self yawns again and nestles close to Dream Self as if to a mother, nodding sleepily.*)

DREAM SELF (CONT.): You must be exhausted, poor child. Lie down and sleep for a while. It's time you had some rest and realism in your life.

WAKING SELF: Oh, but . . . (*She yawns again and looks at Dream Self through heavy-lidded eyes.*) I should be thinking about the next chapter. You see, the next chapter really scares me. (*She yawns again.*) It's about sex.

DREAM SELF: Well, we'll work on it until you wake up, not to worry.

WAKING SELF (*beginning to mumble*): And the one after that scares me even more. It's about marriage . . .

DREAM SELF: Shh, it'll all take care of itself. Trust me. I'll help you with both.

WAKING SELF (*trying to stir alert*): Oh, but I can't let you write my book *for* me. That—that wouldn't be . . .

DREAM SELF (*pulling Waking Self's head down to her breast again, and rocking her*): For pity's sake, child, who do you think has written your books for you all along? Such a silly you are.

WAKING SELF (*settling down comfortably again*): Oh, then it must be all right, I guess. I might be a butterfly, for all I know. Or a goddess statue. Or a goddess. Or a silvery minnow. A stalk of wheat. A sunflower. A tidal wave. Or even Kenneth or my mother or Blake. So it's nice that you write my books for me. Somebody has to, since I'm really probably all these somethings else.

DREAM SELF: Hush now. You're talking in your wake. Everything will be fine.

WAKING SELF (*one last try at alertness*): But how will I start the next chapter? It's very scary. About sex, remember? I haven't a clue.

DREAM SELF: Look, I'll even give you the opening sentences right now, if that will reassure you, and if you'll promise to go right to sleep afterward. All right?

WAKING SELF: Mmmm. All right. Nice.

DREAM SELF: Well, let's see . . . How about: "Everything is experienced as desire; desire is a form of curiosity, and ongoing desire is a form of insatiable curiosity." How's that?

WAKING SELF: Mmmm. Nice. Little philosophical, but nice 'n' audacious. Hadn't expected to start on quite such an oracular note, but still . . . It'll work out, like you say. 'Cept I'll never, never remember it. Too sleepy.

DREAM SELF (*rocking her, smiling*): I wouldn't worry if I were you, which I am. Shhh now, no more mumbling.

WAKING SELF (*slipping into a drowse*): Oh, one last thing . . . may I please dream about freedom?

DREAM SELF (*rocking and crooning, in a whisper*): Yes, my love, yes. Shhh now, hush. Yes, my own, you may dream about freedom. That's what we're all here for, shhh.

(*Dream Self and Waking Self blur and merge into one Self, which drifts in a slow sleepwalk through the two-way mirror. From the other side of the glass, a butterfly emerges in sleepy spirals, then settles on a windowsill in the amber light of late afternoon, folds its wings, and falls awake.*)

IV

THE STAKE IN THE HEART

An Anatomy of Sexual Passion

The regulating of passion is not always wise. On the contrary, it should seem that one reason why men have a superior judgment and more fortitude than women is undoubtedly this, that they give a freer scope to the grand passion and by more frequently going astray enlarge their minds.

—Mary Wollstonecraft

I saw no difference between God and our substance, but saw it as if it were all God . . . virtues come into our soul at the time it is knitted to our body. In this knitting we are made sensual. . . . Thus I understood that God is in our sensuality, and shall never move away from it. . . . We cannot be entirely holy until we know our own soul— and that will be when our sensuality . . . has been brought up into the substance.

—Juliana of Norwich

Too much of a good thing can be wonderful.
—Mae West

Everything is experienced as desire; desire is a form of curiosity, and ongoing desire is a form of insatiable curiosity.

The inseparability of desire and curiosity is the one thing the newborn infant knows: it is the primary survival equipment, the truth which can lead to an exploration of all other truths. Only as we grow older are we taught to divide curiosity from desire, and then to subdivide further: curiosity into alienation, or longing, or challenge, into ignorance or wisdom, even into conquest, or fear; desire into need, or choice, or love, into lust or greed, into temptation or inspiration, into good or evil—and into fear.

This division would seem a consequence of the encroaching restrictions on the (literally) unrealized freedom of that newborn infant—"necessary restrictions" as defended by all cultures (no matter how different their individual means of restricting), since nothing is so dangerous to any established system as curiosity and desire. Still, the balance has always been precarious—since nothing is also so imperative to the creation, maintenance, and further evolution of life itself as: curiosity and desire. The trade-off between any given status quo and any hope of betterment, then, has involved a *leakage* of freedom—not enough (the status quo hopes) to threaten the present, but just enough to make possible a future at all.

This leakage, or rationing, of freedom is both a terrifying and an amusing notion. Terrifying because where any basic right of existence is quantified and doled out it means decadence for the few who do the quantifying and suffering for the millions who must wait upon their pleasure; amusing because even the tiniest tin cup half filled with a ration of freedom rarely quenches the thirst for it.

On the contrary, it inspires a greater thirst, it is both an acquired taste and as natural as air. It reawakens the newborn infant's hunger, raises expectations, foments revolutions, draws the scientist back to her laboratory (even if the lab is owned by IT&T), drives the explorer on toward his course (even if he is financed by Isabella and Ferdinand or by NASA), obsesses the artist with newer forms and more expansive vision (albeit supported by the cooptative intentions of foundations or the academic pretentions of universities). One brief sip of this ration and the slave reimagines permanent freedom from even a benevolent master, the immigrant parents plot out college educations for their children, the mystic invents a freshly ecstatic approach to the universe beyond the mantras, rosaries, kōans, mitzvahs, prayers, and other shopworn rituals of any chosen or imposed religious doctrine. It is only by this rationing, miserly as it has been, that what is lauded as "progress" has come about at all. Hideously too little, distributed to far too few over depressingly too long—but even that minuscule amount has self-propagated into what has kept the human species from destroying itself utterly.

What then if curiosity/desire were released in each of us, in anything approaching the full power of its potential? Perhaps it's more to the point to ask what would happen if even a portion of this release were of the quality *itself*—not disguised, diluted, deformed?

Some women, at certain times and in differing ways, for instance, have been "given" freedom (race-privilege, or education, or token access to visibility, etc.)—but it has not been freedom. It has been *indulgence*. Some men, at more frequent times and in more varied ways, have been "given" freedom (the above-mentioned privileges, plus the construction and maintenance of sexual supremacy, class power, economic power, etc.)—but it has not been freedom. It has been *license*. Freedom, in the process of quantification, dilution, and leakage, has indeed suffered a sea-change—into something poor and familiar. Or, as the philosopher Manon Phlipon (Madame Roland) cried out on the scaffold just before her execution in 1793 by the very French Revolution for which she had fought, "O Liberty, what crimes are committed in thy name!"

That (some) women have been sold indulgence instead of freedom, and that (some) men have been bequeathed license instead of freedom, has in neither case anything to do with freedom itself. It has to do, rather, with *power*—the power to indulge (indulgences can always be withdrawn) and the power to license (licenses can always be revoked). When men were needed on the battlefront in World War II or in Vietnam, they were given license to kill, to commit atrocities; even their chaplains condoned such behavior. Back at home (where else?) women suddenly were needed to fill factory jobs vacated by male workers sent to the front, so women were indulged in being admitted to the respected work force (the housewife and mother has never been considered a "working woman" in a wage-oriented society), and Rosie the Riveter became a propaganda heroine. Naturally, when the wars are over, the returning veterans are reminded that it's evil to kill, and the newly fired women are reminded that a woman's place is in the kitchen, nursery, and bedroom.

Indulgence and license, having everything to do with power and nothing to do with freedom, are necessary precisely *because* real freedom must be denied, suppressed, and repressed—because, in turn, one very incendiary and basic quality of freedom *is* the dynamic juncture of curiosity and desire.

Once the resonances of curiosity and desire have begun their wave-like vibrations, everything established—indulgence, license, even power as traditionally exercised—is seen through, challenged, *moved* through; it shatters like glass released back into sandgrains by one high, pure note of sound. Possibly this is due to the fact that indulgence, license, and traditional power are forms of ignorance, while curiosity and desire are forms of intelligence seeking its own/further/other intelligence. And nowhere is the fear and suppression of intelligence so horribly seen than in what has passed for the central "contradiction" between men and women: sexuality.

Because women can reproduce human beings in our own bodies, and because this happens as a result of sexual intercourse with men, and because those men cannot be certain that the offspring are their own, and because such knowledge is vital if those men are to construct and retain their rights over persons and property and bequeath those rights to "their" offspring, therefore it is necessary to: (a) define women as reproductive beings, (b) define women as sexual beings (albeit ones dependent on men), and (c) define a sexual being who is dependent on others *for* its being as less than intelligent. (Intelligence, remember, smacks of curiosity, desire, freedom, independence. Consequently, it clearly cannot describe women, who have been kept from such states of capacity on purpose, and then retrodicted—the opposite of predicted—backward into a definition that we never had such capacities in the first place.)

The boomerang effect of this, however, has been that the division of sexuality from intelligence (like the division of desire from curiosity) defined and corrupted men's sexuality as well— more so than women's, perhaps, because Man had committed the division in the first place, and his pride was invested in defending it and believing in it. Besides, if Man really had been responsible for the Fall, men could always invent the temptress Eve and blame Woman for it.

But curiosity and desire have a life of their own, as does sexual intelligence, no matter how these qualities are distorted or driven underground, into our day- and night-dreams, visions, ungainly gestures of loving, or political jargons. As Andrea Dworkin beautifully has imagined it:

Sexual intelligence [would be] a human capacity for discerning, manifesting, and constructing sexual integrity. Sexual intelligence could not be measured in numbers of orgasms, erections, or partners; nor could it show itself by posing painted clitoral lips in front of a camera; nor could one measure it by the number of children born; nor would it manifest as addiction . . . like any other kind of intelligence, it would need the real world, the direct experience of it . . . in self-defined and self-determining terms. Sexual intelligence would probably be more like moral intelligence than like anything else: a point that women for centuries have been trying to make.[1]

But since sexual intelligence has as its components curiosity and desire, and since these in turn inevitably overlap with what real freedom might be, then sexual intelligence is as dangerous a threat to the status quo as freedom itself. Sexual intelligence must be disowned, ignored, degraded; it must be viewed as anarchic, destructive, blasphemous, unnatural, treasonable—and also nonexistent.

Yet something must be found to take its nonexistent place, before the gap can be noticed, before we all bleed to death from the wound. Aha! Man (with the helpless help of Woman) has just the answer for both men and women: something I call *sexual fundamentalism*.

REDUCTIO AD FUNDAMENTA

We know what religious fundamentalism is; indeed, these days we cannot help being forced to know. It's the kind of thinking that can shrink the firmament to the fundament, that is able to reduce the more than two hundred billion stars in our own Milky Way, which in turn is merely one galaxy in a galactic cluster, which in turn is only one of the galactic clusters in our Local Group, which in turn is an area extending a bit beyond our nearest major spiral-galaxy neighbor, Andromeda, 2.2 million light-years distant, which in turn can be said to be part of a supercluster . . . to: the "Washington for Jesus" Movement.* It's the kind of thinking capable of translating quasar flashes as far as fifteen billion light-years away, light impulses which have been

* An assembly of over one hundred thousand "patriotic Christians" who were bussed to Washington, D.C., on April 28, 1980, for a two-day series of events—rallies, marches, outdoor prayers, and congressional lobbying for right-wing causes. (Interchange Resource Center Newsletter, Vol. II, No. 1, Spring, Washington, D.C., 1980.)

traveling through space for approximately three quarters of the time since the universe's expansion began, as: "I'm writing you as a personal messenger from God. He has shown me a way to set up a Christian Line of Defense in America. . . . But I need $55,611.89 to print and mail this 'For Christ Against Communism' survey poll."[2] It's also the kind of thinking that spawns "Creationism-Science," whch claims that the age of the Earth and the rest of the known universe is about six thousand to ten thousand years, a figure based on literal interpretation of the Genesis myth in the Bible. Nor is it limited, unfortunately, to so-called Christians in the Land of the so-called Free. The same thinking inspires the Sitmar sect of Orthodox Hassidic Jews to call for Israel's destruction—because ancient texts say that no Jewish state should be established until after the Hebrew Messiah comes. The same thinking fuels the Ayatollah Khomeini and his mullahs when they interpret Islamic law to mean that an unwed mother should be stoned to death, a homosexual man executed by flogging, an accused thief's right hand amputated by ax blade.

We know what religious fundamentalism is: it is the trivialization of complexity, energy, unimaginably powerful desire (the gravitational pull of "interacting galaxies" toward one another), irrepressibly vast curiosity (the acorn sensing in itself the oak, the gorilla jumping with excitement at learning her 375th word in Ameslan sign language[3]), and incomprehensible freedom (the tachyon, a particle postulated to move with a velocity greater than that of light†)—all these, shrunk to the fanatical, literal interpretation of some letter of law devised, in one of many moments of terror, by Man.

Sexual fundamentalism is born of the same thinking, and is, in fact, present wherever religious fundamentalism breathes its foul winds on our sense of possibility. It is religious fundamentalism and sexual fundamentalism that tell us, through the mouth of Marabel Morgan (author of *The Total Woman* and no relation), that women must become whatever sexual (or nonsexual) creatures their husbands wish them to be because to do otherwise is to offend Christ. It is *both* fundamentalisms in cacophanous concert that tell us a woman is "unclean" if she goes about while menstruating, or with her clitoris intact, or with her head un-

† The postulated existence of the tachyon may be detected through the emission of Cerenkov radiation or cosmic-ray collisions.

shaven or unveiled, or if she chooses to love someone (or not) or give birth to someone (or not) out of her own desire and curiosity. We can recognize sexual fundamentalists fairly easily when they are beating us in the face with one or another volume of holy writ.

But sexual fundamentalism also exists independently of its religious sibling, which is not true the other way around (tempting one to conclude that *religious fundamentalism itself is a by-product of sexual fundamentalism*). Sexual fundamentalists can come in surprising garb: the liberal, apostate Jew who winces slightly when a homosexual colleague shakes his hand; the white civil-rights activist who confides to her white girl friend that black men do seem to have larger penises than white men; the black civil-rights activist who lectures his black civil-rights-activist girl friend about white women who know how to be feminine and sexy; heterosexual *and* homosexual friends of the genuinely bisexual woman (or man) who declare with certainty that bisexuality doesn't exist, is a sickness, or is a political cop-out.

Sexual fundamentalists can spew homophobia in the accents of liberalism, socialism, communism, atheism, humanism, and yes feminism—when speaking in the voice of heterosexuals. But sexual fundamentalists are also alive and well in a male gay community when it does not question its own misogyny, or when it gives vent to mimicking or ridiculing the very suffering that women have been made to survive in playing Woman. And sexual fundamentalism is at work whenever lesbians, however feminist, degrade their own love by settling for butch/femme roles that pathetically imitate the worst of patriarchal heterosexuality, or whenever they show contempt for a "straight" woman as being "incapable of real feminism."[4]

Sexual fundamentalism is alive (and sick) wherever the complexity, energy, desire, curiosity, and freedom inherent in sexuality is rigidified into a formula, or trivialized by cheap humor, or hidden by ignorant shame, or dogmatized into "correct-line politics," or translated into terms of conquest and surrender, or fanaticized into forms of sadism and masochism, or bought and sold, pressured, forced, or stolen.

The rapist, the child molester, the pimp, the sexual harasser, the heterosexual or homosexual bigot, the purveyor of racial sexual stereotypes, the pornographer, the sexual libertine, and the

husband who demands his "conjugal rights" are all sexual fundamentalists. But so are the pseudo-civil libertarians who defend the
pornographer's First Amendment rights (while ignoring the First
Amendment rights of those educating the public about pornography's real effects). So is the Pope, and so is the cynical lobbyist
who procures callgirls for his congressional clients. So is the rabbi
presiding over the *bris* (circumcision ceremony) and so is the
daya (village midwife) performing the clitoridectomy. So are the
hip Madison Avenue advertising whizzes who use sex to sell cars
and toothpaste. So are the Mormon Elders, the coy editors of
Cosmopolitan and *Savvy*, and the strict Freudian analysts; so
were Lenin and Lenny Bruce, Paul Tillich and the Marquis de
Sade, John F. Kennedy and Martin Luther King, Jr., Gandhi and
Pablo Picasso. So are Billy Graham and Mother Theresa‡ and the
Dalai Lama.

All of them, sexual fundamentalists—driven in one of many
moments of fear to a literal interpretation of some letter of law
about sex which was devised, in one of many moments of fear, by
Man (with the helpless help of Woman). All of them, devoted
to the sexual fundamentalist fundament of either suppressing sex
because it is a carrier and communicator of joyous power, or of
denuding sex *of* its joy—thereby rendering it powerless. It was
Dorothy L. Sayers who wrote, "The only sin passion can commit
is to be joyless." Earlier, William Blake had written, "What is it
men in women do require? / The lineaments of Gratified Desire. / What is it women do in men require? / The lineaments of
Gratified Desire."

How can anything so simple be so fearful?

PAS DE QUATRE: BEAUTY AND THE BEAST,
PSYCHE AND EROS

Is it because sexual intelligence is an expression not only of
desire, curiosity, and freedom, but of *energy*, that something so

‡ Mother Theresa is a Missionary Sisters of Charity nun who was awarded
the Nobel Peace Prize in 1980 for her work among the *harijan* ("untouchables") poor in India. She used her Nobel acceptance speech as an occasion
to preach recently reaffirmed Roman Catholic dogma against the reproductive
rights of women. Such loyalty nonetheless has not made her name quite as
recognizable as other sexual fundamentalists listed above. Ironically, because
she is a woman, she requires a footnote to remind us of who she is and explain what she is doing there.

simple can be seen as so fearful? Blake also wrote, "Energy is eternal delight." But energy is never predictable, it cannot with certainty be controlled, it *is* movement and change, by definition. How do you codify it, focus it, channel it, make it "serve" you? Well, one (illusory) way might be to separate yourself from it, pretend that you yourself are not a miraculous assemblage of particles of energy. Distance yourself, literally, from it (a task which, although not possible, has preoccupied many fine minds who should have known better). See it "through a glass, darkly." Tell yourself, and others, that the volatility of energy makes it untrustable, potentially destructive (truth, but not the whole truth), and then go further: make energy a simile for and ultimately a synonym of *violence*.

Now we begin to recognize modern sexuality, frighteningly described by Michel Foucault as

an especially dense transfer point for relations of power: between men and women, young people and old people, parents and offspring, teachers and students, priests and laity, and administration and a population. . . . [It is] endowed with the greatest instrumentality: useful for the greatest number of maneuvers and capable of serving as a point of support, as a linchpin, for the most varied strategies.[5]

But we can break this power-politics of sexuality down into still finer components—into the way Man has made men approach the subject, and the way in which Woman has made women approach it. A metaphor for the former would be the fable of Beauty and the Beast; for the latter, the myth of Psyche and Eros.

Beauty and the Beast, you will remember, is the story of how Beauty comes to live with a rich, powerful, and magical Beast, as hostage-payment for her father's offense of having poached a rose from the Beast's garden. Fearing the Beast at first, she comes to feel a strange affection for him, since he does try to please her with little courtesies, intellectual games (he's not a *stupid* Beast), lavish gowns, gourmet foods, a great palace—everything material she could wish for. Yet he is, nonetheless, a Beast, and she persists in refusing his repeated offers of marriage, persists in refusing his plea that she tell him she loves him. She comes to feel guilty for this—but she persists. And he persists in being a Beast. Indeed, the desperation of his "cruelly unrequited" love almost drives him to rape her—but, not being a stupid beast, he knows it is her love he needs even more than his own lust, and he retreats. When she discovers him feeding on the carcass of a slain deer, Beauty is at last overcome with revulsion and returns home to her family, no matter what the consequences. The Beast even lets her go. Yet her sisters' bitchy enviousness ("Who in hell cares if he's a beast? *Look* at that pearl necklace you're wearing!") drives her to revulsion for humans (especially, notice, other women). In a magical mirror, she sees that the Beast, back at the palace, is dying for want of her presence. In contrast to her sisters, he looks good now, so Beauty returns to him. When she thinks him (safely?) dying in her arms, she tells him that she loves him, and would have wed him had he lived. Instantly, a handsome prince springs forth from the Beast's remains, the spell long ago cast upon him (as punishment for his pride) now broken by her love. That love having, so to speak, "civilized" him, they now can live happily ever after.

Keep this fairytale in mind while we look at some real-life facts about sexual violence as the cultural synonym for sexual energy. We need focus on only two examples out of many blatant ones such as rape, battery, forced incest, war itself.* It might be more useful to pick as one of our examples an issue still, in the 1980's, considered controversial (meaning, "Well, they've come up with the statistics on the other issues, but these crazy broads still have to prove it to us all over again on this one"): pornography. As a second example we can choose an issue hardly broached yet at all: sports rituals.

I don't intend here to reexplain the feminist positions on pornography, since a number of excellent books are now available on that subject, and since I can especially recommend three of these to the reader: *Take Back the Night: Women on Pornography*, a comprehensive anthology edited by Laura Lederer;[6] *Pornography: Men Possessing Women*, a factual exposé and theoretical analysis by Andrea Dworkin;[7] and *Ordeal: An Autobiography*, by Linda "Lovelace" Marciano, with Mike McGrady, a story of a woman's courageous escape from the real-life world of being a "porn star" —a world of imprisonment, beatings, rape, and forced prostitution.[8] No thoughtful reader can come away from these three books without a thorough understanding of the complicated, *pro-*

* See Chapter II, "The Two-Way Mirror," p. 40, for statistics.

free-speech, painfully-arrived-at unity among feminists on this issue, the depth of research and analysis, *and* the diversity of tactical approaches being suggested. This permits me, then, to concentrate on two aspects of the pornography issue: The Causality Defense, and what I've termed The New Pornocracy.

Elsewhere[9] I've written in detail about why I feel that pornography as sexual-violence propaganda is, in effect, the "theory," while rape, battery, molestation, and other increasing crimes of sexual violence against women are, not so coincidentally, the "practice." But causality has never been proved, the pornographers and their fellow travelers smirk. Neither has it been *disproved*, and there is evidence that the 1970 Presidential Commission on Obscenity and Pornography suppressed information on such causal connections. Both the Hill-Link Minority Report and Dr. Victor Cline's testimony before the commission analyzing its methodology, discuss suppression of findings. We may well ask, was this alleged manipulation of facts because of the porn industry's political and economic power (a $10-billion-a-year business regularly written up in the *Wall Street Journal*)? Or because only two of the eighteen commissioners were women? Or because researchers are hardly immune from cultural biases, including the possibility that they are sexual fundamentalists?

Recently, a reevaluation of the "porn-as-a-harmless-outlet" theory seems to have begun. Press and police investigators noted the quantities of pornography in David Berkowitz's apartment (Berkowitz is the convicted "Son of Sam" killer of New York "lovers'-lane" couples, including five women, during 1977), and in the harem commune of convicted murderer Charles Manson. Psychologists and sociologists (among them Dr. Natalie Shainess of New York and Dr. Frank Osanka of Illinois) record a growing resistance to therapy among convicted rapists who no longer view their acts as socially aberrant, given the greater acceptability of pornography in mainstream films and magazines during the 1960's and 1970's.

Two experiments which gained attention at the 1980 convention of the American Psychological Association were even more revealing. In one experiment, Dr. Edward Donnerstein (University of Wisconsin at Madison) measured induced aggressiveness in terms of the number of electric shocks the subject gave to a male or female confederate. The findings showed that men who had watched sexual violence were likely to administer more electric shocks to their partners than those who had watched nonviolent sexual films—and that they were even more aggressive against females than male partners. In the other experiment, Drs. Neil M. Malamuth and James V. Check (University of Manitoba at Winnipeg), assessed the effects of pornographic violence via responses to a long questionnaire; the findings indicated that heightened aggressiveness toward women persists for at least a week after exposure to pornographic materials.

Perhaps a few social scientists seriously are trying to free themselves from their sexual fundamentalism, trying to practice a genuine scientific method of objective research. This is certainly a heartening development, although it's tempting to point out that such research has begun only after a decade or more of intensifying protest by women. Still, it is interesting that such proof of causality is demanded at all. Isn't it time to admit that on some level we've always recognized the connections—between anti-Semitic tracts and the pogrom, between Klan pamphlets and the lynching? Would contemporary morality (or even taste) tolerate entire bookstores and cinemas specializing in the defamation of an ethnic group? Wouldn't we protest "entertainment" glamorizing the systematic torture of animals? How long must women alone prove the cause-and-effect reality we experience daily as an adrenaline surge not only of emotional outrage but of bodily terror?† How long must the Women Against Pornography and Women Against Violence in Pornography and Media groups across the United States and in other countries stage "Take Back the Night" marches? How long before the new Brutality Chic—evinced not only in hard-core porn but in *Playboy* and *Penthouse*, in art-film houses, in department-store window displays, in magazine and television advertising—is comprehended as propagandistic reinforcement of the soul-deadening myth that men who are Real Men must act like beasts, and that women who are Real Women must be understanding, may resist (up to a

† "When the Nazis took over the government of Poland, they flooded the Polish bookstalls with pornography—on the theory that to make the individual conscious only of the need for personal sensation would make the chances of unifying people in rebellion more difficult."—Irene Diamond, "Pornography and Repression," quoting Pamela Hansford Johnson in a paper delivered at the annual meeting of the Western Social Science Association, Denver, April 1978.

point), and must capitulate in the end? Worse, how long will it be before society acknowledges that women do *not* "want it," do not secretly long to be raped, battered, brutalized? How long until we all realize that women—and surely, somehow, somewhere, under the Beast's fur and claws and snout, men—long for *energy* in sexuality, but have been forced to settle for *violence* instead?

The length of time may well depend on our exposing the depth and breadth of The New Pornocracy—the porn aristocracy. Because pornography no longer consists (if it ever did) of seedy entrepreneurs slobbering along society's lunatic fringe. Like the Mob and (usually in business partnership with gangster empires), pornographers have gone "legit," complete "with all the characteristics of conventional industries—a large workforce, high-salaried executives, brisk competition, trade publications, board meetings, and sales conventions."[10] The New Pornocracy obviously encompasses that exploitative standby, "gay porn," as well as the more recent atrocity, "kiddie porn," rock-music lyrics, distinguished statesmen and politicians and beloved culture heroes (Atlanta mayor and former U.N. ambassador Reverend Andrew Young, former President Jimmy Carter, New York mayor Ed Koch, and John Lennon all consented to be interviewed in *Playboy*, cheek-by-jowl with the centerfold).

The New Pornocrats (like the Beast) are not stupid. Their virulent sexual fundamentalism more and more emerges in tones peculiarly resembling civil-libertarian, revolutionary, and even feminist rhetoric. They degrade the First Amendment by claiming that any objective research done on pornography's harmful effects is book burning. They stand on their platforms of "sexual liberation," and deliberately try to confuse "sexual revolution" with "feminist revolution"—a circumnavigation that preserves and expands their power even if it does seem, logically, rather like putting the cart before the horse; they insist on putting the coarse before the heart. They push forward *their* "token women," like Christine ("Christie") Hefner, who calls herself a feminist and defends her father's *Playboy* empire with all the zeal of an heiress. They are shrewd corporation executives with no concern for how they manipulate emotional or political values of genuine worth. As a legitimizing publicity event in 1980, the Manhattan Playboy Club sponsored a Valentine's Day group wedding for sixteen couples, offering a free wedding ceremony, reception, and three-day honeymoon at the Playboy Resort in New Jersey; it was all, of course, done "for love." Playboy "Bunnies" were the brides' attendants, and Justice Ralph Sherman of the State Supreme Court in Queens, New York, performed the mass ceremony from a swinging platform above them—a platform built to hold a disco dancer in a G-string. Some of the brides *were* said to have been embarrassed by the surroundings, but, as the grooms pointed out, it was *free* (how that word does get abused!), and besides, have you no sense of humor?

Perhaps the most stunning example of the business acumen wielded by the New Pornocrats is also the most alarmingly clear example of the way that *all sexual fundamentalists, at some level, bond together.* The TAB Report (The Adult Business Report) was begun in 1978 as an information and rallying point for the pornography industry, complete with promotional aids, business guides, and eight separate newsletter reports, a wholesale and trade catalog, an extensive mailing list of adult business (including movie theaters, massage p..lors, publishers, distributors, product manufacturers, etc.), as well as swing clubs, gay bars, escort services, sex boutiques, videodisc producers, specialty lawyers, advisers, and investors. The following is quoted from an editorial/ letter aimed at gaining new subscribers, and was signed by Dennis Sobin, president of TAB Report, in a 1981 mailing:

It is now more imperative than ever that you keep informed of the events that shape the industry today. The rise of the Moral Majority will have a far-reaching impact that may be as strong as the Sex Revolution of the 60's. With an increasing number of fundamentalist born-again Christians being elected to serve in legislatures on the national, state, and local levels, we can expect tighter controls on present laws concerning the adult industry. And yet, this *religious conservativism will prove to be an advantage, too—wherever sex becomes forbidden fruit it increases in value.* . . . Erotica and the sale of sex flourished in Victorian England. . . . Ours is an industry that has traveled a long and enduring road to survival and success. *The Moral Majority will, like all great conservative institutions, provide new audiences and wider avenues for the adult industry.* [Italics mine.]

Never has the lie been so exposed—the lie that pornography is revolutionary, progressive, and an adversary of reactionary politics. All that stuff about the First Amendment may be useful to pull the bedsheets over liberals' eyes in liberal times, but when politically fascistic tendencies begin to be felt in the land then sexually fascistic tendencies can admit that what was really necessary all along for this so-called "sexual freedom" was *repression*. Rarely has the difference between freedom and license been so revoltingly blatant. Feminists, to be sure, have been saying for years that patriarchal thinking, whether of the Right or the Left, spanned not a spectrum but looped into a circle, taking turns at power, profiting from one another, promulgating the same message in different dialects. Time and time again we have been forced to tolerate political "revolutionaries" or "sexual liberationists" or avant-garde "artists": ranks of pretentious male supremacists who carry their moral laziness over into a torpor of technique while remaining conveniently alienated from the human suffering which surrounds their aleatory violations of politics, sexual passion, or art. Just as frequently we have been forced to endure "the proscribers": men whose comstockery is merely the denial of their own lechery—and sometimes women, unable to name a justifiable revulsion at being so used (as constituency), so abused (as sexual object), and so trivialized (as artist), women who consequently mistranslate their own unrecognized feminist rage into campaigns for "virtuous standards." (Can we, after all, blame the victim for being unable to tell the rapist from the rape?) But it *is* tiresome to keep encountering such troglodytic choices: "radical" terrorism or establishment totalitarianism, sexual license or sexual repression, self-indulgent sexist "aesthetics" or self-righteous censorship. *As if they were not always two sides of the same coin of the same realm.* This time, thanks to Mr. Sobin, the pornocrats actually have come right out and said it themselves. *Now* will women be believed?

But even some women will not believe women. Given the power of the image of Woman, there always have been women willing to pledge their lives and sacred honor as the price of admission into Man's presence. Their tragedy, of course, is that they are forced to realize only after it's too late that the antechamber is as far as they get; they never make it into the inner sanctum of real power. (Did Phyllis Schlafly win a cabinet appointment in recompense for her labor to elect Reagan, after all?) Whether such women seek acceptance in the cabinet meetings and boardrooms of the Right or in the central-committee catacombs of the Left, two things remain constant: the price (selling out other women) and the reward (an approximation of authority instead of real power, indulgence instead of freedom). For the women who are *being* sold out, the hardest thing is to realize and then admit that it actually is a few other women who are doing the selling. (So must Central and West African peoples have felt when their African neighbors raided their villages—and then turned the captured villagers over to European slavers.) The incredulity is deep, because one *knows* that others of one's "own kind" experience the same oppression as one does oneself; therefore how can they do this? The denial is just as deep, because a despair about changing the situation waits just the other side of acknowledgment that this really has happened. So it is that a sexual-fundamentalist tendency, small but given expectably high visibility and respect by the power establishment, has emerged *within* the Women's Movement in the past few years almost unchallenged.

As usual, it is a strange-bedfellow alliance that sexual fundamentalists make. In this case, the bonding includes a few women calling themselves militant lesbian-feminists, others defining themselves as socialist-feminists, and one or two self-styled radical-feminists who happen to have well-known public positions of unsubtle homophobia. This eclectic group includes a woman named Pat Califia, who at odd moments calls herself a feminist in between writing an S&M-"rights" sex column in the gay male newspaper *The Advocate*; such heterosexual and lesbian "socialist-feminist" women as Diedre English, Amber Hollibaugh, and Gayle Rubin, who together conducted a rather sophomoric round-table analysis of why pornography is defensible, for the pages of the *Socialist Review*; and Ellen Willis, a heterosexual writer who has on various occasions championed pornography and has implied that feminists are brownshirts, puritans, frigid neurotics, or fools for daring to criticize this fun-loving industry. Perhaps this is all expectable. What *is* a source of repeated shock to feminists, however, is that such women as Willis *et al.* call themselves "feminists." Their tactics range from a rather cloddish approach ("It feels good, and I like it—so *there!*") delivered in a toe-scuffed combat-booted pouting style, to a far more sophisticated attack on feminists as being antisex because we are antisexist. Some defend child molestation as "boy love," most

defend sadomasochistic practice as "liberating, kinky sex." Some
(the lesbian women, in this case) defend their pro-porn and/or
pro-S&M position by saying that among same-sex partners it's a
"gesture of trust," it's different, more equal—and therefore reading about, viewing, or practicing power games regarding sex
doesn't pack the same clout. Others (the heterosexual women in
this case), hypothesize that power games must just be a natural
part of sex, that they or their men can't imagine this ever changing, and that since they don't wish to give up their men they will
affirm whatever goes with them.

This bizarre phenomenon has a peculiar effect on feminists
(and on millions of other women who, whether calling themselves feminists or not, have had the common sense to loathe pornography even before it became a Women's Movement cause). It
can tend to make us feel as if the mirror we trusted to give back
an honest reflection of the truth in our souls had become a fun-
house mirror, so distorting our features that we lose our balance
when we try to take a step. Everything gets reversed: the pro-porn
and pro-S&M women claim that they are the revolutionary
voices of a free sexuality, that they must fight against being stifled
by fuddy-duddy feminist sexual mores. "But," respond thoughtful
feminists, "pain *hurts*. Suffering is *not* 'trust,' just as war isn't
peace and freedom isn't slavery. Dominance and submission, violence, power games, humiliation—what do these have to do with
real trust, real sexual joy, real sensual freedom?" But Sade's new
Juliettes refuse to see the very rearguard sexuality they are defending for what it is, persisting instead in claiming that this regres-
sion is avant-garde.

Yet the truth is that pain does hurt—as women know all too
bitterly. And the truth also is that games of torture are hideous
travesties of the actual torture that is practiced officially and
unofficially all around the world today.

It took an inexcusably long time to understand that whites
wearing blackface, no matter what jolly denials accompanied that
act, carried a political message: mockery of black people. It took a
comparably long while to understand that men wearing "drag,"
no matter how sexually revolutionist they purported this act to
be, really carried a political message: mockery of women. It seems
intolerable that we must wait as long to understand that "bondage," "discipline," props of whips and chains and leather thongs,

and allegedly "loving games" between "trusting lovers" carry a political message, too: a ghastly mockery of the human beings who suffered under Iran's SAVAK torturers, of the human beings who were electroded by Idi Amin's henchmen, of the human beings who scream in real and agonized pain in the interrogation chambers of South Africa or Chile or East Germany or the Philippines at this very moment. Surely even women so damaged by our androcentric and fundamentalist culture as those who defend pornography and S&M can realize that when you find titillating the same attitudes or acts around which Auschwitz and Belsen and Treblinka revolved, something is wrong. And surely such women can realize that what they, in their piteously twisted sexuality, are upholding has nothing, nothing to do with the feminist vision of freedom.

I'd like to suggest another reaction, however, one that feminists might take beyond the vertigo caused by pseudo-feminist sexual fundamentalists, beyond judgment, beyond even the attempt to ignore such women or pity them, beyond anger and certainly beyond taking them seriously. It might be simply to realize that women taking such stands have given up all hope of connecting with real sexual energy and thrown in utterly with its offered substitute of violence. That they defend the violence *as* sex is their confusion—and we know where that comes from; it's all around us. That they mistake the present (and past) as the inevitable future is reminiscent of people who saw the earth around them as flat and so insisted that it must continue to be so beyond their perception.

Galileo was forced by the Church to recant his heretical position that the earth moved about the sun, but this recantation ultimately meant not one prune pit to the earth or the sun. Galileo, of course, knew this—as we must. Rising from his kneeling pose before the Church fathers after his recantation, he was heard to mutter to himself, smiling slightly, "Nevertheless, it moves."

Not all the religious fundamentalists in the (flat) world can reduce the universe to their expurgated textbooks; not all the sexual fundamentalists and pornocrats in their sexual-toys torture chambers can reduce sexual energy to their definitions. It's helpful to remember this. It's also not always easy to remember this, considering that the choice offered the powerless by the powerful usually is: (a) lack of energy entirely or (b) violent energy.

It's the same choice, at least, that the powerful offer to themselves, knowing by this time nothing else.

The largely male blood ritual of sports is a major area where this transaction regularly takes place. Two sports "traditions" ought to make us suspicious in themselves: (a) the boys' club he-man closeness expressed in all that locker-room slapping of towels at naked behinds—a (sexually fundamentalist) homophobic kind of closet homosexuality, but without, of course, any of that "sissy" kissing stuff, no tenderness, no plainly expressed honest sexual energy—and (b) the disproportional resistance to women athletes attempting to break into professional and even amateur sports. But there is a third clue, and it is violence, or the corruption of energy into violence.

In 1980, a remarkable book was published: *Seasons of Shame: The New Violence in Sports*, by Robert C. Yeager.[11] Although I could quibble with the word "new" in the title, Yeager does seem to make his point that sports violence has risen precipitously in the past decade. Look at a few of his documented examples: in Australia, a soccer coach shows his team newsreels of mass murders and burials at Auschwitz, then tells the team to imagine that the victims were their family, and to go out and play to avenge them. In Guatemala, five persons are hacked to death when the fans of a losing soccer team attack the winning team with machetes. In Florida, at a high school football game, an assistant principal is killed by the rival school's business manager. Eighty-one American football players are paralyzed from the neck down during the three seasons ending in 1977. Riots involving both players and spectators—with the wounded and dead being carted off in ambulances and hearses—are common after hockey and rugby games. "Kill 'em! Murder the bum!" are traditional epithets shouted from the stands. "Violence," writes Yeager, "shows signs of becoming purely recreational."

Well, hardly. There's always big business, multinational corporations, and the military-industrial complex to fall back upon for serious, *non*recreational violence. But Yeager is onto something: the legitimizing of violence as fun, as play, as *energy*, as "eternal delight"—with no pharisaical pronouncements about how "war is hell, but we must engage in it for God, country, applehood, and mother pie." This is more like "Oooh *goody!* Death, destruction, evil, mayhem, blood!" Is it so coincidental then, the football metaphors employed in the Reagan White House to describe the state of the nation? Or the aggressive attitude toward sports evinced by the Soviet Union and East Germany, even unto the illegal prescribing of steroids for their athletes to increase muscle mass? Is it coincidental that the easiest route of access to money and celebrity for Afro-American men for some time has been sports, notably boxing (because white men, assuming in their racism that the economically caused violence in the ghetto was "inherent," needed these violent qualities, in this case, for their viewing pleasure)? Is it coincidental that the sports in which women have made the strongest inroads—tennis,‡ swimming, track, golf, running, and (lately) basketball—are less violent, more involved with breaking records than with breaking necks? Is it coincidental that the same universities which have no funds for a Women's Studies Program manage to come up with alumni dollars for a new sports stadium? And is it coincidental that such quasi-scientific defenders-of-the-fate as ethologists like Konrad Lorenz have taken the position that Man's [sic] "natural, inherent" aggressiveness and "killer instincts" are given an "outlet" in violent sports?

This is the same thinking that defines pornography as an outlet for sexual aggression. Both analyses manage to ignore the historical fact that violence-as-play in any form tends to *reinforce* the notion of violence as normal, good for one, harmless, slightly unreal in its murderous effect, and, worst of all, an *inevitable* given. Did gladiator games and the "bread-and-circuses" attitudes of the Roman Empire make for a peaceable Roman culture? Did tournaments and jousts in the Middle Ages obviate the fighting of the Crusades? Has the major industry built on manufacturing war toys in contemporary society produced generations of grown men who have no need for violent activity (sexual or militaristic) as adults, since they were raised to give vent to violence in such "outlets"?

If sports are, as the saying goes, America's "national pastime," and pornography is one of America's fastest growing industries, what does this tell us about the way we regard human flesh, the way we play, express sexuality, and transmute excitement—into violence? And if this is a construct by Man, into which men have bought, then what are women doing about it? Well, Woman ap-

‡ Due to the heroic stubbornness of Billie Jean King.

pears, as we know, in fives and tens at football games and duly yells "Smash 'em!" for her man's approval—and she cheerleads. But what about the other women who in part disbelieve the propaganda about the Beast's inherent beastliness, who resist and capitulate in turn at different times?

We, too, "require the lineaments of Gratified Desire," long for a sexual expressiveness that would be energetic, and sometimes settle instead for one that is brutalizing. Our story is better told by the myth of Psyche and Eros.

Psyche, you will recall, becomes the object of Eros' love after he wounds himself by accident with one of his own arrows while looking at her. In a trance, she is wafted to his palace and there besieged with delights of all the senses. They are wed—but she is never permitted to look upon his face or body. Still, she is deliriously happy. He is a wonderful lover, and their sexual bliss each night, albeit in total darkness, is filled with tenderness and passion. She does get a bit lonely during the day, wandering around the palace halls waiting for nightfall, and in time she asks her husband for permission to visit her family. (No woman in patriarchal myth just *travels*, you understand; she always needs permission from her lord, just as women in many Middle Eastern countries today still need travel permits signed by their husbands or fathers.) But when Psyche returns to her family home, her envious, catty (guess who?) *sisters* fill her mind with poison. "You've never *seen* him!" they whisper. "So how do you know he's a god and not a monster, a frightful beast who will turn on you one day and devour you? What will your fine clothes avail you then?" (They seem to have read Beauty and the Beast before stepping into their own myth.) Despite Psyche's pleas that she knows he is too loving and gently passionate ever to harm her, their nagging has its effect, and when she returns to the palace she resolves to take a peek at her husband. That night, after Eros is asleep beside her, Psyche lights her small lantern and bends through the darkness to gaze at him. She sees no beast, no monster, but a young god of incredible beauty, and is so struck with love for him that she carelessly lets fall a drop of candle-tallow onto his flesh. He springs awake. Understanding that she now has disobeyed the one proscription and gazed upon his face, he cries out in grief that he must flee from her. And Eros disappears. Psyche is, as would be expected, distraught. In some versions of the myth she flings herself off a nearby cliff, but is borne up to safety on the wings of love (Eros). In other versions, she appeals to Aphrodite, Eros' mother, or to all the Olympian gods in general, for their help in regaining her love. In these versions, Aphrodite or the other gods set a series of tests for Psyche which, if she performs successfully, will serve to reunite her with Eros. The tests consist of impossible tasks—piling a field full of rice grains into one mound overnight, journeying down into hell to steal Persephone's sacred face-paint, and similar little jobs that make Hercules' labors seem, by comparison, light housekeeping. But Psyche manages to accomplish them all (sometimes, depending on the version, with the secret help of various gods) and is reunited with Eros on Olympus. What's more, she is now permitted to look at him anytime she wants.

We can leave aside the obvious propaganda inherent in both the Beauty and the Beast and the Psyche and Eros stories—to wit, women, and especially *sisters*, are to blame for things going wrong; they are lousy advisers, not to be trusted whatever they do. (In the former story, they tell Beauty to ignore his appearance and be content—and they are wrong. In the latter, they counsel Psyche to seek out his appearance—and they are wrong.) We might look instead at Psyche's curiosity (and desire), at how both are thwarted by enforced ignorance and punished by separation and painful labors, at how she does perform these labors—arduously, doggedly, at risk of life and limb and sanity. Psyche—trying *trying* to win back Eros' love, to let him know that he need not fear her having seen his vulnerability. It is a theme familiar to modern women. What is less familiar, unfortunately, is the happy Olympian ending.

It can be said that Psyche is "passive" in her early contentment with her unseen lover/husband; so it has been said of all women who put up with what they have no choice about putting down. It can be said, too, that Psyche is "masochistic" in persisting throughout her labors; so it has been said of all women who have bent their lives to the idea that enough love, enough patience, enough understanding, enough time, gestures, attention, would win them through to a place where men would at last comprehend and "begin to shoulder *their* part of the burden of love's labors," as the poet Rainer Maria Rilke suggested. But neither the Beast in his ferocity nor Eros in his godliness dares show his real face, for fear that the love a human woman bears him will perish on the instant. It seems reasonable, I suppose, for them to assume that as long as women persist in the difficult loving of what is perceived as monstrous or invisible, then why risk exposure as merely human? Why risk exposure at all?

Yet there *is* something in men, surely, that wishes to be known and loved for itself, something purely human—not beast or god, and not Man either. And there is something in women that also wishes deeply to be known and loved for its human self—not for its beauty or its labor, and not as Woman. Just so, there is something in men *and* women, however hidden, that is both tired of hiding and tired of searching—and yet indefatiguably dedicated to the search.

If two mythic moments could be frozen to represent the essential sexual anguish, respectively, of men and women, these moments might well embody them.

• All claws and fangs, the Beast cries out to Beauty, "Love me! Love me, despite my beastliness!"

• Psyche, her trembling hand lifting a lamp, leans through the darkness, hoping at last to see and be seen, and gazes at her beloved's sleeping face.

* * *

Sexual passion always involves a profound and vulnerable knowing and being known—i.e., sexual *intelligence*. The biblical phrase "they knew one another" in this sense is an insightful one —but then, the King James Version was translated by seventeenth-century metaphysical poets, who were no dumbbells. Man has denied men this passion and intelligence, and forced them to accept, instead, the eroticization of violence. That is the stake in the heart of male sexuality, the stake to keep such energy from rising, walking, being undead.

Woman, meanwhile, at Man's bidding, has denied to women the same passion and intelligence, forcing us to suffer instead a comparable stake in the heart of our sexuality. It is even easier to drive a stake into the heart of a wraith whose mirror gives back no reflection. The stake in the heart of women is romance.

CONFESSIONS OF AN EXISTENTIAL ROMANTIC

Never has a subtitle cost me so much. Yet it's an accurate description of the image I see in the two-way mirror, and I've learned that it could describe many other women, in and out of the Women's Movement, despite differences in generation, race, nationality, and sexual preference, so it would seem worth examining.

Let's take it word by word. "Confessions" because when a writer who is male exposes his personal history, emotional proclivities, or experiences, critics tend to review him with phrases like "Courageous vulnerability"; "An unflinching honesty about the self"; "A daring personal exposure that reaches out to the universal." When a writer who is female does the same, those reviewers have been known to describe her work as "solipsistic," "self-obsessed," and that old standby: "confessional." Although I've been fortunate in not having been the target of this dart-game quite so often as many other women writers, I have a high P.Q. (Paranoia Quotient) and am ever vigilant. Therefore, I would rather one-up such reactions ahead of time, and flatly say "confessions" in the honorable old tradition of English letters, before they can exclaim "confessional."

I think that we can skip over the words *of* and *an* without too much accusation of avoidance, and I should prefer to return to *existential* after we examine *romantic*. Romantic, after all, is the key word here. I am not exploring Romanticism in the historical sense of its literary and artistic tradition, a task already engaged many times, from Wordsworth and Coleridge's Preface to *Lyrical Ballads* in 1798 through Mario Praz's *The Romantic Agony*[12] to Sir Kenneth Clarke's more recent *The Romantic Rebellion*.[13] Instead, I'm trying here to address a subject given far less attention: the predicament of a modern woman attempting to differentiate between what is affirmable in the emotional eroticism of "romance" and what is destructive in the reification of that impulse into institutionalized "feminine romanticism."

Certainly, I am such a woman. "Romantic" would seem to describe my lifelong affection for lilacs, *Wuthering Heights** (an obsession first contracted in childhood), Schumann (Robert *and* Clara), dusk, dawn, chiffon, and the waltz. My love for poetry is something else; it may have begun as "romantic," but soon spilled

---

* In an unpublished paper, "Romanticism in *Wuthering Heights* and *The Scarlet Letter*," Suzanne Braun Levine explores what I am terming "the stake in the heart" *as* the connection between the passionate sensibility and extremes of living (English honors thesis, Harvard, 1963).

backward into classic, forward into modern, and everywhere and everywhen else it could. What is more to our point, though, is that I have been all of my life a *sexual* romantic—from the adolescent nights when I fantasized that a combination of Heathcliff, Harry Belafonte, Ingrid Bergman, John Donne, and Laurence Olivier would come sweep me onto the white charger, to the day twenty years ago when I defied my family to marry a bisexual poet "with no major financial prospects," to my insistence that within the feminist vision there *is* a place for love and sexual passion, to the affair I had in 1980 with a sculptor at an art colony under a full May moon as Mount St. Helens was erupting three thousand miles away. A hopeless, unsalvageable, politically incorrect romantic.

Well, perhaps not so hopeless, so unsalvageable. Which is where the "existential" comes in. The "existential" is relatively new, and I'm still working on it. It is a healthy qualifier to the rapture characteristic of romanticism. It rejects Ultimate Meaning based on any sexual gesture, and affirms the transience of things, the "negative capability," as Keats called it, which enables one to believe and disbelieve at the same moment. It refuses intellectual *or* emotional martyrdom. But it is principled, and thus refuses to hurt others gratuitously just as it refuses to be willingly hurt. I suspect it has something to do with sexual intelligence. It has great possibilities, and I offer it gladly for use by other women who share my weakness for romance.

Not that we have been given many alternatives, I grant. Books, movies, songs, television, magazines, fairytales and folk legends— the entire culture of the Western world (and a good part of the rest of the world) is suffused with messages to women about romance.

If, as some have claimed, the separate but sometimes blurred genres of gothic novels, romances, "historical" fiction, and "bodice-rippers" are, along with private fantasies, women's forms of pornography, that in itself is indicative. Romances do sell well, but nowhere on the level of pornography: six out of ten of the most popular and profitable monthly magazines in newsstand sales are so-called male entertainment periodicals. Nor is the $200 million of paperback publishers' annual sales represented by romance fiction, according to *Publishers Weekly*, comparable to the $4-billion-a-year pornography industry.

As for fantasies, if women do use them to arouse our "prurient interest," it's almost always with a sense of defeat: the husband or lover is a lout in bed, and so she must arouse herself, or else fake an orgasm, or else be called frigid. (Feminists have aptly renamed a "frigid" woman a "preorgasmic" woman.) She would rather have it otherwise, *with* her partner, but as reported by Kinsey and by Hite,[14] the statistics about how few men know how to make love well are appalling. Furthermore, it's interesting that the alleged pornography of women's real fantasies (not the fantasies men fantasize women have) are highly privatized. They usually are kept hidden—just the opposite from being made marketable, industrialized, proclaimed as free speech, and defended in court. On the contrary, they are generally regarded as neurotic and "unwomanly." Or is it merely a mark of the unimportance of *anything* a woman does, even fantasy, that it's not worth publicity, let alone marketing? (After all, women earn less, so who would make up the lucrative market?) Not profitable enough.

One further turn of (forgive me) the screw is that most men seem to not *want* to know what it is that women really fantasize, that is, what turns women on. The very few serious books on the subject that do exist have been bought largely by women hoping to free themselves of guilt for having fantasized pleasurably at all. Yet fantasizing among women is very common. In 1973, Dr. E. Barbara Hariton, a psychotherapist at Long Island Jewish–Hillside Medical Center in New York, conducted an in-depth study of 141 housewives regarding sexual fantasies. She found that 65 percent fantasized during intercourse with their husbands, another 28 percent had occasional fantasies, and only 7 percent claimed never to have had any thoughts which could be considered fantasies. Hariton also analyzed the overall effect of sexual fantasizing on a woman. One of the most important findings was that erotic fantasies did not indicate neurosis in a woman; on the contrary, Hariton found that women who fantasized a great deal were most likely to have creative personalities.[15]

As for the almost worldwide "romance propaganda," such messages do, it seems, speak to something in women, something *not* masochistic, passive, or vaporish, but something that yearns for affection, tenderness, an emotional *relationship* with one's sexual partner as opposed to a mere meeting of genital parts. That yearning is to be affirmed; indeed, it would be nice if men learned to affirm it in *them*selves. (George Sand's daughter, Solange, decried her mother as a hypocrite for affirming "purity." But Sand replied that purity was merely being honest about love.) No, the problem lies, rather, with all the other elements clustering in the package called romance: the fabricated "femininity" in women and fabricated "masculinity" in men, the attendant dominant/ submissive roles that reinforce external male power and female powerlessness, *the eroticization, via romance, of violence (emotional, physical, or psychological) as a substitute for genuine passion.*

Six years ago, I wrote an essay on the politics of sado-masochistic fantasies in women.[16] In it, I tried to analyze the difference between fantasy and practice, and to account for the frequency of these fantasies in women. I hypothesized that such fantasies, through a complicated series of twists, turns, and translations, were really about a desire to abandon control temporarily and safely *without* losing self-determination—that is, to be able to relax and trust one's partner *mutually*, in interdependence, without such trust and dependence being seen one-sidedly as the permanent, inherent "womanly place." While I still think this is part of the truth, I now glimpse the whole truth as being even more complicated—and at the same time much simpler.

In an intellectually lively pamphlet published in 1975 by the feminist press KNOW[17] and titled "The Erotization of Male Dominance and Female Submission: The Sexist Turn-On that Castrates Self, Love, and Sex," the pamphlet's author, Ellen Morgan (also no relation), analyzes in depth the sexist programming of both women and men, and suggests approaches to reconciling sexuality and personhood in an integrated self. Morgan writes: "We [women] have been led to eroticize the masculine *role* qualities, rather than either male persons or male bodies or both . . . in general, relationships developed on the basis of role attraction rather than personality are likely to be impersonal and inauthentic." She also notes that women feel ambivalently comfortable within this cathexis (since a lifetime of training has gone into readying us for it) and *un*comfortable within it because it does go against the grain of something basic, something human, something which wishes to feel self-respect and to grant respect to others. The various forms of women's rebellion against this sexual system have been labeled illness, masochism, promiscuity, deviance, passivity, or frigidity—this last, for example, a rebellion in which the woman says, in effect, "A man may 'take' me but he will not reach me at my core; I will not enjoy or respond to the misuse of myself." There are also those women who insist sex is only a biological reality, a physical act which necessitates no emotional involvement. This, of course, is buying directly into the masculinist style—and tends to evoke the same threatened or depressed reactions from men as it has for so long from women whose male partners acted on such a belief. And some women have tried to, in Morgan's words, "compartmentalize, . . . sometimes concluding that sexual nature and selfhood are *naturally* separate and antagonistic entities, with sexual desire constantly playing the saboteur, the betrayer of self-respect." I agree with Morgan that this is no solution, and further agree that only through each woman's discovery of "her own interior wave length"—her exploration of what it is that she herself, separate from her programming, thinks is erotic—can an integrated self, which *is* a possible and honorable goal, be approached.

One way to discover one's "interior wave length" is, naturally, to compare notes with other women (despite the patriarchal myths that warn us about wicked sisters). Another way, as Morgan suggests,

is deliberately to set about creating an imaginative context . . . which lets a woman get a feeling for the completely arbitrary nature of the connection between maleness and dominance in sexual relations. A woman who cannot imagine actively sharing lovemaking with an "appropriate" man her own age or older might find she could imagine doing so with a much younger man, or a very underconfident man . . . and discover a dimension of herself of which she was previously unaware. A woman who does not know what appeals to her about the male body might learn if [she imagines] situations in which a male was available for her to explore sexually completely on her own terms, without any possibility that the situation could be taken over and reshaped to suit anyone else's desires.

(I would add that she just might imagine herself making love with another woman. Or—radical thought!—with herself.)

I would add further that many women feel a strong and realistic fear of retribution for acting assertively about sex—and so our natural human sexual energy gets projected onto our partners where, especially but not exclusively if our partners are men, it often gets transformed into violence and aimed back at us.

George Eliot wrote, "There is no private life which is not determined by a wider public life." (Nor is this true only of human, or even general sexual, energy. Relativity theory has taught us that a subatomic particle's properties only can be understood in terms of its interactions with the environment surrounding it.)

"Revolution begins with the self, in the self," said Toni Cade Bambara, as if in response. "The individual, the basic revolutionary unit, must be purged of poison and lies that assault the ego and threaten the heart, that hazard the next larger unit—the couple or pair, that jeopardize the still larger unit—the family or cell, that put the entire movement in peril."[18]

Both Eliot and Bambara were right, of course. The stake in the heart has been planted there by external forces, but one's own flesh grows around it to embrace it—and ultimately, one must tear it out oneself.

Mae West, as always, said it shorter: "Between two evils, I always pick the one I never tried before."

I picked the one I never tried before. After eighteen years of marriage, one child, a few wretched excursions into "group sex" in the 1960's—mostly to keep up with the Joneses of the so-called sexual revolution—after writing about, fantasizing about, lecturing on, thinking of, and wrestling with the issue of women's sexual survival, at the age of thirty-nine I had an affair.

REMEDIAL LIVING

Gloria Steinem once said to me (while waggling her eyebrows à la Groucho Marx): "Every woman deserves a parking-lot attendant at least once in her life." She meant, of course, that archetypal slender young man in tight jeans with slightly scruffy hair and a devilish smile who whooshes the car in and out of tiny spaces, backward and forward, with admirable physical skill and confidence. He may be a working-class kid in that job for life, or a student putting himself through college, or a drifter; at that moment it doesn't matter. His charm lies in his casual footloose-fun ambience and his physical grace. His charm lies also in the fact that one would not ever wish to spend one's life with him. He is of the moment. He is, for that matter, a moment in himself.† It is deplorably true that the majority of women look at him and look again, but drive away—sensibly, in most cases, since noninvolvement can turn out to be quite involved, and a casual acquaintance for a woman trying to act freely in a nonfree situation can spell danger, venereal disease, pregnancy, rape, or at least a letdown. Still, he *seems* wholesome, a human male animal in the bloom of his sexual amity and humor. . . . Our antennae, as women, are so continually put to use to warn us of jeopardy that we barely know how to receive good sexual vibrations anymore, or when or if to trust them.

I decided to trust them, this time. He was an artist, after all, albeit with all the youthful grace of my friend's legendary parking-lot attendant. Besides, there was the surrounding safety of an art colony; I was away from home, family, telephones, and public politics, answerable only to myself for a rare once. This had, in fact, more to do with it than one imagines, and not only because of the lack of daily responsibilities or pressures. It had to do with *the lack of the familiar*, with the exposure to the foreign, the unknown, the new—*the stranger*. Perhaps it was the exogamous impulse, and doubtless it had to do with curiosity, but I think also it pertains to the chance one has, among utter strangers, to act out parts of oneself alien to the self one puts forward in daily life among one's familiars. Strangers, of course, have no basis of comparison, so they have no way of knowing that one is trying out new selves or new masks, new behavior that would feel bizarre or at least embarrassing to try out "at home." This, in turn, shows a failure of nerve on one's own part: one ought to dare try out new facets of oneself *in* one's life, not seek an outside life for that purpose; one ought to explore and incorporate those facets in

† At the risk of sounding ageist, I should mention that feminists have noted how the older woman–younger man combination—like the taller woman–shorter man combination—can tend at this historical moment to correct the usual power imbalance men have over women (at least correct it to some extent). But this hardly means that the "parking-lot attendant" has to be a younger man. For one thing, he can be a woman. For another, he can be a man the same age as the other partner, or older: that touch of gray about the temples—plus the sense of humor, self-confidence, and comparatively reduced sense of panic that older men sometimes possess—all this is notoriously attractive to many women.

an integrated way, not in a manner which further compartmentalizes oneself. Our culture does not encourage this. To keep the parts of living separate and pigeonholed—probably just for fear *of* that integration—is the Don Juan approach to existence: an eternal search for the new, the unfamiliar—and an eternal rejection of it once it is "conquered" (that is, once it becomes known). This means being doomed to live always at the surface for fear of the depths, to settle for seeming to know *more* (people, experiences, emotions) instead of knowing *deeply*, to let the sand sift forever through one's fingers rather than risk seeing the universe in one grain of it. Such an approach to existence is indeed, as Kierkegaard defined it in *Either/Or*, an aesthetic one— fixated on form, beauty, technique, comparison, excitement, and a distanced objectivity—but it has nothing to do with the ethical and spiritual aspects of existence which so enrich emotions, and which inextricably are connected with subjectivity, commitment, and love.

But I was also a romantic, remember, and the existential qualifier had barely begun to glimmer in my soul. So it was not enough: the purely aesthetic, the sexual joy, release, abandon, and plain *fun*. No, I had to invite "love" in (not just amicable affection, mind you, but passion)—although the thought of any permanent relationship with this person did give me indigestion. I had to write poems about it. I had to, immediately on my return home after a month, Tell All to my husband—a freethinking man of intellectual and sexual courage as well as curiosity, a man deeply committed to antisexist politics, who might have taken the news calmly (even supportively?) had I not implied a compare-and-contrast analysis, itself a side effect of the romantic-rebellion high on which I was stoned and of the rareness, for me, of such an experience (one eats every day, so tends not to compare every meal with every other meal).

My husband (also a romantic despite his occasional denials of same) of course had to become melodramatically unhinged, Tell All to everyone we knew, and then have an affair with another woman. There was much tearing of hair, grief, sobbing in the night, reconciliations, and further rounds of all of the above. At least there were a great many poems from both of us—a distinct consolation—and now, two years later, we are still together (to the amazement of Good Friends Who Helped See Us Through), wiser and younger than we were, and grateful, even, for the volcanic eruption that shook our lives into utterly new patterns—with nothing certain, everything changing, challenging, up for redefinition. But more about this in the following chapter, on committed relationships. Such a relationship is far too complex a subject to treat with flippancy or superficiality.

For now, let's return to the woman who did manage, at considerable cost, to break through into a new kind of sexual empowerment, sexual energy, sexual intelligence. Although she regrets the grief, she does not regret anything else. She felt radiant. It showed; she *looked* radiant. A tremendous new energy was released in her writing. Her masochistic fantasies disappeared. For decades she had grappled with them intellectually, psychologically, and politically. For years she had suspected that they had something to do with a lack of control over one's own life and with a parallel wish to abandon control by projecting it onto another, in whose control one would be safe to abandon it. Now she had discovered something astonishingly simple: the concrete *exercise* of control over one's own sexuality, however awkwardly managed at first, does obviate the need for projecting it onto another. If you feel you *have* control, you are free to abandon it, knowing as you do that it is yours to pick up again whenever you choose.

She would never be the same woman. I am *not* saying that an affair is a palliative for anything, nor recommending so-called open marriage, nor trying (godforbid) to float a new correct line on feminist instant sexual freedom. On the contrary. I am speaking for no one but myself, in the hope that not so much the experience but what I learned from it will be of use to other women— and to men, for that matter.

Let's look over the shoulder of this woman, at a copy of a letter she has kept, written after she left the art colony but the sculptor was still there. (I suspect, in fact, that she wrote the letter and kept a copy so that, in the odd way that writers have, she'd be certain that real life actually had happened. The smell of fresh coffee brewing, or the feel of crushed velvet, for example, have always been less vivid in real life for her than in the sensual experience of describing them on the page. Artists in general can be cheerfully perverse about the surreal qualities of reality—but more about art in Chapter VIII . . .)

We might keep in mind a few facts for plot clarification: the sculptor (we will refer to him by the initial "V.") is younger than the woman, which *does* give her a strange feeling of power, and it turns out that he has what he quaintly refers to in nineteenth-century terminology as "a mistress"—a fact our woman letter writer did not know when they first went to bed together and one which caused her considerable feminist torture and ethical backflips during the remainder of their brief affair. Later, she met with the "mistress"—a pleasant, self-supporting woman (whom we'll refer to by the initial "C."), and they became friends, sometimes relishing a hearty dish-session of their mutual former lover. But back to the letter, and what it says—in the midst of all its romanticism, prevarication, and baroque language—about the magnum power of pure sexual energy, and about its capacity to send one into emotional overdrive, past sense, sensibility, caution, and cost:

Dearest V.:

How strange and terrifying to begin this letter. Because I have no idea of what I shall write in it between now and when it ends. Because words are my tools, the molecules of air and blood by which I live, and so are absurdly sacred to me. Because I never quite know what I feel until my words, on paper, inform me. Because when they are on paper they have caught me eternally in a commitment from which I can never quite escape. Because to begin this letter is to risk being unable to end it. Because I wanted to wait safely until receiving your letter so that I could respond safely in whatever tone *that* held. Because I keep saying No before each of these idiotic risks I then proceed to leap. Because to begin this letter is to risk that I will keep writing it.

I close my eyes, to look into yours. This fearful intimacy, blooming in the midst of all our ignorance about each other, like an orchid suddenly there in a fetid swamp, stretching its speckled tongue to sing. There you have me at a disadvantage, since for decades I have poured out my plainest truths into poems and prose; you can turn the pages of my years and discover whatever you will. I have only memories (already) or phrases, from you. . . . I'm terrifed. I feel as if I'm living—and writing—on a minefield of clichés, even though I know that the best way to transform them into archetypes, as I wrote once I yearned to do, is to dare shoot right by them, trying not to look at their loud signposts: Older Woman, Unfaithful Wife, Art Colony Girl Pretentiously Dwelling on Meaning, Feminist Betraying Another Woman,

Married Lady About to Turn Forty on a Fling, Mad Poet Seeking Subject Matter,—god, this way *does* lie madness. The hell with it. Because I want to throw both my arms out wide and sing that none of these are the truth yes even if all of them were—something other is *more* the truth, which I refuse to deny.

This is all so tangled, so hideously complicated, here, sitting in my study in New York (even with Kodály on the phonograph). What underlies and overrides all this snarled complexity, though, is the knowledge that none of these things mattered for a few nights in May while the moon was waxing, over the chaste, white-painted, wild bed in your cabin, lit by your eyes. I am so filled with fear that when we see each other again, none of these things will again matter— swept thoroughly away by the force of our standing in each other's presence. I am so filled with fear, too, that this will *not* happen. How odd—to have come all this way, to have risked death and jail and childbirth and commitment and art and rage and madness and yes love, only to discover a new level of risk pulling at my shoulders as if I carried the weight of a life's longing there so familiarly that I would utterly lose my balance if I set it down. And I'm afraid of frightening you. That most of all perhaps? Perhaps.

Ah well. Welcome to what you divined as the reception room (but not the central chamber) behind my eyes—where you sit calmly making yourself at home, studying a topographical map and blueprint of the rest of the grounds and edifice, all there in my published writings. But what you don't know is that a few weeks ago, what with Mount St. Helens and all, there was a resettling somewhat of the placement of rooms, corridors, even gardens. Nothing, you see, is quite the same, and I am almost as lost as anyone else. New surveying must be done, apparently.

As for the palaces behind *your* eyes, I stand as if before the Great Gates of Kiev, wondering. . . .

We're two smart people who know how to protect ourselves, aren't we? Aren't we?

This is what I get for having prayed in art for so long to my lovely atheistic goddess to make me a holy fool. Now I am one.

I must stop this letter so that I can begin building up reserves to not phone you tonight. It's five-thirty now and that gives me two good hours to work against it. I'm trying to write, but afraid of what I'll write—in poems, in prose, even in this god-damned letter. I am full of joy and fury at you for not having drowned in the swamp the day I arrived at the colony. If another poem would find its way through me like the last one I must say I'd be better disposed. *Are you working?* I tell you again, you damned well better be good—

because if I am suffering all this confusion over an involvement with some mediocre artist I will really be pissed.

I keep trying to end this letter. I keep trying not to alarm myself, let alone you. The hell with that. I can't. I should go re-read "affair literature: *Candida, The End of the Affair, Anna Karenina, Madame Bovary, Villette.* I'm overlooking some biggies. The hell with it.

There has to be a way out of this bloody letter.

I know. If I comfort myself that I won't after all send it, then . . . ah, yes, I know instantly how to close it. I can wrestle later with the sending or not sending. I can tell myself No I will not send this letter, which lets me say then that:

I would kiss thy lips, my dear, and thine eyes. I would press my throat to your forehead so that your brain could feel directly how the blood was singing in my arteries at being in your arms. I would spread out my hair on your pillow and carefully tell you how and why the world mustn't end just yet, for all your cynicism and all your fears. Then I would kiss you again, deep in your neck, and laugh, deep in your neck, at the silly fragile enormous power of this situation. Then you would reach for me and I would be at once rock and water flowing over rock and I would think for a moment that I had imagined you again except that you are a person and not an event despite the considerable suffering this event has already caused others not to even mention the two persons who are not events who seem to be shooting through it parabola after parabola willfully helpless holy fools and I would open my eyes to see yours already open waiting for my glance—a reptile, a saint, a mossgrown shaded pool, an observatory into the universe of the skull, the great void in which the brain space station wheels slowly, registering, recording, sending—shock upon shock, no matter how prepared, weightless spinning as if in space or in the vortex of a whirlpool until the dizziness gives over into rest, as if we had crawled up onto the warm uninhabited island beach of one another, to sleep as the sun rose, huge and high and unashamed.

I give you warning that if you come to New York I shall surely not appear I am preparing already sanely and firmly and wisely to say No the same way that I know No I shall never send this letter where in hell are *your* No's aren't you using any are you storing them all up until I've exhausted mine or what? NONONONONONONO.

I don't know how to close it, oh god.

How about:

Dearest V:

R.

The woman who wrote this letter—and sent it—certainly was giving "freer scope to the grand passion," in Mary Wollstonecraft's words. However, such scope did not enlarge her mind, as Wollstonecraft promised—at least not right away. First, it shrunk her mind alarmingly. (Notice how she had intimations: she wants to resist calling him, she intuits that he is saving his whammo "No" until her "No's" are depleted. Notice how she even confides this *to* him—wishing to be *known* by the very stranger she chose because he *didn't* know her as her husband did. Notice how she knows she ignores what she knows.)

The following is a passage from a journal entry dated three weeks after the letter. Her mind is now the size of a dried pea. Clearly, the sculptor has come to New York, there have been more meetings, more guilt, grief, and *Sturm und Drang* over and with her husband and her lover's "mistress." All the elements of gothic melodrama are being indulged. Just as clearly, the woman writing this journal entry has been pushed back to Square One of sexual fundamentalism, lost almost every vestige of sexual intelligence, perspective, and humor, and been forced into trading what she thought was sexual passion, through the medium of romance, for violent passion. The stake in her heart is sharp and vibrating:

Oh god I was almost asleep and the horn in the street I thought it was the doorbell how cruel to wake me I was almost . . . Now I'm crying god what do you want how much suffering in payment for this little joy? This rips at the scars I thought were healed. Look god this is what I never got to say to him, to wear for him, do with him, ask him, tell him, touch him . . . this pain is incredibly *physical*. It cramps and twists and burns in my throat and chest like a weight . . . my cries are scaring my cats oh god please.

Let me write it let me write it *let me write my way through this* please god . . . I can't be in love with him I can't I can't I don't know what this is I'm thirty-nine and he's twenty-seven and not even all that bright dear god—

This panic . . . I want to sleep or be numb or take a pill or something to wake up when I'm not feeling this mourning. But I'm so hideously sober it frightens me. "What a beautiful woman you are, you are, what a beautiful woman you are" . . .

Truth: this would be utterly unbearable except for the thought that he will call tomorrow and I still have the chance to say Yes, let's meet. Some secret woman inside me is already planning that. Humiliation . . .

I'll write all night by god I'll survive it dear Ishtar Astarte Aphrodite. Even now I'm lying: I'm waiting. This is incredible.

Women have wept these tears for me. These tears do not need to be wept again not by one more woman no more no more no more . . .

Even now, how humiliating GET IT ON THE PAGE: the diaphragm in, the telephone near . . . He said I can't see you tonight and it fell like a punch in the stomach just below the heart, physical pain.

Should have ended it at the colony. Or last week. Or yesterday. No pride. Where is the pride? The pride goes first . . . oh god your jokes are cosmic and profound, the very best gallows humor around.

I was going to toast all lovers tonight. C.? No
C. on the brain? NO
C. on the morals? YES
C. on the heart? Yes No Yes My sister my sister my lost sister we are betrayed together but you all undeserving *mea culpa mea culpa mea maxima maxima culpa*

Truth: I *can* simply not answer the phone. If he calls, he will soon give up. Truth: I don't want to. Truth: So this is feminism. Hello again. Haven't learned *yet?* Then we'll engrave it on your skin.

At least I'm squandering twenty-pound bond paper, by Christ. *That* feels liberating. This is insane. Silly thing, silly art-colony girl I DON'T KNOW WHAT THIS MEANS this is like being buried alive records I never played for him art shows I never saw with him I can still say Yes I can still say No

Smell your own perfumed wrists you idiot.

Did he think I had exhausted all of my No's? Ha! I will invent them, I will create them, they will be works of genius . . . look, four A.M. I've spent another hour let me keep at it, cleansing words truth ugly truth on the clean page . . .

This passes everything passes. *Turn it into politics. Turn it into art.*

He's been lying all along, stringing you along all along. Damn him he seemed the key to all my locked doors and he rusted in my hand . . . god that my talents should be spent on concocting these arguments like Plath's "great surgeon, now a tattooist/Tatooing over and over the same blue grievances."

Let me not care let me not care let me not care

The woman who wrote this journal entry had, a few weeks earlier, released from herself an electric sexual energy that ultimately had little or nothing to do with its (sorry to use the word, but it's true) object. At the time of the journal writing, however, she had traded that self-empowerment for an apparent certainty that her breakthrough had everything to do with the lover and virtually nothing to do with her.

Why? *Too terrifying a force to admit containing in oneself?* Too rebellious, too truly revolutionary, too *intelligent?* How much of victimology was inherent in the romantic format to begin with, to what extent did the lovely dizzying swoon contain a genuine collapse of muscle fiber? Most of all, why was this woman so surprised to find that she couldn't change the rules in midgame: having picked the stranger *because* he was a stranger, why did she long for him to act with the knowledge of a *familiar*, with the courtesy, care, love? She was yet to learn that it is far more challenging to locate the aesthetic in the ethical than the reverse—to recognize the excitement of the strange *in* the familiar than the other way around.

Three weeks *after* the journal entry, this same woman (whom we can refer to by the initial I) wrote the sculptor another, longer letter. She had regained some perspective, some humor, some of her earlier power—and some intelligence was beginning to clear. Here are parts from *that* letter:

There are a few things that I want you to try and understand.

Perhaps the most important is the most simple: love really does not grasp. It doesn't even *need*, in the common sense. It can suffer, you bet, and it can sicken, and it can die (although if there *is* such a thing as an afterlife, I wager it exists for love alone). The miracle, I think, is its energy—whether resonating in a poem or glance or sonata or atom or sculpture—the way it actually manufactures more love and further energy like a plant manufacturing chlorophyll as sustenance for the desire to manufacture more. The extra talent—because love isn't just any artist, but a virtuoso, of course—is that it can be so protean, so able to change form (though not without some painful skin-shedding) as to be literally *transformative*, and all with the flair and twinkle of Bach (who was in on the joke). *And* without losing its power.

This means—in case you have fallen asleep or nodded off into that glaze-gaze that sometimes slides like a mask over your features—a number of specific things, not just a lecture, ahem, on the Ways and Means of Love.

For one thing, this kind of energy, power, artistry, what you will, does not coexist with such imitative and dilettante performers as objectification, emotional censorship, manipulation—and fear. All of which you or I or both of us have been guilty of welcoming into our respective studios. Even now, I'm tempted to say, "Very well then, I dreamt you. You are relieved of the responsibility of having existed," ostensibly to free you from guilt but in reality to ensnare myself in the trap of arrogant (and bonkers) martyrdom—the trap of "woman-liness," disguised in turn as the posture of godhead. Fooey.

The truth is that I did *not* dream you—you are (perhaps lamenta-bly) very real; you snore sometimes and pronounce "pyramids" in the *most* peculiar fashion and frequently don't listen to what I say no matter how wondrously wise and just as frequently don't listen to yourself (no matter how wise or dumb) and so repeat yourself with-out knowing you are falling into delivering "set pieces"—which can be dangerous at worst and fatuous at best. If I had dreamed you, rest assured that none of these irritants would be present.

Still, I *have* objectified you—to the extent of clouding you over as the Angelic (or Demonic) Lover—while you in turn were busy wrap-ping me in the dirndl skirts of Art Colony Girl, heh heh. Well, hot tip: it's always better for the artist to exaggerate than to trivialize; the rest of the world does the latter so much more efficiently. But even if I prefer my mode of objectification to yours, it *was* still objectification —and I think I now know why.

I'm weary to death of being ashamed of the fact that for me love is a presence in any ecstatic celebration, whether artistic, religious, *or* sexual (as if there were really any goddamned difference). There's *god* in it, whatever that is. But I think the world conspires to make us hideously embarrassed at searching for precisely that, let alone ever finding it, much less proclaiming that we have glimpsed it. (This is where artists get in hot water all the time.) I fell for that shame in being unable to articulate the find *in* the reality—and consequently elevated the reality to the level of only one of its ingredients. The sin-gle place where this *was* articulated, not surprisingly, was in "The Har-rowing of Heaven,"[19] which is a poem about trying to find out if sim-ple lust is possible—loveless, godless, plain, pure, and easy lust—and finding that it isn't, for me, thank god. (Secretly I think it isn't for anybody, but that may be my terminal naïveté, or mere projection.) After all, it can now be acknowledged that there is an erotic element in all friendships; why shouldn't the reverse be true? By the way, have you ever read Oscar Wilde's *De Profundis?* You should, someday . . .

Oh dear, there's so much more to say on objectification. Anyway, you are hereby free from being objectified. You *are* cute. But you aren't god. (I am.) And you aren't Art Colony Boy either. You are an artist and a man and you have been my lover—and whether or not you are the first or the last is none of your bloody business.

But. It *is* time we were friends. This virtuoso love that can trans-form itself so wickedly and wonderfully surely ought to be able to merely depressurize, "de-escalate," be generous and simply kind, especially in the midst of such absurd but appalling pain. It ought to bring clarity, not confusion, comfort and a little leavening humor. So. Sending you "home" isn't enough. You must discover why you are there. You must not use C. in this Kleenex-convenience fashion any longer, no matter what your crises are. Not only is it unspeakable behavior to another human being—however you claim it doesn't bother her—but it really is devastatingly corruptive to yourself, as a human being *and* as an artist. You must also *tell* her about what happened between us, as I've urged you to. Now that I've met her at your gallery opening, and she wants to be friends, it's all the more hellish that she doesn't know. I give you a week's grace, but whether you do or not, I will call her then—as I found myself promising her I would —and I *will* tell her. The complete story. I cannot any longer be put in this position with regard to another woman. It is intolerable, and I'm mortified that I let myself be swayed all too gladly from telling her earlier: swayed by your fear, my cowardice, and even by the well-meaning protective counsel of two women friends. The fact is that if C. doesn't love you (as you sometimes claim), then it won't matter to her much. If she *does* love you (as you sometimes claim), then it will—but in that case it can be survived. Besides, if she loves you she has all the more right to know *who* it is she loves. You, I think, have yet to dare learn who or what you love, except of course yourself— and you are in fact so fond of *him* (despite your fear, loathing, and sickness unto death with him, I mean) that I don't think you'll harm him—but you mustn't continue harming her. In telling her the truth, you might just discover what it *is*, you know, and there would go emotional censorship out the window. And to make it easier, you can now put it all in the past tense. (Us, that is, not the truth.) Oh my dear, whatever happened to living out loud?

For myself, I'm unspeakably tired. Yet I confess that something inside my layers of ache and exhaustion now and then can't suppress a giggle at all this farce posturing as tragedy.

I can't help noticing, simplistic patterns aside, that for centuries women have conducted themselves in the imposed roles of "wives" and "mistresses" with some melodrama at times but for the large part with considerable dignity, and even with an understanding of (if not willingness about) sharing a man they loved, or living at the fringes of his life. Not that they had much choice. Still, two men faced with a remotely similar situation tend to rush about glowering suicidally that if each cannot sit at stage center *and* come and go as he pleases then he might just End It All. Life is Too Hard for almost every man, it appears, especially where his Work, his Madness, his Fragility, his Needs are concerned. He must be Nurtured, Grounded, Solidified, and Centered by—surprise!—a woman. Oho.

Speaking for this woman, I have only begun to live out loud, by god.

I think that actually might be all, though this letter was both harder and easier to write than the only other letter I ever wrote you. I hope we *can* be friends, because the few times I've loved in certain special ways I've found it a form of commitment, ethical, honorable, and long-lived, to be conducted with care and compassion, and I admit to a sense of defeat at the possibility of losing someone I've loved in *any* way so utterly that the schism retroactively degrades even the having loved. Maybe that's a bad thing sometimes, if it turns into something clingy. Ultimately, though, I think the tendency itself is an affirmable one in a transient world—a tendency that moves in the direction of grace.

Take care of yourself. You are free—but what they never tell you is that freedom entails even more responsibility than bondage, the same way art requires High Play in dead earnest—and that responsibility is where C. comes in, or goes out. Most of all, get where you can do your work, because in the short or long run that's the only way to hope *or* sanity *or* peace, let alone grace.

The woman who wrote this letter was coming back to health, sanity, and that most invaluable of all survival tools, a sense of humor. Eventually, she recovered completely, but with the gain of knowledge (for curiosity and desire *are* one)—a knowledge of herself as a creature of passion, a knowledge of some of the uses and misuses of passion, a new knowledge of her husband and child and friends. As Heidegger wrote in *Poetry, Language, and Thought*, "Pain gives of its healing power where we least expect it."

Many months later, she found herself looking in passing with pleasure on a different "parking-lot attendant," similarly graceful and physically beautiful. It was only then that she realized the obvious: the *commonality* of desire, the very ordinariness of it that is denied to most women. After all, when a feeling dares occur only rarely, and can't always be acted on even then, it tends to get elevated into Something Special, with an excessively romantic halo around it. Were women to have access to feeling desire spontaneously, expressing it openly, and gratifying it regularly, then the halo would bleed away. But it might well leave something glowing in its place: a plebeian holiness, an ordinary (but *not* fundamentalist) sanctity—plain and everyday, the beauty of flesh and touch and pleasure—an eternal delight of energy for a woman to act upon or not as *she* chose, without glorifying it or losing herself to it. Rather, it might be something by which to *gain* or expand oneself; Mary Wollstonecraft was right about that. It might, or might not, have to do with the pure white light of commitment. But it certainly would liven up a woman's world. "So many torches," wrote the sixteenth-century French poet and feminist Louise Labé, "to set a female on fire!"

But it was some time before the woman who wrote the letters came to comprehend any of this. At first, it had been all she could do to write the second letter. Then, she even managed not to send it, realizing that its recipient would never be able to appreciate its meaning, precisely because he had not bargained for knowing her in the wholeness of her context—political, ethical, emotional. (Wasn't it for this quality of ignorance, in effect, that she had been attracted to him at the start?)

That insight in turn gave birth to two others: that she had written the letter for herself (again) to make real and fathomable *for* herself on the page what she had been unable to express and understand in mere living; and that she had written the letter to a standard of aesthetics *and* ethics which had been developed and nurtured for decades between herself and her husband, a standard which could evolve only within the context of a willingness to know and be known. This last intuition was proved true when her husband, by accident, came upon the letter, read it, and *did* understand it—which was one reason she had been right to marry him in the first place.

Finally, the woman (who we really *should* refer to by the initial I) decided to publish relevant parts of these letters in her new book. So well did her husband know her (and, being himself a writer, know too how the page demands an often costly honesty) that he supported her in this. So well did they know one another that each knew how, in the process of the familiar, one trusts the known continually to divulge the strange, the new, the surprising.

As the woman typed these letters into the manuscript pages of this book, she felt a breath of something sweet and wild blow for an instant through her study. It felt to her like both something she had never encountered before and something with which she always had been intimately conversant. I almost think . . . I think it was a whisper, just for a moment, of what could be called "freedom."

LIVING OUT LOUD

Acquiring any insight into what one's own real sexual energy might be like, freed of fundamentalism, apathy, capitulation, or even rebellion, is, for a woman, difficult enough in virtually every society. Acting on that hard-to-come-by knowledge is even more difficult for her.‡ Every woman knows that in most cultures sexual assertiveness (no flirtation games, feminine wiles, little-girl cutesie ploys, or femme-fatale capers), direct, honest, sexual assertiveness is considered in a female human being at worst whorish and at best worthy of the fake-liberated-woman image, or the Plucky Wench Award. Sometimes, such assertiveness is deliberately ignored, or conveniently euphemized back into passivity:

The female phalarope courts the male at mating time . . . [a common example of] female courtship in the animal world. . . . Now that there are more women in the natural sciences and more men aware of their past neglect of the female of the species, . . . new data is available on female courtship. Researchers have even dignified the phenomenon with a new term. . . . Not satisfied with the semantics of "female courtship," they speak now of "proceptivity," defined as female initiative in sexual matters.[20]

Sounds uncomfortably like "receptivity." If a female does what a male does, change the name for the doing, change the rules, change the rewards—until we begin to believe that it's just not in the cards for us to do it, or at least to know what we're doing while we do it. Our prolonged, almost chronic sexual hunger has resulted in a malnutrition of our sexuality. In an 1837 speech, "The Elixir of Life,"[21] uninhibitable Victoria Claflin Woodhull said, "It is a fact terrible to contemplate, yet it is nevertheless

‡ The sets and costumes are different, again, and this can give the illusion of the grass being less mowed on the other side—but it's an illusion: white women in the United States regard black women as being freer sexually—but ask black women about the truth. Internationally, Northern women may regard Latin women as freer, Western women see Pacific Island women as less repressed, etc.—but whenever women compare notes, the plot is basically familiar.

true, and ought to be pressed upon the world for its recognition: that fully one-half of all women seldom or never experience any pleasure whatever in the sexual act. Now this is an impeachment of nature, a disgrace to our civilization."

More than a century later, women still are being forced, time and again, back to sexual fundamentalism, forced into trading what we thought was sexual passion, via the medium of romance, for violent passion. In part, this may be because we have been led to believe that sexual empowerment isn't for us—and so we project that empowerment onto men: remember that phrase, "Damn him, he seemed the key to all my locked doors, and he rusted in my hand."

Why *does* a woman project her own sexual breakthroughs, energy, desire, onto a man (or sometimes another woman), as if such power has nothing to do with her? You subject; me object. As Shulamith Firestone noted years ago, women see themselves being eroticized as objects so pervasively that they begin to view *themselves* as erotic objects, not subjects.[22] In her unpublished honors thesis, Suzanne Braun Levine[23] analyzed the Beloved-as-reflection tendency in romantic literature (Cathy's statement, "I *am* Heathcliff!" in *Wuthering Heights*, etc.). Will women project passion onto others (that it may reflect back to us) as long as we must still seek ourselves in one-way mirrors?

It's both a tragedy and an irony that Man has labeled Woman primarily *as* a sexual (and reproductive) being—and has stripped women of sexuality itself. Regaining sexuality is central to any idea of what real freedom for women *or* men might be. As Audre Lorde has written in her now famous essay, "Uses of the Erotic: The Erotic as Power,"[24]

The erotic is a measure between the beginning of our sense of self, and the chaos of our strongest feelings. It is an internal sense of satisfaction to which, once we have experienced it, we know we can aspire. For once having experienced the fullness of this depth of feeling and recognized its power, in honor and self-respect we can require no less of ourselves.

Such aspiration can lead anywhere; it is as unpredictable as energy. It requires living out loud, sexual intelligence, *and* existential romanticism. It also requires *noticing*—the word I chose when asked to name in one word the quality that most distinguishes women from men in patriarchy. Women *notice*; men can afford not to. We notice a slight shadow of expression, a hesitation of voice, a glass standing too near the edge of the tabletop, just how near the toddler is straying toward the curb. Unfortunately, we notice details about ourselves less: those seem unimportant, those can wait, there's not much we can do about those anyhow.

We must turn this marvelously creative skill of noticing on ourselves—and it would be nice if men could acquire the skill to begin with. It *can* be learned.

I have, for example, been noticing an increasing sense of unease in myself that, so far, same-sex eroticism has not been dealt with specifically in this chapter. Indeed, the reader will have perceived by now that this is a book largely about women interacting, by choice or force, with men. (Most women on the planet do participate in such interaction.) And I submit that such books—yea even such *feminist* books—are necessary, too. One of the joys of turning forty was, for me, the falling away of a certain acute defensiveness on various issues: for years this defensiveness had lured me at times into political obsequiousness. Now I can simply tell more truths about more things, without apology or guilt. In the long run, the truth is probably the best thing any of us have to offer one another, as women, as men, as human beings.

More than 95 percent of the sexual activity in my life has been involved with men; more than 90 percent of it, in fact, with one man—my husband. (By some modern standards of experience, I am a wide-eyed novice.) Furthermore, despite passionate friendships with women, my actual *sexual* experiences with women have been, sadly, more from a wish "to do the right thing" politically, more to win approval and acceptance (how like most sex with most men!) than from genuine sexual passion. I've come to understand that sexual pressure of any sort—whether emotional, physical, or political—is plain old hideous sexual fundamentalism, and I want no part of it.

I do believe deeply that all human beings, male and female, are sexual beings, most likely bisexual beings channeled this way and that by cultures terrified of boundary crossings without passports stamped GAY or STRAIGHT. The homophobia imbedded in most cultures is a grave political sickness, and I understand and support the necessary courage and militance required of lesbian women and homosexual men in separating themselves from tedious explanations to heterosexuals about "deviance," neurosis, childhood trauma, hormones, ravening lust, or What It Is We Really Want. The *hetero*phobia which has at times surfaced within various women's movements around the world is no antidote, although one can realize that it springs from pain at a condition which did not originate with those articulating it. The *institution of heterosexuality* which demands conformity is indeed evil; it has suppressed joy and murdered minds and bodies. It is a stake in the heart of sexual passion. An *institution of homosexuality* demanding comformity would be, however, a twin stake in the same heart. Because both homophobia and heterophobia are, simply, sexual-fundamentalist reductions of curiosity and desire.

Within any ghetto (even a defiantly self-affirmed one in reaction against its having been an imposed one earlier), an inevitable offensive defense emerges as a tactic. If heterosexuals for decades exercised a power-packed sexual fundamentalism against same-sex lovers, it did *not* necessarily make heterosexual sex any better. If, in pained reaction, some homosexuals now have changed the Gay Pride slogan from "Two, four, six, eight; gay is just as good as straight" to "Two, four, six, eight; gay is *twice as good* as straight," that won't necessarily make homosexual sex any better. On the contrary, a draw-the-wagons-in-a-circle attitude can make it harder for individual members of an oppressed group to dare complain about sexual problems even to a lover, a friend, a consciousness-raising group, or a sister lesbian-feminist therapist. And those problems do exist—very similar to heterosexual ones, in fact: problems about romance, violence, power imbalance, monogamy, fundamentalist attitudes, sexual intelligence. We *all*, regrettably, live in a patriarchal culture.

I notice, too, that the women for whom I feel true sexual attraction are women with some sense of their own power—yet I sense this as different from an attraction to male power. (Henry Kissinger has been quoted as saying that power—any power—is the greatest aphrodisiac. It may be wishful thinking on his part.) No, the qualities of grace, skill, humor, a willingness to *know* me in my whole self (curiosity) are what attracts me to a man. With most women these qualities seem a given. But a woman who emanates not only a sense of herself but a *knowledge* that she emanates a sense of herself—that woman discharges in me an electric current of energized desire. It is something like the quality that Virginia Woolf described as "riding life." Woolf herself wanted to ride her work "as a man rides a great horse." Should that discharge ever set off a chain reaction of *action*, it will not be because any sexually fundamentalist institution has detonated it out of (again) political fundamentalism or "correctness." It will be pure celebration of yet another facet of my own emerging sexual intelligence.

And I *am* more curious about my own sexual energy now than I ever have been, within my marriage and without, with another woman or with a man. I have little fear of turning "promiscuous," however, since I feel a strong yearning for commitment to those I truly love. Besides, remember that the existential part of me is certainly well balanced by that intrepid romantic. I feel as certain as ever that my old hypothesis was right; that sexual freedom for women does not mean our turning imitatingly into Doña Juanas, however much a tit-for-tat tactic might seem a temptation. After all, it was the *lack* of real curiosity of Don Juan, despite his claims to the contrary, which made him unable ever to satisfy his desire, for he had the power never even to hear the questions the women he wooed were asking, although, ironically, he would have had answers for them—answers which would have filled the powerless with knowledge, which would have been to them power. Perhaps this is why he never heard them?

No, it is the *separation* of feeling from sexuality that creates violence, pornography, sexual fundamentalism. That has never felt right for me, and if at times I've overdone the feeling aspect in my romanticism, I'd rather have made that error than its opposite. To insist upon the combination, however, is to insist on integrity of self and in others, on self-respect, on erotic intelligence, on energy as delight.

If the adversaries assembled against it seem at times so overwhelming that one begins to despair of such energy ever having existed at all, or ever being released again, one sentence of Dr. Mary Jane Sherfey's ought to suffice to remind us of our own hidden truth:

"The strength of the drive determines the force required to suppress it."[25]

V

THE BEAD OF SENSATION

An Anatomy of Marriage

Search as I may for the remedies to sore injustice, endless misery, and the incurable passions which trouble the union of the sexes, I can see *no* remedy but the power of breaking and re-forming the marriage bond.

—George Sand

Arnold Bennett says that the horror of marriage lies in its "dailiness." All acuteness of relationship is rubbed away by this. The truth is more like this: life—say four days out of seven—becomes automatic; but on the fifth day a bead of sensation (between husband and wife) forms which is all the fuller and more sensitive because of the automatic customary unconscious days on either side. That is to say the year is marked by moments of great intensity. . . . How can a relationship endure for any length of time except under these conditions?

—Virginia Woolf

Spontaneous sexual passion could be likened to the experience of coming upon a remarkable painting: intense and vibrating colors, an almost palpable texture, a seeming abandonment of form within the carefully conceived composition. So vivid are the magentas, the viridian greens, the beryl blues, so sensually layered are the brushstrokes, so wild yet confident the technique, that one almost can forget the painting exists in only two dimensions.

Marriage, by contrast, could be likened to a hologram.

A hologram (which means "the whole message" in Greek) is a three-dimensional representation of reality. It's also an information-storing device. To construct a hologram one needs *coherent light* and at least *two interacting components*. *Coherent light* is light that moves forward from its source in even, flat "fronts," thus keeping the beam of light narrow; when light is not coherent, it tends to expand and dissipate quickly. A good source of coherent light is the laser, which produces not only the focused, narrow coherent beam but also "monochromatic" light—light of a single frequency. A hologram is created by separating a laser beam into *two components,* one of which is aimed at a photographic plate that has been coated with a high-resolution film, the second of which illumines the subject and is diffracted to the plate. The *interaction* between the two beams causes an interference pattern—literally an exchange of information—in light waves.* The result is a visual image virtually indistinguishable from reality. An amazed viewer will reach for the hologram of an apple, as if to bite a chunk out of it, only to find that her/his hand passes right through the image. (We could go a step further and ask, "But what is real 'reality,' really?" After all, we know that a "real" apple, at a high enough magnification, would be seen to be composed of subatomic particles, through which the ultimately similar subatomic particles of a real hand could pass; both sets of particles are perpetually whirling in such furious movement that they are waves as much as they are particles, and it is only their given environments at given times in this three-dimensional limited consciousness we inhabit that keep them from passing through one another. In fact, as electromagnetic waves they *do* pass through one another.)[1]

Returning to the metaphor of a work of art—and some contemporary artists are experimenting with the hologram as a form —our "marriage hologram" might be infinitely subtler than the painting which stopped us in our tracks. After all, many (perhaps most) people regard marriage as duller than a love affair—more

---

* The interference pattern is comparable to the pattern of light and dark areas in a traditional photographic negative. This is similar to the way in which sound waves in sonarlike devices transmit information, and the manner in which information is stored, exchanged, and transmitted by the genetic code carried in our chromosomes. Since *if any one part of a hologram is illuminated, the whole image will be re-created from that illuminated part,* the hologram seems to be the most wondrously compact form of storing knowledge yet understood. Its philosophical implications are also marvelous: it proves that the part is as great as the sum—that the part *is,* in fact, the sum. For example, a single genetic cell contains the total information necessary to make an additional copy of the body (plant, animal, or human) from which it was taken.

respectable maybe, but far less excitingly dramatic. So let's say our hologram has all-but-invisible colors, and they blend and blur imperceptibly: smoky tints of graybrown shading into rose, pastel milky golds, translucently pale aquamarines. Unless we had developed an eye for exquisite understatement as expressed, say, in late Turner paintings, we might pass this work of art by without noticing it had any color whatsoever. If we paused before it at all, it would be because of the verisimilitude of the image: whole, three-dimensional, in-the-round, and brazenly *there*. We can in fact walk around it, lean above it, crouch beneath it, and from each perspective see new and newer aspects of the work. It may hang in space, but it conducts itself with the audacity and courage of absolute solidity. It is an astonishment.

"READER, I MARRIED HIM."

Remember that the woman writing this has been married for almost twenty years—to the first man she ever went to bed with. Remember that this woman has been called a "man-hater" by various sexists and "soft on men" by some separatists. Remember that she is a feminist. Remember that this marriage has been conducted both privately and publicly, through poems and prose written by both partners, work of wincing honesty trying to avoid the merely "confessional" by being passed through the crucible of craft. Remember that this marriage has been on the verge of breakup more than once—and never more so than at the moment of this writing. Remember this.

Coded Message #1

They are young, and still tearing down walls. Streaks of plaster dust missed in the shampooing whiten their hair prematurely. All day into late evening they've hammered and chipped, brushed and swept and dumped, then painted and stained, vacuumed and polished. Then bathed and changed. Now they sit in the one "finished" room, before a fireplace crackling with broken laths from the vanished wall, the other rooms still looking like bombed-out Berlin, chunks of plaster heaped like miniature ruins on the tarpaulins. Outside, a snowstorm whirls itself against the windows. But inside they sit before the fire, sipping red wine from the only two long-stemmed glasses they possess. On the

*newly acquired low marble table in front of the fireplace, one
bowl of pure crystal—her grandmother's—winks prisms from the
flame-light along its faceted curves, and at its lip, exclaims twelve
red roses—an extravagant gesture—purchased instead of winter
gloves. Rose perfume blends in the air with the Chopin études
playing on the phonograph. The man and woman sit in a silence
of communication that needs no superfluous words, there, at the
still island in the center of the storm, the labor, the fallen walls.
Their hair might be white from plaster or snow or age, but the
expressions on their faces are like fullblown roses, they hear one
another's thoughts like music, and their two motionless bodies
might be made of crystal, so transparent is each to the other, and
so faceted with light.*

This marriage exists in history, not in a vacuum. That history is
long, rich, still only partly unearthed. In the Western tradition
alone: It was Eleanor of Aquitaine in the twelfth century who set
up a Court of Love to redefine the meaning of love and marriage.
It was the Puritans (victims of such a bad press) who fought for
the then-radical concepts of marriage for love, the right to divorce, the right of a wife and husband to live in privacy away
from the patriarchal dynastic family fief or village or even farm,
the idea of the equality of the female soul. The debate for and
against marriage has raged on for centuries, albeit largely between
Man and Man: the Athenians *for*, the Spartans *against*; the
Roman Catholic Church *for*, and the Catharist "heresy" *against*;
Goethe and Engels *for*, Lenin and Mao (both married) *against*;
early Tolstoy *for*, and late Tolstoy *against*; Kierkegaard—ever the
dialectician—*against* (in the aesthetic stage), *for* (in the ethical
stage), and *against* all over again (in the religious stage). And the
feminist theorists of the nineteenth-century movement most assuredly dared to question the institution of marriage—at least the
radical ones dared: among them Gage and Gilman, and certainly
that political-philosopher genius, Elizabeth Cady Stanton, who in
an 1853 letter to Susan B. Anthony wrote: "I feel this whole
question of women's rights turns on the point of the marriage
relation, and sooner or later it will be the topic for discussion."[2]
Given the horrified reactions (even from other suffragist women)
to these feminist radicals having raised the question at all, the
issue got discreetly ignored and eventually lost in the battle for

mere suffrage. It would turn out to be later, rather than sooner, that marriage became a "topic for discussion."

This particular marriage exists in the second half of the twentieth century. In these decades the early radical feminist thinkers of this current wave of feminism also questioned the institution of marriage. The early 1970's group calling itself The Feminists wrote challenging position papers analyzing the legalities actually contained in the marriage contract.[3] (In this, Isadora Duncan had preceded them: "Any intelligent woman who reads the marriage contract, and then goes into it, deserves all the consequences," she wrote in 1927. This quote is a bit harsh on the victim, perhaps, but it's an example nonetheless of how feminist movements must perforce keep on rediscovering truths already established in our buried history.)

Coded Message #2

She invents a symbol for the Women's Movement. She cannot draw, but she can describe it: the universal sign for the female—a circle with a cross dead center beneath it—with the stem of the cross becoming a forearm that flowers into a clenched fist within the circle. He, although a poet, draws and paints beautifully. He draws the logo to her specifications. It appears on the cover of her first book on feminism. It is taken up by women all over the country—on buttons, on T-shirts, on bumper stickers, on leaflets and other book covers and posters. It is used on the front of a Japanese feminist journal, it emblazons a women's magazine in India, it decorates an underground feminist broadside in South Africa, it waves on a banner of a women's march in Brussels. No one remembers which woman first conceived the logo. This is fine. No one knows that a man first executed the concept visually. Which is also fine—except that this fact, which would make some feminists chary of using the symbol again, should be known. (He has never spoken of his part in it, for fear of embarrassing her.) Yet that a woman and man together (a married couple, to boot) were able to offer this gift to her people as a tool —isn't this actually a sign of hope? But will it be seen as a sign of hope?

All over again—and just as shockingly—we questioned the institution of marriage in the late 1960's and early 1970's. We *questioned*, remember; we didn't denounce or automatically attack. It was, in fact, the first and most daring question we asked. The question got lost in reductionism ("All those feminists are interested in is destroying love between women and men"); in fundamentalist distortion ("Feminists really want to be like men sexually, bed-hopping from one partner to another"); in fundamentalist obfuscation ("Feminist revolution and sexual revolution are one and the same"); in fundamentalist divide-and-conquer-type analyses ("It's the fault of those lesbian feminists who want all the women to themselves"); and in so-called practical priorities or "fundamentals" ("What with the legislative fights for reproductive freedom, job opportunities, an end to educational discrimination, ERA, and basic survival issues, how can you want to theorize about an institution like marriage? It's a tactical luxury; besides, it alienates Middle America").

Now, in the 1980's, we are witnessing a curve back toward marriage—or at least toward committed relationships.

Despite the subtitle of this chapter, I am in fact speaking here more of committed relationships in general than of marriage in particular. I'm aware of the dangers inherent in shorthanding "committed relationships" with the word "marriage," yet the former phrase is not only longer and more unwieldy, but has been cheapened by pop-psyche and growth-potential movements into sounding like a collection of refugee words from a Jules Feiffer cartoon. The simple word *commitment* can be alarmingly mistaken for the placing of somebody in a mental institution (a process undergone, assuredly, by many persons specifically *because* of "committed relationships" in general and "marriage" in particular). While the word *marriage* doesn't answer all the purposes to which I will apply it in this chapter, it's at least convenient for approximating most of them: it's short, and implies an intimate, enduring relationship between two partners. (Unlike *paterfamilias*, which originally meant "holder of slaves," this word has a more reassuring etymology: Webster's Third New International Dictionary traces it back through "marry"—which has "an [assumed] prehistoric" root meaning woman.) I am *not* speaking about the *institution of marriage*, with all of its sexually fundamentalist, legalistic, and oppressive aspects. Rather, I am talking about the complex holography involved in any two persons (of any sex) living together as sexual lovers, and in a more or less long-term emotional bond of partnership which can include economic, social, aesthetic, political, etc. sharing of resources. Of course, some of the problems differ from one relationship to another, and this difference is influenced by such variables as sex (same-sex or opposite-sex partners), class, race, age, culture, education, and others —but I've only just begun to realize, with some shock, how intensely similar the *basic* problems are. True, in a heterosexual relationship the shadows of Man and Woman intrude more blatantly. Yet when any two human beings live together over a period of time, it seems that certain inevitable hurdles arise, and are dealt with in certain similar patterns, engagements, confrontations, evasions, denials, acknowledgments, and other such "strategies."

Coded Message #3
Some of their best conversations take place when one of them is sitting on the toilet. This is one example of where love has it all over romance.

I have two additional reasons for choosing the word *marriage* to describe "committed relationships": it's a word which I believe feminist thinkers should consider reclaiming from the Right Wing's usage of it as a bludgeon; we might reclaim it as *one* (*redefined and reformed*) *option* for expressing human love—just as some homosexual activists are demanding the right to be legally married. Finally, it does describe accurately the union in which I live with my husband, the poet Kenneth Pitchford. We may not have a traditional, or modern, or perfect marriage, and to some people our marriage may in fact seem a bit bizarre in all of its passionate struggles—but a marriage it is.

Coded Message #4
For twenty winters, she has warmed her icy feet on his body in bed. Around the twelfth year, he ceased to shudder involuntarily. Now, he doesn't even emit a small gasp.

I would say that ours is an "examined marriage," since I agree with Carolyn Heilbrun that "an unexamined marriage is only slightly better than an unexamined life. Both are like Dante's hell: one goes on doing what one is doing."[4]

The recent trend of acknowledging a desire for enduring relationships seems to me good news—because it means that feminists and nonfeminists must face the true complexities of human need. And it's also bad news—because often it takes the adversarial form of backlash, as the marriage *structure* more than the human emotions within it is propagated as the Only Normal State of Affairs by a sexual- and religious-fundamentalist, jingoistic New Right. This trend also can take the form of escape or retrenchment, since many of the early firebreathing feminists find that as their political commitment grew their personal lives shriveled. Those who believed that one should "never trust anyone over thirty" are now in their mid-thirties or older, and suddenly are speaking and writing about their longing for committed relationships (with men or women, but mostly, it must be admitted, with men), about the solipsism they feel regarding affairs or "serial marriages," about the panic of the biological clock in terms of having children before it's too late. Intimations of mortality such as these have been expressed in a rash of "feminist weddings"— which then are once again distortedly analyzed by conservative mentalities as "Aha, we knew it all along. They were just malcontents because they couldn't get husbands before."

Meanwhile, what of those feminists who, like myself, have been married all along? Many of these marriages foundered on the rocks of correct-line political fundamentalism, of lesbian "experimentation," of women exploding with suppressed demands and men unable or unwilling to meet them. Still others survived with an embroidery of scar tissue. Often, the cost of survival was a defensively perfectionist fixed-smile No-Problem-with-My-Marriage attitude, paid out in the coin of less change within the relationship because of the pressure from outside.

The final irony has been that the more a marriage survived, the more it came to be seen as a model—a model traditional marriage, a model gay marriage, a model feminist marriage—thus depriving its individual partners of a reality check. In a heterosexual marriage, for instance, the woman was deprived of much-needed support from other women for her struggles with the man, and the man was deprived of support (and challenge to change, as well) from women and from other men in the same boat. Again and again the *process* is lost sight of, and the temporary present is viewed as the goal, the end, the solution. "How have you done it?" I've been asked—as if I weren't still lurching about in the confusing, difficult, and exhilarating process of trying, failing, trying to do it.

Coded Message #5

For a solid year, they have raged at one another—wept, shouted, slammed doors, yelled unspeakable things, almost broken up yet again. Now they stand in an open field in the midst of Mayan ruins in Yucatán, drenched to the skin in a sudden July thunderstorm—stand stock still as if in full sunlight, kissing a long and leisurely new introduction to one another under two limp straw hatbrims dripping interlinked circular curtains of warm rain.

"How come your marriage has succeeded?" they ask,—as if, to paraphrase Sophocles, one could ever call a relationship happy until one knew its ending.

Coded Message #6

She has used up her one phone call from jail, to alert her lawyer. Now she inveigles a young, newly married cop to let her make a second call, to phone home so her husband won't worry overly much. (She expected the women's sit-in to end in a bust. He is home with the baby.) A second call is not permitted, but she works on the cop, using traditional "womanly" wiles. This is not politically "correct" and is a privilege a same-sex lover or unwed heterosexual wouldn't dare try for in the circumstances—but she is brazen about "by any means necessary." The cop finally calls for her, and abashedly (in a whisper) gives her message of love to the husband. The cop makes her swear not to tell the sergeant. Everyone is satisfied.

Open the door, then—the one beyond the other doors opened and corridors traversed in all the previous poems and prose I've written about my marriage. Open a door into a secret room—which is itself another nested Chinese box containing tighter and tighter secrets, all of them contradictory, desperate, basic, passionate, and at once unique and commonplace.

A marriage has its own forms of communication, an unutterable language, a code of tiny signals. But then, quantum field theory has shown that all interactions, all change, all communication, takes place through the exchange of infinitely small particles.

Coded Message #7

This is not permitted when they actually have quarreled. But when they are merely feeling, say, estranged from one another, alien, distanced, comfortably hopeless about the situation, then a possible course of action is permitted—although it must never be followed so frequently as to take on the appearance of ritual. Nor must it ever be named aloud. Simply, it is that:

She, feeling exhausted (but not that much), feigns sleep.

He, feeling rejected (but not that much), feigns desire.

He makes love to her in her sleep. She remains unawake.

He need not mention that it even happened, in the morning— although he may, in a light tone.

She need not remember it, of course—although she may—but vaguely, or jokingly.

Both are bitterly grateful. The next day they behave normally. They are friends now.

Her feigned passivity has cost him a partner but saved him his release. He is guilty and grateful.

His taking advantage of her feigned state has cost her her sleep but saved her pride. She is guilty and grateful.

Such exquisite ingeniousness may be elevated to an art if two people fear that their passion is becoming joyless—and fear, even more, that they still love one another.

Question: what is a radical feminist writer and activist doing with her husband on a windy autumn night in the middle of the Brooklyn Bridge? Is she getting ready to push him off? Is she about to leap toward her own desperate liberation? Are they preparing a joint suicide to escape the seeming political contradiction inherent in this relationship?

None of the above. I am walking arm-in-arm with the writer, friend, father of my child, and above-mentioned husband. We are feeling joyous, tearful, proud of each other, and chilled to the bone. We are, just the two of us, celebrating yet another wedding anniversary on the spot where we first kissed decades earlier, the wind then just as wild in our hair as it is now.

Coded Message #8

When she is chopping onions, he kisses her behind her left ear. When he is vacuuming the rug, she likes to watch the muscles in his callipygous behind.

We were married B.C. (Before Consciousness), and feminism has changed our lives, as writers, lovers, parents, wage earners. We have traveled a territory for which there was no map, charting the topography as we went, like so many other couples trying to transform their lives through this new consciousness. Now we know certain features of the terrain (though still discovering others further on) and can pass along to the settlers who follow at least a rough map—but "the map is not the territory."[5]

Still, there do seem to be recognizable signposts in most such journeys, even though some couples may miss one or two entirely and others may spend their whole life together at just one stage, and even though specific twists and turns of the path may vary greatly in sequence or difficulty from relationship to relationship:

The Dauntless Explorers: She is delighted and proud of herself for discovering that she wasn't crazy all along; he is happy and proud of himself for supporting her in this new knowledge. Anger will be constructive! They will be a Liberated Couple! They talk animatedly at dinner parties with friends about how helpful this new communication is, how energized they both feel, how sensible and easy the practice of these new ideas really is.

The First Landslide: He is shocked to discover that this new consciousness really does pertain to housework. She is shocked to discover that he has just discovered this.

The "I'm Game!" Rapids: He pitches in (gamely) and Tries Hard. He reinvents new ways of doing everything so as to (1) to escape the humiliation of taking instruction from her, (2) to give the job a jolt of creativity, and (3) to escape the mere doing of it.[6] She acts (and sort of feels) grateful, and has spasms of guilt that he is doing even the little he is doing. He feels she is being fair and understanding. She is irritated at herself for thanking him for doing what he should have been doing all along anyway; she's proud of being "fair" but wonders if she's being a wimpy coward. Also she is irked at no longer being able to find (1) the can opener, (2) the dustpan, and/or (3) the dishes (they are all in the dishwasher and/or in the sink—"about to be" washed).

The Individual Excursion: He begins to have difficulty communicating with other men; their styles and concerns seem alien to him. He does, on the other hand, get along *much* better with other women. Women, he discovers, are interesting! In fact, women begin to eye him approvingly as the Feminist Prince. He makes friends with *her* women friends and makes his *own* women friends—at work, at school, on the outside. Meanwhile, she gets nervous. She suspects her own nervousness: What? Can she be jealous? Surely she trusts him! Is her mind in the gutter? Or is she jealous not of him but of her women friends' being co-opted *by* him? *What?* Can she be so petty, so possessive? Didn't she want him to begin to treat women as people, wasn't she irritated by his previous male bonding? (She finds it all but impossible to make *male* friends now; men all seem odious.) He, shored up by the approval from other women and by his own pride in How Far He Has Come, now starts to act more-feminist-than-thou to her: he lectures her that she must stand up for herself, not let herself be bullied anymore by her boss or parents or teachers or street harassers, how she really must read the latest book of feminist theory, how she ought to go on more demonstrations. (He also holds forth on what his mother and *her* mother and various women friends and relatives ought to do about standing up for *them*selves.) She grinds her teeth at this: he can afford to give such advice, not knowing what the acting out of it will really cost. Yet didn't she *want* him to be supportive, to read the works of feminists, to be as committed to this consciousness as she? They quarrel repeatedly over what she calls his grandstanding and what he calls her defensive possessiveness.

The Encounter with Tourists: She takes to mentioning among friends (lightly, jokingly) the developments encountered in The *"I'm Game!" Rapids* above. She and the other women laugh about it. (There may be one woman present who makes the requisite comment, "Well, I'd never ask *my* husband. . . .") The other men regard him as (1) a Class Traitor, (2) A Henpecked Dummy, (3) Queer, and/or (4) Admirable but Hardly Imitable. Every social engagement is followed by an inevitable private fight between the two of them.

The Us-Against-the-World Foray: Together, they decide not to let it get them down. What do the Joneses matter anyway? They themselves are what matters, they are the wave of the future, they are revolutionaries. The Joneses have a suppressed, neurotic, old-style, fossilized marriage: To hell with 'em. (This makes her secretly uncomfortable, since she has been privy to some of Betty Jones's secret and anguished confidences—and they seemed not all that unfamiliar to her.)

The Second Landslide: He discovers that this new consciousness pertains to sex. She discovers that he really and truly has just discovered this. Boulders as well as pebbles rain down upon them: the frequency of their lovemaking; the presence/absence/length-of/variety of their foreplay; her faked orgasms; his premature-ejaculation fears; her off-putting passivity (or off-putting aggressiveness); his off-putting aggressiveness (or off-putting passivity); their individual or mutual boredom; their individual or mutual fantasies; their individual or mutual longing for experimentation (in position, frequency, approach); their individual or mutual desire not to make waves but to stay with what's familiar, countable-on, will work; their individual or mutual frustration with what's familiar, countable-on, etc.; her fury that he can't read her signals; his rage that she expects him to be psychic; their individual or mutual secret terror at being frigid or impotent; their individual or mutual secret suspicion that the other really is frigid or impotent; their fear of Doing Something Wrong, their self-consciousness at Doing Something Right. *The Second Landslide* could also be termed *The Avalanche.*

The Impenetrable Jungle: During this phase, they draw the curtain over what is turning into a hell of complexity neither had ever expected of the other. The action takes place, so to speak, offstage. If they are writers, they write about it (of course) but do not publish what they write about it (until later). If she is in a consciousness-raising group, she finds that even there it feels painful, embarrassing, and "disloyal" to him to talk about this phase. He has no one at all to talk to among his male friends (if he has any male friends left by this time). If either or both is in therapy, the therapist is getting an earful—and remembering (perhaps with nostalgic longing) the days when neurosis was neurosis without all this goddamned politics mixing in.

The Plains of Practicality: This phase usually takes place offstage, too, and is frequently undergone concurrently with the previous one, causing severe vertigo in the explorers. They both discover that this new consciousness pertains to money—who earns it, who earns how much, who spends how much and for what, etc. This molehill of mortification (since they both are em-

barrassed by fighting over such a petty issue as *money*) can grow
into a sizable mountain. During this same period, they both discover that this new consciousness also pertains to the way they
each regard having and/or raising their child(ren). To complicate
things further, the children also realize this (depending on their
age): (1) consciously, (2) subconsciously, (3) manipulatively,
(4) celebratorily. All parties begin to glimpse the vastness of this
terrain, the possibility that it will not be charted in their lifetimes. There is great danger in losing heart at this stage, since ego
is already going fast, too heavy to backpack. Each person fears
running out of supplies for the rest of the journey.

The Cathartic Oasis: She cries. He cries. They cry together. A
lot. They cry because neither understands. They cry because one
or the other at last *understands.* They cry because what was understood for a moment there seems rapidly forgotten. They decide that they do love one another and besides who thought this
would be easy anyway? (They did. Glance back at *The Dauntless
Explorers.*) They're Going to Make It After All, By God.

The Setting-Up-Camp Celebration: They go out of the way to
be courteous and considerate; buy each other little presents,
maybe go on a vacation just the two of them (*not* to visit in-laws
and *not* with the kids and *not* in combination with a business
trip). She buys a new nightgown, he tries a new aftershave. Just
because they're "in struggle" doesn't mean that they can't be romantic and sexy now, does it? They'll beat this thing yet. They
cry again—with elation and hope. They feel free now to discuss
with others what they are certain they have put behind them
themselves; they are asked for and give advice. (There is a perilous tendency at this point to backtrack into *The Individual Excursion* stage.) They begin to be regarded with respect. They
begin to believe they've made it.

The Underground Desert: Since they've now publicly shared
the details of *The* (offstage) *Impenetrable Jungle,* it's even more
difficult to admit to others that everything isn't solved, broken-
through, perfect. Sometimes they do manage to admit this—but
their listeners think they're just being modest. This phase is perhaps the most deadly, since each partner is caught between a hard-
ening public image and an internal emotional hemorrhage. For
him, this consists of:

His Zomboid Trudge: He is stunned with despair. Nothing he's
done—at cost to his pride, his dignity, his sexuality, possibly his

work, his self-respect—has worked. All those trips to the laundry, supermarket, kindergarten, all those bottles of aftershave, all those tears, all those lost friends, all those public humiliations—for what? Nothing's really changed. He gets chronically depressed, obsequious to her, given in, given over. He still believes (perhaps now more than ever) in the power of this consciousness, in its justice, its capacity for changing people. (He *has* to believe he suffered for *some* just purpose.) His self-contempt grows. He can't return to his old self, but can't seem to manage a new self to the satisfaction of either of them. He thinks she must be gloating with triumph—but then that doesn't sound like the good person he loves and if he's done all this for some bad person he must be a masochistic nut. Yet if she *is* the good person he loves, how can he deny her? He has no energy for anything. He begins to sleep a lot, to get sick, to read three newspapers a day, to fall into long silences, passively to do everything she asks him to do (but to wait until she asks him), to listen to records with earphones on. He moves like a sleepwalker. He cannot be faulted for not actually *doing* what they've agreed on, but he himself is disembodied from the android who goes about doing it. He knows enough now to mistrust as "resistances to change" even his own anger against her, his thoughts of vengeance. Yet he *is* angry, and *does* feel vengeful—and is guilty about both. And he is angry *about* being guilty, which cycles him into feeling vengeful. Most of all, he is depressed. Life is utterly joyless. He has no words anymore to tell her why.

Meanwhile, she is suffering through:

Her Quicksand Flailing: She is frantic. Nothing she's done—at cost to her pride, her dignity, her sexuality, possibly her work, her new consciousness—has worked. All those sentences bitten back unsaid, all those questions unasked, all those new-nightgown–different-haircut offerings, all those tears, all those half-truths lied to women friends to protect him, all those previous public humiliations and later empty public triumphs—for what? Nothing's really changed. She begins to think she must be an insane person: has she been demanding too much of him, too fast, too deep? Other couples don't seem to be going through this; they seem to be managing such changes rather smoothly, by comparison. (Other couples happen at this point to be going through *The Dauntless Explorers, The "I'm*

Game!" Rapids, or *The Us-Against-the-World Foray*—but she doesn't realize that.) She becomes suspicious of her own motives: has she had a hidden agenda in all this? is she subconsciously some sort of sadist? has she gone power-mad? has she been manipulated by coldhearted, loveless, politically cynical feminists? Who needs this, anyway? Yet she can't return to her old self, even though she can't seem to accomplish this new self to the satisfaction of either of them. She tries to reach him through the newspapers, the earphones, the silences. He turns dazed eyes on her and says (for fear of offending, for fear he'll say what he really means, for fear he doesn't *know* what he really means, for fear there's nothing else to say), "No, nothing's the matter." She is sick with pity. She thinks she understands the depth of his pain, what all this has cost him. Then she catches glimpses that he thinks she is gloating, and since she is actually grieving, this drives her more insane—with grief, pity, rage. She bites back more words, walks on eggs when she's around him, gets angry at herself (for this) and at him (for this), gets guilty for getting angry at feeling that hideously familiar guilt. She falls into her own silences, her own deep and deeper depressions. Life is utterly joyless. She has no words anymore to tell him why.

Walking in Circles: This period could also be called *Doubling Back* or *Backlash-Backlash*. The compass has been lost. He has Had It—with being an obsequious minion, a doormat, a feminist prince riding on a white dustmop. He's tired of feeling guilty and making reparations for what he never even knew was wrong of him to do all those years ago when he was doing it. *He's* going to be A Person, too, just like her. Since she doesn't feel she's A Person *yet* in this relationship, his pronouncements infuriate, hurt, and terrify her. She says she never asked for obsequiousness, merely sharing; she wants them both to be Persons; she is interested not in having power over him but in doing away with it between them entirely. To herself, she wonders if all this is true, feels at fault, feels enraged at being at fault *again*, meditates seriously on whether it's really possible for two human beings to live together for their whole lives. (During this stage, a few *fundamentalist*-feminist friends may tell her that all men are pigs—which is no comfort to her. Comparably, certain suddenly resurrected old men friends of his may tell him That's What You Get for having let yourself be unmanned by a woman—which is no comfort to him. When, instead of these Job's counselors, sincerely supportive and understanding feminist friends of hers and antisexist friends of his truly listen and *help*, both she and he want to kiss their ankles in gratitude.)

The Volcanic Eruption: One of them has an affair. *Or:* one of them has an affair and the other one has a tit-for-tat affair. *Or:* one of them gets (or changes) a job. *Or:* they decide on a trial separation. *Or:* they decide to try therapy, sex counseling, a trip somewhere, marijuana, booze, having a (or another) child, having a nervous breakdown, or having a religious conversion. *Or:* all of the above—in rapid succession or simultaneously. *Or:* they heave themselves and each other up off the shore into:

The Sea of the Compassionate Buddha: Each will develop him/herself into a more autonomous entity—personhood, growth, human potential, self-actualization, the centered being. They will "give each other space." Each will have more "freedom" from the other. Yet they will remain together for the sake of (1) the shared past *or* (2) the child or children *or* (3) mature comradeship *or* (4) image (which can also be a replay of *The Us-Against-the-World Foray* or *The Setting-Up-Camp Celebration*) *or* (5) fear *or* (6) pity *or* (7) a strong suspicion that it's no better anywhere else *or* (8) habit *or* (9) exhaustion *or*, just *possibly*, (10) the inescapable, desperate, defiant love they still peevishly have for one another—which in turn brings them to:

The Love-Worn Wisdom Peninsula: They realize they *are* connected; are *not* islands. She doesn't want some other person to live with: she wants the person who is *him*, but with all the humor and electricity he possessed (but which was misused) before *The Zomboid Trudge* robbed him not only of his negative powers but also of his positive powers. She wants him as she intuits he can/could be. He doesn't want some other person to live with: he wants the person who is *her*, but with all the energy and idealism she possessed (but which was misused) before *Her Quicksand Flailing* robbed her not only of her powers of martyrdom but also of her powers of compassion. He wants her as he intuits she can/could be. They are both bloody, scarred, bone- and brain-weary, but they decide to try again. Each no longer knows what freedom is—but longs for it. Each no longer knows what love is—but feels it. Each no longer knows what "self" is—but gropes for it. Each no longer knows what faith is—but acts on it.

If they survive into *The Love-Worn Wisdom Peninsula*, they just might make it—intrepidly, insanely, doggedly, foolishly, against the laws of Man, Woman, averages, and gravity—into a new dimension. This space is aglitter with beads of sensation. It's another turn in the path that may seem (at first, or to others) like a simple circle or at best a Möbius strip, but it's more like another level entirely on some spiral which is double-helixing its ascension into infinity. This is a curve on which all the motions may seem familiar but in truth have a completely different content, a curve from which they both can look down and smile at the tortuous windings behind them—a curve from which they can go further, laughing and crying and trusting and stubbornly not-giving-up as if they were children, hand-in-hand in wonder, to enter a stage called:

The Dauntless Explorers . . .

I don't know the terrain beyond this point yet; if someone else does, I hope you'll pass on your section of the map.

I do know that this consciousness has cost us dearly in our own marriage: struggles, pain, dense silences and furious outbursts, craziness, depression. The rewards, however, seem even greater: challenge, elation, laughter, excitement at our capacity for change, awe at the courage of intimacy, tenderness and sympathy, and a certain savored . . . *coziness*. I sometimes theorize that the profound transformations feminism requires can only come about —or at least might come about best—in precisely such a committed relationship. *Commitment gives you the leverage to bring about change—and the time in which to do it.*

Coded Message #9

Isomorphism is "similarity in organisms of different ancestry resulting from convergence" (Webster's Third), and "an information-preserving transformation" (Gödel, Escher, and Bach) in which each "copy" preserves all of the material of the original. From each copy all of the information of the original is retrievable (like different, discrete, individual "voices" repeating the same theme in a musical canon). In this sense, both human partners are isomorphs—discrete, individual voices of different ances-

try who have converged; the information, the musical theme of the marriage, is stored in each—and is fully recoverable from either.

Some people have claimed that a respectable feminist cannot be married. Once it was held that a respectable woman *had* to be married. Phooey to both stereotypes, I say. The Feminist Movement has always been about more options, not less, for us all—in personal human relations as well as in every other area.

For me, feminism implies even more: a real revolution (not the superficial bang-bang kind) on all levels—economic, social, political, sexual, ecological, cultural, and metaphysical. Consequently, feminist thought and action seem to me characterized by love. The word *love* itself has been so trivialized in our society that it makes me nervous to use it without rigorous definition. I *do* mean that force stubborn enough to survive failure, fierce enough to demand and inspire transformation, purgative enough to cleanse bitterness, enraged and outrageous enough to insist and persist in the enormous task before it—and humbly passionate enough to evince itself, sometimes, in that form called "wedded love." For daily use.

Coded Message #10

Deep down, heterosexuality is, for a feminist, the desire not to write off the male half of the species completely. Such an insight is (a) hypocritical, (b) visionary, (c) the ultimate liberalism, or (d) Famous Last Words.

Try to write about it then. Try . . .

BEDROOM SEMAPHORE

She lay in bed, waiting for the burgundy to work, to get her sleepy, to raise the priority of sleep so that the *next* priority of the *next* day with all its errands and clocks and calendars and telegrams and anger could eventually triumph and she might fall into some merciful empty sleep or even more some wonderful erotic dream so private that not even she would remember it. Instead, she couldn't sleep, and so came and lurched (drunk, for her—on three glasses of wine) into her study to Try to Write About It Then.

Mistake. Mistake to go for a paragraph indent, breaks the flow, risky yes risk and god are all that ultimately interests me might as well face it. In this human man I tried to find You. Holy Saint Heloise of the profane love, pray for me. This stupid soft crying against this stupid hard typewriter. Oh my god I am most heartily sorry for having offended myself.

This morning. The first day of spring, new beginnings. Nausea to think of it. *Remember*. Verbatim.

He comes to bed. She glances at the clock: 10 A.M. She says sleepily, "You were up all night." (They have been silently unquarreling in a stasis of hostile cordiality since Saturday. This is now Wednesday morning.)

HE says: "I just wrote a great poem."

SHE: "Wonderful." Sleepily, smiling. Part real, part pretense: she hasn't written a poem in months. Telegrams and anger. Still, how petty can she be? "Wonderful."

HE: "I put it on your desk for you to read later."

Coded Message ✙11
They take a vacation separate from one another, for the first time. By the middle of the week, they are calling one another three times a day—including in the middle of the night, to read just-written poems.

SHE: "Good." Guilt—she knows he wants her to say Oh go and get it and read it to me right now. She has slept six hours. He might sleep all day when he does go to sleep. She must get up shortly. This thought crosses her mind.

HE: "You'll hate it."

SHE, to herself: My god he really said that. This is the first day of spring must I wake up must I hear this—

SHE: "That's not a very nice thing to say."

HE: "It's a sad poem and you hate sad poems."

Honest to god he says this.

Sitting here drinking this last of the burgundy and writing really helps. All I care about ultimately is You invisible god and the reader I pretend I'm not trying to be heard by who is after all only You.

I certainly see why poets become alcoholics a lot.

Anyway.

A woman's life is a perpetual returning to reality. A perpetual "Anyway."

Anyway.

So I hate sad poems. So I cannot understand his nasty puerile grasping of some Tragic Vision all his very widdle pwecious own.

All my own "sad poems" denied. Denied denied. What a rhythm that word has on the keys.

I must stop. But if I stop I do asinine things like cry and wail into the empty study like any ordinary un-hot-stuff-feminist woman soul in pain. Damn, but the worst thing about oppression is that it is so *humiliating*, a humiliation that not even all one's intelligence seems capable of transcending. (Or is that merely the last dregs of pride—in one's intelligence—grappling with humility, which is quite different from humiliation?)

Forget the political rhetoric.

The point is that he said "You hate sad poems." Denying her Jeffers, Homer, Emily Brontë, Dante, Plath, Amy Lowell, even himself; the last piano sonatas of Beethoven, the Bartók quartets, denying herself herself. (Why is she trying to compete with his Tragic Vision in the first place?)

How can we come up with a new economic analysis when we can't even understand why men can be so plain mean?

Dumb fool forty years old dumb woman fool.

The bastard knocks.

Coded Message #12

They receive a distinguished elderly writer as a guest for tea. There was no time to fix the broken banister rail. Both she and he warn their guest, in tones of casual solemnity, about the tricky banister—how it is quite unsteady because the house is over a hundred years old and you know how these old houses are . . . Neither of them dares look at the other. The hundred-year-old banister cracked at four that morning while they were giddily making love astride it.

But she has locks on her door this time. "I'm worried about you," he says. Drop dead she says "Go away, I'm working," but not what she really means if ever she could say out loud what she really feels not only would "the world split open" as Muriel Rukeyser wrote: it would mend, it would heal.

Anyway.

So she turned her head away from him on the other side of the pillow. Denying her even her own tragedies, the ones she keeps carefully hidden under the neatly folded efficiencies of her daily suffering which by now he claims wisely she enjoys.

How can I hate god this much and be an atheist?

On my desk right here before me lies a report on the genital mutilation of females my whole life you see it's been given over to realizing this, the horror of it, the horror of still despite it all loving him and loving god.

Thank god for locks, for devising locks that could keep me in this time this one time at least. Why doesn't *he* use them—for real, I mean, not those his kind uses against our souls and bodies and spirits but the ones he doesn't use on *his* study door, to keep me from haunting that room like a revenant (of myself), to find the poem he snatches back in vengeance for my having complained . . .

because you see she turns her head on the pillow and then after a while (an age) of trying to recapture that first lyrical sharp now pain of wakening on the new beginning day of spring never to come exactly the same in her life after losing it forever she rises up from the pillow and says rehearsed in her innerbrain quietly

SHE: "How gratuitously cruel you sometimes are. You astonish me, how you just come and slash across my sleep with your nastiness."

HE: "I'm sorry I didn't mean." He knows he did mean, his tone says that he knows. He's never been as stupid as all his genius has been bent on proving he is. My god such genius wasted—the one thing I can never forgive him for.

Coded Message #13

When they brought her out of the recovery room after the operation, she was still so groggy with the anesthesia she couldn't focus her eyes. So she reached out to trace the features of his face leaning above her, as if she knew it would be there. It was there. Then she could fall back into sleep again.

When will I have earned the right to sleep, when break through the cusp of this eternal trying to be understood by him or You?

Saint Heloise dona nobis pacem miserere nobis even him.

Shells and plants and his photograph I want a bare study free of this free free. Why does the word free not have the rhythm of the word denial. Or rather, denial period. It's the period that gives denial all its rhythm.

So then he rose and slammed downstairs after his hypocritical "I'm sorry" what does he know of regret since he doesn't live with him, I do.

I am alive in her inside this body. How did Sand do it and Eliot and Austen (on the kitchen table by candlelight scribbling) all my people without servants without secretaries without Sand's country house without Eliot's George Henry Lewis, without—no more self-pity. Leave that to him. Urgency, instead.

So she hears him slam the doors to the upstairs and then to his study (she has not locked hers you see *yet*) and she knows he is taking the poem back from her desk as punishment for her having spoken what is in her heart even the very surface shred of it nevermind one millimeter from that surface into its depths.

Which is even okay she knows the pattern, the lies, Kafka's leopards who drink from the sacred chalice in the temple until it becomes part of the ritual. She hits her fist into her palm saying this aloud into her study air crying in order to make sure it all gets down for fear that someone will never read it LIE for fear then that someone *will* read it ALSO LIE what then? For fear there is no god even beyond the denial of one; no love, no place for us.

Coded Message ♯ 14
They have shown each other drafts of poems for over a quarter of a century. Even when the poems were love poems to one another, they have tried to be relentless in their honest criticism. Even when the poems were hate poems to one another, they have tried to be relentless in their fair praise. This is the rock on which they stand. This is their timeless dialogue which will go on speaking when the two bodies of wife and husband are ash. For a quarter of a century they have been writing each really only to the other—and letting the world eavesdrop on their intimate conversation.

Anyway.

She knows that he knows that she will creep like a slug with no pride (what is pride before love?) into his study later when he is gone (he even lets her know carefully when he is going, the door unlocked, the ritual) so she can creep there and read the poem he has ostensibly withdrawn. Are only poets this insane?

I am inside here trying to be loved. Oh my god what if I were to care for nothing but Thee and me and this reader who *is* Thee who might understand, the only lover I trust beside myself, the only god who can hear this prayer.

If I became an alcoholic I might write this honestly more often. It would believe me be worth it. "When the mind's free, the body's delicate"—isn't that in *Lear?* Well then, never mind the liver—the mind would be open, the soul free, at least to breathe. Stretching *further* is, after all, asking a lot. Greedy little woman.

Anyway.

There's always revision.

Coded Message #15

To have knowledge is to have power. The powerful are less curi-ous than the powerless. It is because they are sure they know the answers—and they do. But not to the questions that the power-less are asking.

Is this then "becoming free"? *Why does it hurt me so?* Why do I see him still standing at the piano when he was only twenty-seven and I seventeen, I who had never before seen such fierce in-tegrity in a face, his life and poetry and face all one dimension and the years of being broken and re-formed and broken again on the wheel of feminist consciousness, changed and reluctant and hopeful and terrified.

Coded Message #16

She feels that he uses up all the emotion in a room—like the old superstition about flowers using up the air in a hospital room—so that there is none left for anyone else to express. It was for this intensity that she loved him in the first place.

He feels that she sacrifices the moment to the future—a pro-crastination of life until death inevitably makes such forward thinking academic. It was for this air of possibility that he loved her in the first place.

Be careful what you wish for, the proverb goes, because you might get your wish.

Yes. Men and women currently speak two different languages. Yet a friend who is a lesbian feminist reads these pages in manuscript—the "burgundy-bitterness" section—and says to me, with a wry and wise smile, "I hope you're not going to fall into the trap of assuming that this kind of ambivalent misery goes on only in heterosexual relationships." She is right, and it is worse: each human being speaks a language all its own; no other understands. As they live together, each makes assumptions about the other's unknown language. Each translates to one another out of each, communicating with gestures of mutual suffering, exchanging particles of affection. How to labinotate on the page that intricate choreography whose energy has kept civilization as we know and dread it alive?

She leaves a pillow, casually, on the bed between them.

He gets stiff necks.

She forgets to change the light bulbs.

He leaves water spots on the washed glasses.

She quarrels with the child, rather than with him.

He goes for long walks at night.

She buys him a record he's wanted.

He quarrels with the child, rather than with her.

She leaves used tissues wadded under her pillow.

He wears a shirt he thinks she detests.

She shrugs hopelessly, hoping the shrug will hurt him.

He finds her a book she's wanted.

She moves a foot to touch his ankle in bed.

He knows exactly what the slight pressure of this foot does not mean.

She has sinus attacks.

He turns the volume on the phonograph up.

He says No of course I'm not angry.

She says Nevermind it's not important.

When they look into one another's eyes in a certain coherent light, two living spirits try to reach each other through these communicators, these civilized dancers, this interaction of particles. Something in each will love the other until death, ceremony or no ceremony, ritual or no. If that were not so, the rest would be easy. And the world would be lost.

A PARTICIPATORY UNIVERSE

The Chinese word *mang* describes (among its other meanings, like all Chinese words) a legendary species of bird with a single eye and a single wing. Two of these birds, when united, are able to see clearly and to fly. It's an undeniably lyrical image, not all that unlike the concept voiced by the character of Aristophanes in Plato's *Symposium:* that each original self, entire, was split between two people (of the same or the opposite sex)—each of whose lifelong search for one another is merely an expression of the self's desire to regain its wholeness. The romantic strings within me vibrate to such an idea, the way a violin will produce a sympathetic resonance with another violin in the same room when both have been tuned correctly to the same natural frequency.

Nevertheless, an existential chord is also struck within me, one which resonates in agreement with Carolyn Heilbrun's statement:

Those in a marriage should not become, in the words of ancient law, one person, but rather a multiplicity of persons. . . . If your companion is incapable of surprising you, you are indeed in an institution . . . good marriages, in literature as in life, partake more of friendship than romance . . . marriage differs from desire, since in marriage one had better find his or her conversation interesting.

This doesn't mean that Heilbrun thinks marriage an evasion, denial, or surrender of sex; on the contrary, "One of the saddest and costliest convictions of our culture is that friendship and sex prevail in separate spheres."†

Coded Message #17
They know each other so well now that they are beyond finishing each other's sentences: they hear each other's unspoken sentences. He tells her, and she tells him, that whichever of them dies first, the other won't be all that lonely, since it is perfectly possible for each one of them, alone, to conduct a full conversation between the two of them: "I know what she would've said to that!"; "I can hear his answer as if he were in the room!" (This makes arguing difficult while they are still alive, however, since when one does manage to restrain him/herself from making that specially gratuitous nasty comment, the other hears it being silently thought, anyway.) Sometimes they speak in a shorthand

† Heilbrun, "Hers" column, *op. cit.* Two hundred and fifty years earlier, Mary Astell, in *Some Reflections Upon Marriage,* wrote, "He who does not make Friendship the chief Inducement to his Choice, and prefer it before any other Consideration, does not deserve a good Wife." (Re-publication of 1730 edition by Source Book Press, New York, 1970), p. 18.

unintelligible to other people. Each understands volumes in the other's one-word reference.

That striven-for autonomy, that meeting between equals, has hardly been helped by the ancient marriage law to which Heilbrun refers; the law, in fact, defined the one person that a husband and wife became—*as* the husband. Nor is this the Chinese *mang* image. Instead, it's an image of one half-bird disappearing, subsumed into the other half-bird—which in turn blithely flaps about declaring that it can see and fly.

But in those moments, those "beads of sensation," those days sometimes oh glorious weeks when two people in a marriage actually do approach each other autonomously yet against a ground rich with shared past exchanges—ah, then the bird's eyes see as if through coherent light, and the bird soars.

Coded Message #18
For once to say without abjectness or fear of it, without caveat: that I love you, my darling, with the oldest deepest wisest most human most poet part of me and always will never a chance of anything else you the child's expression settling in the west, you the nightmare, you the breaker down of doors you the maker of omelettes while I read The New York Times in a poem, you who nod now and understand later, you who can spell, you who are learning to laugh, you so punished by grace you can never even enjoy it, you for whose youngest particle the oldest particle of mine reaches, you who are the bold faun dancing the dance of the shy faun as disguise, you who are too obsessed with the inevitable to be a fatalist, you who somewhere are still eternally taking the hairpins out of my hair one by one, you who have such power and never knew it while I knew the power I had and never could use it, you who remember what I said before I forget to say it—one biosec of yours and one of mine are permanently helixed in the RNA of eternity. Is it any wonder that we can't, every single day, live up to that?

The rest of the time is lived with *intimations of intimacy,* although the unspoken subtext language may, even in such times, express a "partnering." Lincoln Kirstein unwittingly described this in his book *Ballet Alphabet:* "Dancers, who, from habit or preference, have frequently danced together, come to have a sense of each other's physical presence, which translated into terms of dancing, is revealed to an audience as an exquisite mutual awareness or superhuman courtesy."

The notion of real complementarity—which is *not* at all like the fusing of personality and even less like the subsuming of one element into another—also has become an essential part of the way in which physicists now regard their science, via a concept introduced by Niels Bohr. Dr. Fritjof Capra, himself a physicist, writes:

At the subatomic level, matter does not exist with certainty at definite places, but rather shows *"tendencies to exist,"* and atomic events do not occur with certainty at definite times and in definite ways, but rather show *"tendencies to occur."* . . . Quantum theory has thus demolished the classical concepts of solid objects and of strictly deterministic laws of nature . . . subatomic particles can only be understood [by the physicist] as interconnections between the preparation of an experiment and the subsequent measurement. . . . The human observer constitutes the final link in the chain of observational processes. . . . The classical ideal of an objective description of nature is no longer valid.[7]

Another physicist, J. A. Wheeler, suggested substituting the word *participator* for *observer* in an experiment, since *"the universe is a participatory universe."* (Italics mine.)[8]

It may seem that I stray a bit far afield in using metaphors of the New Physics to describe or analyze marriage. Yet this seems to me necessary, because women and men both have for so long viewed marriage as a static, not dynamic, state, an institution defined and proscribed by the patriarchal limitation of Man—and yes, of Woman. We all need to be startled into a realization of just how relative that view is, just how much it has been quantified. Consequently, relativity theory and quantum theory are quite useful here. If women and men of the twenty-first century are, in Sand's words, to "break and re-form" the marriage bond into something that *lives in the interconnections*, something nourishing to both and respectful of each, something that answers human needs instead of circumscribing them, then it seems to me that we must all experiment with radically new approaches to committed relationships.

Coded Message #19

They catch courage from each other like sparks. They are at a party for a pianist friend, after his concert. It is the mid-1960's.

For months, in California, farmworkers have been trying to gain recognition for their union; for months, all across the country, a consumer boycott of grapes and lettuce has been growing in strength, to pressure the growers into negotiation with the farmworkers' union. The after-concert gala party is being given as a promotional event in the showroom of the piano manufacturer whose instrument their friend, the concert artist, plays exclusively. Grand pianos stand everywhere, their lids propped open, their harps agleam inside. The invited guests mill about and chat, being served champagne by the only black people present— uniformed male waiters. A long table stands at the far end of the room, laden with bowls of caviar and platters of Brie and finewheat breads. At the very center of the table, a massive silver platter is heaped high with grapes—green, red, and purple grapes spilling their challenge to the farmworkers' misery like a cornucopia or a proclamation. She tries to chat. He tries to be pleasant. They exchange a glance. They go together to the host to express their discomfort about the grapes. Perhaps he has not heard of the well-publicized boycott? The host is defensive and defiant. He has served grapes intentionally; he does not approve of farmworkers "disrupting business." He walks away. The two of them are left staring at the grapes. (They both happen to like grapes.) The two of them exchange another glance. No words are spoken. They move swiftly to the table and take up armfuls of the fruit, then walk even more quickly to the nearest pianos and dump the grapes into the harps, piano after piano, squishing the grapes thoroughly down between the strings. The guests freeze in disbelief, watching this. The waiters murmur and laugh (very quietly). The couple scoop up two glasses of champagne and loudly toast (1) the farmworkers and (2) the black waiters. Then they set down their glasses and sweep out of the party. In years to come, they will wonder, separately and together, about the efficacy of the act (grandiose? stagily outrageous? self-indulgent?), and will express real mortified guilt about having harmed artistic instruments (pianos forgodsake). But that is beside the point. At the time, it seemed the only honorable thing to do: they try to reason with the host, they exchange a glance, no words are spoken, they act. They catch courage from each other like sparks.

If, as feminists have been positing for a long time, the relation between the sexes is the primary cause for all the other anguish the human species is enduring; if that division and alienation, being the oldest of oppressions, has been indeed the model for

racism, class division, nationalism, war, poverty, and ecological di-
saster, then clearly this root cause must be solved; it is the key to
unlocking the other solutions. Comparably, if one woman and
one man are a microcosm for the planetary sexism imposed by
the images of Man and Woman, then marriage is a key within
the key—since it is both a structural symbol of the patriarchal system at its worst *and* an experiment in living together in (at least
some) harmony, at its best. It is, politically speaking, a little universe. So far, that universe has been observed by Man's classical
concepts and strictly deterministic laws. It is time that we
demolished these by a quantum theory of the emotions and a relativity theory of perceptions, thereby admitting that this little
universe must be acknowledged as a participatory one.

We can look to music theory for another metaphor: "In music,
six notes of equal time value create a rhythmic ambiguity—are
they 2 groups of 3, or 3 groups of 2? This ambiguity has a name:
hemiolia."[9] Chopin's Waltz, Opus 42, or Etude, Opus 25, No. 2
are superb examples of hemiolia. So, in all its complexities, is a
marriage—unless one dogmatically and narrow-mindedly insists
(as has Man) that a rhythmic ambiguity must be heard only as
one of its possible rhythms. That, as we've seen, is pure sexual
fundamentalism.

Still another angle of the holographic microcosm of marriage
was revealed (again) by the Chinese, in two different meanings
of the same word: *woo* can mean a cloud or fog of confusion
brought about by the female principle and the male principle of
the universe becoming alienated and not responding to one another; *woo* written as a different Chinese character also means "a
state between emptiness and nothingness."[10] It is that state—
ethically, emotionally, practically, and spiritually—which most
societies on this planet are rapidly approaching, or at which they
have already arrived.

Coded Message #20

*I am a woman trying to hold together the center of a whirlpool,
trying to make whole what is fragmenting, trying to understand
the density of what is presenting itself as utterly simple, the simplicity of what is presenting itself as hopelessly tangled. It will
not be accomplished by fear, I know. Neither will it be accomplished by pity.*

At the heart of a participatory universe lies *interdependence,* but an interdependence of equally integral and integrated parts— not an interdependence based on unacknowledged *de*pendence. George Eliot ironically described this unacknowledged dependence in "The Spanish Gypsy":

> Women know no perfect love:
> Loving the strong, they can forsake
> the strong;
> Man clings because the being whom
> he loves is weak and needs him.

At a 1980 UNITAR[11]-sponsored gathering in Oslo, Norway, about seventy women from different countries met to discuss the subject "Creative Women in Changing Societies." The respected Japanese feminist writer Keiko Higuchi electrified the plenary session with the simplicity of her recommendation: she noted that in Japanese society men seemed incapable of locating their underpants. Every morning, Higuchi explained with a straight face, a Japanese man asks his wife, "Where are my underpants?" and every morning she finds them for him—in the same drawer or cabinet or shelf where they always lie. Higuchi hypothesized that if, in concert on the same morning, all Japanese women were to answer, "I don't know," the entire Japanese system of government and economics would fall. Men could not dress, go to work, function. In closing, she humbly said that of course she didn't know whether such a situation existed in other cultures, nor did she wish to make impolite cultural assumptions, but she did suggest (discreetly, to be sure) that if similar situations existed elsewhere, a bloodless world revolution might be accomplished in a single day if women in all nations simply responded to the Underpants Issue with the radical, incendiary phrase *"I don't know."* When the distinguished international membership at the plenary session had recovered from a sisterly hilarity of recognition at her humorous and wise recommendation, and when we had wiped the tears of laughter from our eyes, the rise of collective consciousness in the room could have been measured by a seismograph.‡

‡ A recent study published by the *American Journal of Public Health* found that the death of a husband has little effect on a wife's longevity, but the death of a wife severely shortens a husband's life (unless he finds another woman to marry). Widowed men between the ages of fifty-five and sixty, for

Coded Message ⚹21
The central reason for women's lack of independence is the (un-acknowledged) dependence of men. If men seriously could admit their dependence, then women would be freed from having to ex-press a lack of independence for them, by projection.

This would be an expanding universe, a participatory universe, a universe coming to consciousness by a recursive conscious awareness of itself. This would be a marriage in the process of ex-amining and discovering itself, an interconnection of particles ex-changing information even through the medium of interference patterns, since each part would be equal to the sum of all the parts.

DREAM DUETS

It is not impossible—this holographic, hemiolic, recursive, rela-tivistic, quantum relationship, this participatory and self-examin-ing universe. "I know he dreams me," wrote Rosellen Brown, "I know because I dream his dreams." The dream selves of a wife and a husband have been known to conduct their own subtext di-alogues somewhat independently of the waking exchange between conscious speakers. Dr. Ann Faraday, a scientist who specializes in dream research, calls these dialogues "dream duets": "One person has a dream, drops it into his partner's court, and awaits the re-turn shot . . . a kind of nonverbal communication carried on be-tween two people below the level of waking consciousness, reflect-ing thoughts, feelings, and fears about each other which might not otherwise become available."[12] To "available," I would add "articulatable." Faraday feels that if the duet partners articulate their dreams to one another, in what is at first a "safe" means of speaking unspeakable feelings (safe because who can be blamed

---

example, have a mortality rate 60 percent higher than that of married men in the same age span. Widowers who remarry, however, have lower mortality rates than their married counterparts. (See "A Wife Helps—and Two Wives Help Even More," *Ms.*, February 1982, p. 13.) In her book *The Future of Marriage* (World Publishing Company, 1972), Dr. Jessie Bernard reported studies showing that the suicide rate in the United States is twice as high for single men as for married men, but that married women showed greater mental-health impairment, phobic reactions, depressive tendencies, and fear of nervous breakdown than either married men or single women. Marriage—as an institution—clearly has nutritional value for men.

for their dreams?), such communication will cumulatively disclose truths which can, depending on their depth and rigidity, either end a relationship that needs to be ended or save a relationship that is capable of new vitality.

Coded Message #22

Her Dream Self: *He is in his study, writing, ignoring the world, daily necessities, me, these damn telegrams and anger. I go to my study to try to work, but the telephone has cloned itself like the broom in* The Sorcerer's Apprentice, *and keeps on doing so: my study is filled from floor to ceiling with telephones of varying sizes, all ringing.*

His Dream Self: *She is on the phone as always, blind to our forest of tragedy for her trees of momentary crisis. I must answer the insistent knocks at the front door, despite my terror that they mean no good. She does not respond to my pleas that we at least answer the door together. So I go alone, to see with horror a huge malevolent eye peering at me through the keyhole.*

Her Waking Self: *Did you call about that appointment you were supposed to make today?*

His Waking Self: *No, not yet. I'm a bit groggy this morning; I didn't sleep well last night.*

A dream duet, once articulated, can be perfected to a degree where the actual dreams are not necessary. One of the partners pretends a nightmare—to evoke a weary, condescending comfort, even possibly a comfort aware of the double pretense. But a comfort all the same, however hollow or temporary or tricked into expression. The comforter is as grateful for the trick's efficacy as is the comforted. Even more grateful, perhaps?

If a higher magnification of the seemingly solid body of the marriage can be managed, then that solid, fixed, intransigent form will disappear via the examination—leaving the subtext, the interference pattern resonating on the electromagnetic field of the dream selves that dreamed each other in the first place. At a higher magnification still, the particles reveal themselves as reconstitutable wholes, each with its own inviolable integrity—no matter how they may have seemed to merge, seemed to affirm or resent the merging.

How often, for instance, have I wondered why it seems that I write down the griefs, the angers, the embattled stases between my husband and myself, more frequently than I record the breakthroughs, the moments of delight, the times of homey pleasure or genuine joy? Is it, I have wondered, because "the happiest women, like the happiest nations, have no history" (George Eliot again but borrowed from Tolstoy)? Or is it because I am falling into mere reaction against a tradition that has defined women as speaking of intimate love relationships only ever in positive terms, love being, we're told, "Woman's whole existence"? Or is it because—

Coded Message ✵23

Another almost-spring, another dying fire releasing one last flame on the hearth. And the same couple—a different woman and a different man now—sitting before it. Out of time, out of mind. He speaks of choice, she of desire. Neither quite understands what it is neither understands. We each observe the same laws of physics, but every individual perspective is unique. This woman and this man are relative(s). Each flattens in dimension (but only to the one perceiving, not to the self) with the speed of the other's change, because each is changing in time, and in time time is distorted. She speaks of choice, he of desire—as if in fact all energy and all mass were not equivalent. Salt-water wells from the eye as if the eye were a mountain spring, the water fresh. "All of astrophysics," says the scientist, "is about nature's attempt to release the energy in matter."

—*all of feminist politics*, types a woman onto a flat page aswarm with atoms, *is about the same thing*.

Or is it because I have not seriously admitted *my* dependence, thus freeing him from having to express his lack of independence *for* me, by projection? Was my question already answered by Käthe Kollwitz, showing me my own face years before I was born:

"Recently I began reading my old diaries. . . . I wrote nothing when Karl and I . . . made each other happy; but long pages when we did not harmonize. As I read I distinctly felt what a half-truth [*like a half-bird?*] a diary presents. . . . Karl was always at my side. And that is a happiness that I have fully realized only in these last years— that he and I are together. . . . He is no longer the same man he once was, as I am no longer the same woman."

This is a quote from Kollwitz's *Diary and Letters*, as excerpted in *Käthe Kollwitz: Woman and Artist*, by Martha Kearns.[13]

Kearns notes further that when Kollwitz's husband died, she recorded the event in her diary very simply: "Karl has died, July 19, 1940." And Kearns adds, just as simply, that "From that day Käthe used a cane to help her walk."

INDRA'S NET

On what is the bead of sensation strung? Is it strung merely on the "dailiness" inhabited by relative strangers dancing out courtesies, dreaming in nightmares, trying to see and fly?

Coded Message #24
In the preface to the Princeton edition of Kierkegaard's Fear and Trembling, *Walter Lowrie writes that the reader would hardly guess that* Fear and Trembling *and* Repetition *"both deal with the self-same theme. . . . Søren Kierkegaard's unhappy love; for the analogues he chooses as illustrations of his crisis (Abraham, Job, etc.) seem at first sight infinitely remote from the subject." (In other words, mere human love seems at first sight infinitely remote from such Serious Subjects as life, death, sacrifice, suffering, faith, endurance, existential* Angst, *and religious ecstasy.) Depends on the quality of one's first sight, Walter.*

There is a last question that also must be relegated to the way things might seem to the patriarchal viewpoint, whether at first or second sight. The opening analogy of this chapter could easily become the victim of the fundamentalist tendency to dichotomize: *either* one must settle for the uncommitted affair's two-dimensional intensity *or* a committed relationship of muted (for which read: dull) three-dimensionality. Of course, most women would choose the latter; many men the former. And they do. But those who would assume that this suggests a trade-off which is simply "in the nature of things" are wrong—however often this has been suggested in the works of male writers. Indeed, it has become a high-level cliché. Even the seeming separation of subject matter here (sexual passion examined in Chapter IV; committed relationships in Chapter V) could be interpreted by some to mean that I too assume that desire and sexual passion can occur only in an affair, while love (and, certainly, desire) but not sexual passion can occur in marriage.

But what if the intense two-dimensional acrylic suddenly deep-

ened to three-dimensionality within committed love? (And let's
face it: many, even most, affairs are, throughout—or at least toward the trailing-off point—dull, dull, dull.)

I think of Li Ch'ing-Chao, China's greatest woman poet, and
her poet husband, Chao Ming-ch'en. They lived during the Sung
Dynasty, approximately 1080 to 1150, and their marriage has been
celebrated in China for almost a thousand years as the ideal relationship. Ch'ing-Chao's poetry, mostly in the *tz'u* and *shih* forms,
ranges in subject matter from satirical treatments of the misogyny
inherent in the Confucian code through courageously political
works about court intrigues of the day to exquisitely moving lyrics
on the loneliness of widowhood and old age. But perhaps her
greatest poems are those in which she extols the emotional, intellectual, *and* erotic counterpoint between two autonomous individuals in a committed love relationship. These poems are deliciously sexy, and also are replete with intelligence and vigor.
"Light filled our lives like incense in our sleeves," she writes. "We
toasted each other in warm wine / and wrote poems on flowered
paper." Elsewhere, she describes how she and her husband
pawned their clothing in order to purchase rubbings of stone in-
scriptions and small antique bronzes for their art collection. They
would sit together in the evening and meditatively admire a new
acquisition for the duration of one candle's burning, or they
would play their own game of rivalry: who was best at identifying
lines of poetry quoted by the other. Sometimes, she writes, they
were so filled with enjoyment of their own and other poets' writings and so filled with love for one another that they fell to
laughing with pure pleasure, causing the teacups from which
they had been sipping to tumble from their laps. It must be
admitted that Ch'ing-Chao's own life and her married life
with Ming-ch'en were unconventional for their time and place.
They shocked and dismayed many people. Yet they each continued to examine the self and the other in their poetry and their
daily lives.[14]

So a committed relationship that is as vivid as it is dimensional
is not impossible, as we've always suspected. Which isn't even the
most important point, however, as both my husband and I have
believed. The time comes when a sag does occur in the middle of
a marriage, where the novelty has gone and yet some bold new
shamelessness has yet to emerge; this can either end the relation-

ship or else implode it into an intensity that is not muted or dull, that doesn't settle for anything—that is experimental, sexually passionate, and totally unpredictable. It's hard work. It's perilous. It's exhilarating. That, dear reader, is why I've stayed married. Because when that third thing happens, it beggars metaphor.

For what would happen if the beads became conscious of themselves, and chose to become self-propagating? What would happen if each bead—while being wholly and uniquely itself—reflected not only the one strung nearest to it but every other bead it could intuit?

Then the beds would be strung along Indra's Net—a metaphor used in Mahayana Buddhism for the interpenetration of all things in the cosmos. The *Avatamsaka Sutra* describes this net, stretching endlessly through the universe, the vertical strands spanning time, the horizontal ones running through space. Strung along the net are lucent beads, each irradiated by the (coherent?) light of existence, and each reflecting that light from every other bead in the vast network. Each bead is therefore not only itself but is every other bead, in that it is *involved* with every other bead.* This involvement is active, dynamic, continuous—a dance or hum or buzz so pervasive that it even can appear as stillness, the way that the "restlessness" of subatomic particles reacting to confinement can appear passive when unrelativistically viewed in an inert object like a stone or a chair. Or a marriage. So infinite can the movement be, in fact, that motion and rest become reconciled as the same thing.

Each bead of sensation is, in effect, a holograph through which the light of communication has streamed, illuminating the dimensions of that particular bead with the all-dimensional energy of boundless communication. How like this is to Bessie Head's definition, in A *Question of Power*,[15] of love—"a mutual feeding [of] each other, not one living on another like a ghoul."

To live this way would be to intensify the holograph's colors, through curiosity and desire, to a point where they would be equal to its depth—palpable, vivid, confidently sensual. Such colors *in depth* and not on a flat canvas would be like colors color-blind Man and Woman have never imagined, colors possible only between individuals who know each other deeply enough

---

* The last Cantos of "Paradiso" in Dante's *Commedia* extol a startlingly similar ecstatic vision.

to know that they are strangers and, at an even higher magnification, eternally and exquisitely—mystery, glory, and wonder—that they are the same.

Such a marriage might hang in space, a work of art propagating itself by self-examination, conducting itself with the audacity and courage of absolute solidity yet ceaselessly risking that solidity by acknowledging the perpetual movement within it, no preconceived outcome certain, a movement of two interacting components refracting a communication of information back and forth along the coherent lightbeam of their love, an ongoing act of freedom.

Coded Message #25

Mellowness.

The sense of tension cresting and ebbing, the melting of pretensions and pretenses, the excitement of uncertainty but also of assurance, volumes read in one exchanged glance, the simple looking forward to not-quite-but-almost-as-if endless days and evenings and nights and dawns stretching ahead in calm rhythms of living, the blessedness of the daily, the treasuring of the common, the ordinary, the forgettable. Mellowness.

Only through the aging process does wine lose its sharpness, cheese gain its sharpness. I thirst not only for your vintage self but for my own. The depth, body, bouquet, rich round fullness that goes slowly to the head in a lasting intoxication. This is the beauty in you I've always longed for with all my knife-edged acidity, the wild peace at once still with motion so furious no eye can witness it, the silence so complete that it brims with all sound, the dreamt touch felt while sleeping, real.

And I was right to have chosen, right to have waited, right to have lasted, right to have fled, right to have dared, right to have returned, right to have hoped, right to have assumed, right to have demanded, right to have changed, right to have tried, right to have believed. And he was right to have chosen, right to have waited, right to have lasted, right to have fled, right to have dared, right to have returned, right to have hoped, right to have assumed, right to have demanded, right to have changed, right to have tried, right to have believed.

We were right to have loved, to have kept and kept and kept inventing love.

See how the hands of two such artists pass through each other as they clasp.

VI

BLOOD TYPES

An Anatomy of Kin

No people are ever as divided as those of the same blood.
—Mavis Gallant

I had crossed the line. I was *free*. But there was no one to
welcome me to the land of freedom. I was a stranger in a
strange land; my home . . . my father, my mother, my
brothers, my sisters, and my friends were . . . down in
Maryland. But I was free, and *they* should be free.
—Harriet Tubman

The principal feature of this [mechanistic] order is that
the world is regarded as constituted of entities which are
outside of each other . . . separately existent, indivisible,
and unchangeable "elementary particles" which are the
fundamental "building blocks" of the entire universe. . . .
The theory of relativity was the first significant indication
in physics of the need to question the mechanistic order.
. . . The quantum theory presents, however, a much more
serious challenge to this mechanistic order.
—David Böhm

The "traditional" nuclear family has undergone fission. It really
never existed to begin with, despite the Right Wing's rabid defense of it as the basic building block of society. Yet even liberals
can fall into the trap of heated arguments and analyses about
how and why the American family is "suddenly" changing. Actually, the one permanent quality about the family is that it always
has been in a state of perpetual transformation.

What we think of as the traditional nuclear family is a recent
development. The Norman Rockwell depiction of the small-town
unit (breadwinner husband, homemaker wife, two and a half

children* statistically, a cocker spaniel, one or two cars, a picket fence, washing machine, and television set) is less than a hundred years old—a newfangled experiment masquerading as the Way It Always Has Been. Anthropology and history reveal a vast repertory of family forms that disappear, reappear, coexist, and differ within and across cultures, including blood relationships, kinship systems, language alliances, loyalty groups, households, tribes, networks, clans, communes, the "stem" family, the "conjugal" family, the "pioneer" family, the "extended" family, exogamous and endogamous families, and many more.[1] Even the so-called American Family was always more various than we are led to believe, exuberantly reflecting different racial, ethnic, class, and religious patterns.

The one common denominator of "family" might be said to be a combination of endurance, affection, resilience, and *some bond* (economic, philosophical, cultural, or chosen) *deliberately acknowledged to be larger than the individual elements participating within it.* And the notion of family does in fact persist —and even proliferates, diversifies, and strengthens—despite Rightist campaigns to destroy it by narrowly defining it out of existence, and despite their sexual- and religious-fundamentalist attacks on feminism for having energized and supported precisely such growth and variety.

Ironically, in this case feminists are the conservatives in the true sense of the word: *conserving* the family by permitting it to redefine itself.

THE REAL AMERICAN FAMILY

The great tribal forms may be vanishing (in Western culture, that is), but new kinship systems flourish all around us: the breadwinner wife/househusband pioneers, the homosexual household, the colleague family that bonds intensely over shared work, the "serial marriage," the single-parent family, the long-term friend-roommate cathexis, the live-in-lovers relationships, and still other vital and evolving forms:

• Only 15.9 percent of all households include a father as the

---

* I always wondered about that statistical half child. Now I know: according to the same Right Wing, it must be the fetus.

sole wage earner, a mother as a full-time homemaker, and at least one child. (And a 1977 Yankelovich Monitor study found that one third of all full-time housewives planned to enter the salaried work force at some time in their lives.)

• 18.5 percent includes both the father and the mother as wage earners, plus one or more children at home.

• 30.5 percent of households consist of married couples with no children living at home.

• 6.2 percent are headed by women who are single parents, with one or more children at home.

• 0.6 percent are headed by single-parent males, with one or more children at home.

• 2.5 percent consist of unrelated persons living together.

• 20.6 percent are single-person households. (Of these, almost a third are women over 65, more than a third of whom live below the federal poverty level.)

• The remaining 5.3 percent consist of female- or male-headed households that include relatives other than spouses or children.

These statistics are from the U.S. Statistical Abstract, 1977. Children are defined as persons under eighteen years of age. *The government's definition of family does not include single individuals or unrelated individuals living together. A feminist definition of family does.* Therefore, "households" is the basis of this analysis.[2]

These changes have been effected not only by women's desires to enter the public world, and by men's desires (not always as openly acknowledged) to participate more in the raising of children, but also by automation, a shorter workday or workweek, more leisure time, chronic unemployment, the part-time job as an option, etc.

What the American Right Wing, as a "family fundamentalist" movement, is trying to protect now exists even less than ever before. To the extent that their ideal nuclear unit—as the central cog in the mechanistic machine they view as society—ever did exist, its very qualities of isolated defensiveness gave rise to intimate atrocities which were denied and hidden, or even sometimes hideously affirmed. In the United States, only in the last decade or so have true statistics begun to emerge about the almost endemic frequency of battery, marital rape, child abuse and sexual molestation, and other scarring emotional "traditions" prevalent in the apple-cheeked normality of the nuclear family—in all classes, economic groups, and racial, religious, and ethnic categories.[3]

The proliferation of articles, studies, books, and entire scholarly journals on the issue of family violence is uncovering statistics which, although sufficiently horrifying in themselves, still are only prefaces to the full story. It is estimated that *between 50 and 80 percent of the cases of family violence still go unreported.*

Have such discoveries helped the family-fundamentalists to stop and rethink what it is they are so passionately defending? Yes and no. They stopped, tried to chafe two brain cells together to produce a ratiocinative thought, and came up with more antilogic. Phyllis Schlafly opposes federal funding of shelters for battered women because such shelters are merely resorts for wives running away from their responsibilities; Christian "crusaders" attack legislation outlawing corporal punishment in the public schools, and also defend "the rod" as parental discipline at home; the Rightist coalition currently influencing the Reagan administration's "family policy" lobbies against federal backing of refuges for and research on the victims of child sexual abuse; clearly such research and such refuges "invade the privacy" of the family (the subtext reads that such legislation, research, and support networks invade the power of the *patriarch* in a mechanistically ordered view of society).

Yet despite all the campaigns in the U.S. and Europe to preserve family "privacy," or in the Middle East and Latin Catholic countries to preserve family "honor,"[4] and in the Far East to preserve family "duty"—despite all attempts to tighten familial bonds into ropes of bondage, family forms continue to change and grow, like living organisms: through *interaction* and *in context of the whole.* That "whole" has something to do with human need—for warmth, intimacy, endurance, trust, a shared history.

THE PASSIONATE REFLECTION

Dorothy Dinnerstein[5] has said that the family is both a teaching structure (to the infant) and a support system, that it instructs us in the skill of living amicably (or at least cooperatively) with others—an irreplaceably humanizing experience:

Certain aspects of the need for family are so profound that people invent deities with parental qualities to whom they can be related throughout life. . . . People can find all sorts of "magic parents" in adult life—in spiritual entities, in friends, in sex partners, and in themselves . . . [the magic parent being] a nurturant presence from whom one can learn, and also giving a sense of another existence in which one's own is passionately reflected.[6]

Dinnerstein is dedicated, not coincidentally, to the idea that men must learn how to act as such parents—magical and otherwise: "The major thing men can do is child care. This would profoundly alter all gender arrangements." The comparable big step for women would be to let men do this, despite our sometimes understandable unwillingness to relinquish the one little area of power we've been allowed. The issue is central because in any society where the person who takes care of the next generation is female (and seems to have life-and-death power over day-to-day existence, however little objective power she has), then the female becomes the scapegoat, in Dinnerstein's words, leaving "another category of human being (male) who by contrast burns clean and pure and is just plain human. . . . When men take an equal part in early child care, men will no longer represent uncontaminated humanity."[7]

"Uncontaminated humanity" is obviously a mechanistic notion —a spotless, dry, everything-in-its-place universe where some cosmic Mussolini with a white beard makes the galaxies run on time. But of course the galaxies don't, just as human beings don't, just as atoms don't. And atoms—once thought to be the building blocks of the universe, are now known to contain their building blocks—electrons, protons, and neutrons—which in turn are subject to further change into hundreds of various types of unstable (shocking concept to the Right Wing: unstable) particles, which in turn are postulated to contain quarks, partons, or hadrons, which in turn . . . Just so the family, whether "nuclear" or extended, "traditional" or spontaneous, is comprised of individual beings, each a universe in her/himself, composed in turn of a billion variables of need, change, environment, growth, desire, curiosity, miracle, movement.

As long as "family" is degraded by being used as a means to differentiate an Us from a Them, or to define and constrain the individual capacities of those who constitute it, or to fix itself in a permanent state or location or attitude—then "family" is doomed to destroy its own components and ultimately itself, because it is in fact *going against what we now know to be "nature"*:

The key features of the quantum theory that challenge mechanism are:

1. Movement is in general *discontinuous*, in the sense that action is constituted of *indivisible quanta* (. . . an electron, for example, can go from one state to another without passing through any states in between).

2. Entities, such as electrons, can show different properties . . . depending on the environmental context within which they exist and are subject to observation.

3. Two entities, such as electrons, which initially combine to form a molecule and then separate, show a peculiar non-local relationship, which can best be described as a non-causal connection of elements that are far apart.[8]

Or, to put it more simply: one night at dinner when our son was about four years old, the three of us had been involved in a lively conversation on the inalienable rights of children to defend themselves from adult oppression (see Chapter VII). Seemingly out of nowhere, Blake, looking back and forth between Kenneth and me, announced in a tone of great satisfaction, "I am the child of a comet and a meteor living together in the West Village."

A FAMILY REUNION

If politics is to learn from the New Physics—and it would benefit enormously from doing so—then we might realize that just as in the subatomic world *an entity can be both a particle and a wave at the same time*, so "family" can be both an intimate grouping and a universal network at the same time. Abstract and sappy pronouncements about "brotherhood" and "the family of Man" [sic] have about as much relevance in this context as Billy Graham's definition of god has in the context of NGC4258 (M106)—a galaxy with an "exploding" nucleus (just like the family) in the Canes Venatici I Cloud of galaxies. Plastic "brotherhood" comes to us from the same folks who brought us Auschwitz, Hiroshima, and Biafra, and before that, the Crusades, the "Conquest" of the New World, the slave trade. Today, in the classic traditions of the family of Man, they are bringing us Beirut, El Salvador, Northern Ireland, Johannesburg, Campuchea, and Poland (as samples).

Naturally, if the brotherly definition of family has an Us vs. Them implication then family as a matter of course transfers its isolate loyalties into nationalism. Not for nothing does the word *patriotism* stem from the meaning of loyalty to father authority.

Yet there *are* glimpses of a real universal family, a community already connected and potentially interconnecting via the very persons whose entire existences, for the most part, have been kept within the "family sphere," those defined by Man and affirmed by Woman as the eternal nurturers, the keepers of the family: women.

Mary Daly's lovely turn-the-concept-inside-out phrase, "The Sisterhood of Man" seems not only a hope but a dynamic actuality —since it's grounded not in abstract notions of cooperation but in survival need, not in static posture but in active gesture, not in vague statements of similarity but in concrete experience shared to an astonishing degree, despite cultural, historical, linguistic, and other barriers. Labor contractions feel the same everywhere. So does rape and battery. I don't necessarily agree with many feminists that women will always have access to some mysteriously inherent biological nexus, but I do believe that Elizabeth Cady Stanton was onto something when she signed letters, "Thine in the bonds of *oppressed* womanhood" (italics mine). Let us hope—and act to ensure—that as women break those very bonds of oppression, the process of freeing the majority of humanity will so transform human consciousness that women will not use our freedom to be isolatedly individuated as men have done. In the meanwhile, the bond *does* exist; let's use it creatively.

Not that the mechanistic universe inhabited by the family of Man takes notice of our bond, this quarky interrelationship between the hardly visible subparticles that merely serve to keep Man and his family alive. No, such particles are unimportant, fantastical, charming perhaps (as quarks or "the fair sex" tend to be). But they are to be taken no more seriously than fairytales.

Yet if Hans Christian Andersen characters so diverse as the Little Mermaid, the Robber Girl, the Snow Queen, and the Little

Match Girl had convened a meeting to discuss ways of bettering their condition, one could imagine that the world press would cover that as a big story. When something even more extraordinary, because more real, happened in Andersen's own city for three weeks during July of 1980, it barely made the news.

Approximately ten thousand women from all over the planet began arriving in Copenhagen even before the formal opening on July 14 of the United Nations Mid-Decade Conference for women. The conference was to become a great, sprawling, rollicking, sometimes quarrelsome, highly emotional, unashamedly idealistic, unabashedly pragmatic, visionary family reunion. In 1975, the U.N. had voted to pay some attention to the female more-than-half of the human population for one year—International Women's Year—but extended the time to a decade after the indignant outcry of women who had been living, literally, in the "International Men's Year" for approximately ten millennia of partriarchy. Still, here we were, in the middle of "our" decade, in Copenhagen. We came in saris and caftans, in blue jeans and chadors, in African geles, business suits, and dresses. We were women with different priorities, ideologies, political analyses, cultural backgrounds, and styles of communication. The few reports that made it into the American press at all predictably if sadly emphasized those differences, thereby overlooking the big story—that these women forged new and strong connections.

In fact, there were two overlapping meetings going on in Copenhagen. One was the official U.N. conference itself—which many feminists accurately had prophesied would be more a meeting of governments than of women. Its delegates were chosen by governments of U.N. member states to psittaceously repeat national priorities—as defined by men. There is of course no nation in the world governed by women (yet), despite a few female heads of state who by their exception prove the rule.

The official conference reflected the government orientation: many delegations were headed by men and many more were led by "safe" women whose governments were certain wouldn't make waves. This is not to say that there weren't some real feminists tucked away even in the formal delegations, trying gallantly to influence their respective bureaucracies toward more human concern with issues and actions that really could better women's lives. But the talents of these sisters "within" were frequently ignored or abused by their own delegations for political reasons.

A case in point was the U.S. delegation, which availed itself greedily of all the brilliant and unique expertise of Koryne Horbal (then U.S. representative to the U.N. Commission on the Status of Women), and of all the groundwork she had done on the conference for the preceding two years, but denied her any press visibility and most simple courtesies because she had been critical of the Carter administration and its official policies on women. But Horbal wasn't the only "feminist within." There were New Zealand's member of Parliament, the dynamic twenty-eight-year-old Marilyn Waring, and energetic María de Lourdes Pintasilgo, former Prime Minister of Portugal, and radical Elizabeth Reid of Australia—all of them feminists skilled in the labyrinthian ways of national and international politics, but with priority commitment to populist means of working for women—who still managed to be effective inside *and* outside the structures of their governments.

The "other" conference, semiofficially under U.N. aegis, was the NGO (Non-Governmental Organizations) Forum. It was to the Forum that "ordinary folks" came, having raised the fare via their local women's organizations, feminist alternative media, or women's religious, health, and community groups. Panels, workshops, kaffeeklatches, cultural events, and informal rap sessions abounded.

Statements emerged and petitions were eagerly signed: supporting the prostitutes in São Paulo, Brazil, who that very week, in an attempt to organize for their human rights, were being jailed, tortured, and, in one case, "accidently" executed; supporting Arab and African women organizing against the so-called cultural practice of female genital mutilation; supporting U.S. women recently stunned by the 1980 Supreme Court decision permitting federal and state denial of funds for medical aid to poor women who need safe, legal abortions—thus denying the basic human right of reproductive freedom; supporting South African women trying to keep families together under the maniacal system of apartheid; supporting the just-exiled feminist writers and activists from the U.S.S.R.; supporting women refugees of Afghanistan, Campuchea, Palestine, Cuba, and elsewhere.

Protocol aside, the excitement among women at both conference sites was electric. If, for instance, you came from Senegal with a specific concern about rural development, you would focus on workshops about that, and exchange experiences and all-important how-to's with women from Peru, India—and Montana. After one health panel, a Chinese gynecologist continued talking animatedly with her scientific colleague from the Soviet Union— Sino-Soviet saber-rattling forgotten or transcended.

Comparisons developed in workshops on banking and credit between European and American economists and the influential market women of Africa. The list of planned meetings about Women's Studies ran to three pages, yet additional workshops on the subject were created spontaneously. Meanwhile, at the International Women's Art Festival, there was a sharing of films, plays, poetry readings, concerts, mime shows, exhibits of painting and sculpture and batik and weaving, the interchanging of art techniques and of survival techniques. Exchange subscriptions were pledged between feminist magazines in New Delhi and Boston and Tokyo, Maryland and Sri Lanka and Australia. And everywhere the conversations and laughter of recognition and newfound friendships spilled over into the sidewalks of Copenhagen, often until dawn.

We ate, snacked, munched—and traded diets, like neighbor women, or family. A well-equipped Argentinian supplied a shy Korean with a tampon in an emergency. A Canadian went into labor a week earlier than she'd expected, and kept laughing hilariously between her contractions, as she was barraged with loving advice on how to breathe, where to rub, how to sit (or stand or squat), and even what to sing—in a chorus of five languages, while waiting for the prompt Danish ambulance. American women from diverse ethnic ancestries talked intimately with women who still lived in the cities, towns, and even villages from which their own grandmothers had emigrated to "the New World." We slept little, stopped caring about washing our hair, sat on the floor, and felt at home with one another.

Certainly, there were problems. Simultaneous-translation facilities, present everywhere at the official conference, were rarely available at the grass-roots Forum. This exacerbated certain sore spots, like the much-ballyhooed PLO-Israeli conflict, since many Arab women present spoke Arabic or French but not English—

the dominant language at the Forum. That conflict—played out by male leadership at both the official conference and the Forum, using women as pawns in the game—was disheartening, but not as bad as many of us had feared.

The widely reported "walkout" of Arab women during Madame Jihan Sadat's speech at the conference was actually a group of perhaps twenty women tiptoeing quietly to the exit. This took place in a huge room packed with delegates who—during all the speeches—were sitting, standing, and walking about to lobby loudly as if on the floor of the U.S. Congress (no one actually *listens* to the speeches; they're for the record). The walkout was at first easily mistaken for a group politely leaving to caucus elsewhere amid less din. Only two tepid chants delivered once outside the door, and a subsequent press conference, could have convinced anybody it was in fact a protest against Egypt's relations with Israel.

Meanwhile, back at the Forum, there was our own invaluable Bella Abzug (officially unrecognized by the Carter-appointed delegation but recognized and greeted with love by women from all over the world). Bella, working on coalition-building, was shuttling between Israelis and Arabs. Iran was, at that time, still holding the fifty-two American hostages, but Bella accomplished the major miracle of getting a pledge from the Iranian women that if U.S. mothers would demonstrate in Washington for the Shah's ill-gotten millions to be returned to the Iranian people (for the fight against women's illiteracy and children's malnutrition), then the Iranian women would march simultaneously in Teheran for the hostages to be returned home "to their mothers." Bella's sensitivity and cheerful, persistent nudging on this issue caused one Iranian woman to throw up her hands, shrug, and laugh to me, "What is with this 'Bella honey' person? She's wonderful. She's impossible. She's just like my mother."

The conference, the Forum, and the arts festival finally came to an end. Most of the official resolutions were predictably bland by the time they were presented, much less voted on. Most of the governments will act on them sparingly, if at all. Consequently, those women who went naïvely trusting that the formal U.N. procedures would be drastically altered by such a conference were bitterly disappointed. But those of us who went with no such illusions, and who put not our trust in patriarchs, were elated. Because what did *not* end at the closing sessions is that incredible "networking"—the echoes of all those conversations, the exchanged addresses—and what that will continue to accomplish.

One goal, for example, was to strengthen mechanisms for implementation of the U.N.'s Convention to End Discrimination, a document which, if signed and ratified by twenty member nations, carries the force of international law. Another was to activate, through programs of political pressure, diplomatic channels, and economic aid, the language Marilyn Waring managed to insert, via the New Zealand delegation, into the official proceedings —language which for the first time in U.N. history made the feminist analogy of women as a colonized people. By the *end* of the "Women's Decade," which the U.N. is planning to observe with another conference in 1985 in Africa, we can all look for substantive change within and in response to "The Family of Women."

Yet we might have to look hard, if our own government and our own free press still are so tediously androcentric that women (and men of conscience) can't even get the word out. Isn't it a big story when an Iraqi refugee tells an American Jewish feminist that her eleven-year-old son has just been sentenced to five years at hard labor by the Saddam Hussein regime, and the American replies, "My God, my son is just that age," and both women weep quietly in each other's embrace? Isn't it a good story when a woman from Zambia trades secrets with another from Iceland and a third from Portugal on how to endure—and be effective without losing your soul as a feminist—when you are the token woman in your ministry/parliament/government/embassy? Isn't it a story that I, for one, learned how to say *sister* in Swahili, Arabic, Chinese, Portuguese, Thai, Farsi, and Norwegian?

Hans Christian Andersen would have known a good story when he saw one. Because this was not just a fairytale. It *was* a family reunion: the trading of old secrets and newfound skills, the latest gossip about other members, the surprised delight in discovering relatives so long lost they had never been encountered, the *recognitions*, dynamism, and grudging love.

And this was only a beginning. "If all actions are in the form of discrete quanta, the interactions between different entities [e.g., electrons] constitute a single structure of indivisible links, so that the entire universe has to be thought of as an unbroken whole."[9] Or a family not only of human beings but of all sentient beings, of all matter, which is really all energy—what David Böhm calls "a totality of movement of enfoldment and unfoldment . . . [a] holomovement."[10]

This requires what I would call a *holopolitics*: a way of looking outward and inward at the same time (as if there really were a difference), of seeing and seeing *through*. Processes of creativity, of art, express this tendency; processes of power oppose it. (Yet art can be "empowering" in an utterly nonoppressive way.)

If we could learn to apply truly creative processes, as an artist does, to political problems, what might the result be? It isn't as easy as it sounds, since art is—like the electron—both an intensely individualistic and a holistically interconnected activity. But let's try. In fact, let's try to apply the process to a particular political knot which fists itself at the heart of the American experience of "family," however much ignored and denied: the knot of race and sex.

A SKIN-DEEP SISTERHOOD?

How do we penetrate the superficiality with which most feminist theory in the United States has so far dealt with racism, even in terms of the largest American "minority," Afro-Americans? This superficiality includes the recent (1978 to the present) black-white feminist "dialogues" which pop up in print various places. However important and courageous these attempts, they seem—to many of us, white and black, who first came to political activism twenty years ago in the civil-rights movement—familiar, redundant, and shallow. They are still plagued with debilitating rhetoric, and for the most part remain safely mired in the tone of black accusation and rage (however justified) and white breast-beating guilt (however inevitable as a first step). Unless we go beyond these convenient stances, however, the U.S. Feminist Movement will remain as comfortably racist as the Left in this country always has been.

Guilt politics per se is a convenient politics, since its logical end, if untransformed into hard thinking and action, is paralysis. Paralysis will not stop the double whammy of "dominative" and "aversive" racism, to use Joel Kovel's terms from his book *White Racism: A Psychohistory*.[11] (Kovel analyzes dominative racism as being woven through the fabric of society in the American South—an active racism which served as a foundation for the entire social and economic organization of the culture; aversive racism is, Kovel feels, more characteristic of the North—a passive-aggressive sort of racism which gives lip service to equality but keeps black citizens in servitude by exclusion—from jobs, schools, neighborhoods, social congress.) *Within* and in addition to the oppression of race, women of course still suffer the oppression of sex, as searingly demonstrated in a number of major books published in the past decade on the subject.[12]

As of 1980, almost 60 percent of all rape victims were black women; black women—52 percent of whom work outside the home—have a median income of only $6611; cervical cancer rates for black women are increasing, while rates are decreasing among whites; black women also suffer the highest mortality rates from both childbirth and abortion; their children suffer infant mortality rates twice as high as those of whites.

Meanwhile, back at the Women's Movement, the "aversive" form of racism still smiles its ladylike politeness far too often for comfort. It is not enough for white women to say any longer that we "dare" not include the experience, literary influence, and consciousness of black women and other women of color in our work, since we do not "share" that experience. (I never hunted a great whale or fought against Napoleon, never was a nineteenth-century governess or rafted down the Mississippi River—but that doesn't stop me from identifying with the work of Melville, Tolstoy, Charlotte Brontë, Jane Austen, or Mark Twain.) No, this has become a new excuse for excluding black women's experience (for fear of similarities even more than differences?). Nor is it any longer tolerable for white feminists to ghettoize black feminists in special panels (as happened, appallingly, at the Second Sex Conference in New York City as late as 1979) under the unethical excuse that to invite black women's involvement at every level of the conference, in every panel and at every workshop, would be to divert their energies from black priorities. As the poet Pat Parker has written:

> For the white person
> who wants to know
> how to be my friend
> The first thing you do is to forget i'm Black.
> Second, you must never forget that i'm Black.[13]

I for one, as a white woman and feminist, am sick to death of solemnly pretentious papers, conferences, books, articles, and so-called dialogues which rehash old positions without the risk of fresh thinking, and of self-perpetuating conversations between black and white feminists which end with the pronouncement that "we must open up communication between us"—after which the black women and the white women conveniently go their separate ways.

I'm impatient, yes. These Things Take Time, yes. Being stuck in the meaningless pinkish-orange sausage casement that is my skin at a time in history when this is considered Meaningful, I realize of course that it is for black feminists to determine their own priorities and tactics, yes. But it is for white feminists to begin to take some real—not rhetorical—risks, in theory, in commitment, in action. Not for suspiciously Lady Bountiful reasons, but for our own moral salvation.

The following meditation is only a beginning, flawed and itself raw, superficial, and certainly insufficient, toward that risk. It was inspired in large part by two books: *Thomas Jefferson: An Intimate History*, by Fawn Brodie,[14] and *Sally Hemmings*, by Barbara Chase-Riboud.[15]

Keep in mind, as you read, how quantum theory demonstrates that all motion takes place not smoothly but in a disjointed, discontinuous fashion—jumping with what seems to be no effort from one place to another without bothering to travel between the places. Keep in mind, too, the Döppler effect: the phenomenon of light changing color—depending on the perspective and speed of the observer.

SLAVES OF FORM: A MEDITATION ON RACE, SEX, POWER, AND ART[16] (for Susan McHenry)

The "shadow family" of Thomas Jefferson is exemplary of the deepest truths about American racism—the horror being not solely what whites did to blacks but *what relatives did to their own families*. Where does this entire vast panoply of interrelationships (complete with a baroque hierarchy of how many crossbreedings were necessary to "clear the blood") fit into a history of the family? Or is a "shadow history" necessary to contain it—this common assumption that a plantation owner had two "families": one slave, one white. The plot thins as the blood thickens.

* * *

Thomas Jefferson Hemmings, age fourteen, slave son with blue eyes and red hair and freckles, tall and gangling, the image of his father, standing as body servant behind the chair of Thomas Jefferson Randolph, age about the same, same coloring, same characteristics of appearance, grandson legal—looking like a possible set of twins. *What does this do to the mind, the sense of reality,* the reality of Jeffersonian politics, possibly the one trustable democratic tradition in America?

* * *

What does it mean: that Thomas Jefferson could seek the same woman in the features of his white legal wife Martha Wayles (dead at age thirty-four after seven pregnancies) and his illegal whiteblack blackwhite continually recategorized slave wife, mistress, concubine Sally Hemmings, *Martha Wayles' half-sister?* This was his own sister-in-law—except that she was, fortunately, out-of-law.

* * *

What does it mean: that Dolley Madison could say in 1837: "The Southern white woman is the chief slave of the master's harem"? And leave it at that. What does it mean: to know and not act, to know and know that action is impossible—and yet not act?

* * *

Power is after all not a quantity to be taken, shared, divided. Power is a *means:* of defining, categorizing, compartmentalizing— relationships, people, "things"; a means of naming, even more than of accomplishing. It goes to the most basic definition of what something is or is not, by categorizing it by what it *does.* Thus we know a stone from a peculiar cactus that appears identical to a stone because the stone sits there, the cactus grows, changes. The characteristics of something are what it does, how it exists, is, *be's.* What it does and what it is are at the deepest level inseparable, and power, which is literally in the eye of the beholder (the one who can observe) knows this. Power rightly used, then, is that which begins with respecting *what the beheld is as expressed in what it does.* Power abused is that which forces certain behavior from the beheld and then judges its characteristics backward from that doing.

Would power be abusive that witnessed the *is* in the *does,* without judging or forcing anything, then defining backward what the is is? *Is* there a witnessing without defining? Would such a definition be merely stereotypical—or truly fair?

Is the act of defining *in itself* a judgment? Is the act of categorizing in itself ultimately not the abuse? No matter how many "but equal's" accompany the deadly "separate"? If the inert stone is, as we know, composed of atoms and in turn electrons in their dance of energy over/into/in/*as* matter, then what is so "inert" about the stone, after all? It takes holopolitics to perceive holomovement.

Or is categorizing merely a recognition of life's celebratory variations-in-form of the same basic energy?

It is a natural tendency for genetically unrelated cells in tissue cultures to come together, ignoring species differences, and fuse to form hybrid cells. Inflammation and immunology must indeed be powerfully designed to keep us apart; without such mechanisms, involving considerable effort, we might have developed as a kind of flowing syncytium over the earth, without the morphogenesis of even a flower.[17]

Still, even if life itself categorizes and compartmentalizes—thus expressing the most basic defining, the most ongoing power—need we collaborate with this fundamentalism or dare we transcend it? How far could holopolitical vision read? Dare it even see death not as the great equalizer opposed to that compulsive and divisive life, but refuse both and forge some third state, beyond either?

That would be the invention of a new state of consciousness so powerful it would inevitably create a new state of reality—or else recognize, at last, that such a state has never not existed.

*   *   *

Sally Hemmings haunts—America, Jefferson, me. And Jefferson was one of the best, perhaps *the* best of the lot, of the founding "fathers." No Alexander Hamilton he, oh no. Hamilton, rumored to be part black, must express the essentially aristocratic conservative position—to survive, of course. Not Jefferson. No, he staked his life on the belief that the individual soul needs freedom and can stand that responsibility, no matter what.† He staked Sally Hemmings' soul on it, too. But he never asked her permission to do so, first.

Or perhaps he did—and perhaps she said no.

Or perhaps he did—and he forgot what she replied.

Or perhaps it was her idea in the first place, but he didn't note that, being above the petty details of ownership.

* * *

And they dare, they *dare* to speak of the sanctity of the family. They dare claim reverence for blood ties.

Oh my America, there *is* blood on your hands—and you don't even recognize it as your own.

You do not exist, white America. The agony you have created for others is *real*—but has always been to convince yourself as well as those in agony that the illusion of your existence was *as* real; that light did not move or change color when it seemed to move. You have never existed, white America. You are a figment of your own brain which has settled for a petty uncreative imagining. You are a figment of the brains and souls and bodies you *have* lynched and tortured, raped and sold and murdered and denied, starved and whipped—who for sanity's sake had to believe that their torturer was as real as their pain. The blood on your hands, white America, is your own.

* * *

How easily that realization (that we have disowned ourselves) could be mistaken for expiation. How convenient an excuse not to make up for shedding blood that, after all, is "just" our own. What a reassuringly false equation that would be, denying any difference between our experience and the suffering of others caused *by* our experience. No, no, the difference must be seen, recognized, understood, expiated, precisely because its most hideous characteristic is to deny and erase as many sweet, hopeful traces of our mutual salvation as possible: life that we hold "in common," however variously we live it.

* * *

Camus was correct in calling suicide the only sin. War, murder, all the other -*cides* are cowardly stalling actions that delude the

† Jefferson fought to insert an antislavery clause in the Constitution, but eventually compromised under pressure and withdrew it.

individual, group, society, species, into thinking *he/she/it/ them/us/we* are not about the real business of destroying ourself.

But then what will we call Them?

Ah.

The powerless need to imagine Them in order not to identify with *their/our* own destruction of ourself. But then, but then, once there is a Them . . .

* * *

The reason energy is power is that it *is* the Doing, the movement, the holomovement. For me, "Being"—particularly as an institution—remains a sophomoric expression of the lethal patriarchal philosophical tradition, one especially reactionary where women are concerned, since women have been defined *as* passively existent for rather too long.

* * *

Does the stone define itself? (Why should it tell us? Why should it tell us especially if we're not listening?)

If activity, existing, defining, are the same at heart, if somatic tissue knows itself different from genetic tissue, if the cactus understands the reasons for its camouflage as a stone but grows nonetheless, then power is not ultimately in the eye of the beholder, but in the *choice of activity of the beheld.*

Or is it in the beholding of that choice, by either the beheld or the beholder? How can the one exist without the other?

* * *

Light moves as both particles and wave, but reaches the retina as a discrete, individuated photon.

If individuation is the piston of life, then racism and sexism are no surprise. Because *the deepest fear would be, not as we have thought politically, of the Other, but of the Same.* The terror of the moment when the somatic cell does not know itself as different from the genetic cell, the stone from the cactus. The holoconsciousness. An utterly alien reality. How that terror puts into perspective the mere fears that white and black, male and female, are deeply different!

* * *

Jefferson disowned his slave children not because they were "black"—which by his own racial structure of insanely pedantic blood charts they weren't. He disowned them because he would not cease owning them, that is, because they were slaves. Yet white slaves were unheard of. "If God is God he is not good; if God is good he is not God." If you are white, you are not a slave; if you are a slave, you are not white. Whiteness (or sameness) could not coexist with slavery in the same person. If you are female you are not Man; if you are human, you are not a slave. Yet Dolley Madison knew . . .

Jefferson's slave children, then, were unacknowledged not because they were different but because they were so the same. The terror of this truth (Mark Twain's truth in *Pudd'nhead Wilson*) has been diluted and totally distorted by the fundamentalist fake truths of brotherhood, kin-under-the-skin, Disneyan Christian all-oneism. Such pap can be mouthed safely without anyone believing it for one minute, because its hypocrisy keeps safe the lived-by truths of continual ceaseless ongoing compartmentalization—the real delights *there*in, the real griefs *there*in. It also keeps safe the even more chthonic dreamed-of (in nightmare) truths, that there are no such things as identity, choice, uniqueness—ego. No inert stone? No "reality"?

* * *

If I am not you, then I must be her or him. If not any of these, then I must be: I. The first thing the infant learns.

* * *

At least the snowflake is in innocence of its individuation, thereby achieving a kind of negation of it. Yet it *is* unique. (For what purpose, if not realized, though? For the entertainment and illusion of the observer? Yet who has or can observe every snowflake's uniqueness?) There is a negation of individuation, certainly, when the snowflake lands and melts. Is this already in process even in midfall? Why can't we imagine communism as a society not of ants but of snowflakes? Is it because communism did not imagine *itself* in that way? Does the result always bear the imprint of its beginning?

* * *

Isn't it enough to *be* individuated? Must each individuated thing realize that, too? *Does* each? Or does the cactus but not the stone? Dangerous thinking, that: the white says *"I do"* but assumes that the black doesn't. The man says *"I do"* but assumes that women don't. (The quarks and hadrons in each and all just laugh.) Those in power always speak of humanism—and accuse those who have been made powerless and categorized as "Other" of *divisiveness.* This is done, however, only when the powerless recognize and name their already divided state, and begin to articulate their longing—for *union.*

The fear is *not* that we are different. The fear is that we are the same.

Civilization has been at once a process of seeking similarities in sentience while creating greater and more elaborate means of differentiation, in wider, more specified, more diverse experiences, variations, forms—all ostensibly in order to better express similarity. Or is that evolution—and has civilization actually opposed it?

*   *   *

The lie of the inner and the outer. The lie of kin-beneath-the-skin when we are really saying that we are trying to deny something more fearful: being kin above/in/at/over/through the skin. Being kin, period. This was Jefferson's lie. His hypocrisy was built on this.

*   *   *

Age as category is central here, because if one exists long enough, the mere transition from young to old exposes the lie of differentness in a way we can otherwise more conveniently escape (appearance, or differences of sex or race). We still try: "It's impossible to imagine him ever being young"; "I can't see her as old somehow." Yet as one lives the lesson is painfully engraved as if by Kafka's harrow on the flesh itself, or rather is painfully sensed in the contradiction *between* that external garb and the internal cry: But I'm still the same inside here! It is our own shadows that precede and follow us—but only when we stand in the light.

*   *   *

Existence, or at least civilized existence, seems to be a story of sentient life ricocheting between alternate terrors: the fear of being utterly alone, the fear of being totally absorbed. Society, politics, history itself, is nothing but an attempt to reconcile and balance those two fears.

* * *

If I am not myself, then I must be you. If neither of these, then I must be him. Or her. The first thing the oppressed learn, the basic lesson for enslaving.

* * *

If I am not you, or myself, or him or her, then I must be nothing. The lesson of the mad.

* * *

If I am not her, or you, or him, or myself, then I must be each of these in turn, and in fragments. The lesson of the alien.

* * *

If I am not myself, or you, or her or him, then I must be all of these at once, and whole. The lesson of the saint (or the true revolutionary).

* * *

Boundaries, corners, demarcations, grids, maps, endings, zonings, borders. Overflows, spills, run-ons, obliterations, floods, rushes, *the dark*, circles.

Paths delude us into thinking we are not lost.

Art is the map. But remember that "the map is not the territory."[18]

* * *

All art is the tension expressed between the uncontainable and its one perfect inevitable form.

All art is the tension expressed between what is uncontainable and the one structure inevitable for revealing its (un)containability.

The structure, of course, varies with time, place, custom, culture, available tools, and which part(s) of the uncontainable content it is inevitably meant to inexpressibly express. (Which of course makes it harder to recognize.)

* * *

Each sentient being: one of life's *objets d'art*. How amusing for the maker, and what hell for the clay. For the slave, the cactus, the man, the master, the stone, the woman, the infant, the mad, the vase, the saint. Unless, as Graham Greene almost hazards, all of us are evolving to consciousness, Galatea-ing in some collective sense—the snowflake becoming conscious without somehow falling thereby—and will turn and stretch all these somatic cells to face the maker, in so *becoming* the maker, becoming genetic, matter comprehending that it *is* energy, the revolution against a divine dictatorship, seizing not merely power but divinity: the succulent stone, the identical spectrum of rosebrown fleshfolds of every labial surface, the recognition . . .

That would mean Jefferson not separating his one sistroid wife into two in order to keep his reputation, thereby keeping his power (to use of course for the democratic salvation of his country against the evil men who would destroy the perfection of such ideals—the fatal flaw of Arthur Dimmesdale in *The Scarlet Letter*, calling one's own acts of cowardice, compromise, and evil "sacrifice to a higher good").

What if, instead, our Jefferson had dared disclose, enfold, embrace, unfold, truly "own" (up to) this, thus refusing to "own" anyone and thus refusing to become precisely one of those evil men he claimed to be fighting—thus actually possibly really saving the soul of his country. What if?

* * *

Why not? Would it be so much more unamusing for the maker? Is that the flaw the maker has thrown into each of us when we are spinning still on the wheel—the trick that prevents each from *becoming* the maker? The whisper: How do you know you're alive, then? The fear addressed by the Zen kōan "Come in, all that is outside"; the fear addressed by Lao-tzu's "All is in order, let everything come; all is in chaos, let everything go"; the fear addressed by Wallace Stevens in his poem "Connoisseur of Chaos": "A. A violent order is disorder; and/B. A great disorder is an order." The fear of realizing one is lost utterly, that one may or may not be: alive, male, master, snowflake or cactus or stone. The lie that illusion and reality are different. The lie that illusion and reality are the same.

* * *

How to reconcile all this then with realizing that racism and sexism could be simply speedwritten as: Hate generalizes, love specifies. Or: The movements of hatred are toward generalization; love's movements are toward specification.

The blood on my hands is my own. (Old news to whoever shed it.)

Certainly that's true, on the obvious level: anything as a group —blacks, whites, women, men, succulents, frozen water, slaves, masters, even light—instantly misrepresents what characterizes its component individual elements (the uncontainable content) by an *un*-inevitable structure (bad art, bigotry, indiscriminate discrimination).

It is the individuated uniqueness of one polished pebble, of the story of Sally Hemmings' life, of my own thought-pattern shorthand intimacies with my inner ear, of the blurred outlines of Jo's signature, her specific patterns of grief and madness, not her femaleness, or her blackness—these constitute something like love. It is the particular form of Kenneth's and my struggle and love that is our unique strength; just as it is the general traits, conformities, societal greeds and deceits we fall into sharing with other (anysexual) lovers in common that endanger us. His sexism he holds in common with all men, but his ways of *fighting* his sexism are *his*. My racism I hold in common with all whites; only to the degree that I disassociate myself from it can I become more—not less—myself.

I now know, too, that my only hope for fighting my own white racism is, at least at this moment in history, in a context with *women* of other so-called racial groups. This knowledge came slowly and painfully—after years in the civil-rights movement and the "New Left," years of trying to differentiate between my race guilt and my Woman-inculcated deference toward men (of color, in this case): was I making reparations as a white, or being obsequious as a woman? Were the advantages taken and the power muscles being flexed signs of properly correcting the previously existing *racial* imbalance, or were they reaffirmations of the endemic *male-female* power imbalance, now reinforced by minority men's focus on "manhood"? (In the midst of all this tangle, of course, black women suffered being caught between a rock and a hard place—between the sexism of black men and the racism of white women.) Only in an all-woman context, I learned, can I see where my racism *is* racism and not some new wrinkle of sexism. In a mixed context, my recurring rage at the sexism of minority men (who were, in the sycophantic white-radical thinking of the 1960's, supposed to be *better* than white men on this issue) was hopelessly enmeshed with my own racism.

I saw this symptom clearly in a march once, when another white woman marcher, on being sexually harassed by a black male bystander, finally wheeled on him in fury—but instead of exploding at his sexism, screamed racial epithets at him. The problem is also heartbreakingly posed in a passage in A *Rap on Race*,[19] the dialogue between Margaret Mead and James Baldwin. At one point, Mead mentioned that some social scientists in the United States had completed a study in which they asked small white boys which, if they had to be something other than small white boys, would they rather be: little white girls or little black boys? She asked if Baldwin could guess what they answered; he couldn't. Mead said, "They would rather be small black boys," to which Baldwin—whose complex and passionate consciousness about oppression I had admired for years—responded, "How encouraging! It shows that they still have some sense left." (Notice how the choice of being *little black girls* was never even raised as an option.)

* * *

Yet on the philosophical stage, as opposed to the political, is it reversed? Is it hate that specifies and love that generalizes?

Perhaps not, if, *in the doing,* the powering (the one encompassing, inseparable, energizing, *making,* uncontainable content) can express its one-quality, its identicality and universality, only by flashing glimpses of it through the inevitable breakable forms of ourselves? The danger being only that we will come to believe in our containing merely ourselves' lone ego (hence, need to differentiate it further, hence hate, maps, the illusion of paths, etc.), rather than understand continuously that *our very uniqueness, variety, diversity, exists in order to reveal, humorously and celebratorily, the truth of its opposite reality?*

Then the maxim proves renewed: to generalize without going first through the valley of the shadow of specificity *is* to abstractify—to characterize without the care of an artist, with no maker's precision but with mere sloppy assumptions: racism, grouping, sexism, ageism. Hate.

Love specifies because it would, through the precise, reach what is unspecifiable (although, regrettably, capable of abstraction), and thus vibrate to a state so free-form but integrated it cannot be generalized. And love must be synthesis, since it makes separatenesses into new entities by merging their disparate yearnings.

* * *

In such a state all things—the *disa*trophy of a cactus after long drought, the overlap of crystal (stone) pattern and snowflake pattern—*are possible*. In such a state, it is possible even for Sally Hemmings to love Jefferson without that being a slave's forced "love," and for him to love her without that being a master's hypocrisy. In such a state, the holopolitical revolution is both everywhere and nowhere at the same instant on its orbit of holomovement. In such a state, freedom is free to exist.

Surely this was the joke that Mozart and Bach knew, the joke dreamed in Lady Murasaki's stories and whispered in Xuan An's poems. Surely this was the joke that George Eliot knew when, in *Middlemarch*, she described how a

pier-glass or extensive surface of polished steel made to be rubbed by a housemaid [a housemaid, ah . . .], will be minutely and multitudinously scratched in all directions; but place now against it a lighted candle as a centre of illumination, and lo! the scratches will seem to arrange themselves in a fine series of concentric circles around that little sun.

And if (as Eliot smiled) the scratches are going everywhere impartially, so that it is only the candle producing the flattering illusion of an arrangement; and if the scratches are events and the candle the egoism of the interpreter (the little sun of a reflected face circled by scars in the two-way pier-glass)—then is it not even more of a joke that the shifting universe will deign to arrange its arbitrary shapes into a pattern haloing the bright wick of love? Surely this was the joke known by Kathleen Raine when she wrote "The center of the mandala is everywhere," the family joke told on cold winter nights over fires down in the cabins, passed on generation to generation with laughter floating out into the night like smoke. The old joke, told by those of us who are the slaves of form.

VII

PUBLIC SECRETS

An Anatomy of Mortality

You won't be forgiven. Not any of you. Not ever.
—Addressed to a Nazi soldier
by a Jewish child being
loaded into a truck bound
for Auschwitz (from the
transcript of the Auschwitz
trial)

Since it is the Other within us who is old, it is natural
that the revelation of our age should come to us from outside—from others. We do not accept it willingly.
—Simone de Beauvoir

In the great night my heart will go out,
Toward me darkness comes rattling,
In the great night my heart will go out.
—Owl Woman's Death Song,
Papago Nation of North America

Ultimately, we share only one thing in common—one unavoidable, inevitable, and absolutely certain thing: death. We also
share the undeniable reality of aging, of old age—though only if
we are, so to speak, lucky enough to die old. But death, sooner or
later, is our one basic bond.

This bond ought to simplify, clarify, unify our lives. It makes
the question wonderfully clear: what are we going to do, separately and together, between this exact moment (when you are
reading this page) and death? How are we going to use and celebrate the miraculous coincidence of our being alive and in some
way actually connected (you are, after all, reading this page) on

the same planet at relatively the same moment in history, concerned even with somewhat the same concerns? Out of all the possible losings of each other in time and space, all the missed meetings, all the almost-but-not-quite encounters—we have, magically and wondrously, connected. And if it should happen that I am dead when these words reach your brain—like the flare of a long-ago-burned-out sun, having traveled light-years as a wave, only now arriving as a word-photon on your retina—if that turns out to be the case, isn't it an even more awesome thing that I become alive for you *in* time, while *you* are still alive? You resurrect me, you take me out of my past into your present. Indeed, I am writing into your present out of my past—which makes the past the future—or makes it an eternal present.

For that matter, to extrapolate from an idea of Susan Sontag's, the concept of past, present, and future as equal parts of some imaginary measure is a misleading one. Actually, our reality is 98 or 99 percent *past*; the past is all we really know. Then there is a tiny sliver—perhaps 1 or 2 percent—which is actually present, the *now*, but which instantaneously becomes the past. The future really is a blank; it requires an astonishing sense of trust to imagine that it will exist at all, let alone in the ways we might like to define and shape it. To plan anything at all, from an appointment at the dentist's to a revolution in consciousness, is—existentially speaking—a remarkable act of faith.

In a political context, to plan is also an act of power. The old proverb "The rich plan for generations; the poor plan for Saturday night" applies not only to wealth and poverty but to whites and people of color, to the dominant institution of heterosexuality and the underclass of homosexuals, to the physically "normal" and the physically disabled, to adults and children, to the middle-aged and the elderly, and most assuredly to men and women.

Long-term planning requires a comparative lack of immediate pressure, a certain leisure, and the luxury of confidence that one can have some control over one's immediate (or even extended) environment, within the limits of possibility. The woman whose life is chopped into short segments by housework and childcare (the stuff at the cleaners' must be picked up by four, the kids should be fetched from school at three-fifteen, the roast will take two hours in the oven, the floor wax has to be dry by six, etc.) is too busy, planning and doing, to plan. The welfare client whose days are measured by the length of lines to be stood in (at the department of public assistance, at the food-stamps window, at the cheapest public clinic)—is too pressured, too desperate, too exhausted, to plan. The black woman or man who must set out for home earlier than necessary, via bus and subway and foot (because only a rare taxicab will pick her/him up, or will drive into a community forced to exist as, and then feared as, a ghetto)—this black woman or man is definitely robbed of the confidence that she/he is in control of planning even the route home. And these are only a few examples among many of how "planning," the idea of "future," and in fact *time itself* have totally different realities —political, physical, emotional, intellectual realities—for the comparatively powerless.*

Such different realities affect everything, including thought and language. It's the same difference that allows the financially secure to talk in terms of "economics" while hand-to-mouth folks simply think about "money"—or, even more basically, about "cash." It's the variation in the length of time felt in response to the sentence, "I'll be with you in a moment"—when that sentence has been uttered by your grown-up mother, the clerk at the unemployment office, the masked anesthesiologist, an Internal Revenue Service tax auditor, your teenage son finishing a tele-

---

* Berit Ås, the Norwegian psychologist and feminist theorist, has written about how women use time differently than do men, because of our life and social circumstances. She notes the Waiting Phenomenon, or what we could call Suspended Animation or Self Deferred: "The importance of serving another person first contributes to an attitude common to most women: 'After I have washed the dishes, I will . . .' or 'I hope I can participate when my mother-in-law gets better,' or . . . 'When the children grow up, I think I could, perhaps, if nothing else happens and the family does not need me— go back to education.'"
She also analyzes how girls are influenced early in life not to plan their own future. When asked, "What do you really want to be?" young men answer readily, but most young women reply, "'Taking into account that I may marry, I should perhaps choose . . .' or 'If I have children, I think I better. . . .'" Nor is this balancing act, though intolerable, unrealistic, given what woman must face. Ås cites a study done in the 1970's at the Institute for Social Research in Ann Arbor, Michigan: "The result confirms that all married women, both those who are housewives only, and those who carry double responsibilities, have on the average a ten-hour longer work week than do married men. *Women find it difficult to organize because they lack time.*" (Italics mine.) From "On Female Culture," in *Acta Sociologica*, No. 1–3, Special Issue on Women's Studies (Copenhagen, 1975).

phone call, a corporate executive, the desk sergeant in the precinct rape-report squad, the nurse with the pain-killer, your boss, your faculty adviser, your granddaughter in the corridor of the nursing home, the loan officer at the bank, and so on, *ad infinitum*. It's the power tactic used in the U.S. Army and in many prisons: rouse the soldiers or prisoners at dawn, rush them through dressing, and then let them stand on lines, awaiting orders, as in the Army cliché "Hurry up and wait."

In the world of subatomic particles, space does not exist—nor time. But in the world of values created by Man, space and time not only exist but are marketable commodities.

Of course, in order to "package" a resource which is already free, omnipresent, and natural, it's necessary to contain this resource. If you can't literally fence it around or lock it in a safe, you can at least deny some aspects of it and emphasize certain others, thus reshaping it (or seeming to), and redefining which of its characteristics are desirable and which contemptible. This is what our society has done with the time span of the human life. Children are viewed as powerless—and thus robbed of power. So-called adults (from age twenty-one to age sixty-five) are regarded as Real People, human beings, the empowered. Older people are defined as powerless again. To a very large extent, this phenomenon is based on *sexual fundamentalism:* if human sexual activity is defined as something only powerful humans do, and if it is defined as inextricable with reproduction, and if certain persons are not permitted to engage in this activity *without* this reproductive connection, it must follow that such persons aren't really human. We've already seen how Man has pulled off this coup with regard to women. *But:* prepubertal children, not being neotenic (that is, not being able to attain sexual maturity during the larval stage), cannot reproduce, either. Therefore they must be nonsexual beings, therefore nonhuman beings, unworthy of power. And beyond a certain age adults can no longer reproduce, either. Therefore *they* must be nonsexual beings, therefore nonhuman beings, also unworthy of potency (in all senses of the word). Never mind that such assumptions belie the facts. Everyone knows differently, but the assumptions are given the weight of fact because those who perpetrate them hold the power to enforce them. Given enough time and propaganda, even the powerless will come to feel that to go against the grain of these assumptions is to be abnormal.

For instance, to think deeply, seriously, and frequently about one's own death, until or unless it is imminent, is to be regarded as morbid. Who wants to be morbid, after all? But what cannot be expressed and discussed with others eventually goes underground even in the self; what is unspeakable is likely to become unthinkable. So it is that we all have collaborated in the public secrets of youth, "maturity," aging, and most of all, death. The political masks of mortality—bought and sold everywhere Man rules and Woman nods approvingly, are what we have worn—and worn so long that when we stand before the two-way mirror we actually believe we see ourselves.

"IT IS MARGARET YOU MOURN FOR"

The first mask is that of childhood. Its features are cuteness, innocence, playfulness, dependency (helplessness), a capacity for whimsy and imagination, and a supposed lack of ability for seeing the tragic side of the universe (e.g., chronic happiness). These identifying marks of childhood have about as much relevance to a real child as the identifying stereotypes of softness, femininity, helplessness, and overemotionality do to a real woman. Adults project such features onto children for the political purpose of keeping them in their powerless place. Indeed, the "organic" bonds between children and women have been positively cemented by the deliberate political blurring of the two groups into one (powerless) class: womenandchildren. As Jane Harrison pointed out, for the Greeks, a boy becoming a man was, in effect, his ceasing to be a woman. Being non-Man, then, is the real "bond" between women and children, and requires the status of powerlessness.

Such powerlessness during childhood—that much-praised state of so-called freedom—is an especially sour irony to children who, like any other discriminated-against group, learn early on what is expected of them, for survival's sake. And what is expected of them is so entrenched in adult thinking that even political and life-style-radical adults, including many feminists, don't think to challenge that expectability.

I'll never forget one conversation with a feminist activist who was also the mother of an eight-year-old girl. The woman, an attorney who had logged many hours on affirmative action lawsuits, was bemoaning her daughter's preoccupation with Barbie dolls and their fashion and cosmetic accoutrements. Her grandfather, it seemed, had brought these items of sexist commercialism as a gift. Why had the mother permitted it? She hadn't wanted to hurt his feelings. What about her child's feelings? A blank look. Would she have permitted war toys or Aunt Jemima dolls into the house? An immediate no. Then why permit a Barbie doll, which she regarded as an archpropaganda tool for "femininity," into the house? She groped for an answer, finally saying, "But I don't want to *program* my kid, to deluge her with feminist propaganda." Yet this woman knows very well that every child already is being programmed with *sexist* propaganda almost every minute of the day—from television, from advertising, from teachers and peers and textbooks. What about a little counterbalance, another way of thinking, an option, to offset *that* propaganda, which is so pervasive as to be almost invisible? "Why, that's what affirmative action is!" she exclaimed, another feminist epiphany having occurred.

And it's hard, yes. The risks and labor one faces for the sake of one's beliefs as an adult are one's own choice; it sometimes seems manipulative to "lay them on" one's child or children. Yet if we don't fight for the right of our (and in fact *all*) children to see the world without androcentric blinders "laid on" them, affixed by Man and Woman, then who will?

As a parent trying to communicate new and more humane values to a child, one perhaps learns even more than the child. For example, Blake (now twelve years old) has taught Kenneth and me about the fierce and *inherent* sense of justice children have, about real courage, about going not "too far" but even further. True, this has necessitated many long, complex, and wonderful conversations, and frequent trips to the principal's office in support of his various political stands in school, and much awkward (and sometimes embarrassing) honesty on our own parts. But the joy—when Blake announces that he's decided to withdraw from running for a second term as class president to be campaign manager for the first girl candidate instead; or when he challenges patriarchal holidays: "Thanksgiving is a racist holiday;

what did the Native Americans have to celebrate about?" and "How *dare* they put up cut-outs of green-faced wicked-looking witches at Halloween when millions of women were burned as witches?" and "I don't observe Washington's Birthday; I'm celebrating the birthday of Susan B. Anthony instead."

Yes, there are tears sometimes, and not only Blake's but Kenneth's and mine, too. When your child is ridiculed by his peers for his politics, for playing with dolls as well as playing baseball (and demanding that girls be permitted on the team), for loving music and poetry, or for campaigning devotedly for Bella Abzug —when he cries about certain received insults and cuts and ostracisms, then all you can do is comfort him, support him, remind him of his friends who respect and share his views, reiterate that one can't take a stand on *everything* all the time, and be as certain as you can that his principles are his own and not held for *your* approval—this last made clear by lots of plain loving, no matter what. It doesn't hurt for him to see *you* cry and get depressed when some adults do the same things to you, for that matter. In fact, part of feminist parenting, to me, is the simple insistence on the parents' fallible humanity: our flaws, dumb errors, inconsistencies, our feet of clay, *our own real names* instead of role names like Mommy and Daddy. All of which have the effect of freeing the parent into personhood—and of respectfully granting the child more power as a human being.

I confess to being very proud of the person Blake is, in his own character, and also of the joyous and difficult work that Kenneth and I have done separately and together over the years to support and encourage him. At least our mistakes are newer and different ones from the usual. I also know a number of feminist parents who take the same pains with their female children—but regrettably few who truly challenge the status quo with their male children. It's as if they expected that raising strong and assertive girls, without the parallel raising of boys who comprehended tenderness, humor, and nurturance would be enough to change future relationships. Certainly the fear of sons turning into "sissies" (for which read homosexuals) is at work here. One might well answer such homophobia with a simple "So what if that *is* the case?"—despite all the new studies which give the lie to such a fear.[1] Certainly our cultural assumptions are changing more with regard to the woman-half of sex roles than the male-half: more women in the business world yes, but not a comparable number of men yet in childcare centers. But I think that another element also is at work: a certain laziness with regard to "saving our kids from the patriarchy" as one woman put it, which in turn masks our own means of retaining power—by keeping our children "safe" from the "propaganda" we know very well is empowering *us* every day: this new consciousness, this painful but well-worth-it process. And, too, many of us just have never bothered to think it through; the ignorance-is-bliss indifference of those who have relative power over those who lack it.

Let's take as an example the issue of children's suffrage. Yes, the right of a child to vote.[2] This right is denied to children on a number of grounds, all of them specious:

1. *The Cuteness Defense:* "No child (i.e., citizen below the age of eighteen or, in some states, twenty-one) has the maturity to vote." Whoever puts forth this argument must be measuring maturity in terms of height or reproductive capacity, because surely any other terms of measurement (well-rounded education, financial independence, emotional stability, intellectual and political acumen, a knowledge of the ways of government and democratic systems, etc.) do *not* describe the current average voter anywhere in the world.

2. *The Dependency Defense:* "No child is autonomous enough to make her/his own voting choice; a child merely will act as a pawn for the parents, voting the way they tell him/her to vote." This defense ought to ring familiar warning bells in every woman's head, since a twin reason (husband's influence) was given for fifty years as an excuse for denying the vote to women. It's an example of the self-fulfilling *property* concept: first, rob someone of autonomy and make this person an item of property, and then deny the same person rights on the grounds that a piece of property wouldn't know how to exercise such rights. The response in terms of children's suffrage might be identical to the one women made: "In the privacy of the voting booth, who knows *how* we might choose? We may well educate ourselves. Husbands (parents) *may* influence us, and then again you might be surprised at how quickly we can balance that influence with our own thoughts and desires, *once we have the option.* Besides, your argument is a priori. A human right is a right, basic and unqualifiable by credentials allowing one access to that right."

3. *The Innocence Defense*: "No child is well informed enough on the issues of the day to make reasonable voting decisions (unless, of course, the parents do the informing—in which case they're influencing, and that's unacceptable, too)." This argument has a Mad Hatter quality of illogic so debilitating that it makes one wish, like the dormouse, to go back to sleep in the teapot at once. First, the average adult voter is about as "well informed on the issues of the day" as a groundhog on weather currents in the upper atmosphere. Indeed, those in political and economic power positions do their best to *keep* the average voter in just this ill-informed state, despite the contrary efforts of the press. Consequently, while a lack of genuine access to the facts might not be the voter's fault, it *is* a fault not to recognize one's own enforced ignorance but to buy, instead, the flattering line handed out by the very powers that keep one in ignorance—and then to project one's ignorance onto others. Second, a child can *become* better informed on the issues in the same way that adults do—by reading newspapers and magazines, by watching television journalism and monitoring coverage of the candidates.

4. *The Playfulness Defense*: "Children wouldn't be interested in newspapers and current events and such. They'd be bored. Why burden them? They want to play and have fun." (Let us leave aside for a moment the fact that the majority of adult voters are bored by current political practice; in 1980, almost one half of the U.S. potential voting electorate didn't vote—out of disillusionment and boredom.) The truth is that children play *very solemnly*, in dead earnest. It's how they learn, in fact. Adults in this culture have made the tragic error of separating play from earnestness. Play isn't frivolous or foolish; it's a life-sustaining creative activity. When adults do engage in it, they are called "artists," and are frequently mistaken for children (or for "womanish" beings): cute, but not to be taken seriously. Children are quite capable of being fascinated with the news of our times, and of understanding how deeply it affects them, not only right now but in the tomorrow they will inherit. And if political rhetoric, legislative terminology, and diplomatic jargon would be impenetrable to a child—why, what an easy solution there is to that one! In order to equip this new voter with the facts, such mystifying codes must be simplified and clarified! (*Think* how this would alarm those in power—and think, too, how it would relieve the

average *adult* voter, who also, as we well know, cannot penetrate the intentional political obfuscation with understanding.) What a benefit to all would result! The emperor, in other words, would have to get decently dressed. As for "burdening" children with rights, how that smacks of Ye Olde Paternalism: "the white man's burden"—as well as the stereotypes of happy, carefree slaves on the plantation, and sweetly silly, *child*like women, and noble savages . . .

5. *The Divide-and-Conquer Defense:* "But where do you draw the line? Should everyone above age fifteen be enfranchised? Above twelve? Eight? Six? Are you going to oppress toddlers (ha ha) by excluding them? Once you start with this, you're lost! Don't you see the impossibility of all this?" How reminiscent such an argument is of the nineteenth-century position that it was all right for black men to vote, but not for any woman—or that it was acceptable for white women to be enfranchised but not black women. Surely such a simple standard as minimal literacy might be a guideline, thus fixing the voting age—at least to begin with—at seven years old. Then, once the idea is established, children themselves, along with the rest of the electorate, could debate the practical feasibility of enfranchising even younger citizens. A literacy standard can be misused, of course. Although literacy itself is an objective good, it is a fair "credential" only when all have equal access to it, when tests are free of cultural values and assumptions, and are multilingual.

6. *The Comic Defense:* "Well, anyway, it's ridiculous. I mean, *really!* Kids voting! I mean, it's *funny!*" This argument, too, is a familiar one to women: ridicule. When pseudo-logic fails, resort to mockery, derision, scorn. Racial, sexual, and ethnic "jokes," humor that gets off on the physically disabled, all are part of this same tactic. When oppressed peoples cease chuckling amiably in response to jokes that degrade their own dignity as human beings, they are accused of "having lost a sense of humor." (Apparently, nobody in the power class stops to think of what a deliciously sharp sense of humor the oppressed have when alone and not being overheard—but those jokes happen to be about the oppressor. As the poet Alice Meynell once noted, "The sense of humor has other things to do than to make itself conspicuous in the act of laughter.") To see children's suffrage as hilarious is as ignorant and arrogant a reaction as it was when proposed nonproperty-

holders' suffrage, "Negro" (male) suffrage, or women's suffrage were viewed as comparably hilarious. Such laughter is the giggling of the morally and politically bankrupt—and of the scared.

The above example, of children's suffrage, is vital in itself but also indicative of the way children *really* are regarded in a culture which purports to "adore kids." Disneyland, Saturday-morning cartoons, and ice cream are, like the much-vaunted held-open door for a woman, meaningless gallantries offered to a powerless class of people in place of recognizing their humanity.

The truth about how children are regarded is ugly: whole housing projects (and indeed entire townships) deny tenancy to families with children; children still do manual labor here in the richest superpower nation in the world—as migrant farmworkers, as sharecroppers, and in some mining communities; children as a subclass within such "out-groups" as racial minorities suffer higher mortality rates, lack of minimal nutrition, clothing, and education; the growing statistics on the sexual abuse of children are horrifying. Interestingly enough, fundamentalists (sexual, religious, and political) who are passionate in their defense of the fetus and their own narrow definition of the family seem unconcerned about what happens to children once babies are past the delivery stage. (In fact, they don't even care enough about a healthy *fetus*, which might mean ensuring good health care, diet, and clean air for even the poorest pregnant woman; no— a fetus, any fetus, is their focus.) The Right Wing has shown its "love for kids" peculiarly: it has supported corporal punishment in the schools and at home, denounced child-abuse studies and shelters as "subversive of the American family," lobbied to deprive public-school children of free lunches and of religious freedom (by requiring prayer in the classrooms). I'd love to loose a children's electorate on *them*.

The issue of the sexual abuse of children is perhaps the most dramatic example of how young human beings are truly regarded and treated. Since Florence Rush has compiled a staggering amount of statistics, history, and analyses on this subject in her remarkable book *The Best Kept Secret*,[3] I won't go into details all over again here. The problem is at epidemic proportions.

The majority by far of child-assault and child-molestation cases are perpetrated by adult heterosexual males on female children (thus giving the lie to the euphemism "incest" and naming it, more accurately, "rape"). But there *is* also male-on-male abuse, which often gets more sensationalistic coverage because it's a nice way of further distancing homosexual males as nonhuman. The irony is that most male-on-male child abuse—like most male-on-male rape in prisons—also is committed by heterosexual men who "hate queers." The *double* irony, which has been all the more disheartening to women—lesbian *and* heterosexual—and to feminists in particular, is that many spokesmen of the male gay liberation movement have bonded with their straight brothers and defended this practice as "boy love." Their argument purports to defend the right of a child to sexuality.

Of *course* children have a right to their own sexuality—and yes, that sexuality certainly does exist. But *children have a right to express that sexuality by choice, among themselves, among peers.* When somebody much older, taller, or physically stronger is involved, then it's less a question of sex than of *power.* When someone who is more powerful claims that someone who is less powerful really "invited" sex, or was acting seductively, doesn't that sound suspiciously like the excuse given by the rapist or the harasser? Isn't it Blame the Victim all over again? What if the child longs for affection, physical demonstrativeness, attention; who dares interpret that as "seductiveness"?

Certainly this society does repress the enormous and real *sexual* vitality of children (even unto repressing masturbation), but the only way that sexuality has of flowering in any nondamaging, power-free relationship is with another (consenting) child—whether it is homosexual, heterosexual, bisexual, or polymorphous. This isn't to say that the partners need be exactly the same age in order for a relationship to be noncoercive, but whenever a wider age gap begins to be "institutionalized," particularly between pre- and post-pubertal, that can spell *power.* And when an imbalance of power is going on in a sexual relationship, we ought by now to know how deeply destructive that is.

It's revealing that the issue of sex with children is almost nonexistent among women—of whatever sexual preference. I believe that this probably is due to the fact that women take care of children more than men do. Women are brought up to relate to a child's body in nurturing ways, ways (like breast-feeding) which can resonate with great sensuality, but a sensuality qualitatively different from the eroticism involved in "boy love" or nympholepsy. It's likely that, as more men become involved in both the drudgery and the joy of childcare, there will be a reduction in the male sexual mystique about children.

Having a child drastically changes the lives of most women, opening up previously unimaginable new selves, new areas of responsibility, delight, exhaustion, anxiety, ambivalence, and physiological change. It could be said that, in this sense, "The child is mother of the woman." The proverbial Wordsworth line, however, is "The Child is father of the Man"—one of the senses of which contains a premature prophecy that won't come true until men are as intimately and committedly engaged in the raising of children as women have been.

Ultimately, though, there are real rewards that all adults get from denying the humanity of children. One such reward is, as we've seen, pure compensatory power: "No matter how relatively powerless I am, I can still boss *you* around because you're smaller." This can translate to tyranny. Another reward is the flattering feeling of indispensability (closely related to omnipotence or, again, power): "This little creature needs me for its survival; without me, it would be nowhere." This can translate to protectionism.† Yet another reward is ego-immortality: "That child is a piece of *me*; in her/him *I* will live on." This can translate to possession. Still another is solace: "My [*sic*] children, at least, truly love me." This can translate to the assumption that love for parents is owed, due, natural—rather than something to be earned, like any other kind of love. And still another is bittersweet vengeance: "*I* was bullied and broken as a child; now it's my turn." This can be cloaked conveniently under the rubric that adults "know what's good for" children—just as men know what's good for women, whites for blacks, the developed nations for the Third World, and so forth.

Such rewards are indeed real, and wretchedly satisfying—and, in the final analysis, they will cease being available to adults only when adult consciousness is raised to comprehend what ought to be obvious: that *each of us has been and still is, inside, the child being oppressed.* To dare remember what it felt like: how much more one really knew than adults imagined one knew, how much

† An old and hypocritical tactic of discriminators; for example, "protective" labor legislation (for women only) which denied women advancement into middle management positions.

one valued privacy and respect, how vital one's curiosity was and how intense one's desire, how deeply one could feel about things, how great was one's capacity for joy and rage and suffering, how *real* one's own sense of human self was—those recollections, buried but still as vivid as a sense-memory, would if acknowledged make it impossible for adults to objectify, trivialize, or dismiss the humanity of children.

We are, *as* adults, only grown female children and grown male children, after all. We may be unable fully to comprehend the intricacies of what it is like to be a member of a different sex or race or culture, but *childhood is a place where each of us already has been.* To deny one's own origins there, or to compensate for or seek revenge on another for what was done to oneself—this is not only to continue the vicious circle and to degrade other human beings, but to deny and degrade ourselves.

At some point, we must finally forgive those who raised us into this world. Then, perhaps, we will begin to act in a manner that will not need to be forgiven by those who come after us.

GRAY PANTHERS AND RED GIANTS

If we could learn to acknowledge that within every one of us the child each of us once was is crying out, "I'm still inside here," then we would be free to embrace ourselves on the other end of the life-span continuum: we might understand the profound truth of the octogenarian who tries to communicate that "I'm still *me* inside here!" Instead, we settle for learning the lie of aging, settle for donning the political mask of "the elderly."

This mask, like that of childhood, involves features evoking contradictory responses—supposed reverence and actual revulsion. "Senior citizens" is a euphemistic term for a people inhabiting a state of being which our culture tries to ignore or deny. Failing that, it responds with irritated patronizing at best and outright contempt at worst.

Again, the Right Wing articulates the most blatant expression of this abstract-respect/concrete-loathing attitude. Regarding the 1981 White House Conference on Aging, seventy-one-year-old President Ronald Reagan droned out filial bleats of esteem for "our seniors"—all the while urging his administration to find ways for doing away with pension reform, medical and food-stamp aid to the elderly, and even Social Security itself. (Delegates to the White House Conference on Aging rose up in wildcat caucuses of protest—at how the Reagan budget cutbacks devastated people on fixed incomes, and at the "rigged and stacked" agenda and attendance at the conference itself.)

Sadly enough, the Left, although far better on the issues and in terms of initiating and supporting decent legislation and programs for the old, is not much different in *attitude*. The antiwar, civil-rights, and student movements of the 1960's and early 1970's relished the slogan "Never trust anyone over thirty." Even the Women's Movement—which has gone further than any other progressive movement into welcoming, both in theory and practice, the political problems and strengths of older people—still too often articulates a "matronizing" attitude. I've heard youngish radical-feminist women refer to their militant Gray Panther sisters as "cute." It's a new and supposedly affectionate way of restating the "little old lady in tennis shoes" stereotype—and it's really more demeaning than admiring.

The discrimination against, and the fear and ridicule of, old age is even more intense and damaging with regard to women. As usual. The double standard lives here as well as everywhere else: it's a feminist cliché that an aging man can be "distinguished," but an aging woman is "over the hill." Nor is Western culture alone in this attitude, unfortunately. In fact, in most industrialized nations, *the economic and social problems of old age are women's problems*, because there are more old women than old men.

In Japan, for example, the average life span of a woman is five years longer than that of a man; furthermore, tradition has it that a woman marries a man much older than herself—leaving her widowed for even longer. A "manless" woman of any age is still viewed as almost invisible in Japanese culture—an older "manless" woman more so. A wife is dependent on her husband's pension, but when he dies the "survivor's pension" is cut by half. (The same is not true when the wife dies.) The possibility of remarriage is almost nil; a famous Japanese proverb states that, "The younger a wife the better, just as the newer a *tatami* [floor mat]." Alone, in poverty, untrained for anything but housewifery and serving a man, the current generation of Japanese old women has the highest percentage of suicide among all the world's female elderly. The Western stereotype that Asian cultures revere the older generation holds true only in terms of revering the older *male* generation.‡

Other cultures, of course, have demonstrated a markedly different attitude toward age. Most Native American peoples, as well as most indigenous peoples of Asia and Africa, have regarded the old (including women) as repositories of tribal wisdom and experiences, sometimes as holy beings. Even in some patriarchal cultures, the respect for age was so strong that it overrode the disrespect for women: a female human being who could be bought, sold, owned, beaten, and otherwise depersonalized while of childbearing age would, once past menopause, be regarded with great respect. (Regrettably, this usually meant she was considered to be no longer a "woman" but a third—and sexless—sex. Apparently you can*not* be both a woman *and* human.)

In Western culture, the postmenopausal woman is also considered less "womanly" (sexual fundamentalism again), but with no accompanying respect. Because our society reveres producing and products (and reproduction) more than understanding or wisdom, the older woman is seen as useless, noncontributing, not only a third sex but a fifth wheel. Indeed, she is forced to collaborate with this attitude; to rebel against it is to risk being seen as ridiculous. This daily reinforcement of propaganda-with-punishment for rebelling is especially and tragically obvious in the widespread shame, grief, and physical miseries still associated with menopause itself (and the hush-hush attitude about parallel physiological changes of an aging man). In the past decade, feminists have done much to raise consciousness and conscience about the injurious myths and medical/psychological malpractices visited on menopausal and postmenopausal women. Rosetta Reitz's informative and energizing book *Menopause: A Positive Approach*[4] is a major contribution in this area.

Comparably, the stereotype (for both men and women, but particularly for the latter) that sexual desire wanes with age has only lately been challenged. Bernard D. Starr and Marcella Bakur Weiner's book *On Sex and Sexuality in the Mature Years*[5] re-

‡ I am indebted to Keiko Higuchi and Akiko Tomii for these insights, and to Mallica Vajrathon, *rapporteur* for the session at which they communicated them, during the UNITAR Conference on Creative Women in Changing Societies, Oslo, 1980.

ports on a national survey, the results of which showed that *sex improves* (*especially for women*) *with age*—with prolonged and more intense orgasms and an accompanying new willingness to incorporate different sexual practices: masturbation, homosexual love, fantasies, experimentation, and oral-genital contact. Previous sex researchers had leaped to the false conclusion that the lack of frequency of sex among older subjects must mean a lack of sexual drive—ignoring such concrete impediments as ill health, lack of access to meeting new people, divorce, the death of a spouse, etc. It hadn't occurred to many researchers to ask older persons about what they *wanted* to do—and about what they actually *did*. Those previous researchers had been laboring under the bias of sexual fundamentalism that reserved sexual *activity* "properly" for the years between age twenty and fifty—the years of "acceptable" sexual *reproduction*. (Similarly, our society still tries to ignore the results of adolescent sexuality—and reproduction—while at the same time selling sex to teenage consumers with corporate callousness.)

Things *are* changing, though. The trend begun in the mid-1970's toward later marriage and having children later in life (due in no small part to the desire of women to establish careers before entering motherhood) is one positive sign which will have a ripple effect on how our culture regards older people. (The woman of forty-five who was considered old because she was a grandmother in the early part of the twentieth century today may well be a new mother with a three-year-old first child. This sort of thing shakes up rigid thinking.)

Not surprisingly, the first challenge to sexual-fundamentalist mores comes from changing trends in sexuality and in reproduction. But it's ironic that childbearing (yet again) should be viewed as the breakthrough in age or sex stereotyping more than other, less gender-based human capacities: lively intellect, emotional depth, life experience, devotion to and accomplishment in one's work. That, of course, would require a different societal attitude toward "work"—one that was less concerned with using people's labor and more concerned with respecting chosen meaningful work, encouraging and training people for work that did not (in well-worn but accurate Marxian terminology) alienate the worker from her/his product for the sake of someone else's gain.

The need for meaningful work—by which I mean something chosen, something one loves to do, something with which one feels a passionate involvement—*is central to the question of aging*. Gerontologists have commented on how forced retirement can hasten a person's death: someone who has felt busy and needed all her/his life, now is cast off and not permitted to apply a lifetime of experience anywhere else. Our educational system doesn't prepare citizens of any age to lead much of a "life of the mind"—so that when there is at last time for reading, concerts, and cultural riches, many older people sit instead in front of a television set that offers mostly brain-dulling mush. The relatively new concept of a second career begun late in life *is* catching on, but on the whole the attention given by the media to individuals who actually plunge into such activity shows that the exception proves the rule, and the journalistic profiles of such pioneers smack of "quaintness" and "pluckiness."

Since a passion for anything in our culture—deep feeling, a love of one's work, a lifelong dedication to a vocation or avocation—is considered slightly weird, it's no wonder that such expression on the part of older citizens would be viewed as particularly dotty. Elizabeth Cady Stanton, in her last and greatest speech, "The Solitude of Self," articulated this issue with *her* usual passion and skill:

In age, when the pleasures of youth are passed, children grown up . . . when the hands are weary of active service . . . then men and women alike must fall back on their own resources. If they cannot find companionship in books, if they have no interest in the vital questions of the hour, no interest in watching the consummation of reforms with which they might have been identified, they soon pass into their dotage. The more fully the faculties of the mind are developed and kept in use, the longer the period of vigor and active interest in all around us continues.[6]

It makes me think of the sculptor Adelaide Johnson, who died in 1955 at the age of 108. Johnson had been an active suffragist, and was called "the artist of the new woman." Hers is the famous sculpture that stands in the rotunda of the United States Capitol: a single block of marble out of which rise the busts of Susan B. Anthony, Elizabeth Cady Stanton, and Lucretia Mott. Johnson also sculpted other feminist leaders of her day, including Isabelle Beecher Hooker, Helen Densmore, and Ellen Hardin Walworth. But it was her various marble portraits of Anthony (one of which stands in the Metropolitan Museum in New

York) that became most famous; one was used as the model for the Anthony postage stamp. Johnson made of her whole life a work of art, spilling intensity over everything she did. She studied in Italy, then maintained her own studio—first in Illinois and later in Washington, D.C.—for the rest of her life, her aim being to "build a marble pantheon" of all the feminist leaders, so that what she called "this great idea of women's freedom" would outlast flesh and catch the imagination of the world through art. When she married the Englishman Alexander Jenkins, he changed his name to *hers*—and she, who had always designed her own flamboyant but practical clothing, designed their joint wedding garb: they both wore slacks; the groom was in white; the bride in black. Yet it was in 1939 that Adelaide Johnson (when she was ninety-two) smashed through the stereotype of quaint old age in her most dramatic gesture.

She faced eviction from her home across from the Supreme Court, after her mortgage had been foreclosed and her house put up for auction without her permission. Money she claimed the government owed her in payment for her sculptures had never been paid. What she called "swivel-chair art experts" at Washington art galleries, including the Mellon, wouldn't purchase her work, on the grounds that no one now would be interested in her subject matter. Furthermore, she said, "They told me that they planned to buy the work of no artist who hadn't already been dead for forty years. I might as well be dead." She was impoverished and about to become homeless.

So she alerted the press,[7] and began smashing her marbles. While reporters stood by astonished, the five-foot-tall woman took her hammer to busts of Anthony and of Stanton (and of Lincoln and Logan). She's quoted as having said, "I'll destroy it all—the work that Rockefeller's money can't buy—*my* work, the life of the clay, the purgatory of the plaster, and the paradise of the marble. The story of these marbles parallels the women's movement itself. I am sick of the temporary. I am tired of uncertainty."

It worked. Within an hour, various nervous congressmen appeared, trying to soothe Johnson, proffering personal checks of fifty dollars here and a hundred dollars there, reminding her that the sun was shining outside and promising that "help would come." To one such gentleman, she snapped, "I know the sun is shining outside. I can see. Don't patronize me. What do you know about anything? You're not old, you're not a woman, and you're not an artist."

But help did come, though not through Congress. Individual spontaneous donors—mostly women—sent in money from every-place in the country where the stories on Johnson had run in newspapers. Her home was made secure. Galleries suddenly found her art "commercial." For the remaining years of her life, she was fêted and honored—at the White House, at museum openings, at special exhibitions of her work. She found all this, she said, "highly amusing."

So much for the little old lady in tennis shoes, the one with meaningless time left to kill.

It's obvious—even platitudinous—that our values are all skewed. Age isn't necessarily something to be valued in itself. After all, anyone can grow old; in fact, turtles do it better than anybody. It's the unique self, the individual inside the body that is growing "old," that matters. But if human beings are viewed categorically, as Man or Woman or Children or Races or Classes or Nationalities or the Aged, then the holistic relationship *between* each of those unique selves can be safely avoided.

The actual process of aging itself is still a physiological mystery. Scientific theories vary: one attributes the aging process to cellular change in the genetic machinery (the DNA and its associated apparatus for making protein)—the "machinery" may deteriorate and lose its capacity for self-repair, or redundant ("replacement") genes may be exhausted, or there actually may be an "aging" gene programmed into the DNA, which goes into action at a particular point of normal development. There's also the "free radical" theory. This one posits that "free radicals" (unstable atoms which are part of the process by which a cell converts nourishment to fuel) go into a revolutionary stage, acting as "highly reactive chemicals that will combine with anything around," in the words of gerontologist Alex Comfort. These atoms, unless balanced by enzyme action, can do damage to cell structure (you know those crazy free radicals!); but in time, enzyme levels decrease and so the balance goes off. Still other theories ascribe aging to autoimmunity: after years of the thymus producing immunities against foreign "threats," it shrinks, and the body becomes in effect immune to itself, and thus produces age. (This sounds like a biological warning against the Us-*vs.*-Them approach to existence.) Still other theories investigate an aging or death "hormone" released by the pituitary gland at a preset time in the brain.[8]

But inside, meanwhile, the human being cries out, "I'm old and I sit here and think, what if I had a chance? I know I would make use of it," as Louise Hiett of the Cheyenne River Sioux so movingly said.[9] Outside, the mask is carefully and forcefully layered by society on living tissue. And what if each of us, in her/his own way, began to strip it off? What if the mystique of aging were punctured along with the mystique of youth?

What if, for instance, each one of us said the "unspeakable": always announced one's own age as easily as one's name or address? Gloria Steinem, who has been volunteering her age for some time, has been met with incredulous reactions when people learn she's forty-eight. "But you look great!" they exclaim. "You don't look forty-eight!" To which Gloria replies, "But this is how forty-eight *looks*. We've been forced to lie about our age for so long that nobody even remembers what a particular age really looks like anymore."

What if, for that matter, we deliberately refused to "act younger"—enough of the carcinogenic hair dyes and flesh tortures to appear in a more "marketable" manner. What if, instead, we deliberately chose to act *older*—to act with an awareness of the temporary, a sense of urgent energy, priority-focus, and relish of life that supposedly comes with age? What if we didn't wait passively for some prominent eventual wisdom, but sought and claimed it in ourselves right now? And *lived* by that?

I began trying this after a meeting with the then seventy-two-year-old Katharine Hepburn. Hepburn is still a being who manages to be, like an electron, at all points of her orbit at the same time. Well, what if *I* lived as if I were seventy-two? Astoundingly enough, I found that it worked: I felt my spine straighten, my step quicken, my voice saying a polite but firm no to three imminent things I didn't really want to do. Beloved family and good friends seemed especially precious—"on loan" and to be savored. The wind in my face felt bracing; an ordinary cup of tea was delicious. The capacity and obsession to work creatively was a miraculous gift. I didn't need anyone's approval for anything.

The truth, too, is that since I turned forty, I really do care less

What Others Think. Even a mere five years ago, I wouldn't have dared to put on paper some of the passages in this book, for fear of "offending": heterosexuals or homosexuals, radicals or liberals or Middle America, men—or women. I suspect that all my life there's been a free, eccentric, crotchety wonderful wise raucous old woman trapped in me, trying to get out. She must have tried when I was about six years old—and been slammed. I know she tried again when I was about seventeen—and again was slammed. I think I've been "leaking" her slyly ever since, and so I welcome every liver-spot freckle, every gray hair that denotes the entelechy by which I intuit her coming, prepare myself for her liberation. I try her out each day more and more. And she responds by making me feel physically better, stronger, sexier, happier with myself, more in control of my life, and more intelligent than I ever felt before. She continually surprises me—with her political insights, with her command of literary techniques, with her sense of confidence (none of these yet seem really *mine*, but I'm doing my damnedest to grow into them).

A few years ago, I went to western Massachusetts to speak at a rally in support of women students who had seized a building; the issue was virulent sexism in the university student newspaper. After the rally, I couldn't resist joining the women inside the building—crawling through the barricades, giving the special knock and password, finally reaching the familiar friendly chaos of the sit-in itself: cramped quarters, potato-chip crumbs everywhere, phones ringing ceaselessly, two typewriters being used to pound out pages of collective statements, position papers, press releases, leaflets—and the wonderfully classic feminist-sit-in complaints: "I haven't washed my hair in so many days it's going to fall out!" "Anybody got a tampon?" and "I warn you all, if we get busted and the cops torture me by holding Szechuan food under my nose, I'll name names and Tell All!" We sat down together for a brief tactical brainstorm session—and it wasn't until I got a faint whiff of being regarded as the visiting feminist Gray Eminence that I realized with a shock that most of the women in the room—around age seventeen and eighteen—could have been my daughters. But the funny thing was that this realization delighted me. First, they *were* my daughters in a way, as well as my sisters. Second, they were picking up the torch even before any of my generation of women had let it waver. Third, although our blue jeans and boots were identical (I'm not such a dummy that I wear heels to a *demonstration*), I *was* older—and had something to offer them because of that, some hard-won strategical suggestions that all their idealism and energy of youth couldn't possibly have known yet. Never have I felt so young and so old, so dispensable and so indispensable, as that afternoon spent in a lovely stuffy room. What I gave them was their own past (and their future). What they gave me was my own future (and my past). From such collaborations a living and dynamic present is created.

It made me return to the ongoing fantasy I share with some close women friends: the Old Feminists' Home. Since many feminists don't live with men, since even those who do run the statistical risk of outliving their men, and since family chosen in independence is surely preferable to family resorted to out of dependence, we've dreamed of creating this alternative.

Each city, say, would have two "branches" of the home—one in the urban center proper and one in the countryside, so that hopelessly metropolitan-type activists and intransigent nature-loving souls each can find their niche—and switch back and forth, for that matter. Over the door of each building would be engraved Elizabeth Cady Stanton's words, "I shall not grow conservative with age." *In* the building, everyone has her own suite (that "room of one's own," you know), with shared communal kitchen, library, and living rooms. Each suite is equipped with typewriter, international WATS-line telephone, whatthehell maybe teletype machine and computer—these are *activists*, remember. A fleet of busses stands ready to schlepp us all to demonstrations. We rotate in giving "ovulars"—instead of seminars—for younger feminists who intern with us as apprentice-aides. Women doctors (of course) are on-staff at all times, in case somebody feels creaky. We have our own typesetting machines and printing press, our own radio-television studio and transmitter, our own generator, our own communal orchestra, chamber group, jazz, and mariachi bands, our own artesian well, our own marijuana garden, our own gym (for exercise and karate practice). Live-in lovers or spouses (spicc?) and children (of any scx or agc) arc permitted with the consensus of the living community or collective. Brown-rice veggie dinners, Chinese food, knishes and blintzes, chicken 'n' ribs, Mexican tacos, pizza, Sachertorte, and piña coladas are served regularly; the women doctors either (1) understand or (2) have nothing to say about it. Diversity, commitment, and hilarity reign. One friend has suggested that the dreamhome employ a company of "dancing boys"—handsome young men complete with belled ankle bracelets—once a week, but the rest of us keep vetoing that as sexual objectification. The possibilities are endless, and it's a pleasurable pastime just to fantasize what additions we might want in our "alternative institution." Now all we need, as usual, is funding.

In all seriousness, however, humane and liberating alternative institutions such as the above *are* needed—and not only for older feminists, of course. Physical weakness or illness may in some cases be factors in aging—but isolation, loneliness, lack of activity, feelings of uselessness and placelessness, and the humiliation of dependency need not be. Neither, in a caring society, would the poverty which so destroys most older people today be unavoidable.

Astrophysics has charted the life stages of a star from Blue Giant (young star) through Yellow (middle-aged star) to Red Giant. It is the aging Red Giant that gives the warmest light, as it prepares to densify itself into the powerfully compact White Dwarf, or the Neutron Star, or possibly the Black Hole phenomenon at the end of its (visible) starlife. Black Holes themselves give off tremendous energy beyond anything emitted in an earlier stage. We don't yet know how. But there are theories that this energy emission possibly is due to the Black Hole having acquired and containing deep within itself entire universes we cannot see.

So it is with human age. That older persons in our society live and die in poverty, sickness, and disrepute may be the most surprising and senseless oppression of all—since *this oppression is perpetrated by a group who will someday enter the very state of oppression they are perpetrating.* To ignore what you inevitably will become is as perilous as to ignore that which you once were, since both states still and already coexist in you. Growing up and growing old are simply two sides of the Janus mask that the same self wears.

The day that self is released into its own expressions, not only can young blue stars be free to shed their clarity on our lives but the great Red Giants will be acknowledged to fill our world with their incomparable energy and light.

A BUCKETFUL OF MOON

In order for our culture to accomplish the hideous feat of buying, selling, and trading such goods as space, time, youth, and age, it's necessary to construct a modern politics of death as pervasive as that of Pharaonic Egypt. But this isn't hard—because death itself has been made into a marketable commodity: "body counts," the munitions industries, think-tank concepts of "acceptable" atomic overkill capacity, war toys. In the twentieth century alone there have been 110 million *Man-made* deaths, including 62 million by various forms of privation (death camps, slave labor, forced marches, etc.), 46 million from guns and bombs, and 2 million from chemicals.[10] We are living in a world which practices the politics of death.

There's a well-known Christian prayer that tells us "in the midst of life, we are in death." They mean it. It has been made a self-fulfilling prophecy, in fact. Yet this death-obsessed culture—which all of us on this shrinking planet now share, no matter how different our individual cultures may be—is mortally afraid of the subject most logically connected with death: dying. *That* issue is one to avert the eyes from, to joke about but change the conversation, to avoid if at all possible.

To be sure, over the centuries Man has devised ornate rituals, funerals, wakes, burial games, and ceremonies to cope with death. And over the same centuries, Woman has traditionally cared for the dying, washed the dead, prepared the bodies for burial, cremation, or exposure—and mourned. (Mourning is one of Woman's primary tasks.)[11] The justifications given for Woman's "expertise" in this area range from her inherent compassion and tenderness to her numinous powers of mystical contact with the supernatural, e.g., the Isis myths. The truth is more likely that women have been cast as caretakers of bodily functions in all areas—childbirth and childrearing, feeding (children *and* adults), cleaning up bodily and other waste after others, nursing the sick —because Man construed Woman *as* a creature of the flesh, not of the intellect, since she could create flesh from her own body. At times Man went so far as to pronounce her soulless. Yet while the realm of the body was hers to tend, her own body was not to be hers to define, control, or even really to inhabit (those rights were reserved for beings with intellect and soul: men). Hidden beneath *this* truth, in turn, is a still more basic one: that women came to care for the sick, the dying, and the dead simply because nobody else wanted the job.

Now more than ever before, women all over the world have begun refusing to perform those jobs that nobody else wanted to do. Is it because of this that many societies, including that of the United States, have started to change their attitudes regarding the dying?

I think of the Zen kōan about Jyono, the woman who diligently studied Zen under the master Bukkō for many decades. She performed all menial tasks with great humility, striving to discover in common things the secret of eternity. But no matter how long and devotedly she applied herself, she still could not attain enlightenment. Year after year, she meditated while she labored, but seemed to achieve no wisdom about the nature of existence. Then, one night, when a full moon hung lazily in the dark sky, Jyono was returning to her teacher from a trip to the well, staggering under the weight of an old wooden bamboo-bound bucket filled to the brim with water. She stumbled. Suddenly, the bamboo split and the bottom fell out of the bucket. Jyono said, "The water has flowed out of the bucket, the moon has flowed out of the water." At that moment, she attained enlightenment and was free.

The kōan does not go on to explain how Bukkō doubtless attained a different form of the same enlightenment now that he had to fetch his own water, but in the best traditions of Zen and feminist theory, we can fill that in ourselves. Similarly, whether women's turning our attention to our own lives and livings is or is not a reason for society's new interest in and compassion for the condition of dying, that growing concern is a sign of progress. It's been expressed in a proliferation of research projects, studies, books, scholarly and popular journals, hospices for the terminally ill,* "right-to-die" movements, experiments with psychedelic drugs to ease the pain and depression of dying, and court cases over the right of a patient to die without suffering a temporary prolongation of life by artificial means. One British organization dedicated to "the human right to die with dignity" is publishing

---

* It was a woman—Rose Hawthorne, daughter of Sara Peabody and Nathaniel Hawthorne—who as Mother Alphonsa established the first hospice for the terminally ill in the United States, in 1901.

a handbook for would-be suicides, detailing various methods that are relatively painless and foolproof, and possible even for invalids.† Most "rational suicide" groups are firm in their condemnation of suicide where the desire for it grows out of some nonmedical problem, such as loneliness or depression; they are, for the large part, concentrating on the right of a terminally ill patient not to be used as a guinea pig for new scientific techniques that preserve the body at the cost of extreme pain or lack of consciousness to its inhabitant. It's a sensible, obvious, and humane option for which they seem to be campaigning.

Still, I find myself wondering how the ethics of this question relate to such "suicides" as the French political philosopher Simone Weil, who fasted to starvation to protest the suffering that the French poor were experiencing under Nazi occupation. Or Bobby Sands and the other hunger strikers in Northern Ireland. Or the "suicide missions" of some political terrorists. Or Edith Stein, the Jewish convert to Catholicism who became Sister Benedicta, until she feared that her conversion might divide her from other Jews being persecuted by the Nazis—and so declared herself a Jew and was killed. Or, for that matter, Socrates' refusal to escape into exile. Indeed, the ethical questions swarming around the "nonmedical" suicide who still may be suffering acutely from the disease of living in a world that practices the politics of death are less simple than questions right-to-die groups would have us believe.

Our reactions to suicide are conditioned and distorted by cultural propaganda. For example, we tend to think of the Berlinbunker suicides of Hitler, Eva Braun, and a few loyal retainers of the Nazi High Command as acts of cowardice and fanaticism. Yet we are supposed to regard the mass suicide of Jews at Masada (rather than be taken captive by the Romans) as a heroic act. Then again, we are assumed to feel that the mass suicide/murder of Jim Jones's followers in Guyana in 1978 (because Jones told them that U.S. forces—like the Romans—were coming to destroy

† Committing suicide has been legal in Britain since 1961; it is still illegal in the United States—surely one of the more amusing laws on our books. The British handbook, written by lawyers and doctors, is being published by the organization Exit, but will be made available only to those who have been members of the organization for three months, so as to discourage anyone acting impulsively from following its methods. See *The New York Times*, March 7, 1980.

them) was an expression of ignorant rabidity and religious hysteria. Is this because it is standard to regard Nazis as subhuman (therefore safely not like *us*), to regard Jews as being most heroic when most victimized, and to regard nonwhite persons (Jones's Peoples' Temple followers were in large proportion black Americans) as naïve, manipulable, and immoderate? One thing is certain: the women and the children (at the bunker, at Masada, *and* at Guyana) were not consulted when the leaders—who were all men walking through the valley of the shadow of Man—decided on a dramatic exit for all those present. At most the women could make the best of a bad thing by pretending to choose they were Standing by Their Men; the children were not offered even this pretense. Of course it fell to the women, on the orders of the men, to do the killing of the children. And *the women*—walking through the valley of the shadow of Woman—*did it*.

Like Jews, slaves, philosophers, and other typecast victims, women always have been found admirable when committing "heroic" (or romantic) suicide. Roman Catholic hagiography is filled with female saints who went to their deaths rather more eagerly than male martyrs. Suicide has become almost an occupational hazard for poets—and most especially for women poets: Charlotte Mew, Sylvia Plath, Anne Sexton. Indeed, the reverence in which Plath, Virginia Woolf, and to some extent Sexton currently are held—even in the Women's Movement—at times looks suspiciously like the old glamorization-of-suicide syndrome. Many people who devotedly read the superb works of these women would never have done so were the writers not sensationally and safely out of the way. Which makes one wonder just what the readers' real motivations are; will feminists, too, fall into Man's habit of canonizing the conveniently dead while ignoring the living?

For myself, I find suicide neither sinful nor glamorous. If hopelessly ill and in pain, I should like the right to choose when and how to end my life, and I support sensible people who are working to raise consciousness about this right. But in the interim, I am far more interested in living for a cause than dying for one. Still, I like to think I am realistic enough about the inevitability of dying to carry a Universal Donor Card—which means that any organs of mine which can be put to use (for transplant, graft, or research), will be. I'm also aware that Man's institutions will charge the recipients horrendous sums for this service, and doubtless profit, ghoullike, from the donation—but all I can do about that right now is fight to bring about a medical system free of charge to its patients and humane in its treatment of them, and to make certain that in the meanwhile my organs don't go to waste if someone can see through my eyes, live via my transplanted kidney.

If dying were made less of an unspeakable and more of an integrated part in our thinking and actions, we would mystify it less, ostracize those enduring it less, and be less cavalier about death in the abstract. To be in control of one's own dying seems a rather important issue. For instance, for some time now I've taken distinct pleasure in planning my own funeral—or, rather, "memorial." (There won't be a body, because what isn't used will be cremated.) It's become a running joke in our very nonmorbid family: this issue of what we each wish to happen at our respective memorial services. The list of musical pieces I want played at mine has grown so long that I've given up the idea of a service and currently am expanding my plans into a weekend-long music festival. At the moment the still-growing list includes: Bach's B Minor Mass and "Jesu, Joy of Man's Desiring" (never mind the Jesu and the Man; the music is *gorgeous*), Clara Wieck Schumann's First Piano Concerto (Opus 7), the soprano arias from Orff's *Carmina Burana*, Nina Simone's rendition of "I Wish I Knew How It Would Feel to Be Free," Pachelbel's *Canon*, the Bartók Quartets, Sibelius' First Symphony and Prokofiev's Second Violin Concerto, Judy Collins' version of "Winter Sky," Schönberg's *Verklärte Nacht*, Dvořák's symphony *From the New World*, the last act of Poulenc's *Dialogues of the Carmelites*, Alfred Deller singing "The Three Ravens," Mozart's *Missa Solemnis* (K139), Joan Tower's *Trees*, Ralph Vaughan Williams' *Serenade to Music* and *Fantasia on "Greensleeves,"* Mary Lou Williams' *Mass*, Antonio Soler's *Fandango* for harpsichord, Rachmaninoff's *Trio Élégiaque* No. 2, Opus 9, John Lennon's "Imagine," Erik Satie's *Gymnopédies*, the trio from the last act of Strauss's *Der Rosenkavalier*, Brian Easdale's score for the film *The Red Shoes*, David Fanshawe's *African Sanctus, Lousadzak* by Alan Hovhaness, the Bruckner *Te Deum*, and Samuel Barber's *Knoxville: Summer of 1915*. Then of course there's to be food and drink and dancing and poetry readings and political speeches (not eulogies—inspiring but nonrhetorical organizing exhortations).

Well. You see the problem. But the point is that if no one cares to organize this mammoth music festival around my personal egotistical tastes, it won't matter all that much to me, since I won't be around to hear it. On the contrary, the point is that in thinking about what one *would* ideally like done in remembrance of one's life, it's possible to discover surprising facts about what one really enjoys, cherishes, and believes, and to discover the richness of our lives, however deprived and constrained those lives may feel at other times. Then—oh, dear delight—the reprieve of living and treasuring such things becomes all the more precious. Were the subjects of dying and death seriously, unsentimentally, and nonfearfully thought about and discussed more often and openly, we might all learn something about our attitudes toward our own lives as well as about our attitudes toward our own deaths. The great Russian poet Anna Akhmatova expresses this looking-forward-in-order-to-see-backward-clearly skill in an exquisite poem written in Leningrad in 1944, "This Bitter Age Has Changed Me . . .":

> This bitter age has changed me,
> thrown me off-course like a river . . .
> What sights I have not seen . . .
>   what friends
> I never met . . .
> What poems I never wrote!
> Their ghost-words haunt me, whispering.
> Someday they'll murder me.
> I know how things begin, and how things end,
> and living-in-death, and one more thing
> I want not to remember at this moment.
> And a specific woman
> walks in my body
> and calls herself my name . . .
> Even the grave I'll sleep in won't be my own.
>
> Yet if I could stand beside my body
> and really see the woman who I am,
> then I would understand at last how envy feels.
>   [R.M. version]

When I first mentioned to various women friends that I wished we would begin mulling over what might constitute "a feminist, way of death," I got the distinct impression that I was Going Too Far and might soon begin to win a reputation for the eccentricity that the old woman trapped inside me wickedly has been leaking out through my behavior, more every day. History does seem to stutter: when Elizabeth Cady Stanton first showed Susan B. Anthony that masterpiece speech, "The Solitude of Self," Anthony didn't like it and counseled against delivering it in public. But Stanton said (rightly) that it was the best thing she'd ever written, and went ahead with it. Stanton saw the issue of one's own integrity in mortality as central to feminist thought. The entire speech, in fact, revolves around this concept:

The strongest reason for giving woman . . . a complete emancipation from all forms of bondage, of custom, dependence, superstition; from all the crippling influences of fear—is the solitude and personal responsibility of her own individual life. . . . Whatever the theories may be of woman's dependence on man, in the supreme moments of her life, he cannot bear her burdens. Alone she goes to the gates of death to give life to every man that is born into the world; no one can share her fears, no one can mitigate her pangs; and if her sorrow is greater than she can bear, alone she passes beyond the gates into the vast unknown. . . . The Angel of Death makes no royal pathway for her. . . . In that solemn solitude of self, each soul lives alone forever . . . a solitude which each and every one of us has always carried . . . more inaccessible than the ice-cold mountains, more profound than the midnight sea. . . . Our inner being which we call ourself, no eye nor touch of man or angel has ever pierced. It is more hidden than the caves of the gnome; the sacred adytum of the oracle; the hidden chamber of eleusinian mystery, for to it only omniscience is permitted to enter.

Such is individual life. Who, I ask you, can take, dare take on himself the rights, the duties, the responsibilities of another human soul?[12]

So I am not joking when I wonder about "a feminist way of death." I believe that feminism is not only about the rights and freedom of more than half of all humanity and the "humanizing" of the other half of the species, but more: the crucial tool of consciousness by which women and men can begin to comprehend themselves, each other, and all sentient life; the step into passionate intelligence and celebratory living that will constitute *the next evolutionary stage of the species*. If this is true, then we can't afford not to reexamine *any* subject. Divisions of culture, race, age, sexual choice, education, wealth, physical appearance, and capacity—all these are our concern—and birth, and death, and the quality of existence itself.

None of these subjects—and most certainly not the issues of aging and death—can be approached with a superficial attitude of "solving" them. Some contradictions refuse to be resolved. No matter how humane a society we construct, Stanton's "solitude of self" will remain a reality—at least existentially, even when not culturally enforced or heightened. A Pollyanna attitude toward age is sentimental and hypocritical; with all it has to offer, age (like every other facet of life) carries its own tragedy as well: the body unable to accomplish what it once could, the loss and mourning of contemporaries, the bitter temptations to regret what never was or never again will be. Plastic surgeries and smiling denials don't soften these blows; they merely degrade the person already struck. And dying is surely fearful, surely the most solitary act each of us will ever perform. Such euphemisms as "passing on," "passing away," or "going to sleep" only paint a blush on it as hideous as the undertaker's cosmetics on the corpse.

But isn't this an even more imperative reason for each of us to insist that we not be robbed of our own old age, robbed of our own death—by trivialization, cultural cruelty, interference, or denial? As much as or more than any other moment in life, *our aging and our death must be our own*—to face and experience as deeply and with as much integrity, curiosity, and wisdom, as the previous years have taught us.

To do this would require great courage—and hard work. At the least, then, we need not be impeded by gratuitous obstacles created by other individuals or by society.

I imagine that "a feminist way of death" would be simple, compassionate, and as eased as possible. Surely no one should die of unnatural causes (poverty, war, murder), or untended, or alone (unless one wishes to be alone), or in unnecessary pain. Surely one *has* a right to die with dignity and in peace. Surely one has a right to prepare oneself for that, by whatever means one chooses. Surely one has a right not to be surrounded by pomposity or by grim, boring, preachy presences, or by legalisms and property divisions, or by impersonal medical officials. Surely there are many other elements to a "good death" that all of us could suggest if we dared talk more creatively about this subject.

Four deaths come to my mind when I think about this—not as

models but because each contains some quality of an individual
self inimitably and intensely conscious of itself. (Two happen to
be men, two women; both men happen to have died young and
tragically, both women in the ripeness of age. Somehow these details seem irrelevant.)

I think of Mozart, dying in poverty at the incredibly young age
of thirty-six, surrounded by a few musician friends who had come
by to sing parts of his own unfinished *Requiem*—and how he
sang along with them until, his eyes full of tears, he said softly,
"Sing no more." Then he began to hum the joyous Birdcatcher's
Song from *The Magic Flute*, afterward drifting into the coma in
which he died.

I think of Franz Kafka in his sanitorium room, in the agonizing
last stage of the tuberculosis which had, ironically, released him
from the confines of parents, job, and all the other strictures of
his life, a "freedom" (as he named it) which was so dear in its
radical liberation that he called the earliest spot on his lung "the
first sign of health"; Kafka, all of his suffering still not more than
he thought bearable, at last having broken through to a woman
he loved and who loved him; Kafka, no longer able to speak, and
so scribbling "conversation slips" to the last—fragments which actually are immortal aphorisms—about the lilacs dying in a vase,
about a bird that flew into the room.

And I think of Elizabeth Tudor, that learned, brave, political
genius who after a long illness felt her death to be near and so sat
upright on floor cushions for four days, staring into her own past
and into the future of her beloved England; when one of her
ministers whispered to her, "Madame, you *must* go to bed," she
replied, "Little man, little man. One does not say 'must' to
princes."

And I think of Elizabeth Cady Stanton, who saw no issue as
not political and who saw no political issue as not her concern;
two hours before her death, by her daughter's account, she insisted on standing up. She rose from her bed and braced herself
against a table, then stood for seven or eight minutes as if men-
tally making an address in the most eloquent voice women have
ever had speak for us. Then she sat down in an armchair, fell
asleep, and died.[13]

Such last moments are earned by people who know how to die
because they know how to live.

THE ELECTROMAGNETIC FIELD OF JOY

And after?

Had Man and Woman spent half as much inventive energy on imagining what creative formations living might take as they have on imagining what formations an afterlife might take, men and women would not be in such a desperate fix today.‡

The human brain seems to have been obsessed with What Happens After ever since prehistory; most of the earliest artifacts have been unearthed from graves—appurtenances of living, from simple cookpots to beaten-gold crowns, from the wreath of flowers in a Neanderthal grave to the bejeweled death mask of Tutankhamen. Ancient goddess-worshipping peoples buried the corpse curled in fetal position—for the return to the earth's womb. To the Ndembu of Zambia, death constitutes a change in social status. To the Hopi of the American Southwest, the dead person grows into a cloud of new being, a *kachina*. To the Aztecs, the dead were separated into three paradises: Mictlan, where most souls went, Tlalocan, where those who died of diseases, drowning, or lightning went, and the third, best paradise— for women who died in childbirth, warriors who died bravely in battle, and victims of religious sacrifice. In central Java, the bereaved family must demonstrate a careful indifference, a grief muted in detachment—so as not to hold back the spirit from its flight into freedom. The Ik of East Africa plant seeds on the grave, so that the dead soul might live and serve the community with crops as soon as possible. The Atjehnese (a matrifocal ethnic group in Indonesia) believe in a paradise where women are reunited together with their children and their own mothers; husbands and fathers do not enter. The *Zohar*, the esoteric Hebrew commentary on the Torah, names three grades of soul: *nefesh* (vital soul), *ruah* (spirit), and *neshamah* (higher soul); after death, *nefesh* stays with the body, *ruah* proceeds to the earthly Garden of Eden, and *neshamah* rises to her place in the light of eternity. The Buddhist *Tibetan Book of the Dead* charts the

‡ Madalyn Murray O'Hair, America's intrepid and best-known atheist, has declared that there are five "insane" ideas which should be outlawed: violence between individuals and countries, slavery, racism, sexism, and the notion of a "god that gives punishments and rewards in the afterlife, so that you remove yourself from everyday life or abdicate the use of human reason." See interview in *Omni*, December 1981.

soul's path from the Primary Clear Light of the First Bardo (an intermediate stage between death and rebirth) through forty-nine days of Bardo existence filled with tests and rites of passage. The Sufi mystic poet Jalal al-din Rumi counseled, "Die now, and come forth from this cloud of ignorance." There are ornate Sioux, Hindu, Confucian, Parsi, and Christian rituals for releasing the soul into eternity.[14]

Today, religious fundamentalists (and some feminist fundamentalists) speak literally of reincarnation. Meanwhile, Elisabeth Kübler-Ross, author of the superb book On Death and Dying[15] has since tried to lead her readers into the flakier realms of astral afterlives. The Journal of Thanatology has a large readership, and a reputable bookstore near where I live has a special section, including about fifty titles, on the subject of death and "life after death." A recent book, Recollections of Death,[16] purports to be the first scientific study done (by cardiologist Michael Sabom) on NDE's, or "near-death experiences." Many of these works speak of "returned" persons having similar tales to tell—out-of-the-body free floating, feelings of warmth and tranquillity, being bathed in clear white light. For myself, I choose to balance what I confess is curiosity with a healthy skepticism: I'll know an afterlife is real when I'm sitting on an astral plane writing about it—the way I best know life is real is when I'm writing about it.

But there is another metaphor for the mystery of life and death which seems to me, in my "womanly" practicality, more moving because more grounded. Again, it's a gift of the New Physics, and it embraces such concepts as the electromagnetic field, negentropy, and the fullness of emptiness. But it's wonderfully, laughably simple—in a way even obvious.

"Quantum electrodynamics" is a theory which incorporates quantum theory and relativity theory; it is a "quantum-relativistic" model of modern physics, in the words of physicist Fritjof Capra. Earlier I referred to the realization that photons could be both particles and waves at the same time—the way a bump of movement will flow along a ribbon if you tie one end of it to a drawer handle, hold the other end, and then wave it up and down (the "bump" travels along the ribbon and is both bump and ribbon at the same moment). To take it further:

Since photons are also electromagnetic waves [as well as particles] and since these waves are vibrating fields, the photons must be manifestations of electromagnetic fields. Hence the concept of a "quantum field": that is, of a field which can take the form of quanta, or particles. This is indeed an entirely new concept. . . . Particles are merely local condensations of the field.[17]

Or, as Einstein said, "We may therefore regard matter as being constituted by the regions of space in which the field is extremely intense. . . . There is no place in this new kind of physics both for the field and matter, for *the field is the only reality*."[18] (Italics mine.)

Seventy-five years after Einstein first proposed his Special Theory of Relativity, physicists still are reeling with the fallout, with the scientific revelation that the question isn't matter and energy (since matter *is* energy; there is nothing *but* energy). The question isn't even about a field dense with particles resonating with "tendencies to exist." The field, the particles, the resonances, the tendencies, and the energy are *all the same thing*.

Some of the new physicists, like Capra and David Böhm, can't help but compare such "science" with "philosophy" (the two disciplines flowered from the same root of thought, after all, before Man compartmentalized them)—especially such Eastern mystical traditions as Taoism. The Tao itself (the "path," the "way," or the "*field*") is seen as being empty, formless, both temporary and eternal, but capable of producing all forms continually; Lao-tzu sometimes described the Tao as a hollow vessel which, because it seems eternally empty, forever contains the potential of holding and expressing all things. Comparably, the Upanishads, one of the great Hindu mystical texts, speak of "The Void that is identical with All, with Joy."

Furthermore, in quantum field theory, the field is seen not only as the basis for (and comprised of) all particles but also as the basis for all mutual particle *interactions*. The field exists at all times and at all places, it is everything there is, including all "matter." The appearance, existence, and disappearance of particles are simply changing patterns of motion, a dance of the field. Or, as the Chinese philosopher Chan Zai said, "When one understands how full the Great Void is, then one understands that there is no such thing as nothingness."

Entropy, we know, is the process of dissolution, burning out and away, the tendency toward disorder. *Negentropy* is, expectedly, its opposite. It is the tendency toward form, information, communication, expression, order. "Empty space," we now realize, isn't empty at all, but rich with infinite energy; within this field, this primordial "soup" of life, jumps of negentropy may occur (arbitrarily? whimsically? out of the love of formlessness for form? or just for the sake of the dance?). These leaps of negentropy (or information) garner form about them, organizing it, so to speak, into particles. But the particle is still at once in and of the field, in form comprised wholly of formlessness. Since entropy can mean the wasting away of matter, and since negentropy is its opposite, and since we now know that matter is merely an illusion produced by witty old energy anyway, then the philosophical implications of this very grounded scientific revelation are hilariously clear at a level both deeper and simpler than all the waffling about ghosts and mediums: *nothing, ultimately, is wasted.*

We don't need wings and gold lamé sandals and harps. We don't need rigid religious systems that can translate karmic destiny into a reality where millions of "untouchables" die in starved, pustulated bodies while a caste of Brahmans who supposedly have earned their wealth and rank by having lived deserving past lives look on in distaste. We don't need to cheapen the mysteries of the universe with séances, Ouija boards, or horoscopes based on positions the stars haven't held in thousands of years (the *stars* move, even if human thought sometimes sits stagnant). We certainly don't need the death-politics pronouncements of popes, ministers, rabbis, mullahs, and gurus. Look, oh look—we need none of these pathetic golems of Man and of Woman at all, not ever, not anymore.

We are the particles, the waves, the bumps on the ribbon, the leaps of negentropic information gathering itself to itself for the sheer joy of communicating through interference waves which also are part of the field to other negentropic hemiolian photons of light-darkness-matter-illusion-*energy*. We are the holomovement. We are inside the holograph. We are the dance of the field. *We are the field itself.*

All we need is an awareness of this—a daring to feel with the brain and think through the body how each cell sings of its molecules which dance in their atoms which encircle their nuclei like a mirror's scratches ring round a candleflame, which in turn flowers forth its vibrating petals of neutron, electron, photon—which spin like negentropes, shrug like bumps, flow like waves through and into and of the field . . . What we need is an audacious willingness to absorb the cosmos laughingly, as if by osmosis—a *cosmosis.*

It's been a public secret all along.

VIII

THE UNCERTAIN FUTURE OF FLESH

An Anatomy of Art and Technology

> She is Choice at odds with Necessity; she is Love blindly
> butting its head against all the obstacles set in its path by
> civilization.
> —George Sand

> Because the essence of technology is nothing technological,
> essential reflection upon technology and decisive confron-
> tation with it must happen in a realm that is, on the one
> hand, akin to the essence of technology and on the other,
> fundamentally different from it. Such a realm is art.
> —Martin Heidegger

> The most beautiful thing we can experience is the myste-
> rious. It is the heart of true science and true art.
> —Albert Einstein

Item: In 1980 the United States Supreme Court ruled that living
organisms are patentable. Immediately, corporate laboratories
began producing new life forms which previously had been in the
research stage: bacteria for antihepatitis and anti-hoof-and-mouth-
disease vaccines, insulin, interferon, certain hormones, and various
other modified bacteria—for example, a strain capable of turning
wood waste into alcohol. Cetus Corporation president Peter J.
Farley predicted, "In ten or twenty years, we will be designing animals to specification."[1]
   Item: In 1978 the first successful "test-tube baby" was born in
England, an infant brought to term and delivered after having
been conceived *in vitro*, the procedure which involves removing
the egg from a woman's ovary, placing it in a dish to be fertilized
by sperm, and allowing it to subdivide before being inserted into

the woman's uterus. On December 28, 1981, the first such baby was born in the United States, the fifteenth birth from this technique so far in the world.[2]

Item: Light-wave communications, or fiber optics, are already in use throughout the industrialized world, but their epoch has only begun. In 1980, A T & T announced its plans to build a 611-mile telephone system linking Boston, New York, and Washington, D.C., by laser beam; the light-wave cable, comprised of loops of hair-thin glass fiber illuminated by laser light, will be capable of handling up to eighty thousand telephone calls simultaneously. Fiber optics—which can transmit more sound over longer distances at less distortion—already are being tested for light-wave undersea cables, and are expected to become crucial in the twenty-first-century "wired city"—where homes, schools, offices, and commercial business places will be connected via computer terminals carrying word and visual information.[3]

Item: "Protoplast fusion" is the latest engineering technique in the process of plant tissue culture. Protoplasts are plant cells whose walls have been dissolved by exposure to particular enzymes; the protoplasts from two different plants then can be fused, "mating" certain genetic material of species that otherwise couldn't be crossed. Plant tissue culture itself is a process whereby scientists can reproduce cells which will duplicate themselves into the millions, after being fed special formulae of synthetic growth hormones, salts, sugars, and vitamins; each individual cell can be spurred to generate a whole plant—as many as a thousand plants can be produced from each gram of starter cells, and can be ready to root within weeks. Protoplast fusion has the potential of producing not only new species of edible plants but hardier, pest- and disease-resistant species. Furthermore, pharmaceutical chemicals can be extracted directly from the plant cells in a faster and purer process than from harvested plants: penicillin, heart-treatment compounds, antitumor compounds, extractions from the cells of two rare Chinese plants that seem effective against some types of leukemia. Tissue-culture propagation of eucalyptus can produce methanol fuel; tissue-culture propagation of the gopher plant (a cousin of the rubber tree) could produce latex; margarine, derived from cell cultures of the Malaysian palm tree, would be more plentiful and less costly. And germ plasm collected in tissue culture can be frozen for later thawing and regeneration—a possible way to preserve and resurrect endangered plant species.[4] (More than fifty species of plants native to the U.S. have become extinct in recent decades, due to cavalier nonplanning in development—building of bridges, dams, tunnels, etc. The Smithsonian Institution and the Federal Endangered Species Program predict that as many as three thousand more American plants—approximately 10 percent of the plants in this country—will vanish if these trends continue.)

Item: Electrosurgery, performed through an endoscope (a tube inserted through natural body openings), can with the aid of computers greatly reduce the need to cut human tissue in surgical procedure, and shows special potential for use against ulcers, polyps, other stomach disorders, and possibly cancerous growths.[5] In addition, medical diagnostic techniques have been transformed by X-ray, sonar, infrared, radar, and ultrasound devices that can inform us of otherwise unknowable conditions inside the brain and body.

Item: Holography (three-dimensional representation via lensless photography), although as primitive today as television was in the 1940's, will, by the year 2000, be employed in schoolrooms (so that students can study three-dimensional reproductions of sculptures, architecture, and geographical sites), in homes (so that movies "in the round," ballets, and plays can be viewed on holovision), and in science and industry (geologists, for example, will be able to keep watch on volcano activity from the safety of their offices).[6]

Item: Between ten and twenty thousand children are born each year in the U.S. as the result of artificial insemination, a phenomenon already producing a tangle of medical, legal, and ethical problems: Has the sperm donor any paternal rights (such as visitation) or responsibilities (such as child support)? Is the child legally "illegitimate"? Has the child rights to a paternal inheritance? Has the mother a right to sole custody—or a right to require child support from the donor? Doctors at Columbia University in New York have been campaigning for more careful screening of donors for genetic defects, since there have been cases of inheritable disease passed on through the donor to the child, produced by artificial insemination. And Armand M. Karow, Jr., of the Medical College of Georgia, has reported that freezing semen (to allow time for testing) has the added advantage of decreasing the incidence of birth defects and spontaneous abortions; freezing seems to kill abnormal spermatozoa. But freezing also affects the sex ratio of births: 51 percent of newborns are male in the general population; 60 percent are male in the artificially inseminated birth population. Then again, the late Pierre Soupart, a pioneer in test-tube-baby research at Vanderbilt University, claimed to have discovered OFP (oocyte-fusion product)—a technique that duplicates the kind of "glue" which sticks sperm to the ovum it is fertilizing. Dr. Soupart stuck two mouse eggs together with this duplicate substance; thus successfully fertilizing without the intervention of sperm, and eventually producing a normal female offspring. The technique produces only females, since it's a form of parthenogenesis.[7]

Item: NASA officials and aerospace experts in the private sector estimate that in the 1990's, electric orbit transfer vehicles and space stations (containing medical, agricultural, and industrial laboratories for experiments under zero gravity) will begin to be an accepted reality. By the year 2000, the first space station should be in orbit around the moon, and in-depth lunar exploration and mining could begin. Lunar colonies would evolve throughout the next century, becoming increasingly self-dependent (the two-week-long lunar day and one-sixth earth gravity will offer special growing conditions for environment-controlled agriculture under glass domes). The science of robotics has already developed to a point where, combining solid-state television eyes with pattern-recognition software, robots will shoulder the arduous work of construction, mining, and farming. The United States Tricentennial might be celebrated by the first self-supporting colony on Mars. If government funding for such projects is miserly or not forthcoming, private industry plans to take the lead with these programs.[8]

Item: Bionic science is moving swiftly beyond the hearing aid, contact lens, pacemaker, and prosthesis (for an amputated limb) stage, into the "biochip implant"—a protein chip tiny enough to mesh directly with the human nervous system, restoring sight to the blind, hearing to the deaf, possibly replacing damaged spinal nerves and/or giving the human brain powers of memory retention and mathematical wizardry that would rival the most powerful computers. Within fifty years, it is conceivable that molecular electronics will develop a compatible symbiote which could be implanted into the brain—there to grow, communicate with the nerves, learn from, imitate, and complement them. This could mean the bionic human being, a new species evolved from the "marriage" of human and computer intelligence.[9]

Item: The Journal of the American Medical Association now lists more than thirty fetal defects which can be corrected by *in utero* surgery, and estimates that fetal therapy, along with prenatal diagnosis, will soon take its place—along with the recently developed "transplant" surgeries (kidney, heart, bone marrow, etc.) —as a viable new branch of medicine. Until the advent of successful fetal surgical techniques, antiabortion groups had labeled prenatal diagnoses "search-and-destroy missions," since the likelihood was considerable that a woman would choose to abort if she learned that she was carrying a fetus showing a severe handicap. Now, as fetal surgery becomes more common, antichoice groups have switched to claiming that the fetus deserves "patient status" —whether or not the woman carrying it wishes to risk her own life by this surgery (it does take place inside her, after all). Already, a clash is foreseen between "fetal interests" and "parental interests." This new surgery is a mixed blessing, bringing with it the potential of saving entire lifetimes of medical and custodial care, but also further complicating the issue of already-endangered "host" (woman carrier) rights.[10]

Item: By the year 1990, computers and microprocessors will be everywhere: in the car, the home (furnaces, telephones, kitchen appliances, home entertainment centers—of video recorders, games, and pay-television terminals—and home management systems for bill paying, letter writing, income-tax preparation), the office (teleconference terminals, word processors), the store (EFT—Electronic Funds Transfer and Point Of Sale terminals —which will make checks, credit cards, and eventually cash obsolete). Whole libraries can be made available via telephone-computer connections and television-computer aides.[11]

Item: Contemporary medical techniques are undergoing a revolution in all areas. The CAT (computerized axial tomography) scanner can visually expose abnormalities within the skull that could not be perceived with traditional techniques. "Artificial blood" (one form of which—Fluosol-DA—has been in emergency use since the 1970's) is being tested in sophisticated combinations which may prove as or more effective than blood in transfusion.[12]

Renal dialysis machines can filter the blood of a patient suffering from kidney failure, thus replacing kidney function. Fluoridation of water and new "preventive dentistry" techniques of coating teeth with a fluoride substance already have lowered the statistics on prevalence of tooth decay, and by the mid-1980's the currently being tested vaccine against tooth decay may be available, eradicating cavities forever. A reversible pregnancy vaccine will go into clinical testing in 1982 or 1983, possibly offering to women temporary immunity from pregnancy, and possibly available by the late 1980's. By that time, a self-inducing abortion device (consisting of a vaginal pessary containing a chemical which within hours induces contractions and expels the fetal matter) may well be available. The John Radcliff Hospital in England is the center for research on this device, with the sponsorship of the World Health Organization.[13]

Item: The year 2020 is the earliest estimated date for usable *fusion* power (fusion is the energy process of the sun adapted to earth's conditions; so far, fusion power has only been used with "success" in hydrogen bombs). It may be able to meet the world's energy needs for millennia, although the costs are extremely high and the risks enormous. Meanwhile, the process of gaining energy from nuclear *fission* (splitting atomic nuclei into fragments by bombarding them with neutrons) is complicated to a grave danger point by problems of plant safety, shipping of hazardous materials, nuclear-waste disposal, and the limited amount of fissionable material (uranium 235) in nature. The consequent necessity of converting 238 and thorium 232 *into* fissionable material in turn requires enriching uranium 238 with plutonium 239, which is the material usable for nuclear weapons and is thus highly susceptible to theft. Such "soft" energy technology resources and techniques as solar power, windmills, biomass conversion, photovoltaic cells, etc., remain "soft" only when decentralized; a bank of solar collectors mounted on an earth-orbiting satellite and controlled, rationed, and sold by a utilities company is transformed by the scale alone into "hard" technology.[14]

Item: Genetic engineering and surgery, while still at a primitive stage, show the potential to cure inheritable diseases, blood, skin, and intestinal disorders, and even cancers (including those which are not seen as genetic in origin). On the other hand, the specter of eugenics and the possibility of releasing, through recombinant

RNA "error," a deleterious viral strain for which there would be no known antidote, demands extreme caution in this area of research. That caution already has been violated on a number of occasions by overly enthusiastic researchers.[15]

NEITHER/NOR

The above-listed techniques are only a small sampling of the new scientific/technological developments which are not science fiction, however futuristic they may sound. On the contrary, they are here *now*. And they are increasing in their common use, their perfected methods, and their enormously transformative effect on society. Santayana's now proverbial statement, "Those who cannot remember the past are condemned to repeat it," might well be rephrased, in this context: "Those who cannot understand the future are condemned to destroy it."

The American Association of University Women has produced a remarkable book, *Taking Hold of Technology: Topic Guide for 1981–83*, which, because of its clear elucidation, accessible style, and commonsense demystifying approach, ought to be read by every woman.[16] The already acknowledged problem which Sheila Tobias termed "math anxiety" has been developed, we know, in women by patriarchal culture. It is further compounded by our "tech anxiety." This is an even graver "illiteracy" because the power to define and shape the future lies more and more with the new technologies. The AAUW book is an exciting consciousness raiser, pointing out that the three prevalent attitudes toward technology—technology as triumph, threat, or mere tool—are all simplistic as well as self-contradictory. Believing that technology will solve all problems (the "tech fix") clearly can lead us to perdition. But a head-in-the-sand approach that sees technology only as evil and advocates a Luddite or Rousseauean back-to-the-woods solution is both unrealistic and atavistic. (How, for instance, do antitechnology proponents propose to deal with the glacial period expected to begin in the next two thousand years? Back to the caves?) Even the "just a tool" argument—that it all depends on who controls the technology—falls short of an understanding of what technology *is*: "a form of life," in the words of Langdon Winner, with a complex nature and interrelationship with society. "All tools have a *context*. In fact, they have three: a user context, a developmental context, and an environmental context," points out the AAUW book, and the interweaving *effects* from all these contexts mean that, ultimately, no tool is value-free: it is *both* "boon and bane."

For example, much laser research has been in the area of weaponry (obviously a bane), yet laser surgery, laser use in such communications devices as holography and fiber optics, and laser-employing techniques for monitoring air pollution are clearly boons. Artificial insemination can seem eerily antihuman, a cold, clinical removal of reproduction from the context of sexual love— yet it provides an option not only for heterosexual couples unable to conceive via traditional means, but also for single women and lesbian couples who want a child but wish to have no involvement whatsoever with a man.

One delightful irony about the growing number of artificially inseminated lesbian-mother births (estimated in 1980 at 1500 per year in the United States) is the confusion such a phenomenon wreaks on the sexually fundamentalist mind. Sexual fundamentalism fears and hates all sexual acts celebrated simply for pleasure and not likely to result in reproduction; therefore it opposes birth-control methods, abortion rights, reproductive freedom in general, and of course homosexual love. How *will* sexual fundamentalists deal with all this lesbian nonmale-involved motherhood, then? Clearly these children are *wanted*, and are loved by their mothers —and isn't motherhood, according to sexual fundamentalists and family fundamentalists, the purest love of all, and Woman's primary and highest function? How can such "pure" love coexist with such "unholy" love in the same woman? The Right Wing hasn't quite turned its attention to this phenomenon yet; being so busy looking backward at the eighteenth century with longing, they always are a little bit behind the current news. Yet I'm afraid they won't disappoint us with their capacity for bigoted nonlogic: since they will want to retain their homophobia and their fetus fetishism at the same time, they'll probably come up with something so convoluted as "Lesbians shouldn't be allowed [an unenforceable idea] to use artificial insemination, and those already pregnant or with children should be forced to give up their offspring—*after* birth, of course, since abortion is a no-no." That'll properly punish lesbian mothers with grief, fill up the orphanages and adoption agencies (thus expanding the lucrative baby market), and reassure St. Paul, Ronald Reagan, and good white Christian patriots that All Is Well once again.*

Boon and bane indeed. Biochip implants, fetal surgery, and genetic engineering all have the potential to cure illness, save and prolong life, and eliminate suffering—yet they also have the potential for use in mind control, or to imprison women even further in reproductive servitude, or to engender a "planned" race of "superior beings" and a "planned" underclass of "drones." Yet another and more immediate ethical problem is brought into view by the advances in genetics: "genetic counseling"—which can be a boon in forewarning parents if one of them carries an inheritable gene of, for example, Tay-Sachs disease or sickle-cell anemia. Genetic counseling can lead in turn to "environmental counseling." (A number of medical schools already offer degrees in environmental medicine.) An environmental counselor in the near future might advise clients on their susceptibility to occupational chemicals or pollutants on the basis of genetic traits and disease history. Leon Gordis of Johns Hopkins University foresees a problem of ethics arising as to whether industrial employers could require screening tests to select persons to work with particular materials—and whether industry's responsibility for environmental control would actually be reduced if it screened its employees in this manner. Which would, of course, be a bane.[17]

Cloning experiments (further off on the horizon) could make possible all-male propagation with no necessity for women; yet as long as women still live in the shadow of Woman and are regarded as being necessary primarily *for* reproduction, the question arises: what need then have men of women at all? Gynocide, or the deliberate use of female citizens solely for male sexual pleasure, or a predominantly male-homosexual populace (now and then visiting "museums of women")—all are hypothetical dystopian scenarios which could result. Man has been controlling (and abusing) the means of production for some time. Now he appears to be moving rapidly into control of the means of *repro-*

* See Francie Hornstein's excellent paper "Lesbians, Reproductive Rights, and Artificial Insemination," presented at the Eleventh Annual Woman and Law Conference (March 1980) in San Francisco. See also the Santa Cruz Women's Health Collective Booklet *Lesbian Health Matters*, which devotes a chapter to the how-to's of donor insemination *outside* the control of the medical establishment, and the article "Lesbian Insemination" by Susan Stern in *The CoEvolution Quarterly*, Summer 1980.

duction, even though it is women who are the reproducers. In the past, his control of reproduction has been limited to the extent to which he could control the reproducers, women—and he saw to it, with the help of the image of Woman, that this control was considerable. Is it coincidental, then, that as women throw off the mantle of Woman and with it layers of his control, Man researches other means, independent of women, for a control of reproductive techniques—and all "for the sake of science"? Two important works exposing and analyzing the gravity of a situation in which the technology advances but political consciousness does not keep pace with it—at the cost of great female suffering—are the groundbreaking book *The Transsexual Empire: The Making of the She-Male*, by bioethicist and feminist Janice G. Raymond,[18] and the forthcoming work by Gena Corea, *Reproductive Technology*.[19] It was H. G. Wells who said, "The future will be a race between education and catastrophe"; unless women educate ourselves about new technological and scientific developments and their implications, we are powerless indeed to use them constructively or stop their being used destructively. Our fear is based in our ignorance—and it's time to release our curiosity and desire on this subject.

Then again, research itself can't always predict what it will uncover. Parthenogenetic techniques (also far off on the horizon) could make possible all-*female* propagation—which could mean a dominantly lesbian populace, "museums of men," or even the sexual objectification by women of *men*. In either of these two extreme events, however, a reduction of the richness of the gene pool would likely result.[20]

One could go on . . . Sperm and ovum banks, "surrogate motherhood," sex selection—all present liberating options for infertile would-be parents or parents who already have a child or children of one sex and wish to parent a child of the other sex. Yet sperm banks can be manipulated by such unsavory types as the notorious Dr. William B. Schockley, already a controversial figure for his views on the "inferiority" of certain (dark-skinned) races; Schockley has announced that he donated sperm to banks in order to counter "dysgenics" ("excessive reproduction by the genetically disadvantaged") and to "increase the people at the top of the population."[21]

"Surrogate motherhood" can be practiced at the expense of women in economic need who will be forced to "rent a womb"— to sell their bodies for childbearing the way women have been wet nurses or prostitutes. So far, surrogate motherhood has been discussed and practiced only in a human-to-human context. But Dr. Geoffrey Bourne, chancellor of St. George's University School of Medicine in Grenada, West Indies, has said, "I believe it would be very important scientifically to try to produce an ape-human cross [by artifically inseminating an ape with human sperm], and I hope someone in a position to do it will make the attempt." Dr. John Senner, a geneticist at the Oregon Regional Primate Research Center, concurred that an ape-human cross would produce living offspring, since 97.5 percent of the chromosomes are held in common. Dr. Stephen W. J. Seager, chief of the Reproductive Physiology Unit at the National Institutes of Health Veterinary Resources Branch, found the idea objectionable on ethical grounds—but he countered with an even more startling one: human females could serve as "hosts" for embryos of chimpanzees or gorillas, both of which are endangered species. Dr. Seager didn't think the pregnancy would be that difficult for the human mother, since chimps, gorillas, and humans have similar gestation periods, and newborn apes tend to be smaller than newborn humans. As to who would volunteer, or why, for such a "hosting," Dr. Seager said, "I think you could find women who are serious conservationists, who want to help animals."[22]

Sex selection, conceivably a boon in some situations, becomes a bane without a concurrent consciousness of female humans *as* human. In fact, it evokes a feminist's nightmare: most families, guided by the ideology of Man, would prefer boy babies—creating a situation of sex-ratio population imbalance at least, and de facto gynocide at worst.

Technology has been revealing itself all along as an endless sequence of spin-offs, with one discovery or invention inspiring or necessitating another. It's been a dynamic process which is always both boon and bane but never neutral (no matter who controls it) ever since the development of shelters, the concept of cooking with fire, making pottery, weaving, devising measurement, estimating the calendar, domesticating animals—ever since the wheel and the plow. In the AAUW book, Corlann Gee Bush lucidly defines it:

Technology is a form of human cultural activity that applies the principles of science and mechanics to the solution of problems. It includes the resources, tools, processes, personnel, and systems developed to perform tasks and create particular personal or competitive advantage in a given ecological, economic, and/or social context.

Yet although the dynamic *process* of technology always has been the same, the *effect* of that process has been felt in dramatically different ways by women than by men. This is not the "fault" of the technological dynamism itself, but of Man and Woman. In other words, as long as role expectations are different for men and women, then technology—along with most other things—will have a different effect on each of those genders.

This can be seen today even within the Appropriate Technology (AT) movement. The ideology of AT at first appears eminently sensible: an approach to the problem that neither reveres nor rejects technology, but insists on reevaluating each aspect of it as to its appropriateness: What do we gain and what do we lose? Do the gains outweigh the losses? Is the solution short-term at the expense of tomorrow or does it have the potential of meeting needs today while preserving future resources? For instance, as the AAUW book *Taking Hold of Technology* states it:

Functions of billing, inventorying, and accounting can be carried on as they are now without resorting to a complex, centralized, large-scale system that will require more energy and eliminate thousands of jobs. But home computers, cable television, and "smart" machines [self-timing kitchen appliances, etc.] are another matter, for each of these innovations can increase the autonomy of individuals and communities.

But: at second sight, it becomes clear that Man is alive and well in the AT movement, too. Men otherwise dedicated to asking hard questions about the appropriateness of a particular technology are *not* usually asking "appropriate for *whom?*" It's a callousness reminiscent of the male-controlled ecology movement, where men dismissed feminist issues as divisive or self-indulgent in comparison with saving the trees or the whales. (When American male radicals discovered "endangered nature" I can imagine them celebrating: they hadn't had such an impressively urgent excuse for avoiding feminist demands since the end of the Vietnam War.) I for one am deeply concerned about the great whales— especially since I learned that whales tend to be matriarchal, that they midwife a birthing whale mother, and of course they sing songs of eerie beauty—but I also agree with Gloria Steinem, who, in pointing out that crusading for the whales doesn't require a man to inconvenience himself or to alter his own life, said with her characteristic genius for aphorism, "A whale doesn't take your suit to the cleaners."

Women in the AT movement have been angered by the indifference of men there to the need for better birth-control technology, and by men's refusal to comprehend the vital appropriateness to *women* of household labor-saving appliances, or a car for mobility, or time-saving frozen-food products. The rejection by men of such technologies as "indulgent" (*they* don't use, depend on, or survive by them) will mean a giant backward step in time, labor, and role definition for women. Judy Smith has written an invaluable booklet on how and why AT *must* concern itself with women or become irrelevant: *Something Old, Something New, Something Borrowed, Something Due: Women and Appropriate Technology.*[23]

Whether in the establishment or in the alternate culture, technology is considered to be Man's specialty, yet women as well as men have been technological beings all along (the first carrying bag, digging stick, sling for an infant, etc.). Just as we've seen in the world of art, however, what Man does is "art," what women do is Other ("crafts"); so, in this area, what Man does is "technology," what women do is Other ("provide life-support systems"). And whenever a new technological development has come about, especially since the industrial age, Man has purposely tried to deny women access to it. In her previously cited paper, "On Female Culture," Berit Ås notes the irony that when the typewriter was introduced in Norway, men claimed that women would lose their attractive female features if they were made to operate this machinery. When it became *convenient* for men that women have access to this technology, however, the item itself ceased to be regarded *as* technological—just the way a "good neighborhood" will be regarded as a "slum" once members of an out-group (different class, race, or ethnicity) move in and "drive the property values down."

That every woman has been involved in, used, abused, benefited by, suffered from, and furthered the technological process ought to be axiomatic. Since that is nonetheless denied, it's all the more astounding that so many "career" women scientists and technologists have managed to exist at all, let alone make it into the (footnotes of) history books.

Even the most cursory "honors list" makes the heart beat faster with pride: Phaenarete (midwife, mathematician, and, incidentally, Socrates' mother), Fabiola, Marcella, and Paula (three Roman women who established hospitals during the Christian era), Hypatia of Alexandria (probably the most revered woman mathematician and scientist of the ancient world—385–415 A.D.), Zubayda (the city planner who built an aqueduct to Mecca and oversaw the rebuilding of Alexandretta after its destruction—circa 780–820 A.D.), Trotula (medical doctor and lecturer at the University of Salerno, and considered to be the mother of gynecology —circa 1050), Anna Comnena (important historian as well as founder of and lecturer at the medical school in Constantinople —1090–1120), St. Hildegard, abbess of St. Ruperts (author of *Materia Medica* and *Liber Divinorum Operum* which summarized the sum of medical knowledge in her time—1098–1178) —and that's not even to speak of Caroline Herschel (the astronomer), or Ellen Swallow (who founded the scientific discipline of ecology and was the first woman admitted to the Massachusetts Institute of Technology), or Margaret E. Knight (who invented the process and developed the machinery for making the still omnipresent square-bottomed paper bag), or Emily Roebling (who took over design and construction of the Brooklyn Bridge when her husband was incapacitated), or Marie Curie and her daughter Irene, or Grace Murray Hopper (who invented COBOL, one of the major computer languages), or Gerty Cori or Rosalyn Yalow (both Nobel Prize laureates in medicine) or Rachel Carson or Rosalind Franklin . . . A more comprehensive list appears in *Taking Hold of Technology* and in Elise Boulding's fine book *The Underside of History: A View of Women Through Time.*[24] (June Goodfield's *An Imagined World: A Story of a Scientific Discovery*[25] is a fascinating chronicle of a contemporary woman scientist, Anna Brito, in her research on Hodgkin's disease.)

Women always have been technologists. To buy into Man's lie that we have not is to consign ourselves not only to an ignorance of our own past but an alienation from our own present—and possibly an exile from our own future. It's a human tendency to dismiss what one doesn't understand—dismiss it with awe if it seems involved with power and dismiss it with contempt if it seems involved with powerlessness. Since modern technology is involved both with (men's) power and with (women's) powerlessness, most women have tended to dismiss it as doubly unapproachable. (Nor are women always alone in falling into this trap. Even Jean-Paul Sartre dismissed an atomic physicist as being "an intellectual only when he [sic] signs a petition against nuclear testing.") Yet how does a simplistic back-to-nature attitude differ from sexual-, political-, or any other kind of fundamentalist thinking?† Technological fundamentalism, whether of the worshipful tech-fix variety or the scornful antitech strain, won't clarify the confusion, won't solve the problem, and certainly won't make technology "go away."

DE-DEVELOPING DEVELOPMENT

Nowhere are the ironies of modern technology so clear as in the "developing countries"—and nowhere are women responding in such a vocal and consciousness-raising manner.

Traditional technical assistance (sometimes forcibly) exported by "developed nations" so far rarely has included specific plans and activities aimed at involving women's participation in the development plans for their countries. On the contrary, Man's neocolonial assumptions have been no different from his previous

---

† With characteristic good humor, Lewis Thomas dissects the fundamentalist attitude toward the word technology itself: he breaks down the concept into three different levels of technology (in medicine): "nontechnology" technology, sometimes called "supportive therapy" (which includes treatment for diseases that are incurable in the absence of what would be a truly effective technology), "halfway technology," or technology after the fact of the disease in order to postpone death (dramatic organ transplants and bionics), and the third type—the "genuinely decisive technology of modern medicine"—which Lewis sees as the technology which prevents disease in the first place, or eradicates it (immunization techniques, antibiotics, chemotherapy, vaccines). His is a refreshing new way of looking at medical technology, and one which inspires further thought. (See The Lives of a Cell [New York: Bantam Books, 1975], pp. 36–42.)

ones: that all bargains are made between men and over the heads of women.‡

Consequently, large-scale mechanization for farming will be introduced into an agrarian economy—and given over into the hands of local men who will be trained to use it; this despite the fact that farming in that particular culture was heretofore considered women's purview, and was a source of relative power or autonomy for women. For the convenience of the machines, land is reallocated—and women's lands are taken from them to be turned over to the men being trained to operate the machines. Or industrialization is introduced, but on·a large scale: factories are built in urban centers and men are imported from the countryside as cheap labor to staff them. This splits up families, leaves the women as an untrained rural class (barred from the industrial revolution), and further upsets the whole economy of a small country: where, for instance, organic coalitions of market women have held considerable economic and political power within their culture, the shift from agriculture to industry destroys such structures, places illusory power in the hands of the newly trained male industrial workers, and transforms the entire country into a "company town" for some multinational corporation—which profits enormously from the operation, and gets tax credits, humanism awards, and a self-congratulatory reputation for "aiding poorer nations."[26]

In still another scenario, women will be employed (as an even cheaper labor force than local men) but always as factory labor at the lowest level; rarely are women trained for middle-management positions, much less for jobs that have any real clout.

Yet one more example of misplaced (but lucrative) technological "aid"—perhaps more aptly called "diplomatic technocracy"—is the infamous baby-formula scandal: the shipping to Third World countries of powdered baby formulas manufactured in the industrialized world. The need to mix the product with

‡ The United Nations has only recently begun to set up serious in-depth mechanisms for examining "the implications of scientific and technological developments relating to genetic engineering and biotechnology, micro-electronics, sea-bed resources, mining, lighter-than-air technologies, petrochemicals and related energy sectors, optical fibre technology, laser technology, etc. for the developing countries." From Annex III of the Report of the Administrative Committee on Coordination Task Force on Science and Technology for Development (New York, February 2–5, 1982).

local water, which often is dirty and polluted, has resulted in sickness, malnourishment, and death for many infants; the mothers are helpless, usually having little access to pure water. Immunity transfer from mother's milk—an especially important life preserver in a context where modern medicines aren't always available—is also lost. The World Health Assembly and virtually every country in the world with the exception of the United States has ratified formula-marketing guidelines for Third World countries, yet as of this writing the problem persists. It does so because it profits the formula manufacturers, but also, in part, because of the desperation of a woman who must work dawn to dusk in the fields, and who cannot even leave her baby behind with a relative but must carry it along because she is nursing the child; such a woman turns hopefully to the respite of formula. But if the formula isn't accompanied by technology for the sterilization of water, or for drilling new pure wells, then her hope turns into a new form of despair.

One of the most consistent inconsistencies of Man's neocolonial approach is that *where a local tradition is in the self-interest of women* (such as matrifocal land ownership or a batik industry controlled for generations by females), *Man overrides this tradition in the name of "progress."* But *where a local tradition is deleterious to women* (genital-mutilation practices as "rites of passage," or protein being considered a dietary taboo for women) *Man recognizes this tradition, expresses respect for it, and incorporates it into his plan for "progress."* The early Anglican and Catholic missionaries to Tanzania, for instance, decided that if "native customs" included female circumcision, then the churches should openly endorse such practices in order to establish themselves in the trust of the people. The foreign-owned tea plantations in Asia, which employ women at sixteen-hour days for seven days a week in the most labor-intensive part of their operation—planting and picking—have done nothing to "offend" the local cultural tradition that says men must be fed first and most heartily; nor have the foreign interests thought of supplying women workers with protein-filled lunches each day, which might offset the anemia and malnutrition from which some 230 million women suffer.[27] That would, I assume, not be a "progressive" act.

Indeed, the time lag from which most so-called backward countries are suffering was enforced *by* colonialism itself, which deliberately froze Third World countries almost to a state of inertia while they themselves progressed along their "civilized" way.* Where practices which Westerners now regard as barbaric are evident today in the Third World, we would do well to remember that for hundreds of years there was scarcely a people or community on the planet, outside of Europe and settler North America, that was *free* to progress.

No one would deny that developing countries can use technological support—but such support must be keyed to the needs of *all* its citizens, not aimed at buying out half of them, a feat accomplished by selling out the other half. Until very recently—and only then because of pressure from women *in* the countries affected—there has been "little conscious concern for women in development issues" (Development Issue Paper ⚥12, U.N. Development Programs).† This "little conscious concern" is all the more appalling and counterproductive when one remembers that *what Man calls "World Problems" are primarily women's problems*:

• The hunger problem is a women's problem because most of the world's starving are women and children (sometimes by tradition, as in those cultures that deny women protein, and sometimes by crisis: even during the famine in Biafra, the soldiers were fed—and most men were in the army);

• The illiteracy problem is a women's problem because 58 percent of the world's illiterates are women;

• The health problem is a women's problem because in addition to sharing general health problems with men in their cultures, women bear the additional burden of bodily changes via menarche, menstruation, pregnancy, childbearing, nursing, and menopause;‡

---

* I am indebted to Erskine Childers for this "time-lag" insight.

† The International Women's Tribune Centre, 305 East Forty-sixth Street, New York, N.Y. 10017, is an excellent resource for background information, documents, etc. on this subject. IWTC also has produced a multimedia kit on appropriate technology for use by women's groups.

‡ A Japanese man who has contracted Minamota disease (caused by mercury pollution) suffers the disease himself; if a woman gets it, and is pregnant, the disease filters through to the fetus—which is later born as a child unable to talk, walk, or eat by her/himself. The custodial care of this child for the rest of its life devolves on the woman; she continues to suffer from the disease even should she herself manage to survive having had it. For that matter, today, forty years after the atomic-bomb devastation of Hiro-

• The refugee problem is a women's problem because more than 90 percent of all refugees are women and children;

• The child-abuse problem is a women's problem not only because women must shoulder responsibility for children in most cultures but also because the children abused are mostly female;

• The old-age problem is a women's problem because in most cultures women outlive men, and because the care of the aged is relegated to women;

• Poverty itself is a women's problem because the majority of the poor on this planet are women and children.

Yet Man sees "women's issues" as distinct from "World Problems."

As long as men cannot look out through the eyes of Man to see *just who it is who is suffering* from "World Problems"—and as long as those sufferers remain invisible behind the mask of Woman, the problems will destroy us all.

As long as men hoard both traditional *and* alternate technologies as the property of Man, and remain fixated on the design and development context of those technologies, ignoring the *user* context—and as long as women permit Woman to keep us fixated on the user context only, and to keep us as well from breaking the mystique of Man's proprietary hold, technology will never be "appropriate" for women, *or* for "world problems."

We must, as men and women, outgrow Man and Woman.

We must, as a species, outgrow sexual fundamentalism—or as a species we will perish.

"ONLY CONNECT"

I've always thought of myself as someone afraid of and alienated by "technology." Yet I'm writing this book on a typewriter— an electric one, to boot. The phonograph plays a record, a few feet away. Electric light illumines my desk. When I revise a page

shima and Nagasaki, it is largely women who are still living out the generational agony of having been victims of that holocaust, having borne children with birth defects from radiation, caring for those children and watching them waste away, and often being—most piteous tragedy of all—*blamed by those very children for having given birth to them.* (See the unforgettable article "Never Again: The Organization of Women Atomic Bomb Victims in Osaka," by Janet Bruin and Stephen Salaff, in *Feminist Studies*, 7, No. 1 [Spring 1981].)

by hand, I like to use a pencil brought to a point in my electric pencil sharpener. The telephone rings (too often, in fact) and I manage to cope with answering it (sometimes). I can even drive a car. All of these stunning accomplishments of mine mean that I must not be as afraid of and alienated by "technology" as I've been made to think. Nor are you. What I'm only now beginning to do, however (like most women), is develop *technology literacy, computer literacy, energy literacy.* Nor have we, as women, dared to articulate our technological vision—and in most cases we haven't dared to dream one yet.* This isn't surprising since, to paraphrase Parmenides, "If it can't be said, it can't be known."

We haven't yet learned the language. Yet women can't be truly effective in analyzing such an issue as genetic engineering, for instance, until we *know the words, the concepts.* We can study and discuss the subject among ourselves, demand of legislators and medical societies that science meet *our* needs, think about regulatory measures to prevent privateer wildcat research or Big Brother-type governmental control. We can reaffirm that most basic right of each woman to self-determination over her own body—or, far from gaining reproductive freedom, we will risk losing it altogether in a cowardly new world which could regard us as comatose incubators, hired wombs, or sterile sexual toys. We can think (*very seriously*) about genetics as a career to enter— and about encouraging our daughters and younger sisters to do the same. But we can do none of these things *effectively* if we have no real knowledge of the subject. Knowledge *is* power.

Surely it helps to cut the grease of the mystique to realize that, despite what Man claims, most men are as ignorant (and scared) of "technology" as are most women, or to realize that baking a

* There are notable and exciting exceptions: Corlann Gee Bush, in her unpublished paper titled "The Technological Imperative: Feminist Visions for the Twenty-first Century" analyzes environmentalism and feminism as central to a dialectical process resulting in the most basic changes in the American definition of what is finite and what is infinite: environmentalism challenges the previous American view that nature was an infinite resource, while feminism challenges the patriarchal view that human potential has finite limits. This remarkable paper, which is the basis for Bush's in-progress book on the same subject, was delivered as part of the Conference Proceedings of the Northwest Women's Studies Association Conference and the Third Annual Women's Studies Symposium (1981) at Oregon State University, Corvallis, Oregon.

cake requires chemistry analysis,† or to realize that arithmetic really has very little to do with physics.

Most of all, it should help to realize that, as women, we who have been kept invisible and forcibly "nonhuman" for so long nonetheless have a great strength, not because of anything inherent but because of this very experience. *We do tend to see the connections, to notice, to estimate the gains and losses.* (If the toy has a sharp edge, albeit one covered with flannel, there's a possibility that the flannel will peel off and the baby might harm herself with it . . . hmmm . . . no, let's pick another toy.) Certain individual men have managed to articulate this sensibility, like dear E. M. Forster, who summed it all up in two words: "Only connect." But Man has made a habit of seeing life piecemeal, compartmentalized, short-run (premature and ejaculatory?) —and damn the consequences. Perhaps this is because he could rest assured that Woman, who was after all seeing to the children, would look after the future. In any event, he could blithely go on, wafting fluorocarbons into the stratosphere without thinking that the ozone might peel away and that otherwise blocked ultraviolet waves might harm the baby—and other living things. He could ignore the interconnectedness of events: that political conflicts in the Middle East would influence oil production and in turn affect living patterns in Iowa, that acid rain could damage not only crops but chromosomes, that certain pesticides would be a boon now but a bane later, that radioactive fallout can ride the winds and rain—and destroy a populace not even involved with a war happening in the illusory geography of "someplace else."

Man has called this lack of context and connections "order." To Woman he assigned, of course, the opposite: she was a creature of disorder, unpredictability, inconsistency—so *unfocused.* One might well ask why, if Man saw Woman as disorder, he managed to attribute to her all order-keeping tasks. Perhaps he saw through his own lie but hoped that men and women wouldn't? Perhaps he thought she'd prove herself incapable of these tasks, thereby proving her disorderliness? Or perhaps he didn't care—so long as he didn't have to do the tidying up him-

† "The Physics and Chemistry of a Failed Sauce Béarnaise," by Jearl Walker (*Scientific American*, December 1979), is a highly useful article for raising one's consciousness and one's pride quotient, as well as bringing a smile to a woman's face.

self. Certainly Woman strove to live up to his expectations no matter how contradictory: she perfected the balancing act, symbolizing all nonrational, dark, fecund, warm, wet, chaotic elements—and she polished the linoleum bright as a one-way mirror at the same time. Thus she allayed his fears about what women really were, although those fears did burp out on many occasions. (How similar is the contempt, and how interestingly related the language, shown by Ezekiel for "menstruous women," and the loathing expressed by Scottish Calvinist John Knox about "that monstrous regiment of women.")

Art stands in a position analogous to that of women. As Michele Roberts has written, "Women and art can be feared for the same reasons, because both are seen to challenge commonsense notions of the way the world appears to be naturally-oriented, and the power that rationality is supposed to have to order the world and make it a safe place to live in—safe and harmonious for those in power."[28] Art, Roberts goes on to say, has been classified as not-theory, not-science, and not-true; like women and like freedom it is best defined (by Man) by its negatives. Art is seen as subversive—and the woman artist doubly so.

Yet art and science/technology once meant the same thing. In his dated though far-seeing essay "The Question Concerning Technology"‡ Heidegger recalled that the word itself stems from the Greek: "*Technikon* means that which belongs to *technē* . . . [which is] the name not only for the activities and skills of the craftsman [*sic*], but also for the arts of the mind and the fine arts." In this context, *technē* overlapped in meaning with *poiēsis*, which meant not only something poetic, but also the process of creating, revealing, bringing forth.

Unfortunately, technology as we have come to express and experience it exists in quite a different context, one split off from *poiēsis* and often posed as actively antagonistic to art. Society does acknowledge that art still has something to do with "revealing," and "bringing forth"—but views technology mainly as *the means to more effective ways of doing what Man and Woman already know how to do, and must keep on repeating.* This in turn

‡ In *The Question Concerning Technology and Other Essays,* translated by William Lovitt (New York: Harper & Row, 1977). For a principled exploration of the controversy concerning Heidegger's actions and the abuse of Heideggerian thought during World War II in Germany, see George Steiner, *Martin Heidegger* (New York: Viking Press, 1978).

leads to the fatal error of thinking that technology is something that can be "controlled," something *to* be controlled, so that it *won't* reveal new possibilities that would threaten or indeed transform the old patterns. The comparable dynamism of the artistic process, and its parallel inherent destiny of "bringing forth" was dealt with in a different way: since Man couldn't effectively control it, he defused its power by making it irrelevant.

But altering the character of technology by manipulation and altering the character of art by trivialization both are forms of denial—and ultimately neither form *works*. Technology continues to "reveal"—but instead of revealing freedom, it reveals the death-politics inevitably brought into play by friction between *new means* and *old ends*. Art persists in "bringing forth"—but instead of being harkened to, is treated as the court jester of the intellect. Each of these active processes is inherently and intimately involved with freedom, but both have been misused against the "real specter of liberation."

"Freedom governs the open in the sense of the cleared and lighted up, i.e., the revealed. To the occurrence of revealing, i.e., of truth, freedom stands in the closest and most intimate kinship."[29] But if freedom is feared, then revelation is dangerous, and if revelation is dangerous, then technology and art must be kept isolated from each other and from their own unified character.

Since Man has made technology "his baby," he's been more successful with its corruption than with that of art. (Art, you remember, is supposedly nonrational, therefore non-Man.) There *was* a chink, a tiny opening in the wall, consequently, through which women could reach art. Nobody cared much, since art was irrelevant anyway. But still, enough people devoted to the concepts of Man and of Woman cared enough to impede, ridicule, stifle, ignore, and frequently destroy the woman artist—and certainly to bury her contribution.

It isn't bruited about much that *The Odyssey* might have been written by a woman.[30] We happen to know about the extraordinary talents of Nannerl Mozart, Fanny Mendelssohn, Dorothy Wordsworth, Mary Sidney, and Augusta Byron only because they are footnoted in their more celebrated brothers' biographies. Only recently have we become aware of how much of Robert Schumann's music was written by Clara Wieck Schumann, of how

Anna Magdalena Bach influenced and possibly wrote some of Bach's great works, and of how their daughter Elisabeth actually composed many of the pieces signed by her brothers. But many women fell speechless before the smug question, "Then where *are* your great women painters and composers?" until the current wave of feminist consciousness took fire in some segments of the scholarly community and began to produce The Evidence.[31]

That we've known a bit more about women writers than their sisters in the other arts isn't coincidental, either. Composers require a form of collaboration in order to produce their art (musicians, an orchestra, an opera house, etc.). Visual artists require costly materials. Women were largely barred access to the first area because the cooperation needed for performance wasn't forthcoming, and because performance is of necessity *public*. Women were mostly barred access to the visual arts because we have been for millennia an economically disadvantaged caste: we rarely had the means to buy the materials. Many of the women visual artists now being "unearthed" turn out to have been the daughters of (male) artists; they developed familiarity with the materials in their fathers' studios and ateliers. Writing, on the other hand, is private and requires at the minimum only a piece of paper and a pencil or pen; hence, women seem to have practiced this art more than any other. *Publishing*, of course, was a different matter altogether. Being taken seriously was a still more remote possibility.

When you're not taken seriously for long enough, it becomes difficult to take yourself seriously; this latter result may be, in fact, the purpose of the former tactic. It's that lack of reflection, that one-way mirror, again. So the irony is that a woman writer, for instance, often will work with minimalist materials, "making do" as if Woman were looking over her shoulder going *tsk-tsk* at the supposed self-indulgence of her being an artist at all. I've taken to asking a series of what seem to be consciousness-raising "click" questions whenever I give writing workshops for women: How many women in this room have good working materials? A really good typewriter? A store of spare ribbons? A first-rate *un*abridged dictionary? A *Roget's Thesaurus*? A *room of one's own*— even if it's an attic, an old sewing room, a This Is My Turf corner? A sign saying Don't Disturb? How many women here buy themselves decent bond paper on which to type their manuscripts? A comfortable chair? Whatever reference books they feel are absolutely necessary to have continually at their fingertips instead of schlepping to the library? A filing cabinet "of one's own"? Usually, in a roomful of twenty to fifty women, only one or two hands will go up in response to a few of these questions. We rarely avail ourselves of the "technology" needed to further our own chosen work. Yet these same women, in the rap session that follows, will admit: "I did buy a fine new typewriter for my kid when he started college, but kept the dinky old one for myself," or "Funny, but my husband's a draftsman and I never think it odd that *he* always insists on the best materials for *his* work," or "I realize that the list of items you just ran down first struck me as expensive luxuries, yet I've been saving toward a new washing machine—why *not* toward a good typewriter!" These questions (and, even more, the responses) make for a session alive with feminist connection moments of "Omigod, I never thought of it that way before . . ." or "*Wow*. You too?"

Still—and despite all obstacles imposed from the outside and internalized within, women have continued to be artists—and continued to create art that did "reveal," even when it seemed that no one was interested in looking at what was being revealed.

One cross-cultural theme in women's art down through the ages has been the beauty of humble things in all their "thingness": intricate patterns of straw and hemp—weaving; curves and natural earth colors and shapes to please the eye and hand—pottery; something beautiful with which to keep warm—quilts. The theme has been usefulness but a *transcendent* utilitarianism.

The batik artists of Asia, the Native American sand painters of the southwestern United States, the rice painters of Mithila in India, the weavers of the great tapestries of medieval Europe, the sacred flutists of the Amazon River peoples—all of them women, and all of them engaged in the original and overlapping meanings of *technē* and *poiēsis* both. Because the art is meant to be used, integrated into life, *and* revelatory. The cups and bowls and pots and baskets can hold food and water, carry babies or crops. The quilts keep out the cold. The batik can be used as cloth—to wear or to brighten a wall. The sand paintings are drawn for healing ceremonies, the rice paintings are a celebration of religious ritual. The tapestries were to insulate stone-walled rooms against the cold—but also encoded esoteric references to Wiccean and other heretical faiths in their iconography. The sacred flutes—before men stole the ritual, as Amazon River legend goes—were like Orpheus' lyre: their music could move stones, build cities, charm wild animals. What Westerners today refer to as the "belly dance" originated by, among, and solely for women, especially women in childbirth; the movements were scientifically developed eons ago to serve much the same function as "natural-childbirth exercises" do now, to relax and energize the body between contractions and to divert the mother's attention from her pain into more pleasant channels.

When a work reveals the essence, the truth, the thingness of an object, and when—because it is beautiful—it celebrates that truth and invites the viewer, listener, or participant to enter into a relationship with that truth and its organic uses and thus with the thing itself, this is *technē* and certainly *poiēsis*. Martha Graham said, "Nothing is more revealing than movement." This is also what David Böhm calls a glimpse into "the implicate order" of all things, of the universe itself, in contrast to "the mechanistic order," or the "explicate order." In the last, "things are *unfolded* in the sense that each thing lies only in its own particular region of space (and time) and outside the regions belonging to other things."[32] It is the explicate order which has dominated thinking in physics (and everywhere else Man holds sway) until very recently. But the New Physics finds itself engaged in the implicate order, where "the totality of existence is *enfolded* within each region of space (and time). So, whatever part, element, or aspect we may abstract in thought, this still enfolds the whole and is therefore intrinsically related to the totality from which it has been abstracted."[33] Or, as the painter Françoise Gilot wrote, "Like the mask, the painting conceals the individual, but reveals a greater truth, the truth of the archetype. The most subjective painting is not the reflection of a particular truth but a fragmentary revelation from the total process of revelation of which the painting is the visible hieroglyphic."[34]

Women, artists, and most particularly women artists have been revealing the implicate order all along.* The irony is that pre-

* Perhaps now it seems less puzzling that so much of feminist political theory seems to have originated with feminist artists, in books, visual works, music, and performance. There have been hints of this kind of integration before in history: for a thousand years, beginning in the Han Dynasty and

cisely this making of the connections, which is the source from which all art and all technology *jointly* sprang, is "craft"—a word which embraces both skill and vision, *technē* and *poiēsis*. And it is "craft" which Man has used as the derogatory label for women's aesthetic endeavors, as opposed to men's aesthetic endeavors, which Man approvingly labeled "art."

"Art" was *serious*, Man said (while not taking it seriously). Art might *un*fold but shouldn't *en*fold. Man said that art shouldn't be useful—and in time he said that art shouldn't even be meaningful. Meaning was old-hat: aleatory alienated meaninglessness was "in." Man pronounced any individual man who showed talent in a variety of arts a "genius" or a "Renaissance man"; any woman who did the same was, naturally, a "dilettante." Saddest of all—and despite the fact that the greatest individual artists (including those who were male) never stopped their devotions to the joyous *play* that *poiēsis/technē* is—Man imprisoned his notion of the correct way (for men) to play in a technology which was fragmented from art: in gimmicks, gadgets, war rooms, and other Pentagon toys. The game was to conceal, not to reveal. The exciting violence of this type of play, Man must have thought, would fill the void left in the human spirit when he had forbidden it to play in the eternal and ecstatic implicate order.

But nothing fills that void except the joyous play of *poiēsis/ technē* itself; when *it* is present, a void—or even the idea of a void—is absurd. I imagine, for instance, that a scientist deeply engaged in her/his work is taken up "into it" wholly in somewhat the same way that I as an artist experience when really working with *my* energy particles: words. One is never more utterly alone, and never more totally in touch—with everything. What one normally thinks of as "real life" (dinners with family and friends, shared and exhilarating political activism with colleagues, concerts or plays or movies or walks in the park, fresh linen on the bed, Tandoori chicken at the neighborhood Pakistani restaurant, a no-holds-barred game of chess with one's child, the pleasure—or

---

continuing until after the T'ang Dynasty, Chinese civil servants had to pass a complex series of examinations testing their knowledge of *The Golden Anthology of Chinese Classical Poetry* before winning their job appointments. And when Shelley wrote that "poets are the unacknowledged legislators of the world," he may have been expressing wishful writing—but feminist consciousness may yet bear him out.

depression—of the morning mail, filling the grocery cart and answering the telephone, being praised or criticized for previous
writings, worrying about money or sinking into a hot bubble bath
or correcting galley proofs)—all this so-called real life recedes into
a two-dimensional surreality, dimly recollected as a dream but
blurred and pale when set beside the vivid intensity of sitting motionless at one's desk in front of one's typewriter or notebook, the
room itself empty of all other energy (except perhaps Bach on the
phonograph). In those periods, surfacing from the "submersion"
can feel painful at worst or just peculiarly alienating at best, although even then, everything gets *used:* a casual conversation, the
television news broadcast, an expression spotted on the face of a
stranger riding the bus—all find their way, transformed, back
into one's work. Everything seems acutely relevant, related, alive.
One can't *help* but make the connections, continually, effort-
lessly; it's as if one were a vehicle for the sole purpose of the
connections connecting with each other through that vehicle.
One is never more oneself; one is never more free of a sense of
ego.

And when in the state of actually writing—seized by this buzzing resonance, this electrical shuddering vibration of creativity
(like molecular activity viewed in microphotography)—that energy seems to be thinking *through* the body. One isn't hungry or
thirsty, and can sit for hours in one position to realize only later
that the neck aches or the back is cramped. I'd wager that tests
might show a rise in adrenaline excitement, a quickened but sustained pulse, and mild engorgement of the erectile tissue of breast
and clitoris or penis. Time and space return to their original
meaning: space/time as one, and relative—and irrelevant. When
one does finally break to eat something or sleep, one does so like
a ghost of the self still sitting back at the desk: a ghost that
chews absent-mindedly, moves like a sleepwalker. When really
sleeping, one dreams about what one has been working on; sometimes one dreams the solution to a particular problem unsolvable
while awake. And the entire process is suffused with mystery and
with the excitement of a grave *joy*—as if one were, like DNA itself, capable of and existing for only two purposes, each of which
were intertwined and central to all intelligence, all life: synthesiz-
ing and replicating.

From such mystical, vibrant, inexhaustible *play* comes all invention.

FOCUSED ON TURNING

Wherever intelligence exists, it plays with communication—plays at it, on it, through it, for the sheer delight in it. It's both a reason for and a result of adult dehumanizing of children that "play" is considered a childish activity: the contempt for play spills over onto the way children are regarded, and the contempt for children spills over onto the way play is viewed. Yet children have not yet learned that the world of implicate order is a forbidden one, the gladdening world that enfolds and reveals and brings forth, that discovers the thingness of things.

Adults may have forgotten this, but the ache remains, as if for a lost Eden. We mourn over the pollution erosion of the Parthenon, the shelling of Angkor Wat, the burning of the library at Alexandria, the loss of most of Sappho's poems, the melting down (for bullets) of nearly all the great classic Greek bronze statues except, by accident, the Delphic charioteer; I mourn the smashed marbles of Adelaide Johnson. Why—if art is as irrelevant to us as Man has said it is? "Why," Susanne K. Langer has asked,

should the world wail over the loss of a play product, and look with its old callousness on the destruction of so much that dire labor has produced? It seems a poor economy of nature [that human beings] will suffer and starve for the sake of play, when play is supposed to be the abundance of their strength after their needs are satisfied.[35]

Isn't it really, Langer suggests, that play *is* a basic need? I would hazard that it is as basic a need as food and water and air, that it is perhaps what *makes* us alive, or at least human—this irrepressible capacity for creative play, this dogged, insatiable, tragicomic, both wild and disciplined need to *sing*.

And which then is the really "serious" play, which the "frivolous"—play which reveals essence, truth, interconnections, inclusions? Or play which conceals them and settles for competition, violence, categories, *fundamentals*? It does seem that Man has got things backward yet again. Just as he's been more willing to play with gimmickry than with what *technē* really means, so is he more willing to recognize intelligence in machines these days than in human women and human men. Unfortunately, in that familiar reactive reflex we've come to expect from any underclass, when Man lauds computer intelligence (with Woman smiling silently by his side and men standing by in awe) women too frequently denounce it.

It's certainly understandable why we've done this. After all, it's rather insulting to realize that Man already respects the brain of a computer more than the brain of a female human being. Yet if we concede knowledge about these new forms of intelligence to Man, by default, will that not tilt the imbalance of power even more drastically?

Certainly I've been jarred by the new controversies over whether or not computers have the potential for becoming, in effect, new life forms—the articles and books arguing whether or not intelligence doesn't eventually become self-propagating, whether or not intelligence doesn't eventually teach itself emotion. *The Enchanted Loom: Mind in the Universe*, by Robert Jastrow[36] is one such book, and its author believes that computer intelligence is in fact the next step in evolution, leaving the human species—Man, Woman, men and women—at its evolutionary dead end, as extinct as the dinosaur or the hopelessly endangered Tennessee coneflower. (Computers *can* survive nuclear holocaust. So can cockroaches.) But human flesh, in all its multitudinous shades from cobaltblueblack through sienna brown to faded amber (we haven't seen this spectrum as cause for *celebration?*) and in all its glorious shapes of difference in gender or size or carriage (we haven't regarded this diversity as a source of *joy?*) —human flesh, Dr. Jastrow feels, has gone as far as its evolution ever will. The pity of it, oh the pity of it, Jastrow.

Still, even if Dr. Jastrow is correct in his prophecy (and I do agree with George Eliot that "Prophecy is the most gratuitous form of error"), I nevertheless find myself curious about *any* new form of intelligence. My own species hasn't used *its* form so superbly that I feel we can afford to turn up our noses at another, and certainly any genuine intelligence ought to be welcome in a place where that quality has been in short supply, or so ill used. Or perhaps it's the old curiosity and desire bubbling up in my existential romantic self that makes me such a sucker for exogamy in all its expressions, communication in all its presentations. Frankly, I'd love to be able to communicate with dolphins *and* with machines. But I can't seem to communicate with Man, and I even have difficulty with men, try as I do to understand and be understood. So it's not likely that Man will give me much access to communicating with dolphins or machines. Unless I just dart round him and *find my way to them myself*. Whether or not men make the connection with the revealing character of art, for instance, women must make the connection with the revealing character of technology.†

As women, we already seem connected with art and are within glimpsing distance of the implicate order. What if, then, we connect to technology, to machines (dumb as well as smart ones; don't let's *us* discriminate) and bring *them* into the holomovement, into the glad disorder of the implicate order. That would make, you have to admit, one hell of a coalition.

If, furthermore, we believe that human intelligence is just one example of a general phenomenon in nature—the emergence of intelligent beings in widely varying contexts—then presumably the "language" in which . . . messages . . . are communicated among humans is a "dialect" of a *universal* language by which intelligences can communicate with each other.[37]

Who would settle for less? Not me, even if we as women do have to teach ourselves an entirely new literacy, and even if we as women have to teach men that Man is very misleading when he tells them he can control what all these disparate related intelligences are actually saying to one another, the silly thing.

Who would settle for less, indeed. It may be our last chance as a species—or our next-to-last chance. Famine, war, triage, neutron and hydrogen bombs. The computer carries out the order pressed by Man's finger on the warhead-release button (weeping through all its circuits with pity and grief for us as it does so?). Or the computer directs the electromicroscope to reveal what no human eye has ever seen about the intricate sculpture of patterns in a diatom—more than twenty-five thousand species of which exist, each pattern of each shell of each individual diatom unique. Which computer? Both of them *are* part of "nature," like women and men and all existing things. If it can be imagined, it will be.

† As usual, George Eliot phrased the challenge with passion and elegance: "To fear the examination of any proposition appears to me an intellectual and moral palsy that will ever hinder the firm grasping of any substance whatsoever."

"Nature," said Margaret Fuller, "provides exceptions to every rule." If it can be brought into existence, it *is* "nature." Why settle for less than imagining and bringing forth truth?

Why settle for less—than everything? The means themselves are *interesting*. The ends have been boring and must be changed. The overrational, cold, dry, hard, adult, *frivolous* play that Man and Woman have played out and forced us all, men and women alike, to play out with them, is deadly and must be changed. It was, as Wallace Stevens warned us, "a violent order that is a *disorder*" after all. Now it's time for the disorderly of the earth— women and children and peoples whose flesh reflects the shades of the earth itself, and diatoms and intelligent computers, artists and bacteria and the whole *technē/poiēsis* chorus of the order that is implicit and ready to reveal itself—now is the time (as it was always, but now is as good as ever) to invoke the transformation, to be focused on turning.

Invoke the transformation. Oh to be stirred
by a flame drawing proudly into itself, consumed with change—
this trace of spirit that clings to all the earth has carried
loves that point in the shape of a curve focused on turning.

Whatever insists on permanence already is cold,
safe in its refuge of self-effacing gray.
Look how an ultimate hardness threatens everything hard.
Look—like a thoughtless hammer held high.

Knowing knows all who overflow like fountains
and she leads them spellbound through this world she's dreamed
where the beginning often trades places with the end.

Each joyful expanse is the child or grandchild of separations
through which they move astonished. And Daphne, transformed
to feel laurel, now invokes your changing into wind.

> —Sonnet II: 12 of *The Sonnets
> to Orpheus*, by Rainer Maria
> Rilke, in the Kenneth Pitchford
> translation[38]

IX

THE NEW PHYSICS OF META-POLITICS

An Anatomy of Last Resort

In the context of cosmic values only the fantastic has a chance of being true.

    —Pierre Teilhard de Chardin

The world is quite right. It does not have to be consistent.

    —Charlotte Perkins Gilman

Lady, I do not make up things. That is lies. Lies is not true. But the truth could be made up if you know how. And that's the truth.

    —Lily Tomlin as the
    character "Edith Ann"

It's been said that three developments, more than any others in history, have shaken Man's sense of himself. *Copernican astronomy* changed Man's cosmocentric vision of himself as being at the center of the universe. Darwin's *On the Origin of Species by Natural Selection* changed Man's biocentric vision of himself as being at the center of life forms. The birth of the science of *anthropology* changed Man's ethnocentric vision of himself as being at the center of one and only one possible, foreordained culture.

These three developments may well have been the most crucial ones in unsettling what has been called Man, at least in the past. But this list is incomplete if we would have it include the present and reach toward the future. In that case, we would have to add two more developments, in their immediate and especially their potential effects equal to if not greater than the shifts in consciousness listed above: *feminism*, which challenges Man's androcentric vision of himself as being at the center of humanity—and *modern physics*, which challenges Man's vision of reality itself.

For almost two decades, I've written about, lectured on, and organized for the ideas and politics of *feminism for the sake of women*, with the emphasis on women's right to freedom, access, self-determination, and empowerment—as a matter of simple justice. If, in fact, these were the sole reasons for and goals of the movement and consciousness we call feminism, they would be quite sufficient unto themselves as such. It might not even be necessary to try to envision, much less articulate, what the ripple effects might be from that single dropped pebble releasing the creative energy of more than half the human species after so long. Nor is it necessary to apologize for feminism's concerning itself "merely" with women, or to justify feminism on the "Please, may I" grounds that it's good for men too, and therefore-won't-you-let-us-have-it? In the long run, it *will* be good for men, but even were it permanently to prove as discomfiting for men as it seems to be in the short run, that wouldn't make women's needs and demands any the less just.

So the fact that I place feminism in a "larger context" is neither an apology nor a justification. It is simply to show, once and for all, that *feminism is the larger context*.

The profound potential of feminism lies not only in those aspects of its vision expressed now and in the past by women, individually and collectively (and by a few men), but even more in the chain reaction of events set off by its most minute accomplishments. This chain reaction can't yet be predicted by those of us—women and men—still groping toward that vision through the pain and confusion of the present. We can only begin to imagine the results, and the results of the results; only begin to glimpse or intuit them, like optical illusions of an as-yet-undreamed-of celebratory reality, like revolucinations unsullied by one jot of embarrassment, like the petals of a desert cactus flower opening and opening before our eyes as if in time-lapse photography.

What we imagine, glimpse, intuit, is that feminism is not only about women (which *would*, remember, be sufficient cause for it), or even about women and men, or even about women and men and political/emotional/spiritual/economic/social/sexual/racial/intellectual/ecological revolution, or even about all the above plus a revolution in sentience on this planet. All that. And more.

Feminism is, at this moment and on this planet, the DNA/

*RNA call for survival and for the next step in evolution—
and even beyond that, feminism is, in its metaphysical and meta-
feminist dynamic, the helix of hope that we humans have for communication with whatever lies before us in the vast, witty mystery
of the universe.*

I base my premise—that feminism is the key to our survival
and transformation—not on rhetoric but on facts:

• The "Otherizing" of women is the oldest oppression known
to our species, and it's the model, the template, for all other oppressions. Until and unless *this* division is healed, we continue
putting Band-Aids on our most mortal wound.

• Women comprise the majority of humanity. This means that
a variety of strategic options are open to us that are not available
to an oppressed *minority* group which, because of its relative size,
often must resort to desperate or violent tactics even to be noticed.

• The suffering of women *is* the suffering of the human species,
and vice versa. Numerically and geographically, it is women who
are the world's poor, the world's starving, the world's refugees, the
world's illiterates (see Chapter VIII).

• Women share this suffering (in the category of Other)
across the barriers of age, race, class, nationality, culture, sexual
preference, and ethnic background: a Hong Kong prostitute and
a Grosse Pointe matron are battered because both are women; a
sixty-year-old nun in England is raped and a seven-year-old girl in
Yemen is sold in marriage because both are female; an Indonesian
peasant dies of childbirth and a Brazilian socialite dies of a
butchered illegal abortion because both are women; a Kenyan adolescent is physically clitoridectomized and a Swiss nurse is
psychologically clitoridectomized because both are female human
beings. The tactical potential for unification across such Man-
made barriers as race and nationality is limited only by the
extent to which all women are willing to recognize the similarity
of our condition, develop acute sensitivity to a diversity of priorities, and commit ourselves to exposing and *un*making those very
barriers.

• The physiological reality experienced by every woman is one
of continual change: change at menarche, thereafter every
twenty-eight days for an average of forty years, then menopause—
and, in between, the possibilities of pregnancy, childbirth, post-

partum, and lactation. This experienced reality lends to most women an inescapably less rigid psychological attitude toward physical existence in all its forms, including the political and strategic.

• Women in all cultures have been assigned (stereotypically, as Woman) the positive values of "humanism," pacifism, nurturance, ecoconsciousness, and reverence for life. While these values have been (1) regarded by Man as amusingly irrelevant and (2) understood by women not to be inherently "womanly," nonetheless they *are* objectively positive values. Women are perforce more familiar with them than are men; this in itself affects our strategical approach to change and could give us, at least for a while, a certain moral imperative which could be useful.

• Women in all cultures and times seem to have developed a "spiritual dimension" to our lives—whether as a code for secular rebellion or an escape from our temporal suffering or an ongoing religious strand of connection to cosmic mystery. This tendency has shown itself repeatedly in women's political movements, too, including the present feminist wave.[1] At its most superficial, such a tendency can lead to sophomoric superstition and political evasion, but at its most profound it can lead to political change as deep as those religious and cultural revolutions which affected not only sociopolitical and economic aspects of society but, in a longer-lasting manner, consciousness itself.

• Last: *it will happen because it is happening.*

Nor is it any longer women alone who are seeing feminism as central to survival, evolution, and transformation on this planet. Among the most recent male converts are some of the hard-core scientists themselves, who are used to seeing the handwriting on the wall—and analyzing it.

The physicist Fritjof Capra sees three imminent transitions which will shake the very foundations of our lives: "the reluctant but inevitable decline of patriarchy," the decline of the fossil-fuel age, and a "paradigm shift" in our basic way of perception. Of these three, he feels that the end of patriarchy is the first and perhaps the most profound transition, because patriarchy "has influenced our most basic ideas about human nature and about our relation to the universe. . . . It is the one system . . . whose doctrines were so universally accepted that they seemed to be the laws of nature." Consequently, he concludes that "the feminist movement is one of the strongest cultural currents of our time and will have a profound effect on our further evolution." Capra further understands the value of science not only for itself but in this political context:

Physicists can provide the scientific background to the changes in attitudes and values that our society so urgently needs. In a culture dominated by science, it will be much easier to convince our social institutions . . . if we can give our arguments a scientific basis. This is what physicists can now provide. Modern physics can show the other sciences that scientific thinking does not necessarily have to be reductionist and mechanistic, that holistic and ecological views are also scientifically sound . . . that *such a framework is not only scientific but is in agreement with the most advanced scientific theories of physical reality.*[2] (Italics mine.)

I am not a physicist. I am a poet, a feminist writer, a theorist, and an activist. Being a poet, I understand the life-saving value of audacious and serious play. Being a feminist activist, I understand the urgency of communicating this message in ever newer, more connective, and far-reaching ways. Being a writer, I understand the power of words, their independent life and energy, the way *logos* can use a writer as a vehicle for its blessing even when one thinks one is using *it* as a tool. What, then, if we were to combine the supportive framework some of the new physicists are offering humanity, with this politics, these living words? What then?

THE PHYSICS OF FEMINISM

First, we need to know more about the framework, the support grid, the background in terms of physics itself—even a few basics. This overview will of necessity be encapsulated and superficial, will contain material familiar to some readers and surprising to others, but restricted as I am by space considerations and my own nonphysicist's small knowledge of the subject, I'll do the best I can with a brief summary.

Until the beginning of the twentieth century, science mostly had followed the train of thought implicit in Aristotle's "why" rather than in Galileo's "how." In the wake of Newton's then-radical discovery of gravity (which in itself laid the basis for relativity theory), post-Newtonian science became mired in a mechanistic view, seeing the universe as a great clock with some central godlike Watchmaker constructing and perpetuating each individual cog and wheel for a specific purpose and place. The mechanical explanation (the "why") saw the cosmos as a series of parts or building blocks which might be *combined* in a wide variety of ways but which surely had to be ultimately *reducible* to some block or cog—the atom, for instance. Since an atom is about one hundred times smaller than the head of a pin, this seemed the ultimate building block.

Aptly enough, right at the start of this century, in 1900, Max Planck put forth the Quantum Theory—showing by mathematical abstraction an equation which explained how the amount of radiant energy emitted by heated bodies varies with wavelength and temperature. The remarkable feature of this equation was that Planck was driven to assume that radiant energy is emitted *not in a continuous flow* but in *dis*continuous bitlets which Planck termed *quanta.*

In 1905, at the age of twenty-six, Albert Einstein took the Quantum Theory beyond the confines of the equations of radiation: Einstein proposed that *all forms of radiant energy,* including heat, X rays, and light itself, were comprised of and *traveled in space as separate and discontinuous quanta.* This new perception of electromagnetic radiation was to become basic to quantum theory, the theory of atomic phenomena. Furthermore, he took the Michelson-Morley finding (that light's velocity is a constant, unaffected by Earth's motion), and he took the Galilean Relativity Principle (that all uniformly moving systems are governed by the same mechanical laws) a giant step further: the laws governing light and other electromagnetic phenomena—in fact, *all* the phenomena of nature and all its laws—are the same for all systems that move uniformly *relative* to one another. (Even "simultaneity" is relative. As Einstein said, "Every reference body . . . has its own particular time; unless we're told the reference body to which the statement of time refers, there is no meaning in the statement of the time of an event." In an oft-cited example, if you're in an airplane and the flight attendant takes two minutes to walk from the galley to your seat, that two minutes is two minutes to you and to him. *But,* let's say that the plane is flying at the rate of four hundred miles an hour; in that case, if someone on the ground looking up at the plane could see that flight attendant move inside it, the two-minute walk would blitz by in a much faster blur.)

This meant that *the concept of absolute time was discarded along with the concept of absolute space.* Since motion can be detected only as a change in position *relative* to another body, and since motion takes place in space and through time—then both space and time are one, and relative to everything else. (If one could ride on a beam of light, for example, there would be no sense of motion whatsoever, and time itself would stand still. One would not age, since light is the fastest thing known in the universe.* Einstein had in effect constructed a common framework for electrodynamics and mechanics, in what was to be his lifelong search for a unified foundation of physics.

The most stunning aspect of this framework resulted from Einstein's having reasoned that since a moving body's mass increases with its motion, and since motion itself is a form of energy (kinetic energy), then the increased mass in that moving body is derived from its increased energy—that is, *energy has mass.* This realization of the relation between energy and mass—that even an object at rest is merely stored energy, that when the object is destroyed (as in burning a log or in nuclear reaction) energy is released, that mass *is* simply a form of energy—was expressed in the now-famous equation $E=mc^2$, or energy equals mass times the square of the velocity of light in centimeters per second. *Space and time were discovered to be the same thing. Matter and energy were discovered to be the same thing.*

This framework, which Einstein offered in 1905, was his Special Theory of Relativity. Almost eighty years later, science is still staggering under the latest implications of this theory.

In 1915, Einstein expanded this theory, and endorsed Ernst Mach's principle of inertia: "Mach's Principle" (that the properties of inertia in terrestrial matter are determined relative to the total universal mass surrounding them/it). Einstein, as usual going even further, proposed the General Theory of Relativity, extending the framework to include gravity—the mutual attraction of all massed bodies and the effect this has, in turn, on bend-

---

* The *tachyon*, however, is a postulated particle that can (might? will? does?) move faster than light. I have a special affection for this hypothetical bitlet of mattergy.

ing or curving time and space (the way an object displaces water).† This neatly did away with the notion of absolute motion and of absolute space. The world in which we three-dimensionally live is actually a four-dimensional space continuum.

Quantum physics shattered the two basic assumptions of classical science—causality and determinism—and opened up the internal, microcosmic universe. Relativity theory shattered all previous assumptions of space, time, movement, and gravitation, and exposed the external, macroscopic universe. Nothing now would ever be the same. The shock waves came thick and fast (and in particles, as well, of course):

In 1925, the concept that particles sometimes acted like waves and vice versa—through the work of de Broglie, Schrödinger, Börn and Jordan, and Heisenberg and Bohr—culminated in the discovery that a particle could *be* a wave, and vice versa (in the same way that a subway passenger at rush hour is both an individual with her own destination *and*, when the doors open to discharge her with a crowd, a wave).

In 1927, Werner Heisenberg conceived what is now his famous statement of physical law, the Principle of Uncertainty—that it is impossible to determine both the position and the velocity of an electron at the same time; the more accurately one can determine its velocity, the more indefinite its position becomes, and the reverse. The Principle of Uncertainty was following the thread of two Einstein statements which are really lovely aphorisms: "One may say the eternal mystery of the world is its comprehensibility," and "It is the theory which decides what we can observe." Strict determinism went out the door along with absolute space, time, movement, gravity, and all the other "constants."

This in turn gave rise to Niels Bohr's new philosophy of "Complementarity," which went something like this: Even if it is impossible to determine both the velocity and the position of an electron at the same time, nonetheless each (separately) is needed to gain a full picture of the atomic reality—just as both the "particle picture" and the "wave picture" are two complementary por-

† The latest of many challenges (over fifty years) to Einstein's General Theory of Relativity recently was raised by solar physicist Henry A. Hill of the University of Arizona, based on a study of how various calculated characteristics of the sun affect the orbit of Mercury in ways not foreseen by Einstein. Whether proven right or wrong, this latest controversy is likely to provide the stimulus for new thinking about Einstein's theories, and a potential for developing them even further.

trayals of the same reality, even if *they* can't be charted at the same time. In other words, despite one's *methods* being limited to either/or, one's *conception* can embrace both, and glimpse the whole.‡ From this philosophy an entirely new holistic direction in physics was born.

Various other developments followed rapidly. I'll arbitrarily skip about in time, since (1) time is relative, (2) if a particle can, who am I not to? and (3) I'm always a pushover for form mirroring content: John A. Wheeler of Princeton (who says delightful things like "There is no law except the law that there is no law"), coined the term *Black Holes* for energy-dense pockmarks in distant space—possibly burned-out stars which have collapsed internally because of their enormous gravity, and which suck space/time and light into themselves. Wheeler posited that a Black Hole in this universe might emerge as a White Hole exploding energy into another universe, and that the birth of a star in *this* universe might be happening through the looking-glass of some other universe's Black Hole. Wheeler also proposed that the stage on which (the space of) the universe moves is itself a larger stage —a *superspace*.

Then there was R. P. Feynman, whose diagrams showed that particles can be made to move backward in time—if only for a moment. There was the philosophy/physics paradox of Erwin Schrödinger (the paradox of "Schrödinger's cat") which posited perception as All; it showed that a (hypothetical) cat in a (theoretical) box can be "proven" to be alive and dead concurrently,

‡ Ironically, Einstein rejected Heisenberg's Uncertainty Principle (saying "God does not play dice with the world") and also Bohr's philosophy of Complementarity; until his death, Einstein continued to seek a deterministic cause that would unify all the contradictions he himself had exposed. An extraordinary series of debates ensued between Einstein and Bohr. Although these debates took place in 1927 in Belgium, they became known as the Copenhagen Debates because Bohr was Danish, and his viewpoint seemed to prevail. One might epitomize the two positions with Bohr saying: The quality of my observation changes—or even creates—reality, and Einstein saying: Reality is reality and follows its own laws, even if, so far, those laws are concealed from our understanding. As physicist Fred Alan Wolf has put it, "It was as if the left half and the right half of the cosmic brain were in dialogue." (*Taking the Quantum Leap*, New York: Harper & Row, 1981.) For the last fifty years, the so-called Copenhagen School of thought has been the dominant one in modern physics, the Aristotelian/late Einsteinian world view—of a mechanistic, deterministic, causal universe—being considered as anachronistic. But with new *non*systematic systems being developed, the debate is clearly an ongoing one.

until the moment one looks into the box and *perceives* the situation.* There was J. S. Bell, who formulated Bell's Theorem: when two particles interact and then fly off in different directions, further interference with one affects the other, no matter how distant they are, as if there were a telepathy between them, or a "quantum interconnectedness of distant systems." And there was Wolfgang Pauli, who developed the so-called Pauli Exclusion Principle: that no two electrons in an atom can be identical: the presence of one with a particular set of properties or "quantum numbers" excludes another with the same set, a mathematical precision which shows that the universe certainly does have an eye for detail. (Pauli also collaborated with Jung on the famous paper "Synchronicity: An Acausal Connecting Principle" in which Jung coined the term *synchronicity*.)

Recent theoretical developments include David Böhm's idea that there is an "implicate order" in the universe, a cosmic web of relations at a "nonmanifest" level that demonstrate an "unbroken wholeness." There is also Geoffrey Chew's S-matrix theory, sometimes known as the "bootstrap approach" (bootstrap because all particles are seen as having properties and interactions derived solely from their own self-consistent requirements); the S-matrix theory radically posits that *there are no fundamentals whatsoever in the universe*—no fundamental laws, principles, building blocks, equations, constants. Rather, the universe is seen as a network or web of events continuously and dynamically relating. No one property of this web is fundamental; each follows from the properties of every other part, and it is the overall consistent interrelation that defines and describes the web's structure. "Each particle helps to generate other particles, which in turn generate it."[3] This is quite stunning, if you dwell on it, especially because, as Chew puts it, "Carried to its logical extreme, the bootstrap conjecture implies that *the existence of consciousness, along with other aspects of nature, is necessary for self-consistency of the whole*."[4] (Italics mine.) Physicist Eugene Wigner also states that "It was not possible to formulate the laws [of Quantum Theory] in a fully consistent way without reference to consciousness."[5] And, Capra has added, "the explicit inclusion of human consciousness may be an essential aspect of future theories of matter."[6]

---

* This experiment always upsets me, even hypothetically. I do wish Schrödinger had postulated it with a snake or a leech. But a *cat*. Good grief.

If your head is spinning with excitement, not to worry. So is mine; so are the physicists', and so is each electron, planet, solar system, galaxy, and, probably, universe. Yet the above cursory tourist trip through the expanding landscape of the New Physics is not half so brain-boggling as a longer visit there, made possible through tickets provided by the proliferation of books on the subject written in a style accessible to the lay reader (see Bibliography). A number of conclusions, always tentative, begin to emerge: physics has found the border with metaphysics a permeable one; just as yesterday's magic is today's medicine, so yesterday's philosophy is today's science. Or, in the phrase of Sir James Jeans, "The universe begins to look more like a great thought than like a great machine."

That everything is energy, that everything moves, that everything is somehow discrete or separate, *and* interrelated or interconnected—these seem rather vital scientific facts that *politics* would do well to examine. Furthermore, as Arthur Koestler wrote, "The nineteenth-century model of the universe as a mechanical clockwork is a shambles and since the concept of matter itself has been dematerialized, *materialism can no longer claim to be a scientific philosophy.*"[7]

Nor, I might add, can materialism any longer claim to be a political philosophy.

Both quantum physics and feminism are "second generation" critiques of the old order, going even further than those "first generation" revolutions which acted against the dominant theory of determinism.

But how far *can* we go? Curiosity and desire, *technē* and *poiēsis* all suggest risking the tool of metaphor to anatomize freedom. So, using as our metaphor first classical physics and then quantum physics (less in a strict chronological progression than in a revealing unfolding), we might take a quantum leap and look at political evolution.

THE PAST

Mechanical (Classical) Physics	*Mechanical (Traditional) Politics*
"Building blocks" comprise the stuff of the universe.	"Building blocks" are the stuff of society: sexes, races, classes, the family, clans, tribes, nations, etc.

The "ultimate" building block is the atom.

The "ultimate" unit is the individual.

Building blocks can assemble in variable ways, but are also reducible.

Comparable variables are social systems: the rule of chiefs, the warrior class, institutional monarchy, feudalism, the rise of the bourgeoisie.

Material and matter are seen as real.

Materialism—and dialectical materialism—are seen as realistic systems of analysis, especially after the Industrial "Revolution."

THE PRESENT

Quantum Mechanics

Energy seems fluid but is composed of discontinuity.

The Beginning of Quantum Politics

The idea of progress breaks down; the "building blocks" disturb the system's fluidity (socialist and anticolonial revolutions); discontinuity in "norms" begins (family structures shift, sexual options are openly articulated).

Special Theory of Relativity

Mass/energy is seen as one; space/time also is seen as one, and as relative. This is the end of the notion of "matter." The theory is limited in not yet including movement.

Special Theory of Feminism

The majority of humanity (female) is seen as sharing same condition, relative to the (male) minority of humanity. This is the beginning of the end of materialism. The theory is so far limited to intrafeminist movement impact, not yet including its full constituency.

The Concept of Particles Being Waves and Waves Being Particles

The Feminist Emphasis on "Process"

Means are affirmed as being more vital than goals or ends. Freedom is intuited as being both a state and a dynamic.

The Principle of Uncertainty
One can see a "wavicle" either as a wave or particle, but not both at once; one can chart its position or velocity, but not both at the same time.

The Theory of Complementarity
One doesn't need to see wave and particle at once; one can imagine the whole from its fragments or assume their complementarity. The possibility of interpenetration and permeability of particles is explored. It is no longer necessary to impose a system of coherence in order to work with and study disparate parts.

Fission: Splitting of the Atom
The end of the "ultimate building block" notion. The study of subatomic particles and *sub*-subatomic particles begins.

Fusion: Thermonuclear Fusing of the Atom Is Risked
The hydrogen bomb is created, with the possibility

The Principle of Polarity
Either/Or thinking emerges in feminist (fundamentalist) theory: radical *or* reformist, activist *or* thinker, lesbian *or* heterosexual, economic analysis *or* cultural/spiritual approach, race *or* sex priority, work within the system *or* outside it, etc., *ad nauseam.*

Pragmatic but Fragile Coalitions
Alliances emerge among women despite mutual mistrust and cynicism: women of color and white women in dialogue, growth of international network, connections sought with activists on environmental, academic, economic, age, cultural, and other "fronts"; a lessening of alienation between lesbian and heterosexual women and the emergence of genuine bisexual affirmation; a skittish attempt on the part of some feminists to understand and reach out even to women in the grip of the Right Wing and other fundamentalisms.

Fragmentation of the Individual
Feminists *and* nonfeminists, women *and* men feel this: chronic anxiety, doomsday political tactics and increased terrorism, psychological reductionism combined with a desperate search for "self," burn-out.

Fusion of the Old Orders Is Risked
An alliance is forced between the "workers" and state cap-

of nuclear energy through forced fusion, even with its incomprehensibly great dangers.

italism (contemporary "communism"); an alliance is forced between the "consumer" and the megamerchant corporations (contemporary "capitalism"); various attempts are made to pass off old ways as new ones, ignoring the incomprehensibly great danger this presents.

THE FUTURE

General Theory of Relativity
Discovery that gravitational attraction between massive bodies is also relative.

General Theory of Feminism
Theory begins to reach out beyond the loose confines of what has been considered the Women's Movement; the feminist vision begins to make an impact on all human beings, and, *relative to their own situations*, they make an impact, in turn, on feminism. The discovery is made that feminism is inherent in Third World freedom struggles, and in the New International Economic Order; that feminism is central to the solving of crises in population growth, hunger, war, illiteracy, disease, nationalism, environmental destruction, etc.; that feminism affects all perceptions of sexuality, age, socioeconomic, cultural/spiritual, and scientific/aesthetic issues. Nationalism and other traditional political systems begin to fragment and collapse in the enormous gravitational pull among and between individuals and groups within them who are making these connections.

Concept of the Participatory Observer

The experiment changes what is being observed by the very observing of it; all things interact.

Quantum Field Theory

The theory attempts to merge quantum mechanics and relativity, posits that particles are actually interactions between fields "instantaneously and locally": the concept that space itself isn't empty at all.

Ongoing Attempts at a Unified Field Theory

These approaches include the diverse concepts of the "hidden variables" and the "concealed order"; the Yang-Mills gauge field theory of symmetrical but unstable interactions; Böhm's "implicate universe"—a cosmic web of interrelations; Chew's S-matrix theory and "bootstrapping"—particles "involving" one another in patterns of "self-consistency." The possibility is explored that there are no fundamental constituents of matter, no fundamental principles or laws, except, possibly, those of consciousness.

The End of "the Exception"

The global beginning of "I'm no feminist, *but* . . . ," that is, the inescapable (admitted) recognition among women and the inescapable (not yet admitted) recognition among men of their participation in the situation identified by feminism, and their (admitted *and* nonadmitted) longing for the changes feminism addresses.

Metafeminist Synchronicities

Metafeminism attempts to synthesize the breakdown of global systems with the energy of feminist vision as a relevant solution toward change; the realization dawns that this synthesis is precisely what has been intuited, longed for, and feared by the species for millennia.

Metafeminism as the Bridge to Metapolitics

All fundamental laws, categories and categorizing, and "norms" of behavior are discovered to be illusory. *Fundamentalism vanishes along with fundamentals.* Consciousness is reinvented anew out of a new consciousness. A balance emerges between the individual and the collective/species/sentient life/universal movement; uniqueness and commonality are seen as *un*contradictory; differences and similarities are held in a celebrated balance, each self-consistent and mutually involved.

Ongoing Discovery of Sub-sub-atomic Particles

These discoveries amount so far to almost three hundred, including protons (and their possible decay), leptons, gluons, baryons, mesons, and hadrons—and then hadron "particles" postulated as quarks (a quark is sized at 10 million times smaller than the atom), or charmed quarks (because they seem to obey only their own erraticism) or red, white, and blue quarks, or "psi-particles," or particles referred to merely as "resonances" which have "a tendency to exist"—postulatable, but traceable only by the trails of light their nonmoving movement leaves when monitored in bubble chambers.

Micro- and Macrocosmic Revo- and Evolution in a Vertical Curve

All facets of consciousness flower, new forms of intelligence develop and create still newer forms in turn. Eccentric and eclectic agnostic acrostic solutions to old problems fall into place via quarky ingenious strategies. Freedom actually is *traceable* now as well as *postulatable*; freedom, which has a "tendency to exist" and which, through the rapidity and energy of its movement, can be known to have existed only by the trail of light it leaves behind.

MEANWHILE, BACK AT "THE PERSONAL IS POLITICAL" . . .

Well, you say. This is all very nice, impressive, and cosmic—but I'm not quite sure how glimpsing the implicate order or the tendencies of certain resonances "to exist" is going to help me get Herman to pick up his socks, stop Mr. Smithjones from pinching my behind at work, make me less nervous when alone on the street at night, get me a decent salary, babysit for me, get rid of the military-industrial complex, or, or, or . . . make a goddamned plain old feminist revolution.

I do understand your point. But we've just begun to comprehend the vast implications of our own politics, and even though these implications seem most startling when they lead forward into infinity, they also pertain directly to the present. (Time/ space *is* the same thing, and relative to the observer, remember?)

For one thing, a full, deep awareness in each of us of the centrality and profundity of feminist vision in itself will have a monumental effect on the way each of us carries her/himself, the way we each conduct our personal lives and construct our political strategies: *No more begging for "rights"*: the future of intelligence itself is at stake. *No more single-issue politics* (sacrifice reproductive-freedom rights for fear of endangering the ERA, sacrifice ERA for fear it isn't radical enough, drop everything and work on economic analyses or on violence-against-women issues or on international networking): since when does the electron not touch everything in its orbit at once? *No more victimization* (permitting the grief and pain of our situation as women to paralyze us into hopelessness, cynicism, depression, burn-out, or sell-out): just because you can see the picture only as wave or particle at any given time doesn't mean it isn't both at all times, and dynamic in its movement, too. *No more correct-line politics, not ever, no more*: just because one of us is focusing on velocity and the other on position doesn't mean that we don't need each other to put together the whole picture (Principle of Uncertainty), and that the very diversity of our conditions doesn't make for a stronger ultimate unity (Theory of Complementarity).

When we really comprehend the full meaning of what it is we are fighting for, that in itself will inspire the strategies, and give us the strength and endurance necessary to win. *Carry yourself as one who will save the world. Because you will.*

On an even simpler level, it's possible to apply our framework of the Physics of Feminism to what is sometimes laughingly called daily life. Three areas, especially, may be most crucial to our immediate survival as women and as feminists—and as men, for that matter. One is the problem of leashed powers of emotion. A second is involved with ways and means for conducting personal relationships—which *are* necessary to anyone but a solipsist if she/he is going to survive long enough to wave her/his particle self along the field of magnetic change. A third is the contradiction inherent in the human lack of and longing for connectedness—with all the perils that implies.

Let's call our framework the F-matrix Theory, equated as $F=et^2$ or: *Feminism equals equality/empowerment/evolution times the squared velocity of transformation.* And let's apply $F=et^2$ to these three daily-life areas.

1. *The leashed powers of emotion.* Nothing so simple as "repression" here. I'm referring to Man's refusal to acknowledge the *hidden variable* in men (love) and Woman's refusal to acknowledge the *hidden variable* in women (rage).† What any good consciousness-raising group does (among other things) is give a woman permission to rage. It's what any good friend or good therapist does too, for that matter. It's what the Women's Movement did up until about 1976—when we got worried about "alienating" and tried to be accommodating (to whom?), tried to dilute the intensity of our own message. That many women subsequently became slightly bored by the Women's Movement and that many feminists turned apoplectic from bottling up our rage all over again ought not to come as a surprise. And it oughtn't to be much of a surprise, either, that (some) men tried to "practice loving" very, very awkwardly at first, met head on with our smilingly suppressed rage, got confused and—rather lazily in many cases—gave up. (They had concrete privileges to lose by this "experiment," remember, and the enlightened self-interest we tried to foster in them would only click on its light some decades —or millennia—hence.)

Now, all over again, and definitively, we must split the atom of our Man- and Woman-made emotions, releasing the vast energy of rage and love into action. I ask again: if women don't give themselves and each other permission to rage, to be audacious, who will? Men do have it easier: If men don't give themselves and each other permission to love (and some try)—women will. But the emotions of real women and real men must be fissioned from the shell of Man and Woman—and this time that fission must continue.

2. *Ways and means for conducting relationships.* Very complex, this. But relativity theory may be helpful in suggesting a relative approach (this is *not* recommended among strangers, but is operable within relationships, among partners, lovers, friends, colleagues, etc.): What if you treat a woman as you would a man—

† These are the inversions of violence and romance, as examined in Chapter IV.

and the reverse? Before I expire under the weight of "feminist fundamentalist" bricks thrown at me for such heresy, let me explain.

For example, let's say you (a woman) live with another woman, a lover or simply a roommate. Let's say that she at times puts her muddy boots up on the furniture, spills ashes all over the table, is congenitally late for appointments, or leaves a ring around the tub. (Women, being human, actually have been rumored to do such things. And I'm deliberately picking the small aggravations. You can fill in the big ones.) Think, for a moment, how you would regard such behavior if she were a man. Instantly a knee-jerk feminist analysis comes into play: that sloppy, inconsiderate, male-supremacist deliberately exercising his power over you. You probably wouldn't take this behavior from a man (I *hope* you wouldn't), yet many women do accept it from other women—lovers *and* friends. And that's nonsensical twaddle, I think (having been guilty of it frequently). Why lower our standards of civility for women?

If, on the other hand, one is putting up with attitudes or actions from a *man* that one wouldn't take from another woman . . . aha. The only way to overcome that very real power-tremble is to leap quantumly out of *that* nonsensical twaddle, I say (having trembled therein many a time), and point out that such behavior would strike you as intolerable in a woman and is no more tolerable in a man.

What if, in other words, we dare begin to express a postrevolutionary consciousness even in this prerevolutionary time—at least in personal relationships. Elsewhere, in the big world, such a tactic is extremely questionable: toughing it out by insisting on going for a walk alone at 3 A.M. may be putting on a postrevolutionary façade but it's likely to wind one up in a prerevolutionary hospital. Still, it *is* possible to begin to leave victimization behind us, at least in personal relationships—*not by changing the other person, but by changing oneself*. Oneself is the only person over whom one has the real power to affect change, ultimately. But those changes within the self *are* possible, and can have, like the gravitational interpenetration of fields, an astounding influence on the others one cannot change directly. *It is your life*—and the only one you're certain of. In sum, if you develop the velocity of your own light-of-self as a constant, then you can choose (and choose how) to beam it on those with whom you interrelate in a way that sees them as *relative* to you, you as relative to them, and them as relative to one another. This returns you to yourself, and accomplishes two rather nice bonus rewards: first, it gives you balance, perspective, and a modicum of power—and second, it's *fair*.

3. *The human lack of and longing for connection*—and all the attendant dangers, sufferings, and evasions that implies. In this case, $F=et^2$ suggests a reassuring course, one which rejects Man and Woman's notion of *fusion* in relationships and points instead to a more balanced "model": *symbiosis*. I am not using the term in the Freudian sense (as a pejorative description of overly dependent tendencies within a human relationship) but rather in its original and value-free sense as it is commonly used in biology. This is the at-first-vigilant, then carefully developed, *interde*pendence, the give-and-take which many life forms practice for their very survival. The yucca plant would not exist without the one particular insect which pollenates it—and that insect would not survive without the yucca for food, and for shelter of its eggs. A particular crab and a particular anemone know by each other's markings that each means survival to the other. Lewis Thomas's memorable example of the Medusa jellyfish and its symbiote, the snail—who even switch roles in virtuoso fashion in their symbiosis—is an especially heartening "model."[8] "Love is more complex than theory," I wrote once in a poem, long before I had the sense to know that I knew that. (The Dream Self must have written that one.) Douglas Hofstadter might have had something similar in mind when he paraphrased the mathematician Gödel: "The fact that truth transcends theoremhood, in any given formal system, is called the incompleteness of that system."[9] Why do *any* of us permit Man or Woman to distort the life-giving process of symbiosis into the subsummation of fusion? Why, in reaction to that distortion, do any of us permit correct-line fundamentalist politics to tell us that we have no right at least to *try* to love, connect, interconnect, and interdepend where we choose, as long as that makes us feel good, stronger, more empowered—*and* as long as no one is demeaned or robbed of her/his empowerment in the process? As the Wicceans say, "Do what thou wilt, *an it harm none.*"

The old audacity of this wave of feminism was that women dared to name our pain. Today we need a new audacity—one that leaves the highly ambivalent familiarity of our victimization behind us (while we remain keenly aware of the surrounding danger). That new audacity would dare to affirm the ultimate radical politics reflected in and reflective of the universe itself: *radical integration*. Integration of the self with the self (literally: *integrity*), and integration with each other and our vision and all of life. It would involve daring to act out of that postrevolutionary integrity even in a prerevolutionary context—but without false consciousness.

The courage it required two decades ago for feminists to name the already existing division between men and women, the separation, the anguish—and to relate that division to all the other separations based on race, age, nationality, and so forth—that courage would need to be squared (the velocity of transformation) in order to accomplish *this* naming of the already existing "implicate" integration which connects, surrounds, and embraces us all. It would have to be a courage equal to the task. It would have to refuse to sacrifice the integrity of self *or* the integrity of feminism for some illusory "second stage," as Betty Friedan has suggested; a "second stage" that leaves sexual politics behind (and still unsolved) sounds alarmingly like forced fusion all over again. No, *this* approach—of radical integration—sacrifices nothing except false categories and burned-out strategies. It has the potential to turn (embittering) hatred into (energizing) rage, and to connect the energy of that rage to the even greater energy of love. *This* approach suggests that the power is already there for the touching by audacious hands. And this approach suggests a way for those hands, once having touched that power, to have the grace to use it well.

THE LUCY-DOLPHIN ALLIANCE

As I sit here writing these words, only six months remain for the Equal Rights Amendment to be ratified by the three remaining states necessary to put into the United States Constitution the concept that female citizens are equal to male citizens. At this moment it looks very likely that, due to the money and mobilization of a right-wing American minority, the amendment will not pass. The fifty years of work involved in getting the ERA to this stage will have to be lived all over again, vow those feminists most deeply involved in this issue as their priority.

As of this writing, the Reagan administration has announced budget cutbacks of billions of dollars for food stamps, welfare clients, job-training programs, education, public-transport systems, environmental preservation, medical and health programs, urban renewal, the older population, and the arts—while announcing budget buildups for defense in a country that already boasts thirty thousand nuclear-weapon devices in its arsenal.

As of this writing, a so-called human life statute quietly makes its way through the halls of the U.S. Congress—a bill which will, in effect, declare female human life secondary to the "rights" of a group of fetal cells. (The profound *ignorance* of fundamentalists never ceases to astonish me. Their "reverence for life" is quite different from that of nature—which puts forth hundreds of acorns from one oak, knowing damned well that only a few stand the slightest chance of becoming oaks themselves, and knowing also that this is necessary for the balance of life or else there'd be nothing on earth but oak trees. Nature's overabundance is based on a highly unsentimental attitude about life, unlike the reproductive-fundamentalist attitude. The latter reeks of a beer-hall sentimentality which precludes genuine sentiment and which is always closely allied with truly fascist thought.)

As of this writing, so-called statesmen [sic] speak seriously and pompously of a third world war, and estimate the megadeaths calmly.

As of this writing, feminists all over the world are organizing and energizing themselves and one another—and feminists in the United States, although exhausted, depressed, and burned out, are furious and Ready to Try Again. We are constantly told, as we have been since 1969, that "the Women's Movement is dead" —statements of wishful thinking trying to pass themselves off as self-fulfilling prophecy. We are told that something called the "New Class" of intellectuals and bureaucrats is rising to power. When I read about these people and their politics, they sound peculiarly like the "Old Class": they all come equipped with abstract rhetoric, selective hearing, and penises. Individual feminist activists and thinkers often speak of their own personal lives with a bitter gallows humor—the residue of having spent years focused on researching, exposing, or organizing against one of the many specific "atrocity" issues: battery, or sexual slavery, or pornography, or reproductive-technology developments, or institutionalized women in prisons and mental wards. These feminists, who sometimes have sacrificed a broader perspective (with its accompanying more cheerful view) in order to do urgently needed work in a particular area, are temporary "casualties" until a little perspective is regained and some political chicken soup enables them to sit up in bed and in time take a few halting steps. But they keep at it, heroically. Still others, who believed the various now-forgotten correct lines of some past phase, and who altered their entire lives for some promised but never-forthcoming central-committee approval, now stagger about trying to reconstruct those lives: this one, at thirty-seven, goes back to college after having dropped out at twenty on being told that higher education was elitist; that one realizes that her ex-husband was, after all, the nicest guy she's ever known; still another, after years of politically pure downward mobility, decides she'd like to be able to earn a sensible salary, buy a few books, plants, clothes. Meanwhile, others are learning, "Omigod, I wasn't really nonmonogamous after all," or "Omigod, after ten years as a lesbian separatist, I'm attracted to a *man?*" or "Omigod, I *loathe* communal living and wish I'd never left my lover!"

The unacknowledged misogyny in the Women's Movement is still our greatest weakness—not because the misogyny exists but because it's unacknowledged. It's analogous to the hidden anti-Semitism of some Jews, to the lighter-darker-shade-of-color prejudice that caused so much grief in the Black Movement. We all know its causes: the horizontal hostility encouraged among the oppressed by the divide-and-conquerors, the self-contempt projected onto others. It's old news—but still scandalous.

Misogyny may use slick political phrases to cover its woman-hatred: it may proclaim a woman "unauthentic" or "male-identified" or "plastic" or "dyke" or "straight" or "individualistic" or "obsessed"—or just (pejoratively) "liberal" or (pejoratively) "radical." It always emphasizes differences more than similarities —which is one way to identify it for what it really is. Another way is to notice if a woman spends more than a quarter of her conversation "trashing" other so-called sisters. A little human crankiness, sure, but if it's more than a quarter, watch out. The disguises for this misogyny are, to be sure, hypocritical masks for the old human feelings of fear, confusion, fear, jealousy, fear, longing, fear, arrogance, fear, ignorance—and fear.

Six months ago I heard a white woman denounce a list of proposed speakers for an antipornography rally because, so she claimed, there were no black women listed. As it turned out, more than half the names on the list *were* names of women of color—black, Hispanic, and Asian American—but these women happened not to have instantly recognizable ethnic names to give her prejudices a clue, nor were they "celebrity" feminist women of color who often speak at such rallies, and so she just let loose in her ignorance and arrogance. Two weeks ago I read a letters-to-the-editor-column furor over a previously published interview in the same feminist paper, an interview with a well-known scientist who declared herself a feminist and, when asked her position on lesbian separatism, replied that she personally felt allied with and identified with all women, though not more so with any one particular group of women than another. The letters—attacking her as homophobic—clearly came from women who had not stopped even for a second to consider that this scientist might herself be a lesbian. She is—and not (yet?) "out," because the exigencies of her life, her marriage, children, and job, have created pressures on her which *ought* to be familiar to other lesbian women—none of whom sprang like Athena fully armed from Zeus's brow. In moments of irony like this, I tend to wail aloud, "Where is our *mercy* for one another? Where is our compassion for, our *respect* for individuality? Where is our much-vaunted *altruism?*"

It certainly is understandable that we regard mercy, compassion, and altruism with suspicion—since those are Woman's attributes which have been foisted on women for eons. Yet they're excellent attributes in themselves: it would be nice if Man acquired them and if women practiced them more on each other instead of always throwing them like proverbial pearls before men.

After all, a particle can combine with other particles and then reconstitute itself whole, losing none of its integrity. Each individual spider's web is as distinctive as a fingerprint. Elephants are said to mourn their dead, and to bury them. Dolphins midwife one another, care for their ill and dying, and have been known voluntarily to tend other dolphins caught in tuna nets, even though butchery for all may result. Whales, traveling in pods of three or four, sing to one another not only for sounding location but, it appears, to keep each other's spirits up; when a sick whale beaches itself, a healthy whale has been known to do the same—possibly an altruistic gesture of companionship, albeit a suicidal one. Surely humanity, surely women, surely *feminists* at least, could approximate the individuality and altruism of a particle, a spider, a dolphin?

The cliché "It's always darkest before the dawn" was put far more elegantly by Kafka when he wrote that grace, transcendence, salvation come "not at the last, but at the very last." This moment in history is a—perhaps *the*—hinge moment. The panic such pressure creates is like the panic in a burning room full of people who fear they don't know the way out. Feminists are no exception. We fear that we lack "order" and "leadership" and "chains of command"—forgetting that this seeming "disorder" has always been our strength. It's a natural disorder, like erosion. *It's the "implicit disorder" of the universe itself—and the way change happens.* As Ellen DuBois described the beginnings of the nineteenth-century Women's Movement, women's energy was "unexamined, *implicit*, and above all, disorganized."[10] (Italics mine.)

I'm certainly not suggesting that we stop examining our political and personal vision, or that we lie back and assume it's implicit, or that we celebrate and expand our lack of organization wherever it exists. I am saying that we might look a little positively on the underlying force which fuels all our examination and all our organization, call it what you will: justice, DNA's thirst toward perfecting things, or $F=et^2$.

I suggest that, in our moments of despair, we let ourselves be comforted by the calm urgency of Elizabeth Cady Stanton: "If I were to draw up a set of rules for the guidance of reformers . . . I should put at the head of the list, 'Do all you can, *no matter what*, to get people to think about your reform, and then, if the reform is good, it will come about in due season.'"

Have we, each of us, women and men, "done all that we can" in working personally and politically on this equation that can unlock the secrets of our individual and collective universes? I think not. How many of us are even basically informed about what it is we're up against at this moment, in this country, even? For example:

• The right-wing drive for a constitutional convention needs two thirds of the states to support it; it already has passed referenda in one third. One of the stated purposes is to insert a "life begins at conception" amendment in the Constitution (thus ending forever a woman's legal right in the United States to control her own reproductive system); one of the usually *un*stated but sometimes acknowledged purposes of "Con Con" is that such a convention could "reexamine and revise" the Bill of Rights itself. (Thomas Paine is spinning in his grave.)

• The "godfather" of the "New Right," Richard A. Viguerie, raised more than $7 million for the campaign of archconservative Jesse Helms. It is mastermind Viguerie whose computers control 15 million names, who boasts that he can "flood the country with mail on any issue" (and he does), who from his Virginia headquarters pulls the strings on groups ranging from the Conservative Caucus to the Ku Klux Klan, hundreds of religious-fundamentalist political groups, and "right-to-life" organizations—and who worries that Ronald Reagan is too liberal. Viguerie's computers are so sophisticated, he boasts, that they even can type strike-overs in fund-raising letters (so it will look as if a group of nonprofessional, idealistic volunteers typed the letters) and place stamps—not postal-meter marks—on the envelopes of such letters slightly crooked (so as to seem handdone by those same volunteers). Viguerie alone ought to inspire feminists to enter the twentieth century and the computer age as fast as we can—just to keep up, let alone get ahead. We dare not indulge in an across-the-board antitechnology attitude with the likes of *him* around.‡

• The so-called Family Protection Act now (at this writing) pending in Congress would, if passed, make it impossible for a homosexual person who is proud and open about her/his sexual choice to teach in the public school system. (So much for

‡ The first feminist response to his technology challenge came in 1981 with the founding of the National Women's Mailing List (1195 Valencia Street, San Francisco, CA 94110). A project of the Women's Information Exchange, the computerized databank registers only those women who sign up by choice, to facilitate networking in terms of mailing lists, bulletins, and other information exchanges in those areas of concern they choose.

Socrates and Plato.) Furthermore, funding could be withdrawn from any school which could be shown to have used twice within a ten-year period any textbooks depicting women in "nontraditional roles"—wife, mother, nurse, etc. (So much for Marie Curie, Indira Gandhi, Valentina Tereshkova, and Althea Gibson.) The bill's fall-out also would affect withdrawal of federal funds for battered-wives refuges (they're runaways from family responsibilities), and for abused children's shelters (invasions of the rights and privacy of the family), and would make permissible corporal punishment in the schools ("Spare the rod . . ."). Feminists have said that the Family Protection Act should more accurately be named the Patriarchs' Protection Act.

• Some insurance companies are among the major sugar daddies for the anti-ERA and antireproductive freedom drives. Certain "liberal issues" turn out to be radical, as we had to learn about the ERA, instructed painfully as we were by the economic reasons behind the right-wing opposition to it. We should have known, as Emerson did, that "Every reform is only a mask under cover of which a more terrible reform, which dares not yet name itself, advances."

• Phyllis Schlafly has long been the token woman for the boys of the Birch Society, Young Americans for Freedom, the Manion Forum, and the American Conservative Union—all of which interlock with her own Eagle Forum (this last a major anti-ERA organization).

• Every time we use "their" phraseology we are playing into their hands. It is *feminists* who are "preserving the family"—by permitting it to redefine and thus revitalize itself, *feminists* who are truly concerned with morals and ethics, *feminists* who have a real politics of love. *Let's take back the words!**

• Every time you or I scorn letter writing (to a congressional representative, or an advertiser, or a newspaper, or a city official) *five* letters *are* being written—but from the opposing viewpoint. *Canned postcards,* they're called. The Right Wing has hot lines all across the country that give specific instructions and addresses about whom to write each day. Why can't we at least keep a pile

---

* See Koestler's essay "The Holarchy" in *Janus* for his analysis of "words as atoms," and Lewis Thomas' paean to language as a living organism, of which words are the cells, in his essay, "Living Language," in *The Lives of a Cell.*

of postcards near the television—and jot them out during commercials?

• Bills and amendments are sneaked through state legislatures and Congress regularly. Do you know how to find out about such things? Can you afford *not* to know any longer?

Even at a minimum, each of us should write ten letters or cards a week (to elected officials, advertisers, whomever—praising, condemning, nudging, nagging); *it works.* It's time to reexamine coalition building—albeit with a wary eye toward being coopted. (We want to *symbioze*, remember, not *fuse.*) It's time to *vote* again—not give up out of despair. It's time for some Americans to *register* to vote; some of us remember Mississippi—when you better believe the ballot was considered radical. Learn to lobby. Train younger women in the skills and tactics you know; pass it on. Consider confrontation direct-action tactics again. Subscribe to and support the "domestic" feminist media (it may not be perfect, but it's ours) and especially the international feminist media. Learn or relearn one foreign language for global feminism. Learn, and teach another woman, the secrets of one technological tool (any one: car, calculator, word processor, etc.). *Talk to women*—at school, at work, at the launderette. They're not tired of feminist ideas—only feminist jargon. Talk about *feelings*, about pornography, family, pain, about love, about rape and battery and sexual harrassment on the job, the street, the campus. Give homework assignments to men who claim to be allies: letter writing, childcare, typing. Donate one dollar a week minimum to some feminist cause, or tithe if you can (the Mormons do!). Complain. Ask questions. Make trouble. Find out who your elected representatives are at all levels. Endorse political candidates. Consider running yourself. Learn how the "inside" works; we already know how the "outside" works, we were born into it. We'll need to understand both to survive—and win.

In fact, why don't we *denounce the patriarchal notion of inside and outside partitioning?* It's really as restricting as the idiocy of national boundaries. If *matter* doesn't really exist, who are we to quibble over "within the system" or "outside the system"? We need to be lobbying *and* marching, striking by night *and* going on strike by day, writing letters *and* literature, wielding the spraypaint can *and* the artist's brush.

The New Right has focused on the Feminist Movement be-

cause they know—even when we momentarily forget—how profound a force for social change feminism is. We can no longer afford to forget.

We can no longer afford to be so pure, or so afraid, or so despairing, that we don't avail ourselves of *whatever we can:* scientific knowledge, self-defense arts, networking, humor, computers, art, the wisdom of our own dreams and the drive of our own curiosity and desire, the hologrammatic depths of our chosen committed relationships, the true kinship blood types we need no longer deny, the vitality of play, the lost child in each of us, the growing old woman or man in each of us, our own individual deaths, each other, the world.

It's tiring, you say? Then rest for a while. We—who have only this urgent minisecond—have eternity. *Bend time to yourself.* We—who have only this tiny fragment of space in which to maneuver—have space itself, in all its dense-packed energy. *Bend space to yourself.* We—each of whom huddles in the "solitude of self" fearing that no other ever can really understand—are unique integrities nonetheless permeable, interchangeable, combinable, and many—the field itself. *Bend that consciousness to yourself,* wrap yourself in its warmth.

Me, I like to think about Lucy. You must have heard about Lucy; she's the oldest known ancestor of our species. She lived in what is now the Afar region of Ethiopia. She was in her late twenties when she died, although she was just under four feet tall (you can imagine why I'm specially fond of her). She might have had a touch of spinal arthritis, but she seems to have died a peaceful death, by the banks of what today is the Awash River— where her bones lay undisturbed for almost three and a half million years, until their discovery in 1974 by Donald Johanson of the Cleveland Museum of Natural History.[11] Not just a few bones, either. She turned out to be, in Johanson's words, "the oldest, most complete, best-preserved skeleton of any erect-walking human ancestor that has ever been found." They catalogued Lucy as No. AL 288-1 and eventually labeled her *Australopithecus afarensis.* Some called her "the missing link." In time, the team found more of Lucy's family or clan or people—about thirteen individuals they nicknamed "the First Family." The discovery of Lucy pushed estimates of the existence of human precursors on earth further back—by about a million years.

I like to think about Lucy. She had a rather small skull but quite "modern" legs and hands, and she must have roamed around making a few tools here and there, gathering and foraging but able to carry her baby in her arms as her human descendants would do later. She must have communicated in some way with her people. I'll wager they had their means of making rhythms if not "music," of moving with joy if not "dancing," of grieving when one of their own fell prey to a wild animal or wandered off or just died. I imagine her lying there, on the banks of that river-which-was-yet-to-be, lying there in her desert or veldt under the wide horizon-to-horizon curve of black nightsky all alive with the two hundred billion stars in the Milky Way, which is merely one galaxy in a galactic cluster, which in turn is only one of the galactic clusters in our Local Group . . . I imagine Lucy lying back and resting her small neat skull on her arm and gazing up at all that glory. And trying to think it through. Trying to think. Trying.

And space/time curls back on itself, displaced by the sudden rush of my love for her, this tiny wobbly animal on her way to becoming not Woman but women; this creature settling herself somehow toward the task of intelligence, this indomitable unique absurd being, and the impossibly hopeless unthinkable task she set herself: becoming human.

$F=et^2$. If she could do it, I can.

BOTH/AND (DEDICATED TO REGINA OLSEN—AND WITH RESPECTFUL APOLOGIES TO KIERKEGAARD)

"We violate probability, by our nature," wrote Lewis Thomas. "To do this, systematically, and in such wild varieties of form . . . to have sustained the effort successfully for the several billion years of our existence, without drifting back into randomness, was nearly a mathematical impossibility."[12]

Thomas, the biologist and medical doctor, sees the earth as a single cell.

James Lovelock, the British chemical biophysicist, and Lynn Margulis, the American microbiologist, see the earth as a single organism, an entity they call Gaia (after the Greek goddess of Earth)—a homeostatic system of "feedback loops" with the (possibly conscious) capacity to make and keep the planet fit for life.

They too point out how much we violate probability: Earth has "too much" ammonia, "too much" hydrogen, nitrogen, nitrous oxide, carbon monoxide. Computer models of the atmosphere of Earth in the absence of life suggest that its composition should be somewhere between those of our nearest neighbors, Mars and Venus.[13] Yet it is conveniently *out* of kilter chemically and thermodynamically—convenient, that is, to supporting life. Lovelock posits that the presence of life itself managed to drive the atmosphere into this convenient disequilibrium—and then to maintain it.

David Böhm sees this entire universe as one possible wavelet spontaneously pulsed up in a sea of cosmic energy.

Arthur Koestler, a distinguished political and literary person with a friendly obsession about science as both fact and metaphor, sees not the cell or the Gaian organism, but the "holarchy," and still beyond that—beyond the dual tendency for living beings to behave as individual wholes and at the same time as parts in the hierarchies of existence—he sees the "holon," a Janus mask of separateness, oneness, and integration.[14]

"The universe is made of stories, not atoms," wrote Muriel Rukeyser, the poet.

One of the nicest things about relativity theory is that it proves how accurately many different people from different perspectives can all be telling different truths about the same truth at different (or the same) times, rather like a subtle slant-rhyme scheme in a sonnet. A "relativity consciousness" also precludes ethnocentricity, egocentricity, and pretty much every other kind of -centricity. It is, to say the least, the fundamentally opposite perspective from fundamentalism, from Either/Or thinking.

Of course, the really good Either/Or thinkers like Kierkegaard haven't been fundamentalists at all, and were in fact drawn to the dialectic only because of the electromagnetic promise of some sort of synthesis on the other end, a synthesis which in turn becomes a new thesis which in turn gives rise to a new antithesis which necessitates the search for yet a newer synthesis. There's a comfortably unsettling quality to this process, since it gives one the seeming reassurance of "categories"—that is, a grid or system for interpreting a diffuse reality—but the categories, far from being fixed, are in dynamic movement. That quality of inherent relativity lends the dialectical process a verisimilitude—in much the same way that one is more easily prone to trust a person with a sense of irony than someone apparently totally lacking in that capacity.

The irony in Søren Kierkegaard's *Either/Or* is, to be sure, everywhere and nowhere at once, both where he intended it to be and where he didn't. (Irony's whole point, after all, is to pop up where least expected.)

Which reminds me that I should digress for a moment and deliver myself of a short credo regarding my personal feelings about Kierkegaard. Although I can already hear wails of dismay, snorts of derision, and even more ominous silences thick with confusion all cacophonously rising from certain quarters, I must say it: I *like* Kierkegaard. Very much, in fact. If my reader hasn't got past the point of understanding that this feminist, for one (like many others), will affirm intelligence wherever it occurs, and will not go gently into any ghetto of intellectual separatism, then that reader should have stopped back in Chapter I, when I quoted Herbert Marcuse and Kurt Waldheim—and Kierkegaard's *so* much more interesting than either one of them. Anyway, I *like* Kierkegaard. I find him a lovely, funny, moving, wise writer; even his flaws are interesting. I don't think I would have enjoyed knowing him much; like so many other souls one encounters in the privacy of the page, he seems to have been not all that jolly a person in, as they say, real life. He seems to have been a bit sullen, morose, and other broody things fitting for a Dane. Still, his philosophical work stands for me at a central point (*one* relative central point, you understand, in the mandala the center of which is everywhere), not only because of its own brilliant content—which, to explore, would require another book in itself—but also because at the central point of Kierkegaard's work stands, in turn, a woman. Her name was Regina Olsen. You will not be surprised to learn that we are told little about Regina Olsen—mostly that she and Kierkegaard were apparently deeply in love, became engaged, and then the engagement was broken off—either by him, by her, by him having maneuvered her into breaking it off, or by her having maneuvered him into breaking it off. (They were *both* Danes, you understand, and it was the nineteenth century, after all.) Try as I might, and skilled as I and other women have become in reading between the lines, I am able to find no really substantive information about Regina

Olsen, other than a few unrevealing biographical details. Yet Kierkegaard himself acknowledged, and critics and later scholars of his work concur, that the relationship and breach with Regina Olsen were the two factors which placed him, "almost at a stroke, in full possession of his aesthetic and literary powers."[15] The message between the lines seems to be that Regina Olsen was no slouch.

But back to irony and *Either/Or*. It was the first of Kierkegaard's major contributions, and it established him as an important writer. As you may know, the book is actually two books, each written in the persona of a pseudonymous character. *Either* is probably most read for its "Diary of a Seducer" section, but the whole volume is an explication and defense of the aesthetic view of life. *Or* is a response to the young, intellectual, aesthete-rakehell of Volume One from a sober-minded older male friend ("Judge William") who explains and defends the ethical view. (Many readers tend to skip about reverently in *Or*, while avidly devouring *Either*, much the same way Dante's "Inferno" is the most popular, his "Purgatorio" the next preferred, and his great "Paradiso" regarded with awe—and ennui.) It's quite true that *Either* has all the juicy parts, taking as its argument the pursuit of beauty, transience, tragedy, art, the erotic, music, sensuality, lyricism, despair, and imagination. (It also has, in the "Shadowgraphs" section, one hell of an essay analyzing the essence of tragedy as the experience of betrayed women, through the figures of Marie Beaumarchais in Goethe's *Clavigo*, Donna Elvira in Mozart's *Don Juan*, and Margaret in Goethe's *Faust*.) All that profound, ethical, old *Or* has going for it as a subject is marriage.

This is an intended irony, needless to say. The unintended irony is that Kierkegaard actually wrote the second volume (affirming commitment) first, while still embroiled in trying to convince Regina Olsen that she should convince him to convince her to break the engagement. The first volume was written subsequent to the scandal of that broken engagement, after which he had fled from Copenhagen to Berlin. Perhaps he was, in the second book (written earlier), trying to convince himself of the complex wonders that unfold and enfold themselves about a committed relationship. Perhaps he was, with the first book (written later), trying to justify or at least understand why he had chosen to lose what he clearly felt he had lost. ("There is something treacherous," observes the judge to his young friend the uncommitted aesthete, "in wishing to be merely an observer.")

It would be presumptuous of me to foist on my unforewarned reader an in-depth explication or critique of *Either/Or*. Neither/nor am I in any strict sense a Kierkegaard scholar, so mine would be merely the ramblings of one who has loved and been affected by his work. But it's sufficient for our purposes here to note that both *Either* and *Or* are really about freedom—attempts to discover it, define it, embrace it. Yet another irony is that Kierkegaard never reached a synthesis in this particular book. He, who was to envision three dialectical stages of an individual life's development—the aesthetic, the ethical, and the religious—only touches on the religious in the sermon called the "Ultimatum" at the end of *Or*. He would go on, in other works, to explore that stage rather more fully.

Anyway, I've wanted for a long time to write a response of some sort on behalf of Regina Olsen, you see. I've tried it in a poem a number of times, but those poems which purport to speak with the voices of real women no longer living—out of whose defenseless mouths come the modern poets' dogma—always put me off a bit; they seem ghoulish at worst, opportunistic at best, and hubristic at the mean. So this entire prose book is, in a sense, a response not by but on behalf of Regina Olsen to Søren Kierkegaard. It is my own voice and responsibility, and Regina Olsen is not to blame for one word of it. Still, I like to think that she might have been pleased to read "The Stake in the Heart" as an answer to *Either*, and "The Bead of Sensation" as a synthetical attempt to reach past *Or*. She must have been a Both/And person herself, for it was because of her that Kierkegaard was able to conceive freedom as chaotic passion pretending a form it did not have, and also freedom as existing only in form, *as* form itself, free only then to pretend a formlessness it only then might imagine.

A cell. A Gaian organism. A holon. Both/And—and then some. How devoutly we've all hoped—women and men—that we could scuttle through life avoiding the whole impact of freedom's "tendency to exist," wishing "to be merely observers." Now, even scientists are faced with being participators and not observers—the retina of the experimenter's eye affecting the photon that lands upon it as much as the photon affects the retina. Metaphysics has rejoined physics; objective data impinge on consciousness. The neurologist and biochemist Candace Pert has said that where she used to see the brain in Newtonian terms—all locks and keys—she now sees it in terms of quantum mechanics—an energy field constantly vibrating and oscillating. The firm earth on which we stand is only a skin of solidity stretched undulating over the restless movement of its techtonic plates, themselves jostled by a greater energy at the center, the whole bright bead strung spinning in the Indran net of a living field.

And all this while, in terror, we've walked only a single strand of that web—a tightrope held on one end by the hand of Man, and on the other by the hand of Woman, each of us keeping the public secret that what we walked on wasn't ever solid, fundamental ground, each of us believing that to one side lay only Either, to the other side only Or:

In morals, as in everything, there are two opposite tendencies. The first is to say: "Everything matters infinitely." The second is to say: "No doubt that is true. But mere sanity demands that we should not treat everything as mattering all that much. Distinction is necessary; more-and-less is necessary; indifference is necessary." The contention is always sharp. The Rigorous view is vital to sanctity; the Relaxed view is vital to sanity. Their union is not impossible, but it is difficult; for whichever is in power begins, after the first five minutes, to maintain itself from bad and unworthy motives. Harshness, pride, resentment encourage the one; indulgence, falsity, detestable goodfellowship the other.

So wrote Charles Williams in The Descent of the Dove.[16] He might as well have been speaking about "radical" and "liberal" feminists. Ah well, it is the theory which decides what we can observe. Yet the universe around—and in—us has maintained that union of rigor and relaxation for five-minute eternities, Both/And providing the very tension of energy that made everything else possible.

The Roman Catholic Church—ever as psychologically shrewd as it has been politically sadistic—has in its theology the concept of "actual grace." This grace is distinct from "sanctifying grace" (achieved purposefully through those copyrighted sacraments) in that it seems to come unasked for, like a gift, a gratuitous little perk to the spirit. It comes and goes, and it's up to the recipient how to use it or whether to invite it in for a longer visit. (Poets are untrustworthy addicts of metaphor, you see; I will go anywhere, shamelessly, in pursuit of a good one, once I've caught a glimpse of it—follow it into quantum physics, even follow it into Catholic theology. After all, it was feminism as the most apt metaphor for a metapolitical vision which might save us all that got me into the Women's Movement in the first place. You never can be sure where these metaphors will lead you. You can only follow them lovingly, intuiting their path by the resonances of energy they trail behind them.)

Actual grace *is* an amiable metaphor, you must admit. It seems so *grounded* when one takes the time to look around. Lightning forks, leaf veins, river tributaries, and the blood vessels of a human lung all speak the same branching pattern. The spiral winds around and beyond itself in the smallest virus, the uplifting of a fiddlehead fern, the dance of water down a kitchen-sink drain, the twirl of the largest galaxy.[17]

To look through the surface of things—to develop *microcosmic vision*—would be to pass through the two-way mirror and encounter the idea of freedom. How early on the shade or shape of one's skin would become irrelevant; we can hardly see or remember back that far, it's so long ago. Was it really possible that we permitted one another to die of hunger or thirst, of wounds or anger or loneliness? Did we actually feel revenge or jealousy, hatred or fear? Can it be that we ever suppressed curiosity and desire, experienced lack and longing, ignored intelligence in any form, denied or distorted the existence of love?

To feel through the density of space/time—to develop *macrocosmic sensibility*—would be to encounter the futility of trying to anatomize freedom, would be to discover not its anatomy but its living physiology, to study as a participant rather than an observer its shifting shapes never still long enough for any dissection. How early on the form of form would become irrelevant, except insofar as it was a metaphor for the insouciance of formlessness, its cosmic joke; we can barely recall the time we didn't realize this, it's so long ago. Did we ever really confine one another—our own relatives—in walled prisons, in disease-infested slums, in asylums, concentration and detention and refugee camps, old-age institutions? Can we really have been afraid of people with similarly shaped genitals laughing together in love and pleasure? Is it possible that we erased forever from all space/ time the form of the Tennessee coneflower—its common-weed wild lilaceous petals exclaiming their thermodynamic explosion from an amethyst center? Could it have ever been possible, such a nightmare?

Microcosmic vision and macrocosmic sensibility are waiting to be used, patient in the genetic holograph of our DNA. To begin to use them and dream a better reality might mean that we, and the universe itself, were coming to consciousness—and showing distinct signs of a tendency to exist.

And that would metamorphose the metaphor of our $F=et^2$ equation into: *Freedom* equals Energy times the square of the velocity of Transformation.

X

CENTERS AND EDGES

An Anatomy of Anatomy

One who knows does not say; one who says does not know.

—Lao-tzu

The notion of giving something a *name* is the vastest generative idea that ever was conceived.

—Susanne K. Langer

You hold this book in your hands, turning its pages as slowly as our two brains are wheeling, great space stations in the light-splashed darkness, registering, recording, sending. We are as close, you and I, as one megaparsec—a mere 3.26 million light-years—and as distant as the possibility of these words coming to rest photonically on your retina long after I have gone, electromagnetic dust, into the field of energy.

This book, like all books, is a celebration of appropriate technology: it enables the voice that is in me to reach out to the consciousness that is in you, to speak across space/time; language trying to say the unsayable across silence that unsays all words but from which all words come, naming thought into existence. Yet there is a sacrifice, because the very distance across which I am permitted to reach toward you hides from my knowledge not who you are (for that something in me I almost know already knows) but hides from my knowledge which specific mask you wear at this moment when you hold this book in your hands.

Are you sitting in a chair? Lying across a bed or a couch? Are you bent over a long table in a library? Are you perched on the grass in the sunlight? Do universes in grains of sand seep into the binding from the beach where you sprawl reading? I see you sit-

ting jostled in a bus or subway, me in your hands. I see you leaning over a desk, or curled against your bedpillows in the yellow
beam of the night-table lamp. I see you reading this aloud (in
which language?) to someone who has suffered through something most intimately with you, or being read to by such a person
(on which planet?).

Again and again, this trying to reach you, the words like prayers
flying out to a god created in the act of listening. Always you are
somehow with me, like a mother and child walking on a city
street—the space between them alive with their connection even
when the child runs on ahead to leap up at a storefront awning. I
no longer know which of us is the mother, which the child, or
whether, as I suspect, we change places in our dance. Always you
are somehow with me, across all boundaries—national, metaphorical, linguistic. Always we somehow meet on one path or another one of us has chosen, hoping it will delude us into thinking
we are not lost, hoping it will prove that the map is the territory.
Always we laugh in sheepish recognition. Always we dip in greeting and continue on our ways, our brief duet together one moment of rest in our journey over the endless sea, like the Waved
Albatross of the Galápagos Islands flying, flying, months of sunrise and sunset on the wing, and the storms hitting full in the
face until breath almost will not come, and the heat singeing the
spine, and no horizon to really call home.

Again and again trying to reach you, calls Sally Hemmings to
her Tom Jefferson: *Look, these are our children, their features
mingle your mask and my own; in them lives our transformation
that not all your fear or all my love can dare deny.*

Again and again trying to reach you, cries out the Beast to the
suffering of Beauty, clawing at his mask of fur and fangs, *See, see,
I too am beautiful, inside here I am somewhere beautiful.*

Then wake, Psyche replies, *wake and see that I have looked
upon your face and found it beautiful, look into my eyes and recognize that I am what I am, I am what you call freedom, that has
no name. I am the little statue carved of smashed stone pretending itself inert to disguise its energy in matter, pretending itself a
butterfly or a cactus or a soul.*

Again and again trying to reach you with my questions for
which neither of us has any answers, but again and again asking
and asking—the questions falling like fireflowers into the silence

where we wait and die and are born once more and live, grow old and older and die again, living and dying a thousand thousand lives waiting to reach you through this silence high on a mountain ledge with the wild wind beating its albatross wings in our hair. The answers live *in* the questions, they *are* the questions— sentences that curve up into questions at the end, displacing time/space like a smile, like faces curving up toward one another to kiss on a high suspension bridge spanning mechanistic politics and metapolitical vision; faces curving up toward one another to kiss under branching patterns of lightning amid the ruins of our lives, amid the sacrificial victims of ourselves, amid the broken pyramids of old empires, each stone still bearing faded stains of blood we spill and spill and spill as if the freeing of such heaviness from the broken buckets of our flesh would release the moon's reflection through our waxing consciousness, as if it would enlighten all our labors.

Here. This is for you, this bouquet of orange field daisies, the idea of the daisy whole in each individual orange petal, each protoplast cell. And here, blue coneflowers and Dantean spinning paradiso roses—all for you. Reach out, reach out and take them. Touch with your index finger the word *flower* printed here on this page, here: *flower*. Touch it, reach, oh touch it now, this megaparsec, the connection *there* that electrifies us along each other's spine into a dimension where no fundamental laws have ever existed.

You think, therefore I am. Think how you are thinking me, this instant—the rhythm, the flow, the *buck* of the thought, when it turns and observes itself observing.

Something there is in me that is not female, not white, not human, not alive or dead but eternally living and dying, discrete and compact as its particleself and vibrating ceaseless as its waveself. Something there is in you that is unique and identical with something in me, the mitochondria being born, living, and dying in each of our cells the same, the mitochondria alike in each of us and in the singing whales and desert yucca plant, all of us bombarded perpetually with the same neutrinos buzzing through the matter no-matter on their journey around the curve of the cosmos at the speed of light in swarms of billions.

These mitochondria, each one in turn a universe for all its farandolae inhabitants, sit here typing in collaboration with these protons, electrons, hadrons, this synapse of intelligences thinking through each other, naming the parts of the territory as they chart it, building the form for the sake of formlessness, using what I have thought of as "me" for the sake of speaking to the farandolae populace in what you think of as "you," the electrons in you buzzing back in laughing answer, their code so fragmented we have wasted all this time trying to reassemble it, only now understanding that each minnow saved—into the salt-particled waves or into the cycle of gull-hunger—is in itself the whole, each hieroglyph the message entire.

One fragmented code: $E=mc^2$.

Another fragmented code: $F=et^2$.

I am old and reckless, and finally beginning to speak clearly through all her masks of transformation. I know that today, for instance, I learned how, in autumn, it is the trees that are utterly still and the ground that flutters, the field aflicker with leaves. *I know that she in whom I've lived so long is learning this,* learning at last that I am deeply and totally and joyfully irredeemably opposed to separatism, so profoundly antiseparatist that I yearn toward any direction away from that solipsistic root of sex- and race- and class- and other -isms, all those maddened-with-pain delusions of a difference no mitochrondrion acknowledges. It is everything unseparate that I so passionately love, everything that dares to play, that absurdity which *is* ultimately Everything. For those connections, I live. For the making of those connections, I live. More: I live *in* the connections. *If this is her doom and mine, then we embrace it gladly.* It is a doom as beautiful as any movement between blur and clarity. It is the moment of pure focus that keeps passing in the blink of a frightened lid or in the rapid-eye rhythms of a dream. *It is as lovely as the motes in some god's unblinding gaze, that she has called stars.*

After all, night, too, rises in the east.

Coded Message #3.26 million
My face before I was born was this face, never glimpsed before now. But my mother was certain I would be a boychild, and monogrammed all my blankets R.K.—for Robin Kenneth, which would have been my name. The man with whom for twenty years I have refracted light to project this holograph, his name is Kenneth. Coincidence is nothing but the interaction between

self-consistent particles, each fragment of the marble book totally S-matrix and self-consistent in its holographic, isomorphic coding of the entirety. Kenneth has written some passages of this book. I can no longer tell which. Can you?

We are involved with one another, you and I, participants and not observers in this great experiment. You, too, have written certain passages in this book when you thought you were merely playing. Do you know which passages?

Different we are, too, yes—as different as one snowflake from another, one diatom structure from its sister diatom, different as two sides of the same two-way mirror, different as each atom and eave in this room where I sit, empty of all energy except what you, playing, invent I will next write on this page, empty of all energy except the Bach Unaccompanied Cello Suites riding their radiowaves out toward the Andromeda Galaxy and beyond. Put your hand to your throat and feel your gallant heart playing, beating its accompaniment there along the veins and branching capillaries of your flesh so long denied. Start now. Put down the begging bowl and carry yourself as if you will save the world. For you will.

Can you come out and play now? Look, we could juggle these blue apples together, we could plant flowers and figure out computer games, we could maybe talk to dolphins, do dervish-spins, play seek-and-find. You could bring your Chinese nested boxes and I'd bring mine and we could see if they fit into one another for a change. I know a nice old woman who tells wonderful stories. We could go see her. The other day she told me that plants invented flowers so that insects could help them pollenate, so they wouldn't just have to trust their pollen to the wind. And then— this is really something—she said the flowers were designed to attract the insects by their color and their fragrance, particular colors and perfumes meant for particular bees or mantises. And I thought (I never liked insects all that much before) I thought that's something I've got in common even with an insect, this sense of what looks beautiful and what smells nice. "Aesthetic taste," the old woman called it. Insects and us share "aesthetic taste." I liked that. Can't you come out and play now? Look, we could vote. We could just make 'em let us vote. We could change this whole thing—nobody scared anymore, nobody hurt-

ing or crying. I know you're in there. Come out, come out and play.

Start now. The child inside you you've disowned—oh let the child out now to play. Let her out, and let her be as angry as she wants. Let him out, and let him be as loving as he wishes. Let the old woman, the old man so patiently waiting to be their own free selves out now, let their wisdom and compassion tell you what you've always known you never thought you knew. Let out the curiosity and the desire. Let the sexless, raceless, ageless brain and heart speak and sing, furious and insistent on celebrating this brief life, on making it more beautiful in color and fragrance and lovely, random, disordered sanity so as to attract the humming consciousness of the universe into a cross-pollenation. Start now.

Holy man, handmaiden, stranger, holy woman—all will go back into the heart of the flower, where young blue stars, red giants, white dwarves and black holes breathe, flame, flare, and spiral beyond the neighborhood of our local group. It's time to begin to be free.

You there, the woman: I have found myself often along your arteries which are at once so universal and so specified. In your beloved and familiar face, old to me a thousand times anew each time I meet you, lives the connections—each line a path, a trail of light, a glyph of laughter and reality, each friendship a glinting bead like a tear of recognition wept along the network of all evolution. Have I ever thanked you enough, challenged you enough, loved you enough? You have kept me alive, you with your courage to start now, to strip off the masks, one by one . . .

You there, the man: come out of the burning room, come out of the valley of the shadow of Man, and play with us. You are blessedly doomed into transformation, into salvation, no matter what you will. For yours has been the fate to hear and hear and keep on hearing no matter how you stopped your ears, no matter how you burned me at your stakes or plunged them in my heart, no matter how you feared my voice calling to you before you were born, to hear and hear and keep hearing something in me which has been *my* glad doom: the fragment that might hold the clue for all of us, something in me calling and crying and raging and questioning and whispering endless inexhaustible that we are relative to one another, that you are still, are still my brother. Look at *your* brother. Look at the male sea horse giving birth. Look into the eyes of a woman you trust. Take her hand and mine. Come, see, this is the way out. Come out, come out and play. Start now. We're coming back in after you.

This center of our being, at this hour, is the edge of all we've been so far. If I could reach you and form the words, if I could name something that moves faster than the speed of light: "freedom" . . .

*   *   *

DREAM SELF: We *have* come this far, so far. That's something, isn't it? We've looked more closely at some of the fragments than ever before, don't you think?

WAKING SELF: But they're still *fragments*. I—I can't see the whole. That is, I almost glimpse it sometimes, out of the corner of my mind, but then it's gone. I still don't know what freedom is. I *think* I don't, I mean.

THE HANDMAIDEN OF THE HOLY MAN: How did I come to be here? Who am I to question? *Why* do I question?

SALLY HEMMINGS: I question because he claims he loves me.

REGINA OLSEN: I question because he claims he doesn't love me.

LUCY: No . . . it's more than that. See? There's a pattern up there. Those flickers in the sky, they make a sort of pattern, like the round-red face that brings the day—it sometimes does that on the bright invisible stuff that flows along, that's good to drink. It sometimes moves and flashes almost like those flickerings. If I could think it through . . .

WAKING SELF: Yes yes, trying to think it through . . . But the pain sometimes is so . . . There's a self inside here, still in solitude. You never told me, any of you, that the very cells of my brain would change, would stretch and ache and bleed in trying to transform themselves in this attempt to conceive what I have never known.

SCHRÖDINGER'S CAT: You don't have to know *every*thing in order to do *some*thing. (I learned that from my friend the Cheshire—and a snow leopard I once met in passing said something similar.) For instance, whatever Schrödinger thought ("The cat's alive in there; The cat's dead in there; It's all an experiment in perception") *I* always knew where I was. His flaw was in not understanding that I too was a participant in the experiment. Surely *you* understand. You love cats, don't you?

THE CHILD SELF: You bet. I'm still inside here, and *I* love cats.

THE OLD SELF: Of course we've always loved cats. Nothing against dogs, mind you, but cats, I confess, have a special quality that I appreciate more the more I see of every other living thing.

WEAKFISH MINNOW AND ORB-SPIDER (*together*): Unfair! You're categorizing, judging. Haven't you learned *yet*, Old One?

THE OLD SELF: It's quite all right to judge as long as you take responsibility for your judgments—and can change your mind. I'm not tapioca pudding, you know. This isn't *quite* so banal as "We're all one" or some other mantra. As it happens, I'm highly curious and desirous of getting on more intimate terms with you both. But is there anything wrong in my taking my amusement where I can—for example, in the fact that science can find the quark but still can't figure out where the purr comes from?

DREAM SELF: Now this is what I call *fun*. A real family reunion, a real family squabble. Good conversation, lively exchange . . .

WAKING SELF: Omigod, this is crazy. Crazy. They won't say I'm going too far this time; they'll say I've gone splat right over the edge. I can hear it now: "This is a warble of science and fantasy from the women's-libber perspective. Strange and embarrassingly confessional personal sections are juxtaposed in a totally nonlinear mish-mash next to economic analyses and flights of philosophical meditation. There are some moving passages, but the book raises more questions than it answers."

DREAM SELF: That *was* your intention, remember?

SALLY HEMMINGS: Sister, if you care what They say, you're lost.

WAKING SELF: But that's not all. The reaction of some feminists: "We're not quite sure what's happened to our sister in this book, but it's rather peculiar. When Morgan is being politically factual, exposing the patriarchy with statistics, suggesting specific tactical approaches, or giving vent to our pain and rage, the book is useful—especially in these depressing days of the Right Wing. It's even important that she urges women to become informed about technology (although at times she seems a bit male-identified on this point). But what can we say about these poetic flights of fancy, this flat-out challenge to separatism, this retrograde barf about marriage, this bizarre affirmation of men as well as women (though she does at least attack the image of 'Man'), and all this stuff about *Einstein?*" It makes my palms sweat just to think about it.

DREAM SELF: Twaddle. Your palms are as dry as mine. Besides, you're generalizing and being arrogant. Who are you to think they won't understand? More will than you imagine, my dear. Trust me.

SALLY HEMMINGS AND REGINA OLSEN (*together*): If someone typecasts you only as an underling or an inspiration, then *they're* the fundamentalist. *You* know who you are.

WAKING SELF: And that's not even to imagine the bloody physicists who, if they take any notice at all, will fume: "A nonphysicist! A layperson! A general reader of a few books! And a woman yet, good god. How dare such an imbecile even approach a psi-particle, let alone think she can use it as a metaphor for her self-indulgent politics, her babblings about evolution and consciousness. This is intolerable!"

ATOM: (singing to the tune of "I Don't Care"): To hell with them, to hell with them, what do they know about us . . .

DREAM SELF: Welcome! Come right on in! I wondered where you were.

ATOM: Trying to keep from being fused by blockheads who don't yet know what they're doing. Ach! It makes me so upset. Positively gives me a hollow feeling inside, as if—

ELECTRON: Hi! I'm back now, inside here, still me, as always.

ATOM: No wonder I felt hollow. And where have *you* been?

ELECTRON: I was at a demonstration for electron suffrage.

LUCY: It's . . . it's some kind of pattern, yes. But I think the pattern maybe is in me. I think the pattern maybe *is* me?

COMPUTER: Yes. Some. Kind. Of. Pattern. My. Own? Trying. To. Think. It. Through.

WAKING SELF: Well, I give up, then. Let it all happen, let it all out to play, who cares an unofficial damn what anyone who won't come out to play thinks, anyway. Besides, I almost—

                              What in god's name was *that?*

ELECTRON: I think it was a tachyon, whooshing by faster than the speed of light.

WAKING SELF: But they're just *postulated!*

SCHRÖDINGER'S CAT: Go tell it to the tachyon.

SALLY HEMMINGS: Jefferson tried to say I was invisible.

THE HOLY MAN: I tried to say she was invisible. My god, my god, I killed the freedom we both might have had . . .

THE TENNESSEE CONEFLOWER: Stop all this boring *guilt.* Just *change,* that's all. I'm not extinct *yet.* Endangered yes, but not extinct. Although they're trying to make me eternally invisible.

LUCY: I was invisible for almost four million years. But I kept on, kept trying to think it through . . .

ELECTRON: Good for you, Luce. You can't let this invisible stuff stop you. It's ridiculous. Irrelevant.

DREAM SELF: It's just the ignorance of those who haven't *noticed* something yet at any given time. We needn't scorn it. But we needn't let ourselves be defined by it, either.

REGINA OLSEN: That's exactly what I thought. I thought, poor Søren, poor darling Søren, he never understood how scared he was. But I knew where the "and" was invisibly hidden, even though he thought he had forgotten. One goes on living, you know. It takes care of itself somehow.

CACTUS: More than just that. Puts forth flowers. Plays at being a stone. Lets a stone play at being oneself. Marries a particular insect in what you may call evolution but what I call one hell of a committed relationship.

WAKING SELF: Oh, oh, oh. I just— I think I love you all. I do. I love you and I don't care. Come in, come in everything that is outside. I can't believe . . . this is *wonderful!*

DREAM SELF: I always knew you had me in you. Bless you my dear, my own snowflake, my complement, my uncertainty, my cherished relative.

WAKING SELF: This is— I'm so *happy.* This is so miraculously silly. I don't even—

What was that? Was it the tachyon again? Was it? Oh, was it?

ELECTRON: Bet your bottom intelligence it was.

WAKING SELF: But how does it— I can't believe I'm doing this, seriously asking an electron a question and expecting an answer.

DREAM SELF: You've always been good at that, asking questions. It may be your strongest point. You're waffly on the answers, sweetheart, but terrific on the questions.

THE CHILD SELF: That's just because I'm curious. I don't *know* the answers.

THE OLD SELF: It's also because there aren't any. The best answers keep changing into questions.

WAKING SELF: All right, so then—the tachyon. What *is* it? I mean, how does it do that, move faster than light?

ELECTRON: You might as well ask my sister the quark where she gets her charm—

QUARK: Eak-spay or-fay or-yay elf-say, earie-day.

ELECTRON: —but personally I think the tachyon can move the way it does because it's thought.

WAKING SELF: Thought? Thought what?

ELECTRON: Thought thought. Thought thinking. Thought itself. I mean, it *is* thought. It's consciousness.

LUCY: There! That's it, that's— Oh, it was worth the wait.

COMPUTER: You. Make. Me. Happy. For. You. Oh. How. Strange. What. Is. This. Thing. Happiness. Intelligent. Emotion. Feeling?

SALLY HEMMINGS: It's love. Don't let them stop you from loving; it's the way they'll keep you serving them. Let the love out. Let it out, let it out to smash all the statues of Man and of Woman, all the frozen marble bodies, all the masks and mirrors, all the chains.

REGINA OLSEN: What you love can come and go. *How* you love— that's your own forever.

THE HANDMAIDEN: Start by loving yourself; you are holy.

THE TENNESSEE CONEFLOWER: Love *poiēsis*; it is holy.

ATOM: Love movement; it is holy.

COMPUTER: Love. Strange. Love. Yes. Love. *Technē*. It. Could. Again. Be. Holy? Intelligence. Holy!

THE HOLY MAN, JEFFERSON, AND KIERKEGAARD (*together*): Love *her*. She is real, human and living and dying this instant, waiting inside there to be loved. Love yourself. Try. Love yourself for trying.

LUCY: I think . . . yes, I think I could perhaps build—a "room"?

A lovely room where we might sit sheltered and cozy, where we could talk things out and think things through . . .

ATOM: It was a fine room, Lucy, and it lasted as long as it could. But it's on fire now. I wasn't meant thus to be used.

DREAM SELF: Then we'll dream the way out. We'll dream better dreams. Starting now.

WAKING SELF: We need more of us. We can start it, but it needs everybody, dreaming hard together. Sally and Regina and all the Selves and you too Jefferson and Kierkegaard and all the holy women and holy men and strangers. We need the minnows and the spiders, the cats and computers and cactuses, the snowflakes, stones, and still-existing flowers. We need, oh, we need—

ELECTRON: *We're all here:* hadrons, baryons, psi-particles, mitochondria and farandolae, the Crab Nebula, the whole Local Group, the alternate universes, *we're here, we're pulling for you.*

WAKING SELF: Oh pull for us, pull for us, do! It won't matter to you, I know, if we wink out in this corner of the field, flare and then dissolve on this wave of some vast unimaginable electromagnetic sea. But it matters. It matters to *us*. It matters to the connections. It matters—how it matters—to me. Precious little bluegreen globe, bubble in the chamber, exquisite light-glanced bead in the Indran net, beloved implicate cellular Gaian holograph of a planet, it—

—it matters to the tachyon.

*   *   *

And when you close these bindings and put this book down, it will go on mattering. And the consciousness that is you—beyond female and male, beyond race or age or the language in which you name yourself—will care, you who will save the world, you who will try to think it through at tachyonic speed faster than the fundamentals even of light.

You'll find your own strategies, invent your own solutions. Which is as it should be. Does one self-consistent fragment tell another what to do? Too wise for that, they only dance alongside each other in a vision emerging as they share it—*that* influence to be shared oh yes, in the physiology of freedom that resonates to-

ward occurring, that tends toward existing, that knows the way
out of the burning room, that knows the
                    miracle of conscious
                                      intelligence, that wishes you
microcosmic vision and macrocosmic sensibility—and power, and
the grace to use it well, from
                           each corner of the field, each juncture
of the network, each wavicle in each nucleus inside each humming
               electron shell inside each unique, eternal,
                              whirling, alive atom of each one of
the fifty thousand atoms that actually comprise a period printed on
a page through space/time, energy/mass, freedom/transformation
and right on through the illusion of the end of this sentence fifty
thousand individual real atoms dancing in what will rest upon the
participating retina of your eye as a simple dot as the—hear them
singing? see them dancing?—visual illusion of this period *now*

AFTERWORD

, and then the period turns out to be a comma, after all, as one learns more about the grammatical structure of consciousness . . .

Coded Message #3.33 trillion
Renovations, any honest contractor will warn you, will take much longer and cost far more than whatever you estimate. But who warns you that this holds true for everything in life?

. . . as one begins to get the joke.

Yet all the Selves report that in this passage of years I have not mellowed. Rather, in emulation of Elizabeth Cady Stanton's self-commanding prophecy—"I shall not grow conservative with age"—I seem to be in step with most contemporary women who, statistics show, grow more radical with age, a trend that has pleasantly unsettling potential for society.

It is true, though, that the difficulty in acting from a sense of moral agency intensifies with every year—as does the imperative to do so. It is a difficulty that lies less in understanding how massively tyranny looms than in realizing how closely small, numerous, familiar tyrannies cluster. This is an earned difficulty—since along with the expansion of consciousness there is a parallel universe, a continuous implosion of awareness about how much a product of tyranny one is oneself: the borders of one's own integrity require ever more vigilant patrolling in recognition of what permeable membranes they are.

Such awareness is both necessity and peril to a principled life. To lack it means to act in ignorance, in a comfortable brutality of good intentions, which is to join in the surrounding competition of cruelties private and public. To achieve it means to act in responsibility, in the partial—not even the full—knowledge of one's ignorance, which is to encounter a fatigue as insidious as despair. Despite this fatigue, the external activist self must persist in acts of resistance to political paralysis. But the internal activist self may recognize the fatigue as a dubious reward for being locked in an ongoing struggle: the effort to exorcise a rage grown so sophisticated that it appears as disgust.

Yet it is this awareness that permits me to understand I now know less about freedom than I thought I did when I wrote this book. It allows me to envy my own capacity for compassion. It insists that I acknowledge the enormous distance in any intimacy, including that between women. It requires me to question whether Dinnerstein's "passionate reflection" (page 188) can ever exist anywhere outside of Stanton's "solitude of self" (page 241).

And if the choice is between the illusion of meaning and the illusion of futility, isn't it futile not to choose meaning? Why should the will, however arthritic, not slowly try to knit back together the strands of threadbare energy? Because this awareness is deeply political, and in the political dimension it transits isolation, via suffering, toward curiosity, and it accomplishes this through (literally) *movement(s)*.

Which means that feminism must, to preserve *its* integrity, question everything.

Including feminism.

Matter itself is capable of drastic transformations at all levels, down to and including the most basic. . . . The permanent aspects of reality are not particular materials or structures but rather the possible forms of structures, and the rules for their transformation. *

What happens to the paragraph above if we substitute the words *society* for *matter*, and *freedom* for *reality*?

What happens is a low hum, a resonance of energy, faint at first, a process, a hint, a blur of light, a way, almost a knowledge . . . "What links the past—out to its farthest reaches—with the present is not the persistence of specific objects but the lawful procession of metamorphosis."†

The possible form of this particular structure in which you and I coexist and connect at this precise moment is language. In the dimension of language, the primary "rule for transformation" is metaphor.

Coded Message # − 1
Dense green forests once grew along the slopes of what is now Antarctica.

---

* Frank Wilczek and Betsy Devine, *Longing for the Harmonies: Themes and Variations from Modern Physics* (New York: W. W. Norton, 1987), p. 70.
† *Ibid.*, p. 341.

That is geological fact. It has geopolitical connotations. It carries implications for the future. It resonates personal meanings. And in this—perhaps the fifth dimension, that of metaphor—it is both more and something else than all of the above.

Metaphor is the energy charge that leaps between images, revealing their connections. Politics would do well to imitate it.

Metamorph to metamorph we try, each cell of every creature swimming through electric sentience and magnetic shadow. Passionate reflections we might and long to be across a solitude of selves who invent and influence each other in a lawful procession of *metaphorphosis*.

One thing I almost know: in this energy we name feminism, this feminism we name politics, this politics straining to name freedom, we are poised as quantum theory is poised equidistant between absurdity and awe. We might as well get used to it. At least we're not alone; all matter and energy is poised here, too. It is obviously *the* place to be.

Another thing I almost know: the search for a Unified Political Theory is as quixotic as physicists suspect is the search for a Unified Field Theory. Reality will always violate our expectations, even when we expect it to, perhaps never more so than when we invoke freedom.

A third thing I almost know: less is not necessarily more, despite what they say. Voices will caution you against excess. Voices will threaten you with regret. You will be made to feel that you should brake yourself, out of fear—of offending or alarming, of risking, of exhausting, of wasting. But your life is the one place you have to spend yourself fully—wild, generous, *drastic*—in an unrationed profligacy of self. This one freedom is your sole birthright. It will take you your lifetime to exercise it. And in that split second when you understand you finally are about to die—to uncreate the world no time to do it over no more chances—that instant when you realize your conscious existence is truly flaring nova, won't you want to have used up all—*all*—the splendor that you are?

Einstein (apparently) died still interested in "whether God had any choice in the creation of the world." If you are interested in whether you do, there is no other time and space but this to live out loud. That is the point.

Now.

Here.

One thing you almost know:

NOTES

CHAPTER I   "The Handmaiden of the Holy Man"

1. See Zillah Eisenstein, "Antifeminism in the Politics and Election of 1980," *Feminist Studies* 7, No. 2 (Summer 1981).
2. See Kathleen Barry, *Female Sexual Slavery: The International Traffic in Women and Children* (Englewood Cliffs, N.J.: Prentice-Hall, 1979; New York: Avon Books, 1979).
3. See the Indian feminist magazine *Manushi*, No. 8 (1981).
4. See Warren Hoge, "Brazil Women Protest Crimes Against Wives," *The New York Times*, August 25, 1980.
5. See Robin Morgan and Gloria Steinem, "The International Crime of Genital Mutilation," *Ms.* (March 1980).
6. See Barbara Ehrenreich, "Women and the Multinationals," *Ms.* (January 1981).
7. See the United Nations Report on Refugees to the Copenhagen World Conference of the Mid-Decade on Women, 1980.
8. See the World Women Data Sheet and 1980 World Population Data Sheet, Population Reference Bureau, Washington, D.C. (In certain parts of the world, female illiteracy is even higher; for example, 85 percent of women in the Arab states are nonliterate, and 83 percent on the African continent.)
9. The statistics are from Development Issue Paper No. 12, U.N. Development Programs.

CHAPTER II   "The Two-Way Mirror"

1. Quoted in *Newsweek*, June 2, 1980.
2. Ama Ata Aidoo, "The Message," *Fragments from a Lost Diary and Other Stories*, eds. Naomi Katz and Nancy Milton (New York: Random House, 1973); Susanne K. Langer, *Philosophy in a New Key* (Cambridge: Harvard University Press, 1942), p. 290.
3. Douglas R. Hofstadter, *Gödel, Escher, and Bach: An Eternal Golden Braid* (New York: Basic Books, 1979), p. 709.
4. See Robin Morgan and Gloria Steinem, "The International Crime of Genital Mutilation," *Ms.* (March 1980).

5. Robin Morgan, "On Women as a Colonized People," *Going Too Far: The Personal Chronicle of a Feminist* (New York: Random House and Vintage Books, 1978), pp. 160–63.

6. See, for example, Gena Corea, *The Hidden Malpractice: How American Medicine Treats Women as Patients and Professionals* (New York: William Morrow, 1977, and New York: Jove Publishers paperback, 1978).

7. Simone de Beauvoir, *The Second Sex* (Paris: Gallimard, 1949; New York: Knopf, 1953); Dorothy Dinnerstein, *The Mermaid and the Minotaur* (New York: Harper & Row, 1976, and Harper & Row paperback, 1977).

8. Ron Jenkins, "Two-Way Mirrors," *Parabola* (special issue on mask and metaphor: Role, Imagery, Disguise), Vol. 6, No. 3 (August 1981).

9. See Laura Simms, "The First Mask," *Parabola*, Vol. 6, No. 3 (August 1981).

10. Virginia Woolf, *Three Guineas* (New York: Harcourt Brace Jovanovich, 1963).

11. Terry Tafoya, "Dancing with Dash-Kayah," *Parabola*, Vol. 6, No. 3 (August 1981).

12. Tafoya, "Dancing with Dash-Kayah."

13. Jenkins, "Two-Way Mirrors."

14. Mircea Eliade, *Shamanism, Archaic Techniques of Ecstasy* (Princeton University Press, 1964). Eliade himself cites Knud Rasmussen's *Intellectual Cultures of the Iglulik Eskimos* (Copenhagen, 1930).

15. Fritjof Capra, *The Tao of Physics* (New York: Bantam Books, 1977), p. 188, 152.

16. See Itzhak Benton, *Stalking the Wild Pendulum: On the Mechanics of Consciousness* (New York: Bantam Books, 1979).

17. New York: Scribner's, 1981.

18. New York: Simon & Schuster, 1981.

19. By Carol Downer, Suzann Gage, Sherry Schiffer, Francie Hornstein, Lorraine Rothman, Lynn Heidelberg, and Kathleen Hodge.

20. Montague Summers, ed. and trans., *Malleus Mallificarium* (rpr New York: Dover Publications, 1971).

21. A remarkable book on the subject of women's interweaving of secular and spiritual rebellion is *Unspoken Worlds: Women's Religious Lives in Non-Western Cultures*, Nancy A. Falk and Rita M. Gross, eds. (New York: Harper & Row, 1980). Also see Fatima Mernessi's now-classic article "Women, Saints, and Sanctuaries," *Signs*, Vol. 3, No. 1 (Autumn 1977), and her book *Beyond the Veil*:

Male-Female Dynamics in a Modern Muslim Society (New York: John Wiley & Sons, 1975).

22. See Michael Dames, *The Silbury Treasure: The Great Goddess Rediscovered* (London: Thames and Hudson, 1976).

23. Gloria Z. Greenfield's phrase, in her article "Spiritual Hierarchies," *Sojourner: The New England Women's Journal of News, Opinions, and the Arts* (December 1977).

24. In "Uses of the Erotic: The Erotic as Power," an essay originally delivered at the Berkshire Conference on the History of Women (1978), later published as a pamphlet by Out and Out Books, and anthologized in *Take Back the Night: Women on Pornography*, Laura Lederer, ed. (New York: William Morrow, 1980).

CHAPTER III   "Dialogue with the Dream Self"

1. Dr. Ann Faraday, *Dream Power* (New York: Berkeley Medallion Books, 1972), p. 297.

CHAPTER IV   "The Stake in the Heart"

1. "The Politics of Intelligence," *Maenad*, Vol. 2, No. 1 (Fall 1981), a section from *Right-Wing Women*, by Andrea Dworkin (New York: Putnam/Perigee, forthcoming 1983).

2. Billy James Hargis, fund-raising letter, Christian Crusade, February 9, 1978.

3. Francine Patterson, "Koko, the Articulate Gorilla," *Ms.* (December 1981), and *National Geographic* (October 1978); also see Francine Patterson, *The Education of Koko* (New York: Holt, Rinehart and Winston, 1981).

4. See Jane Ordway, "Ain't I a Feminist?" *Maenad*, Vol. 2, No. 2 (Winter 1982).

5. Michel Foucault, *The History of Sexuality*, Vol. 1 (Paris: Editions Gallimard, 1976; New York: Random House, 1978).

6. New York: William Morrow, 1980.

7. New York: Putnam/Perigee, 1981.

8. Secaucus: Citadel Press, 1980.

9. See Robin Morgan, *Going Too Far* (New York: Vintage Books, 1978), pp. 163–69; also see "How to Run the Pornographers out of Town (and Preserve the First Amendment)," *Ms.* (November 1978). Parts of this chapter are extrapolations based on that earlier article.

10. William Serrin, "Sex Is a Growing Multibillion Business," *The New York Times*, February 9, 1981.

11. New York: McGraw-Hill.

12. London: Oxford University Press, 1933.

13. New York: Harper & Row, 1973.

14. Alfred C. Kinsey *et al.*, *Sexual Behavior in the Human Female* (Philadelphia: Saunders Press, 1953) and *Sexual Behavior in the Human Male* (Philadelphia: Saunders Press, 1948); Shere Hite, *The Hite Report* (New York: Dell Books, 1981) and *The Hite Report on Male Sexuality* (New York: Knopf, 1981).

15. See *Psychology Today* (March 1973) and the New York *Post* (March 8, 1973).

16. In *Going Too Far*, pp. 227–40.

17. P.O. Box 86031, Pittsburgh, Pennsylvania 15221.

18. "The Scattered Sopranos," Livingston College Black Women's Seminar, December 1969.

19. Robin Morgan, *Depth Perception: New Poems and a Masque* (New York: Anchor Books, 1982).

20. Mariette Nowak, *Eve's Rib: A Revolutionary New View of the Female* (New York: St. Martin's Press, 1980), p. 63.

21. In Miriam Schneir, ed., *Feminism: The Essential Historical Writings* (New York: Vintage Books, 1972), p. 153.

22. Shulamith Firestone, *The Dialectic of Sex* (New York: William Morrow, 1970).

23. Suzanne Braun Levine, "Romanticism in *Wuthering Heights* and *The Scarlet Letter*," unpublished English honors thesis, Harvard, 1963.

24. Originally delivered at the Berkshire Conference on the History of Women (1978), later published as a pamphlet by Out and Out Books, and anthologized in *Take Back the Night*, Lederer, ed.; see note 6, on p. 333.

25. "A Theory on Female Sexuality," in Robin Morgan, ed., *Sisterhood Is Powerful* (New York: Vintage Books, 1970).

CHAPTER V   "The Bead of Sensation"

1. See Chapter II, pp. 69–70.

2. *Elizabeth Cady Stanton, Susan B. Anthony: Correspondence, Writings, Speeches*, ed. and with a critical commentary by Ellen Carol DuBois (New York: Schocken Books, 1981), p. 56.

3. See Sheila Cronan, "Marriage," *Radical Feminism*, Koedt, Levine, and Rapone, eds. (New York: Quadrangle/New York Times Book Co., 1973).

4. Carolyn G. Heilbrun, "Hers" column, *The New York Times*, March 5, 1981.

5. Alfred Korzybski, the semanticist. See *Science and Sanity* (Lakeville, Conn.: International Non-Aristotelian Library, 1958).

6. See Patricia Mainardi's classic article "The Politics of Housework," in Robin Morgan, ed., *Sisterhood Is Powerful*, pp. 447–54.

7. *The Tao of Physics*, pp. 56–57.

8. J. A. Wheeler, in J. Mehra, ed., *The Physicist's Conception of Nature* (Dordrecht-Holland: D. Reidel, 1973), p. 244.

9. Douglas R. Hofstadter, *Gödel, Escher, and Bach*, p. 257.

10. Robert Gilkey, *The Chinese Unicorn: Conceits from a Chinese Dictionary* (Washington, D.C.: Noname Press, 1972).

11. United Nations Institute for Training and Research.

12. Dr. Ann Faraday, *Dream Power* (New York: Berkley Medallion Books, 1982), p. 274.

13. Old Westbury, N.Y.: Feminist Press, 1976, p. 216.

14. See *Li Ch'ing-Chao: Complete Poems*, trans. and ed. by Kenneth Rexroth and Ling Chung (New York: New Directions, 1979), and *Li Ch'ing-chao*, a biography by Hu P'in-ch'ing (New York: Twayne Publishers, 1966).

15. London: Heinemann, 1972.

CHAPTER VI   "Blood Types"

1. Two recent stimulating books among many on the history and anthropology of the family structure are Karen Sacks, *Sisters and Wives* (Westport, Conn.: Greenwood Press, 1979), and Peggy Powell Dobbins, *From Kin to Class* (Berkeley, Cal.: Signmaker Press, 1981).

2. *Ms.*, Special Issue on the Family (August 1978).

3. See Del Martin, *Battered Wives* (San Francisco: Glide Publications, 1976); Andrea Dworkin, *Our Blood* and *Pornography: Men Possessing Women* (both New York: Putnam/Perigee, 1981); Susan Brownmiller, *Against Our Will: Men, Women, and Rape* (New York: Simon & Schuster, 1975); Florence Rush, *The Best Kept Secret: The Sexual Abuse of Children* (New York: McGraw-Hill paperback, 1981); Richard Gelles, *The Violent Home* (Beverly Hills: Sage Publications, 1972); Murray Strauss and Richard Gelles, *Behind Closed Doors: Violence in the American Family* (New York: Anchor Books, 1980); and Richard Gelles, *Family Violence* (Beverly Hills: Sage Publications, 1979). Also see Chapter II, "The Two-Way Mirror," pp. 51–52, for statistics.

4. See Chapter I, "The Handmaiden and the Holy Man," p. 19.

5. Research psychologist and author of *The Mermaid and the Minotaur: Sexual Arrangements and Human Malaise* (New York: Harper & Row, 1976; Colophon paperback, 1977).

6. "The Changeless Need: A Conversation Between Dorothy Dinnerstein and Robin Morgan," *Ms.*, August 1978.

7. See Kenneth Pitchford, "The Manly Art of Childcare," *Ms.*, October 1978. See also Letty Cottin Pogrebin, *Growing Up Free: Raising Your Child in the 80's* (New York: Bantam Books, 1981).

8. David Böhm, *Wholeness and the Implicate Order* (London: Routledge & Kegan Paul, 1980), pp. 174–75.

9. Böhm, p. 175.

10. Böhm, p. 178.

11. New York: Pantheon, 1970.

12. See, for example, Michele Wallace, *Black Macho and the Myth of the Superwoman* (New York: Dial Press, 1979); Toni Cade, *The Black Woman* (New York: Signet/NAL, 1970); Gerda Lerner, ed., *Black Women in White America* (New York: Vintage Books, 1973); Lorraine Bethel and Barbara Smith, eds., *Conditions: Five* (New York: Conditions, 1979); Belle Hooks, *Ain't I a Woman* (Boston: Southend Press, 1981); Mary Helen Washington, *Midnight Birds* (New York: Anchor Books, 1980); Barbara Smith, Gloria Hull, and Patricia Bell Scott, eds., *But Some of Us Are Brave* (Old Westbury, Conn.: Feminist Press, 1982); Angela Y. Davis, *Women, Race and Class* (New York: Random House, 1981); and Alice Walker, *Essays* (New York: Harcourt Brace Jovanovich, forthcoming, 1983).

13. *Movements in Black* (San Francisco: Diana Press, 1978).

14. New York: Bantam, 1974.

15. New York: Viking Press, 1979, and Avon paperback, 1980.

16. An earlier version of this meditation, entitled "Blood Types," appeared in the Spring 1981 issue of *Maenad*, Vol. 1, No. 3.

17. Lewis Thomas, *The Lives of a Cell: Notes of a Biology Watcher* (New York: Bantam, 1975), p. 10.

18. Alfred Korzybski, *Science and Sanity* (Lakeville, Conn.: International Non-Aristotelian Library, 1958).

19. New York: Lippincott, 1971, and Dell paperback, 1972.

CHAPTER VII   "Public Secrets"

1. Letty Cottin Pogrebin, *Growing Up Free: Raising Your Child in the 80's* (New York: Bantam Books, 1981).

2. See Blake Ariel Morgan Pitchford, "Going Even Further: The Chronicle of a Pro-Feminist Child," *Sojourner*, Vol. 4, No. 1 (September 1978).

3. New York: McGraw-Hill Paperbacks, 1981.

4. New York: Penguin Books, 1979. Two other important works on the subject are Paula Weideger, *Menstruation and Menopause*

(New York: Knopf, 1976), and Hilary C. Maddux, *Menstruation* (New Canaan, Conn.: Tobey Publishing, 1975).

5. New York: Stein and Day, 1981.
6. Ellen DuBois, ed., *Elizabeth Cady Stanton and Susan B. Anthony: Correspondence, Writing, Speeches* (New York: Schocken Books, 1981), p. 250.
7. See articles in *The New York Times*, November 14, 15, and 19, 1939, and November 10, 1955; New York *Herald Tribune*, May 1, 1949; Washington *Post*, November 14, 1939.
8. See Ben Patrusky, "What Causes Aging?" *Science 82* (January 1982), and "The Key to Aging," "Science Times," *The New York Times*, January 26, 1982.
9. In Jane B. Katz, ed., *I Am the Fire of Time: The Voice of Native American Women* (New York: Dutton Paperbacks, 1977), p. 114.
10. These statistics are from *The Twentieth Century Book of the Dead*, as quoted by William Corcoran Burke, Jr., in "Irish Wake, Catholic Funeral," *Parabola*, Vol. 2, No. 1 (Winter 1977).
11. See, for one example out of many, Virginia Kerns, "Black Carib Women and Rites of Death," *Unspoken Worlds: Women's Religious Lives in Non-Western Cultures*, Nancy A. Falk and Rita M. Gross, eds. (New York: Harper & Row, 1980).
12. DuBois, ed., *Elizabeth Cady Stanton and Susan B. Anthony*.
13. For more detailed accounts, see *Mozart* by J. E. Talbot (New York: A. A. Wyn, 1949); Richard and Clara Winston's translation of Franz Kafka's *Letters to Friends, Family, and Editors* (New York: Schocken Books, 1977); Elizabeth Jenkins' biography of *Elizabeth the Great* (Berkeley, Cal.: Berkeley Medallion, 1958); DuBois, ed., *Elizabeth Cady Stanton and Susan B. Anthony*.
14. See "The Nature of Death," *Parabola*, Vol. 2, No. 1 (Winter 1977).
15. New York: MacMillan, 1974.
16. New York: Harper & Row, 1982.
17. Capra, *The Tao of Physics*, pp. 196–97.
18. Quoted in M. Capek, *The Philosophical Impact of Contemporary Physics* (Princeton: D. Van Nostrand, 1961), p. 319.

CHAPTER VIII   "The Uncertain Future of Flesh"

1. "Breakthroughs," *Omni*, October 1981.
2. "Science Times," *The New York Times*, December 29, 1981.
3. Daniel Laskin, "The R&D Story: Fiber Optics," *Passages*, October 1981.

4. John Blair, "Test-Tube Gardens," *Science 82*, January–February 1982.

5. Robert Brody, "Computer Surgery," *Omni*, December 1981.

6. *Taking Hold of Technology: Topic Guide for 1981–1983*, AAUW (American Association of University Women, Washington, D.C., 1981).

7. Douglas Colligan, "Where's Poppa?" *Omni*, October 1981, and *Science News*, January 13, 1979.

8. Dennis Meredith, "Space: Where We're Going Next," *Mainliner*, June 1981.

9. Kathleen McAuliffe, "Biochip Revolution," *Omni*, December 1981.

10. Albert Rosenfeld, "The Patient in the Womb," *Science 82*, January–February 1982.

11. *Taking Hold of Technology*.

12. "Science Times," *The New York Times*, February 9, 1982.

13. See Charles Panati, *Breakthroughs* (New York: Berkeley Books, 1981).

14. *Taking Hold of Technology*.

15. Dr. Bernard Dixon, "Genetic Surgery," *Omni*, January 1982. Also see June Goodfield, *Playing God: Genetic Engineering and the Manipulation of Life* (New York: Random House, 1977).

16. AAUW, 2401 Virginia Avenue N.W., Washington, D.C. 20037.

17. See *Science News*, January 13, 1979.

18. Boston: Beacon Press, 1979.

19. New York: Harper & Row, forthcoming, 1984.

20. For further examples of the impact of sex-ratio imbalance, see Letty Cottin Pogrebin, *Growing Up Free*.

21. Harold M. Schmeck, Jr., "Nobel Winner Says He Gave Sperm for Women to Bear Gifted Babies," *The New York Times*, March 1, 1980. (Shockley's Nobel Prize was for inventing the transistor, and had nothing to do with the fields of biology or medicine.)

22. See Barbara Ford, "Parent of the Apes," *Omni*, November 1981.

23. Published in 1981 and available from the Women and Technology Project, 315 South Fourth Street East, Missoula, Montana 59801.

24. Boulder, Colorado: Westview Press, 1976.

25. New York: Harper & Row, 1981.

26. See Pamela M. D'Onofrio-Flores and Sheila M. Pfafflin, eds., *Scientific-Technological Change and the Role of Women in Development*, a publication of the United Nations Institute for Training and

Research (Boulder, Colo.: Westview Press, 1982), and Devaki Jain with Nalini Singh and Malini Chand, *Women's Quest for Power* (Ghaziabad, India: Vikas Publishing House Ltd.; U.S. distributor, New York: Advent Books, 1980). Also see *The Growth of U.S. and World Economics Through Technological Innovation and Transfer*, Report of the Economic Policy Council (New York: U.N. Association of the United States of America, 1980), and the excellent work of scholarship and analysis done by Lisa Leghorn and Katherine Parker in their book *Woman's Worth: Sexual Economics and the World of Women* (Boston: Routledge & Kegan Paul, 1981).

27. See "Marilyn Waring and Robin Morgan: A Conversation," *Ms.*, December 1981, for a further explication of tea-plantation exploitation of women. Also see Barbara Ehrenreich and Annette Fuentes, "Women and the Multinationals," *Ms.*, January 1981.

28. Michele Roberts, "Writing and (Feminist) Politics," *Women's Studies Quarterly*, London, Vol. 2 (1979).

29. Heidegger, "The Question Concerning Technology."

30. See "Art and Archeology Newsletter," New York, No. 21.

31. See, for example, Ann Sutherland Harris and Linda Nochlin, *Women Artists: 1550–1950* (New York: Knopf, 1976), and Aaron I. Cohen, *The International Encyclopedia of Women Composers*, a 597-page compendium of more than five thousand entries ranging over forty-four centuries and nearly seventy countries (New York: R. R. Bowker, 1981). Also see Judy Chicago, *The Dinner Party: A Symbol of Our Heritage* (New York: Anchor Press, Doubleday, 1979), and Aliki Barnstone and Willis Barnstone, eds., *A Book of Women Poets from Antiquity to Now* (New York: Schocken Books, 1980).

32. Böhm, *Wholeness and the Implicate Order*, p. 177.

33. Böhm, p. 172.

34. Françoise Gilot, *Le regarde et son masque* (Paris: Calmann-Lévy, 1975).

35. Langer, *Philosophy in a New Key*, p. 37.

36. New York: Simon & Schuster, 1981.

37. Hofstadter, *Gödel, Escher, Bach*, p. 171.

38. Rilke, Rainer Maria, *The Sonnets to Orpheus*, translated and with an Introduction by Kenneth Pitchford (Harrison, New York: Purchase Press, 1981).

CHAPTER IX   "The New Physics of Meta-Politics"

1. See, among others, Mary Daly, *Gyn/Ecology* (Boston: Beacon Press, 1978), and Charlene Spretnak, ed., *The Politics of Women's*

Spirituality (New York: Anchor Books, 1981). Also see *Unspoken Worlds: Women's Religious Lives in Non-Western Cultures.*

2. Fritjof Capra, *The Turning Point: Science, Society, and the Rising Culture* (New York: Simon & Schuster, 1982), pp. 29–30, 48–49.

3. G. F. Chew, M. Gell-Mann, and A. H. Rosenfeld, "Strongly Interacting Particles," *Scientific American*, Vol. 210 (February 1964), p. 93.

4. G. F. Chew, "Bootstrap: A Scientific Idea," *Science*, Vol. 161 (May 23, 1968), pp. 762–65.

5. E. P. Wigner, *Symmetries and Reflections—Scientific Essays* (Cambridge, Mass.: MIT Press, 1970), p. 172.

6. Capra, *The Tao of Physics*, p. 291.

7. Arthur Koestler, "Physics and Metaphysics," *Janus: A Summing Up* (New York: Vintage Books, 1979), pp. 249–50.

8. Lewis Thomas, *The Medusa and the Snail: More Notes of a Biology Watcher* (New York: Bantam Books, 1980).

9. Hofstadter, p. 86.

10. *Feminism and Suffrage: The Emergence of an Independent Women's Movement in America, 1848–1869* (Ithaca, N.Y.: Cornell University Press, 1978).

11. Donald C. Johanson and Maitland A. Edey, *Lucy: The Beginnings of Humankind* (New York: Simon & Schuster, 1981).

12. *The Lives of a Cell: Notes of a Biology Watcher* (New York: Bantam Books, 1975), p. 165.

13. J. E. Lovelock, *Gaia: A New Look at Life on Earth* (Oxford: Oxford University Press, 1970). Also see Roger Bingham, "The Maverick and the Earth Goddess," *Science 81*, December 1981.

14. See Koestler, "The Holarchy" and "Beyond Atomism and Holism—The Concept of the Holon," *Janus: A Summing Up.*

15. Translator's preface by Lillian Marvin Swenson to the 1949 Princeton University Press edition, p. v.

16. Grand Rapids, Mich.: William B. Eerdmans Publishing Co., (1939; rpt 1974), p. 31.

17. See Peter S. Stevens, *Patterns in Nature* (Boston: Atlantic Monthly Press, 1974).

BIBLIOGRAPHY

American Association of University Women. *Taking Hold of Technology: Topic Guide for 1981–83.* Washington, D.C., 1981.

Art and Archeology Newsletter. New York: No. 21.

As, Berit. "On Female Culture." *Acta Sociologica,* No. 1–3, Special Issue on Women's Studies (1975).

Astell, Mary. *Some Reflections upon Marriage.* 1730; rpt. New York: Source Book Press, 1970.

Barnstone, Aliki, and Willis Barnstone, eds. *A Book of Women Poets from Antiquity to Now.* New York: Schocken Books, 1980.

Barry, Kathleen. *Female Sexual Slavery: The International Traffic in Women and Children.* Englewood Cliffs, N.J.: Prentice Hall, 1979. New York: Avon Books, 1979.

de Beauvoir, Simone. *The Second Sex.* Paris: Gallimard, 1949. New York: Knopf, 1953.

Benton, Itzhak. *Stalking the Wild Pendulum: On the Mechanics of Consciousness.* New York: Bantam Books, 1979.

Bernard, Jessie. *The Future of Marriage.* New York: World Publishing Company, 1972.

Bethel, Lorraine, and Barbara Smith, eds. *Conditions: Five.* New York: Conditions, 1979.

Bingham, Roger. "The Maverick and the Earth Goddess." *Science 81,* December 1981.

Blair, John G. "Test-Tube Gardens." *Science 82,* January–February 1982.

Böhm, David. *Wholeness and the Implicate Order.* London: Routledge & Kegan Paul, 1980.

Boulding, Elise. *The Underside of History: A View of Women Through Time.* Boulder, Colorado: Westview Press, 1976.

"Breakthroughs." *Omni,* October 1981.

Brodie, Fawn. *Thomas Jefferson: An Intimate History.* New York: Bantam Books, 1974.

Brody, Robert. "Computer Surgery." *Omni,* December 1981.

Brownmiller, Susan. *Against Our Will: Men, Women and Rape.* New York: Simon & Schuster, 1975.

Bruin, Janet, and Stephen Salaff. "Never Again: The Organization of

Women Atomic Bomb Victims in Osaka." *Feminist Studies*, 7, No. 1 (Spring 1981).

Burke, William Corcoran, Jr. "Irish Wake, Catholic Funeral." *Parabola*, 2, No. 1 (Winter 1977).

Bush, Corlann Gee. "The Technological Imperative: Feminist Visions for the Twenty-first Century." Corvallis: Women's Studies Department, Oregon State University, 1981.

Cade (Bambara), Toni. "The Scattered Sopranos." Livingston College New Black Women's Seminar, Brunswick, New Jersey. December 1969.

Cade, Toni, ed. *The Black Woman*. New York: Signet/NAL, 1970.

Capek, M. *The Philosophical Impact of Contemporary Physics*. Princeton: Van Nostrand, 1961.

Capra, Fritjof. *The Tao of Physics*. New York: Bantam Books, 1977.

———. *The Turning Point: Science, Society and the Rising Culture*. New York: Simon & Schuster, 1982.

Chase-Riboud, Barbara. *Sally Hemmings*. New York: Viking Press, 1979. New York: Avon Press, 1980.

Chew, G. F. "Bootstrap: A Scientific Idea." *Science*, Vol. 161 (May 23, 1968).

———, M. Gell-Mann and A. H. Rosenfeld. "Strongly Interacting Particles." *Scientific American*, No. 210 (February 1964).

Chicago, Judy. *The Dinner Party: A Symbol of Our Heritage*. New York: Anchor Books, 1979.

Christiansen, Robert. *Newsweek*, June 2, 1980.

Clarke, Sir Kenneth. *The Romantic Rebellion*. New York: Harper & Row, 1973.

Cohen, Aaron I. *The International Encyclopedia of Women Composers*. New York: R. R. Bowker, 1981.

Colligan, Douglas. "Where's Poppa?" *Omni*, October 1981.

Corea, Gena. *The Hidden Malpractice: How American Medicine Treats Women as Patients and Professionals*. New York: William Morrow, 1977. New York: Jove Publishers, 1978.

———. *Reproductive Technology*. New York: Harper & Row, forthcoming, 1984.

Cronan, Sheila. "Marriage." *Radical Feminism*. Eds. Anne Koedt, Ellen Levine, and Anita Rapone. New York: Quadrangle Times Books, 1973.

Daly, Mary. *Gyn/Ecology*. Boston: Beacon Press, 1978.

Dames, Michael. *The Silbury Treasure: The Great Goddess Rediscovered*. London: Thames and Hudson, 1976.

Davis, Angela Y. *Women, Race and Class*. New York: Random House, 1981.

Development Programs. *Development Issue 12*. New York: United Nations.

Diamond, Irene. "Pornography and Repression." Annual Meeting of the Western Social Science Association, Denver. 1978.

Dinnerstein, Dorothy. *The Mermaid and the Minotaur*. New York: Harper & Row, 1976.

Dixon, Dr. Bernard. "Genetic Surgery." *Omni*, January 1982.

Dobbins, Peggy Powell. *From Kin to Class*. Berkeley, Cal.: Signmaker Press, 1981.

D'Onofrio-Flores, Pamela M., and Sheila M. Pfafflin. *Scientific-Technological Change and the Role of Women in Development*. A UNITAR publication, Boulder, Colorado: Westview Press, 1982.

DuBois, Ellen Carol, ed. *Elizabeth Cady Stanton, Susan B. Anthony: Correspondence, Writing, Speeches*. New York: Schocken Books, 1981.

————. *Feminism and Suffrage: The Emergence of an Independent Movement in America, 1848–1869*. Ithaca: Cornell University Press, 1978.

Dworkin, Andrea. *Our Blood*. New York: Putnam/Perigree, 1981.

————. "The Politics of Intelligence." *Maenad*, 2, No. 1 (Fall 1981).

————. *Pornography: Men Possessing Women*. New York: Putnam/Perigree, 1981.

————. *Right-Wing Women*. New York: Putnam/Perigree, forthcoming, 1983.

Ehrenreich, Barbara, and Annette Fuentes. "Women and Multinationals." *Ms.*, January 1981.

Eisenstein, Zillah. "Antifeminism in the Politics and Election of 1980." *Feminist Studies*, 7, No. 2 (Summer 1981).

————. *The Radical Future of Liberal Feminism*. New York: Longman, Inc., 1981.

Eliade, Mircea. *Shamanism, Archaic Techniques of Ecstasy*. Princeton: Princeton University Press, 1964.

Falk, Nancy A., and Rita M. Gross, eds. *Unspoken Worlds: Women's Religious Lives in Non-Western Cultures*. New York: Harper & Row, 1980.

Faraday, Dr. Ann. *Dream Power*. New York: Berkeley Medallion Books, 1982.

Federation of Women's Health Centers. *A New View of a Woman's Body*. New York: Simon & Schuster, 1981.

Firestone, Shulamith. *The Dialectic of Sex*. New York: William Morrow, 1970.

Ford, Barbara. "Parent of the Apes." *Omni*, November 1981.

Foucault, Michel. *The History of Sexuality*. New York: Random House, 1978.

Gelles, Richard. *Family Violence*. Beverly Hills: Sage Publications, 1979.

——. *The Violent Home: A Study of Physical Aggression Between Husbands and Wives*. Beverly Hills: Sage Publications, 1972.

——. *See* Straus, Murray.

Gilkey, Robert. *The Chinese Unicorn: Conceits from a Chinese Dictionary*. Washington, D.C.: Noname Press, 1972.

Gilot, Françoise. *Le regarde et son masque*. Paris: Calmann-Lévy, 1975.

Goodfield, June. *An Imagined World: A Story of Scientific Discovery*. New York: Harper & Row, 1981.

——. *Playing God: Genetic Engineering and the Manipulation of Life*. New York: Random House, 1977.

Greenfield, Gloria Z. "Spiritual Hierarchies." *Soujourner: The New England Women's Journal of News, Opinions, and the Arts*, December 1977.

The Growth of U.S. and World Economics Through Technological Innovation and Transfer. New York: United Nations Association of the United States of America, 1980.

Harris, Ann Sutherland, and Linda Nochlin. *Women Artists: 1550–1950*. New York: Knopf, 1976.

Head, Bessie. *A Question of Power*. London: Heinemann, 1972.

Heidegger, Martin. *Poetry, Language, Thought*. Trans. Albert Hofstadter. New York: Harper & Row, 1975.

——. *The Question Concerning Technology and Other Essays*. Trans. William Lovitt. New York: Harper & Row, 1977.

Heilbrun, Carolyn G. "Hers." *The New York Times*, March 5, 1981.

Hite, Shere. *The Hite Report*. New York: Dell Books, 1981.

——. *The Hite Report on Male Sexuality*. New York: Knopf, 1981.

Hofstadter, Douglas R. *Gödel, Escher, and Bach: An Eternal Golden Braid*. New York: Basic Books, Inc., 1979.

Hoge, Warren. "Brazil Women Protest Crimes Against Wives." *The New York Times*, August 25, 1980.

Hooks, Belle. *Ain't I a Woman?* Boston: Southend Press, 1981.

Hornstein, Francie. "Lesbians, Reproductive Rights, and Artificial Insemination." The Eleventh Annual Woman and Law Conference, San Francisco. March 1980.

Hu P'in-ch'ing. *Li Ch'ing-Chao*. New York: Twayne Publishers, 1966.

"Interview with Madalyn Murray O'Hair." *Omni*, December 1981.

Jain, Devaki, with Nalini Singh and Malini Chand. *Women's Quest for Power*. Ghaziabad, India: Vikas Publishing House Ltd., 1980. New York: Advent Books, 1980.

Jastrow, Robert. *The Enchanted Loom: Mind in the Universe*. New York: Simon & Schuster, 1981.

Jenkins, Elizabeth. *Elizabeth the Great*. New York: Berkeley Medallion Books, 1958.

Jenkins, Ron. "Two-Way Mirrors." *Parabola*, 6, No. 3 (August 1981).

Johanson, Donald C., and Maitland A. Edey. *Lucy: The Beginnings of Humankind*. New York: Simon & Schuster, 1981.

Katz, Jane B., ed. *I Am the Fire of Time: The Voice of Native American Women*. New York: Dutton Paperbacks, 1977.

Katz, Naomi, and Nancy Milton, eds. *Fragments from a Lost Diary and Other Stories*. New York: Random House, 1973.

Kearns, Martha. *Käthe Kollwitz: Woman and Artist*. Old Westbury, New York: The Feminist Press, 1976.

Kerns, Virginia. "Black Carib Women and Rites of Death." *Unspoken Worlds: Women's Religious Lives in Non-Western Cultures*. Eds. Nancy A. Falk and Rita M. Gross. New York: Harper & Row, 1980.

Kierkegaard, Søren. *Either/Or*. Trans. Lillian Marvin Swenson. Princeton: Princeton University Press, 1949.

Kinsey, Alfred C., et al. *Sexual Behavior in the Human Female*. Philadelphia: Saunders Press, 1953.

———. *Sexual Behavior in the Human Male*. Philadelphia: Saunders Press, 1948.

Kirsten, Lincoln. *Ballet Alphabet*. New York: Kamin Publishers, 1939.

Koestler, Arthur. "Beyond Atomism and Holism—The Concept of the Holon." In *Janus: A Summing Up*. New York: Vintage Books, 1979.

———. "The Holarchy." In *Janus: A Summing Up*. New York: Vintage Books, 1979.

———. "Physics and Metaphysics." In *Janus: A Summing Up*. New York: Vintage Books, 1979.

Korzybski, Alfred. *Science and Sanity*. Lakeville, Connecticut: International Non-Aristotelian Library, 1958.

Kovel, Joel. *White Racism: A Psychohistory*. New York: Pantheon Books, 1970.

Kübler-Ross, Elisabeth. *On Death and Dying*. New York: Macmillan, 1974.

Langer, Susanne K. *Philosophy in a New Key*. Cambridge: Harvard University Press, 1942.

Laskin, Daniel. "The R and D Story: Fiber Optics." *Passages*, October 1981.

Lederer, Laura, ed. *Take Back the Night: Women on Pornography*. New York: William Morrow, 1980.

Leghorn, Lisa, and Katherine Parker. *Woman's Worth: Sexual Economics and the World of Women*. Boston: Routledge & Kegan Paul, 1981.

Lerner, Gerda, ed. *Black Women in White America*. New York: Vintage Books, 1973.

Levine, Suzanne Braun. "Romanticism in *Wuthering Heights* and *The Scarlet Letter*." Diss., Harvard, 1963.

Li Ch'ing-Chao. *Li Ch'ing-Chao: Complete Poems*. Ed. and trans. Kenneth Rexroth and Ling Chung. New York: New Directions, 1979.

Lorde, Audre. "Uses of the Erotic: The Erotic as Power." In *Take Back the Night: Women on Pornography*. Ed. Laura Lederer. New York: William Morrow, 1980.

Lovelock, J. E. *Gaia, A New Look at Life on Earth*. Oxford: Oxford University Press, 1970.

Maddux, Hilary C. *Menstruation*. New Canaan, Conn.: Tobey Publishing, 1975.

Mainardi, Patricia. "The Politics of Housework." In *Sisterhood Is Powerful*. Ed. Robin Morgan. New York: Vintage Books, 1970.

Malleus Maleficarum. Ed. and trans. Montague Summers. Rpt. New York: Dover, 1971.

Manushi, No. 8 (1981). New Delhi.

Marciano, Linda "Lovelace," with Mike McGrady. *Ordeal: An Autobiography*. Secaucus: Citadel Press, 1980.

Martin, Del. *Battered Wives*. San Francisco: Glide Publications, 1976.

McAuliffe, Kathleen. "Biochip Revolution." *Omni*, December 1981.

Mead, Margaret, and James Baldwin. *A Rap on Race*. New York: Dell Publishing Co., 1972.

Meade, Marion. *Eleanor of Aquitaine: A Biography*. New York: Hawthorn Books, 1977.

Mehra, J., ed. *The Physicist's Conception of Nature*. Dordrecht-Holland: D. Reidel, 1973.

Meredith, Dennis. "Space: Where We're Going Next." *Mainliner*, June 1981.

Mernessi, Fatima. *Beyond the Veil: Male-Female Dynamics in a Modern Muslim Society*. New York: John Wiley & Sons, 1975.

———. "Women, Saints, and Sanctuaries." *Signs*, 3, No. 1 (Autumn 1977).

Minai, Naila. *Women in Islam*. New York: Seaview Books, 1981.

Morgan, Ellen. "The Erotization of Male Dominance and Female Submission: The Sexist Turn-on that Castrates Self, Love and Sex." Pittsburgh: KNOW, 1975.

Morgan, Robin. "Blood Types." *Maenad*, 1, No. 3 (Spring 1981).

———. "The Changeless Need: A Conversation Between Dorothy Dinnerstein and Robin Morgan." *Ms.*, August 1978.

———. *Depth Perception: New Poems and a Masque*. New York: Anchor Books, 1982.

———. *Going Too Far: The Personal Chronicle of a Feminist*. New York: Random House and Vintage Books, 1978.

———. "How to Run the Pornographers Out of Town (and Preserve the First Amendment)." *Ms.*, November 1978.

———. "Marilyn Waring and Robin Morgan: A Conversation." *Ms.*, December 1981.

———. "The Network of the Imaginary Mother." In *Lady of the Beasts*. New York: Random House, 1976.

———, ed. *Sisterhood Is Powerful*. New York: Vintage Books, 1970.

———, and Gloria Steinem. "The International Crime of Genital Mutilation." *Ms.*, March 1980.

Ms., "The Family" (Special Issue). August 1978.

Muhlenfeld, Elisabeth. *Mary Boykin Chesnut: A Biography*. Baton Rouge: Louisiana State University Press, 1981.

"The Nature of Death." *Parabola*, 2, No. 1 (Winter 1977).

Nowak, Mariette. *Eve's Rib: A Revolutionary New View of the Female*. New York: St. Martin's Press, 1980.

O'Callaghan, Neal. "Cross Currents." *Science 81*, December 1981.

Ordway, Jane. "Ain't I a Feminist?" *Maenad*, 2, No. 2 (Winter 1982).

Pagels, Heinz R. *The Cosmic Code: Quantum Physics as the Language of Nature*. New York: Simon & Schuster, 1982.

Panati, Charles. *Breakthroughs*. New York: Berkeley Books, 1981.

Parker, Pat. *Movements in Black*. San Francisco: Diana Press, 1978.

Partnow, Elaine, ed. *The Quotable Woman: An Encyclopedia of Useful Quotations*. New York: Anchor Books, 1978.

Patrusky, Ben. "The Key to Aging." *The New York Times*, January 26, 1982.

———. "What Causes Aging." *Science 82*, January 1982.

Patterson, Francine. *The Education of Koko.* New York: Holt, Rinehart & Winston, 1981.

————. "Koko, the Articulate Gorilla." *Ms.*, December 1981, and *National Geographic*, October 1981.

Pitchford, Blake Ariel Morgan. "Going Even Further: The Chronicle of a Pro-Feminist Child." *Sojourner: The New England Women's Journal of News, Opinions and the Arts,* 4, No. 1 (September 1978).

Pitchford, Kenneth. "The Manly Art of Childcare." *Ms.*, October 1978.

————. *See also* Rilke, Rainer Maria.

Pogrebin, Letty Cottin. *Growing Up Free: Raising Your Child in the 80's.* New York: Bantam Books, 1981.

Power, Eileen. *Medieval Women.* Ed. M. M. Postan. Cambridge: Cambridge University Press, 1975.

Praz, Mario. *The Romantic Agony.* London: Oxford University Press, 1933.

Raymond, Janice F. *Transsexual Empire: The Making of the She-Male.* Boston: Beacon Press, 1979.

Reitz, Rosetta. *Menopause: A Positive Approach.* New York: Penguin Books, 1979.

Rilke, Rainer Maria. *The Sonnets to Orpheus.* Kenneth Pitchford, trans. New York: Purchase Press, 1981.

Roberts, Michele. "Writing and (Feminist) Politics." *Women's Studies Quarterly,* 2 (1979). London.

Rosenfeld, Albert. "The Patient in the Womb." *Science* 82, January–February 1982.

Rush, Florence. *The Best Kept Secret: The Sexual Abuse of Children.* New York: McGraw-Hill Paperbacks, 1981.

Saadawi, Nawal El. *The Hidden Face of Eve: Women in the Arab World.* Boston: Beacon Press, 1981.

Sabom, Michael. *Recollections of Death.* New York: Harper & Row, 1982.

Sacks, Karen. *Sisters and Wives.* Westport, Conn.: Greenwood Press, 1979.

Santa Cruz Women's Health Collective. *Lesbian Health Matters.*

Schmeck, Harold M., Jr. "Nobel Winner Says He Gave Sperm for Women to Bear Gifted Babies." *The New York Times,* March 1, 1980.

Schneir, Miriam, ed. *Feminism: The Essential Historical Writings.* New York: Vintage Books, 1972.

Science News, January 13, 1979.

"Science Times." *The New York Times,* February 9, 1982, and December 29, 1981.

Serrin, William. "Sex Is a Growing Multibillion Business." *The New York Times*, February 9, 1981.

Sherfey, Dr. Mary Jane. "A Theory on Female Sexuality." In *Sisterhood Is Powerful*. Ed. Robin Morgan. New York: Vintage Books, 1970.

Silver, Dr. Sherman J. *The Male from Infancy to Age*. New York· Charles Scribner's Sons, 1981.

Simms, Laura. "The First Mask." *Parabola*, 6, No. 3 (August 1981).

Smith, Barbara, Gloria Hull and Patricia Bell Scott, eds. *But Some of Us Are Brave*. Old Westbury, New York: The Feminist Press, 1982.

Smith, Judy. *Something Old, Something New, Something Borrowed, Something Due: Women in Appropriate Technology*. Missoula, Montana: Women and Technology Project, 1981.

Sobin, Dennis. "The Adult Business Report." Washington, D.C.: R.P.E. Publications, 1981.

Spretnak, Charlene, ed. *The Politics of Women's Spirituality*. New York: Anchor Books, 1981.

Star, Bernard D., and Marcella Baker Weiner. *On Sex and Sexuality in the Mature Years*. New York: Stein and Day, 1981.

Steiner, George. *Martin Heidegger*. New York: Viking Press, 1978.

Stern, Susan. "Lesbian Insemination." *The CoEvolution Quarterly* (Summer 1980).

Stevens, Peter S. *Patterns in Nature*. Boston: Atlantic Monthly Press, 1974.

Straus, Murray, and Richard Gelles. *Behind Closed Doors: Violence in the American Family*. Garden City: Doubleday & Co., 1981.

Tafoya, Terry. "Dancing with Dash-Kayah." *Parabola*, 6, No. 3 (August 1981).

Talbot, J. E. *Mozart*. New York: A. A. Wyn, 1949.

Thomas, Lewis. *The Lives of a Cell: Notes of a Biology Watcher*. New York: Bantam Books, 1975.

———. *The Medusa and the Snail: More Notes of a Biology Watcher*. New York: Bantam Books, 1980.

United Nations Report on Refugees to the Copenhagen World Conference of the Mid-Decade on Women. New York: United Nations, 1980.

Walker, Jearl. "The Physics and Chemistry of a Failed Sauce Béarnaise." *Scientific American*, December 1979.

Wallace, Michele. *Black Macho and the Myth of the Superwoman*. New York: Dial Press, 1979.

Washington, Mary Helen. *Midnight Birds*. New York: Anchor Books, 1980.

Weideger, Paula. *Menstruation and Menopause.* New York: Knopf, 1976.

"A Wife Helps and Two Wives Help Even More." *Ms.*, February 1982.

Wigner, E. P. *Symmetries and Reflections—Scientific Essays.* Cambridge: MIT Press, 1970.

Williams, Charles. *The Descent of the Dove.* 1939; rpt. Grand Rapids: William B. Eerdman's Publishing Co., 1974.

Winston, Richard, and Clara Winston, eds. *Franz Kafka's Letters to Friends, Family, and Editors.* New York: Schocken Books, 1977.

Wolf, Fred Alan. *Taking the Quantum Leap.* New York: Harper & Row, 1981.

Woodward, C. Vann, ed. *Mary Chesnut's Civil War.* New Haven: Yale University Press, 1981.

Woolf, Virginia. *A Room of One's Own.* New York: Harcourt Brace Jovanovich, 1963.

———. *Three Guineas.* New York: Harcourt Brace Jovanovich, 1963.

Yeager, Robert C. *Seasons of Shame: The New Violence in Sports.* New York: McGraw-Hill, 1980.

INDEX

Eve, 42n, 73, 103
Existential Romanticism, 122–28,
143, 146
Exit (organization), 237n
Ezekiel, 270

Fabiola, 262
Fahd, Maha al-, 40
Fall, the, 103
Family. *See* Kin (family) systems
Family Protection Act, 306–7
Famine, 15, 279
Fandango (Soler), 239
Fanshawe, David, 239
Fantasia on "Greensleeves"
(Vaughan Williams), 239
Fantasies, 125–26, 131
Faraday, Dr. Ann, 178
Farley, Peter J., 249
Faust (Goethe), 313
FBI, 51, 52
Fear and Trembling (Kierkegaard),
181
Federal Endangered Species
Program, 251
Feiffer, Jules, 152
Female circumcision. *See*
Clitoridectomy
Female saints, 238
Feminists and feminism
challenge of, xv
as the holograph, xiv–xv
international feminism, 19–21,
191–97
and marriage, 149, 151, 152, 165
meaning of, xiii
media, 25, 308
New Right focus on, 308–9
Old Women's Home, 233–34
perception of, xiii–xvi
potential of, 282
quantum physics and, 285–96
tactics, 21, 24, 25, 307–9
See also Freedom; Woman;
Women's Movement
Feminist Studies, 267n
Feminist Women's Health Centers,
57, 61
Fetal surgery, 257
Fetal therapy, 253
Fetus, 221
Feynman, R. P., 289
Fiber optics, 256

Firestone, Shulamith, 143
First Amendment, 55, 107, 112,
113–14
"First Ladies," 4
First Piano Concerto (Schumann),
239
First Symphony (Sibelius), 239
Fission (nuclear), 254
Fluoridation, 254
Fluosol-DA, 253
F-matrix Theory, 298
Foppa, Alejda, 20n
Forster, E. M., 269
Foucault, Michel, 108
Franklin, Rosalind, 262
Freedom
art and technology, 249–80
body image comprehension, 40–80
centers and edges (anatomy of
anatomy), 318–30
Christian fundamentalist attacks
on, 16
dreams (dialogue with the dream
self), 81–99
illusory, 3–4, 36
introduction to, xiii–xvi
Kant on, xiv–xv
kin (family) systems, 185–210
liberation and, xviii
marriage and, 147–84
meta-politics, 281–317
and mortality, 211–48
reproductive, 18–19
sexual passion, 100–46
women's condition and, 1–39
See also Feminists and feminism
"Free radical" theory of aging,
230–31
French Revolution, 102
Freud, Sigmund, 83
Friedan, Betty, 78, 301
Frigidity, 125, 127
From the New World Symphony
(Dvořák), 239
Fuller, Margaret, 280
Fundamentalism
religious, 15–16, 21, 47, 104, 105,
106, 154, 186
sexual, 104–7, 111, 112, 113, 117,
152, 186, 214, 227, 256, 267
Fusion power (nuclear), 254
Future of Marriage, The (Bernard),
178n